YVES BONNEFOY (1923–2016), regarded as France's greatest poet of the last fifty years, was the author of many volumes of poetry and poetic prose, and numerous books of essays on literature and art, including studies of Baudelaire, Rimbaud, Goya and Giacometti. Between 1981 and 2016 he was Professor (and then Emeritus Professor) of Comparative Poetics at the Collège de France, a position he inherited from Roland Barthes. His work has been translated into scores of languages and he himself was a master translator of Shakespeare, Yeats, Keats, Leopardi, Seferis and others. He received a wide variety of literary prizes.

STEPHEN ROMER is a poet and the translator of Bonnefoy's prose book *L'Arrière-pays* (1972/2012). He has served as Maître de conférences at the University of Tours since 1991. His anthology of twentieth-century French poems was published by Faber in 2002. His poetry collections include *Tribute, Idols* and *Yellow Studio*. He was elected Fellow of the Royal Society of Literature in 2011. His latest collection, *Set Thy Love in Order: New and Selected Poems*, was published by Carcanet in 2017. He is Stipendiary Lecturer in French at Brasenose College, Oxford.

JOHN NAUGHTON is Harrington and Shirley Drake Professor of the Humanities at Colgate University. He has authored or edited seven books in the area of modern French poetry, including *The Poetics of Yves Bonnefoy* (1984) and *Shakespeare and the French Poet* (2004). His translations have been honoured by the British Poetry Book Society and by the Modern Language Association. He has received the medal of the Collège de France in Paris for 'distinguished contributions to the study of French literature'.

ANTHONY RUDOLF is a poet and the translator of books of poetry from French, Russian and other languages. He was associated with Bonnefoy for more than half a century. He founded Menard Press in 1969, now dormant after nearly 50 years and 170 titles. He is Chevalier de l'Ordre des Arts et des Lettres (2004), Fellow of the Royal Society of Literature (2005) and Fellow of the English Association (2010). His collected poems, *European Hours*, was published by Carcanet in 2017.

Prose
of
Yves Bonnefoy

edited & translated by
Stephen Romer, John Naughton & Anthony Rudolf

with other translations by
Iain Bamforth, Michael Bishop, Hilary Davies,
Jennie Feldman, Emily Grosholz, Mark Hutchinson,
Steven Jaron, Viviane Lowe, James Petterson, Hoyt Rogers,
Richard Stamelman, Jean Stewart, John Taylor, Chris Turner

CARCANET

First published in Great Britain in 2020
by Carcanet Press Limited
Alliance House, 30 Cross Street
Manchester, M2 7AQ
www.carcanet.co.uk

This publication was made possible by a translation grant from the Institut
français du Royaume-Uni.

A CIP catalogue record for this book is available from the
British Library: ISBN 978 1 78410 811 3

Typeset by XL Publishing Services, Exmouth.
Printed & bound in England by SRP Ltd

The publisher acknowledges financial assistance from Arts Council England.

Supported using public funding by
ARTS COUNCIL
ENGLAND

Contents

Notes on the Translators

Iain Bamforth is an independent scholar, writer and physician living in Strasbourg. Author of five volumes of poetry, he has also published several works of prose which include *The Good European: Essays and Arguments*(2006), *A Doctor's Dictionary: Writings on Culture and Medicine* (2015) and *Scattered Limbs: A Medical Dreambook* (2020). Based on experiences related to his professional activities as a health care consultant in the region, he is currently working on a collection of pieces about Wallacea, the exotic geographical entity that marks the farthest orbit of the many fugues of Rimbaud – 'the man with soles of wind'.

Michael Bishop is emeritus McCulloch Professor of French and Contemporary Studies at Dalhousie University. He has written widely in the fields of contemporary poetry and art. He is also poet, translator and publisher of Editions VVV. His most recent publications include *The Endless Theory of Days : The Art and Poetry of Gérard Titus-Carmel* (2007), *Contemporary French Art 1* (2008), *Contemporary French Art 2* (2011), *Dystopie et poïein, agnose et reconnaissance. Seize études sur la poésie française et francophone contemporaine* (2014) and *Earth and Mind: Dreaming, Writing, Being. Nine Contemporary French Poets* (2018). His poetry includes *Snowing, with Grace* (2007) and *La Genèse maintenant* (2011).

Hilary Davies has published four collections of poetry from Enitharmon: the latest, *Exile and the Kingdom*, was published in November 2016. She is also a translator, essayist and critic, and for ten years co-edited the poetry magazine *Argo*. Hilary has won an Eric Gregory award and 1st prize in the TLS/Cheltenham Poetry Festival Competition and has been a Hawthornden Fellow and Chairman of the Poetry Society. She was Royal Literary Fund Fellow at King's College, London, 2012–16 and is now an RLF Fellow at the British Library for 2018–19. She is currently Fellow of the English Association and for many years was Head of Languages at St. Paul's Girls' School in London. Hilary was married to the poet Sebastian Barker, who died in 2014.

Jennie Feldman studied Modern Languages at St Hilda's College, Oxford. She has published two collections of poems, *The Lost Notebook* (2005), shortlisted for the Glen Dimplex Poetry Award, and *Swift* (2012). Her translations include poetry by Jacques Réda – *Treading Lightly: Selected Poems 1961–1975* (2005) – and his autobiographical work, *The Mirabelle Pickers (Aller aux mirabelles)* (2012). A Hawthornden Fellow, she is co-editor and translator, with Stephen Romer, of *Into the Deep Street: Seven Modern French Poets, 1938– 2008* (2009), awarded a special commendation by the judges of the 2011 Popescu Translation Prize. *Chardin and Rembrandt* (2016), her translation of Marcel Proust's essay, was published by David Zwirner Books.

Emily Grosholz is Edwin Erle Sparks Professor of Philosophy, African American Studies and English at the Pennsylvania State University. Her latest book of poetry *The Stars of Earth: New and Selected Poems* appeared in 2017 with artwork by Farhad Ostovani. It was preceded in 2016 by *Starry Reckoning: Reference and Analysis in Mathematics and Cosmology*, winner of the Ferndando Gil International Prize for Philosophy of Science in 2017, and was then followed by *Great Circles: The Transits of Mathematics and Poetry* in 2018, which brings the two aspects of her life's work together. Her English translation of Yves Bonnefoy's *Beginning and End of the Snow, Followed by Where the Arrow Falls*, also with artwork by Farhad Ostovani, was published in 2012. Her book *Childhood*, with artwork by Lucy Vines Bonnefoy and published in 2014, has to date raised $3500 for UNICEF.

Mark Hutchinson is a freelance translator who has lived for many years in Paris. His translations include Emmanuel Hocquard's *Of Mist & Clouds* (1994), *The Gardens of Sallust* (1995) and *The Library at Trieste* (1995), René Char's *Hypnos: Notes from the French Resistance* (2014) and *The Inventors and Other Poems* (2015), and Anne Serre's *The Governesses* (2018) and *The Fool and Other Moral Tales* (2019).

Steven Jaron is a clinical psychologist and psychoanalyst working at the Centre Hospitalier National d'Ophtalmologie des 15–20 in Paris and in private practice. He holds a doctorate in French and Comparative Literature from Columbia University and is a visiting lecturer on psychology and psychoanalysis at the medical faculty of Sorbonne University. He is the author of *Edmond Jabès: The Hazard of Exile* (2003) and he gave the 2006 ADAM lecture at Kings College London on the painting of Zoran Music. His essay on 'Francis Bacon's Nervous System' appeared in *Bacon and the Mind: Art, Neuroscience and Psychology* (2019).

Viviane Lowe is a Swiss translator, editor and copywriter based in Geneva. She studied anthropology at Stanford University and at the Australian National University in Canberra, where she focused on the cultural history of late 20th century Vietnam. She has translated short fiction from the Vietnamese as well as numerous exhibition catalogues, academic studies and articles in the field of art history, literary studies, contemporary history, theology and architecture, both from and to the French. Her recent published translations include J. Kuntz, *International Geneva: 100 Years of Architecture* (2017); M. Jeanneret and N. Ducimetière, eds., *The Italian Renaissance: A Zest for Life* and M. Faini, *Pietro Bembo: A Life in Laurels and Scarlet* (2016), and F. Elsig and S. Sala, eds., *Hell or Paradise: The Origins of Caricature, 16th–18th centuries* (2013).

James Petterson is Professor of French at Wellesley College, specializing in the study of contemporary French poetry in relation to philosophy and the visual arts. He is the author of *Postwar Figures of L'Ephémère: Yves Bonnefoy, Louis-René des Forêts, Jacques Dupin, André du Bouchet* (2000) and *Poetry Proscribed: Twentieth-Century (Re)Visions of the Trials of Poetry in France* (2007). The latter book was republished in French in 2013. Petterson is also the translator of French poet Jacques Dupin's monograph *Miró*, as well as of essays by Jean Baudrillard and Yves Bonnefoy. He is currently working on a book-length project provisionally titled 'Dominique Fourcade: *Tout arrive*' examining the poet's interconnectedness with American poetry and modernist traditions in the arts, specifically painting, music, dance choreography and film.

Hoyt Rogers is the author of a poetry collection, *Witnesses* (1986), and a volume of criticism, *The Poetics of Inconstancy* (1997). His poems, stories, essays, and translations have appeared in a wide range of periodicals, including *Agni*, *The New England Review*, *The Kenyon Review*, *Harper's*, and *The Fortnightly Review*, where he is a Contributing Editor. He has translated dozens of works from the French, German, Italian, and Spanish. With Alastair Reid and others, he collaborated on the *Selected Poems* of Jorge Luis Borges (2000). With Paul Auster, he published *Openwork*, the first anthology of André du Bouchet in English (2014); *Outside*, his latest translation of du Bouchet (with Eric Fishman), is forthcoming at Bitter Oleander Press. He has translated four works by Yves Bonnefoy, including *The Curved Planks* (2007); a fifth, *Rome, 1630*, will be appearing soon from Seagull Books.

Richard Stamelman, Professor emeritus of French and Comparative Literature at Williams College, is a specialist in nineteenth- and twentieth-century French poetry. He has authored studies on Baudelaire, Apollinaire, Breton, Jouve, Ponge, Jaccottet, Bonnefoy, Jabès, Giacometti, and Garache, among other French poets and artists. He is also the author of: *The Drama of Self in Guillaume Apollinaire's 'Alcools'*; *Lost beyond Telling: Representations of Death and Absence in Modern French Poetry*; *Perfume: Joy, Obsession, Scandal, Sin; A Cultural History of Fragrance from 1750 to the Present*; and editor of *Yves Bonnefoy, The Lure and the Truth of Painting. Selected Essays on Art.* He has been awarded a Guggenheim Memorial Fellowship and is a chevalier dans l'Ordre des Palmes Académiques.

The late **Jean Stewart** was a prize-winning translator of many French authors. She translated among other works, Louis-René des Forêt's *The Children's Room* (1963) and Yves Bonnefoy's monumental *Alberto Giacometti: A Biography of his Work* (1991).

John Taylor is an American writer, critic, and translator who lives in France. Among his recent translations are books by Philippe Jaccottet, José-Flore Tappy, Catherine Colomb, Pierre Voélin, Jacques Dupin, Pierre Chappuis, and Pierre-Albert Jourdan, as well as the Italian poetry of Lorenzo Calogero, Alfredo de Palchi, and Franca Mancinelli. Taylor's essays on Yves Bonnefoy can be found in his books *Paths to Contemporary French Literature* (vol. 1, 2004), *Paths to Contemporary French Literature* (vol. 2, 2007), *Into the Heart* *of European Poetry* (2008), and *A Little Tour through European Poetry* (2015). He also writes short prose and poetry. His most recent book is *A Notebook of Clouds & A Notebook of Ridges* (2019), a 'double book' written with the Swiss poet Pierre Chappuis.

Chris Turner is a freelance translator living and working in Birmingham, UK. He has translated more than eighty books from French and German, including twenty-one by Jean Baudrillard and five by André Gorz. Among his most recent published translations are Pascal Quignard's *Villa Amalia*, Pascale Casanova's *Kafka, Angry Poet* and five short volumes of previously untranslated texts by Roland Barthes, all with Seagull Books. He has recently completed the translation of a biography of André Gorz, also to be published by Seagull in 2021.

Introduction

STEPHEN ROMER

The present volume of essays constitutes the second part of the Yves Bonnefoy *Reader*; the first part, containing the poems and poetic prose, was published in 2017. As my co-editor Anthony Rudolf wrote in the Preface to that volume, Bonnefoy's work has always been a 'two-track' adventure in poetry and prose. And as John Naughton, my other co-editor, points out in the Introduction to the same volume, in both his poetry and the essays that constitute his poetics, 'Bonnefoy makes clear that his aim is above all onto-logical'. The subjective drama and the ontological quest that haunts the poems and poetic prose, is indeed carried over quite naturally, and with equal fervour, into the critical prose essays gathered here. The high seriousness of the undertaking, and its urgency, has for its source the same need to locate authentic plenitude of being, and for its aim the same desire to affirm hope, though any idea of super-natural revelation must be dissociated from these terms. Whatever his subject matter, and it ranges widely, Yves Bonnefoy's instinct is resolutely to drive back to origins, to return to fundamentals – to the 'original act' of consciousness, or of being, behind a poem or a painting. To a place most often upstream of, or outside of language – though language itself, the existence of the written sign, visually or as sound, or passages of colour in a painting, can already point the way to an escape from the conceptual mode of thinking against which the poet has always done battle. Certain paintings, and all true poems, partake of Bonnefoy's *double postulation* – by which it seems possible, by astute use of systems (language, or perspective, or form), to disturb our mental habit that instantly categorises, and thereby 'neutralises' phenomena. By avoiding those formulations, the particular use of language that is the poem, attentive to the visual and phonic proper-ties of the sign, is able to deliver us back to an instant of plenitude, or to use his by now famous term, of *présence*. And it may be, as he suggests in 'Image and Presence', one of the key essays included here, that what is signified, what the reader is delivered up to by the poem, is simply 'intensity as such'; and the reader then pledges to the author that he or she, too, 'will remain in intensity'.

Before his death in 2016, at the time this *Reader* was being planned, Yves Bonnefoy engaged in some fairly detailed discussion with the editors regarding contents, in particular where the poems and poetic prose were concerned; but he was equally anxious that as regards the critical essays, the full range of his interests should as far as possible be represented, and where it has not, due to constraints of space, then at least registered in prefatory material. As it stands, we have taken pains to represent his major areas of interest: the 'foundational' essays on poetics are here, including the important riposte to the critic Georges Poulet; essays on painting, sculpture and architecture, notably on Medieval wood carving, Piero della Francesca, the Quattrocento and the Italian Baroque; there is a sustained analysis of a painting by his beloved Poussin; a rare excursion into music, on Mozart's operas, in which Mozart is essentially considered as a poet; a piece on Blake's drawings, which are a revelation to him; a consideration of two modern artists, Giacometti and Henri Cartier-Bresson. Two complex essays, 'The Unique and his Interlocutor' and 'Our Need of Rimbaud', represent the passionate lifelong 'discussion' he has sustained with the *incontournables* of the nineteenth-century, Baudelaire, Mallarmé and Rimbaud, whose key phrases are scattered like manna throughout this book. A further sidelight is thrown on Baudelaire, in contrast with Maupassant, in the important late study, 'Poetry and Photography'. In 'The Other Language in my Head' he delivers himself of his personal view of translation, supplemented by his essay on Yeats's poetics, also here, which in this view requires an act of singular empathy, but also of 'making his own' the thought of the poet to be translated. There is the late 'Letter to Shakespeare', that attests to his continuing, at times almost playful, engagement with the dramatist: it is in this spirit, given the familiar tone of the 'letter', that we have included it in the 'Memoirs' section. Although he was not given to memoir writing, when commissioned to do so he could write movingly on friends and mentors; hence the inclusion here of his luminous early memoir of Sylvia Beach in Greece, and of his three encounters, separated in time, with Jorge Luis Borges.

As it stands, the present volume contains twenty-six essays, and of the twenty-six half are newly commissioned translations. The first was published in 1961, and the last in 2013. It must be said, however, that Bonnefoy's prose bibliography (critical prose only) includes, at the last count in 2016, sixty items, several of them major volumes (including fourteen collections of essays on literature and painting). Alongside these stand volumes of art history: *Rome, 1630,* an illustrated full-length study of Bernini and the Roman Baroque; the monumental *Alberto Giacometti, biographie d'une oeuvre* from 1991; the long-pondered *Goya, les peintures noires* (2005). Then there are the free-standing short monographs, no less than ten of which were published since 2006 by the Editions Galilée, that seemed to take over the rôle formerly occupied by the Mercure de France, though important volumes continued to come from them, and from the major houses, Editions du Seuil and Gallimard. True, many of the shorter monographs have been subsequently gathered in the essay collections, but by any standard the production rate is prodigious – probably unequalled – and it was gathering pace towards the end, with the poet entering his ninth decade, concluding with the astonishing and moving prose memoir of his parents and his childhood, *L'Echarpe rouge* (2016). By contrast there are only nine major collections of poetry listed, and a further fourteen lesser volumes, some of them poetic prose: and it should be thus, for authentic poetry itself comes much more rarely. The lists so far exclude Bonnefoy's extensive work as a translator: this includes ten Shakespeare plays – to which he appended long introductions – the *Sonnets* and the two long narrative poems; and collections of Petrarch, Donne, Leopardi, Keats and Yeats.[1]

This production rate, these statistics should give us pause. If the poet was anxious that the range of work not included in this volume be signaled, it was not out of some strange fear of falling short; there is a deeper anxiety here, namely that the resolutely philosophical-

---

1   Bonnefoy has, in fact, been well-served in English translation. Of the critical prose, three full-length volumes have been published by Chicago: *The Act and the Place of Poetry* (ed. John Naughton); *The Lure and the Truth of Painting* (ed. Richard Stamelman); *Shakespeare and the French Poet* (ed. John Naughton); 1989, 1994, 2005 respectively. More recently Seagull Books (Calcutta/Chicago) has published *The Arrière-pays* (tr. Stephen Romer, 2012); *Rome, 1630,* on the early Baroque, (tr. Hoyt Rogers), and *The Red Scarf,* the late memoir, (tr. Stephen Romer) are both forthcoming.

ontological approach, the *gravité enflammée* of his rhetoric, to use once more Philippe Jaccottet's phrase, might baffle the Anglophone reader not brought up in the tradition of French philosophical discourse, or with the sacred tripartite, 'dialectical' method of argument that is inculcated from high school on. Bonnefoy is acutely, and defensively, aware of this, and the anxiety is expressed in several places, notably in the Preface he wrote for *The Lure and the Truth of Painting*, a collection of his essays on painting edited by Richard Stamelman (1995):

> On the one hand, I believe that what is essential and specific to great works is their defiance of language, rendering all the more necessary the perception and understanding of this foundational event; and on the other, I believe that this comprehension, or at the very least some sort of designation, is possible, if one learns to call into question the conceptual discourse, which comes so naturally to our lips, so as to replace it with another way of speaking about – or speaking with – works.

I quote at length because it seems essential, at this stage, to let Bonnefoy explain his project in his own words. Not that it makes it easier to grasp – following on from the passage above, he fears he offers his reader 'a vague hypothesis and an even more uncertain hope.'[2]

The reader should thus be warned: the essays that follow are frequently arduous. As Richard Stamelman has remarked: 'Bonnefoy is not a poet who is also a philosopher but a poet who is *always* a philosopher'. His unique style, long sinuous sentences that follow the movement of his thought as it unfolds, require concentration. Bonnefoy's method – and he is quite idiosyncratic in this – is time and again to explain his very particular view of what poetry *is*, before settling to the matter in hand. In that sense there is nothing of the casual aphorist about him, we do not get the disjunctive flashes of insight to be found, say, in the *Cahiers* of Paul Valéry. Bonnefoy's essays were conceived, for the most part, as formal articles, university lectures, catalogue essays, or Introductions; he eschewed literary journalism; the brief, incisive literary 'review' is not his medium. A

---

2   Yves Bonnefoy, *The Lure and the Truth of Painting: Selected Essays on Art*. Ed. Richard Stamelman, Chicago: University of Chicago Press (1995), p.XIII.

Bonnefoy essay is a serious business, and needs to be set up in the proper way. But for those with the patience to follow him, and who come to appreciate how his frequent digressions, and reiterations, bear down ever closer upon his object, the rewards can be great. This introduction is merely an attempt to provide some context, and some *points de repère* or signposts to the intellectual adventure that follows.

The paradoxes in his thinking will become apparent; they arise chiefly from the singular belief, that 'defiance of language' is specific to great works, and Bonnefoy will set about looking for signs of this, and even if he ranges over vastly differing material he will express these things in similar terminology. And one paradox that has certainly not passed unnoticed, is that he uses abstract terms to designate the earthly elementals – stone, fire, tree – he would have us cleave to. Time and again, the categories recur: presence, being-in-the-world, *hic et nunc*, plenitude, the One – which refer to a primal state of unity, to be found once we have escaped conceptual discourse; and to do so involves the necessary acceptance of 'finitude' (our mortality) and chance and death; and certain phenomena strike us – notably in the irreplaceably important apprehensions of the young child, in their sudden standing-forth – *surgissement* is the word he uses – both in plenitude but also as if emerging *ex nihilo,* from a terrifying void; and against these presences we are constantly lured by the conceptual, Platonic world of the Idea, the essence, the image, the chimera, the phantasm; but also of the daydream, and the utopian lure of a better 'elsewhere', a road not taken, all these latter states are contained in the graphic word 'excarnation'. These and a few other terms will be encountered frequently, they are the engine and dialectic of Bonnefoy's thought, and it is to be hoped, (it is certainly his hope when he gives voice to this anxiety of his) that their meaning be clarified and nuanced by each fresh context.

*

In this sense, a *Reader*, which is necessarily a sampler, actually seems a satisfactory approach to Bonnefoy, because his gist, his ardent 'message' does not vary in any great degree, and the consistency of his thought, its trenchancy, from the first declarative texts, is remarkable:

The concept, which is our way of philosophising, is a profound rejection of death, regardless of the subject it explores. It is clearly always a means of escape. Because we die in this world and in order to deny our fate, man has constructed with concepts a dwelling place of logic, where the only worthwhile principles are those of permanence and identity. [...] Yes, there is truth in them, which I do not claim to judge. But there is a lie in concepts *in general,* which allows thinking, thanks to the vast power of words, to abandon the world of things. [...] Is there a concept for footsteps in the night, for a cry, for a stone rolling in the brushwood? For the feeling evoked by an empty house? No, nothing of the real has been kept except what suits our peace of mind [...][3]

Remembering, and praising the sarcophagi around San Vitale in Ravenna, which seem to the poet to acknowledge death, by inscribing it upon stone, Bonnefoy stumbles upon his great theme, and he keeps it constantly before him thereafter. How much does a given work acknowledge 'finitude', and chance and mortal change? This is the measuring stick. One can see instantly, that this is a subjective measurement – and this leads to polemic and philosophical difficulties. But as we shall see, Bonnefoy too is fascinated, and tortured, by the alternative, idealist vision. 'The Tombs of Ravenna', an 'excited reverie', to use Yeats's lovely phrase, was written in 1953, when the poet was thirty. It represents his coming of age. We have included sections from it in volume 1, but it equally serves as a source text to the prose. The inaugural piece here, 'Byzantium', from 1961, which is incidentally steeped in the poet's readings in Yeats, takes up the theme, while varying it.

Painting & the Visual Arts

Byzantium, of course, took on decadent accretions in the *fin de siècle* – hieratic despots that mingle with figures in *Hérodiade* or *Salomé*, that Yeats in part dispels, in his great poems on the subject, and in

---

3   See 'The Tombs of Ravenna' in Yves Bonnefoy: *Poems*. Manchester: Carcanet (2017), p.3.

passages of *A Vision*, where he describes the unity of the project: 'I think that in early Byzantium, maybe never before or since in recorded history, religious, aesthetic and practical life were one', but also describes 'Byzantine eyes of drilled ivory staring upon a vision'.[4] Bonnefoy, following his own theme, or vision, must reject the mechanical bird of the artificer, that represents autonomous art. He remarks: 'the soul sought to survive in a room full of carefully chosen objects, but the choices were made on the basis of form alone and so were indifferent to the incarnation that forms take in life and in passing time(…)'. But where Yeats sees in the mosaics of the Virgin in Sicily and in Torcello, where the *Panagia Hodigitria* floats in the apse, the 'harsh Byzantine image' – Bonnefoy attends to a different image, or hears a different voice:

> I, for my part, no longer heard in it Theodora in her gold but Mistra in ruins: no longer the peacock but the stone – and thus from the very outset I associated it with a desire deep within me that sought its homeland: the desire to confront our world in those aspects that are most fleeting, that seem the least charged with being, and to give sacred meaning to them so that I might be saved with them. It's true: each time a bird cry has echoed in some forest far away, each time I have come to the threshold of a stony arena in which my own absence seems to reign, each time that the mortal and limited *here* has thus asked me to break the seal of the modern rejection of being, it was a ray of Byzantium I seemed to touch, as though by premonition, and from the very moment I first learned the name of the city of images.

Once again, I have quoted at length, not only for the beauty of the passage, but because it represents a crucial aspect of all this poet's writings on art: we too shall always, as we follow him, find ourselves on that stony arena of his own subjectivity; if we look to Bonnefoy for 'art history' in anything like a conventional sense we shall end up frustrated. A preference for Mistra in ruins is not in any traditional sense a contribution to our understanding of Byzantine art – though

4 See .W.B.Yeats, *A Vision*, London: Macmillan (1978), p.277. The whole chapter, 'Dove or Swan' is germane to the sort of cultural sweep present in Bonnefoy's essays, when taken together.

it instantly brings it alive, and gives it a bearing on the present, even an urgency, which reams of scholarly research concerned with origins and influences rarely does. It is important to grasp from the outset, as he has said himself, that we are being given to share in a poet's particular subjective drama, aspects of which emerge from his unconscious. And yet, remarkably, this drama casts itself in terms – the tension between the real and the ideal, between finitude and the deathless, between presence and image, between the lure of the floating signifier, of the authorless text and an assumption of intentionality – which are sufficiently universal to compel us as readers. This does not mean he has not read and studied deeply, for example, in the art of the Quattrocento – he undertook postgraduate research on the subject, under André Chastel: the essay here on Piero, 'The Strategy of the Enigma' shows that. And the long essay on Poussin's *Bergers d'Arcadie* does qualify as art history in the more conventional sense. But Bonnefoy's main concern, his *default position*, is always with the measuring stick of Being I mentioned above; how much or how little can he respond to a work for what it reveals, or defends, of this world, *hic et nunc*, and its mortal changing condition.

In the Byzantium essay he is drawn to the moment when, as Yeats puts it, Christ, 'shall grow more like ourselves, putting off that stern majesty', and hence he concentrates on the fresco in the monastery of Sopocani in Serbia representing the *Dormition of the Virgin*. Here, an almost disarmingly simple statement arises out of his fast-shifting thought: Christ is the 'mindful son of the *Dormition* who, out of love, returns to the mortal condition; before him lay the remains of the old woman, long and black', and therefore he can empathise with Christ to the extent that He is a dutiful son mourning a beloved mother (something that goes deep with this poet). Throughout the essays, in his search for, or affirmation of human life in its mutability, this startling directness, sometimes without psychological nuance, emerging from layers of complexity is a recurrent feature. Bonnefoy frequently seizes upon what corresponds to his own 'requirements', explicitly here, speaking of the Christ figure in this fresco, for he goes on: 'Never has a divine archetype more closely resembled the highest moment of subjective ambition, or been so easy to internalise for one striving to be a poet, or seemed so intimately related in its nature to the poetry of our time.' He does not hesitate to seize upon a detail, often obscure in the background, to work his thesis; hence in *The Arrière-pays* (1972) he remarks the landscape of little hills winding away in the background of certain paintings by Piero della Francesca, and relates them to his own obsession with finding a 'true place', forever concealed, just over the horizon, over the crest of the next hill. This sort of thing can lead to some idiosyncratic, even eccentric readings; but, equally, they frequently contain within them brilliant and valuable insights.

The two essays on Piero della Francesca, even though they are separated by more than forty years, are a case in point. Piero has always engaged Bonnefoy, like one of Baudelaire's 'phares' or beacon-figures, from his early studies in the Quattrocento and his first, revelatory visits to Italy in the 1950s. It is this painter's obsession with the new science of perspective, and his brilliant deployment of it, that will become part of Bonnefoy's own subjective drama in *The Arrière-pays*, where perspective becomes another 'lure', creating an ideal space at the expense, once more, of the real.[5] But in 'Humour and Cast Shadows', an essay from 1961, he seizes on a curious detail, the exaggerated headgear worn by characters in a painting from the *Legend of the True Cross* series in Arezzo, the hats become a 'humorous' detail (not a category frequently admitted by Bonnefoy) that shows how even in a moment of high spiritual tension, the presentation of the Cross, a humorous detail can occur: one is reminded of Auden's poem 'Musée des Beaux Arts' where at a similar moment of crisis, 'dogs go on with their doggy life and the torturer's horse/ Scratches its innocent behind on a tree'. And only Bonnefoy, surely, could make the astonishing leap, and land on his feet, when he inquires what would be the 'opposite' of the huge hats of Piero, and replies without hesitation, it is the 'cast shadow'. He cites here the work of the Surrealist painter Giorgio de Chirico, whose ideal arcades and piazzas, that obey the rules of perspective in their turn, but are now

---

5   See Yves Bonnefoy, *The Arrière-pays*, tr. Stephen Romer. Calcutta/Chicago: Seagull Books, 2012. Brief passages were published in Volume 1 of this *Reader*, but the whole volume, first published in 1972, is of key importance, especially as a 'source-book' for Bonnefoy's adventures in the visual arts, notably in Italy. It is here that the narrator's 'deliverance' from the idealizing science of Tuscan perspective, into the Roman Baroque, is most fully played out.

seen 'from the outside' and in the declining light; this light casts long shadows, and ushers in 'an intuition of nothingness, the glory of a sun setting in the west'. This is an example of Bonnefoy's bold associative approach which, if not exactly *verifiable* in a scientific sense, creates a vibrant, plausible *correspondance* between two painters of divergent epochs, that is intellectually thrilling.

The second, much longer essay from 2006, and published in English for the first time here, *The Strategy of the Enigma*, sets out to suggest something on the face of it quite radical; in this account, when painting *The Flagellation*, now in Urbino, Piero turns away, albeit in the loftiest, most tactful way, from the gospel event in the background, and from the urgent discussion – most probably political and involving war – being carried on in the foreground. As if, while commissioned to portray events of great moment, Piero chooses this moment to construct a 'strategy of enigma', whereby rather than trying to identify the personages and details in the painting, rendered deliberately opaque, the viewer is encouraged to see 'all the more directly and strongly what in the picture is not meaning and is, precisely, colour, form, the exchanges that colour and form have amongst themselves (...)'; the lesson drawn here is summed up: 'Not to understand allows one to see'. In Bonnefoy's reading, which he coaxes out with subtlety and precaution, Piero is thereby cast, in his easing apart of form and content, as a forerunner of a decidedly modern sensibility. And the comparison that is drawn this time, similarly bold, but still brilliant, is with Edward Hopper.

From the Quattrocento, two further essays move us on to the Baroque; a short piece on Bernini, and a major study of a painting by Poussin, *Les Bergers d'Arcadie*, which demonstrates Bonnefoy's claim to be taken seriously, when he so desires, as a scholarly art historian. He states his position on the Baroque ardently, in the short extract we have included here from his early monograph *Rome, 1630*, devoted to Bernini's great coiled 'barley sugar' Baldaquin in Saint Peter's, Rome, raised above the apostle's tomb and the high altar. This example of flamboyant baroque may seem a surprising locus for Bonnefoy to find so many conflicts resolved in the drama of representation initiated by the science of perspective in Florentine art, which 'regards the object externally, and thus reduces it to its appearance'. In a remarkable passage, he finds the angels atop the baldaquin, literally represented in a position that suits his own subjective requirements perfectly: 'With a foot, with the movement of a hip, they find a toehold in palpable existence, with its blinded entanglements; but their whole body already seems poised for a rebound.' The angels seem to be grounded – that toehold - in a moment before flight, but for the poet all is in that moment – the rare moment of immanence, celebrated in so many of his poems. And it is, crucially, a moment freed from Catholic dogma – 'since it will resolve into pure *presence*, and cease to hold us back in what is no longer sin'. Original Sin is a dogma rebarbative to Bonnefoy, with its concomitant mistrust of sensuality, and of the body – of what Pound, similarly repelled, called the 'hell-breeding belief'; and 'the new atheism', the secular mind he sees emerging at this time, and names in the Poussin essay, will deliver enlightened man from its toils. The poet discovers to his joy that Bernini's triumphant but grounded angels, describe not an object, but an 'encounter', a turning towards the viewer, an invitation to unabashed plenitude to which he finds he can assent. This idea of 'encounter', of communion with another, or with others, as against perfection-seeking unearthly solitude, increasingly informs his poetics. The counter-intuitive word that Bonnefoy uses, relating to Bernini, usually regarded as exultantly extrovert – is *interiority*; because the viewer is drawn in, invited in, to an encounter where, finally liberated from the anxiety of spatial idealism, he or she is released into a spiritual freedom that is a 'dazzling interiority'.

Like Bernini, but even more so, more intensely since the drama of identification is stronger with the French painter who settled in Rome, Poussin's struggles, and eventual triumphs, are grist to the poet's mill. Poussin! To the uninitiated, he may seem a magnificent but perhaps a rather cerebral, coldly classicising painter; in Bonnefoy's mind and eye he is anything but. Indeed, it is Poussin, notably in his great series of paintings *Moïse sauvé des eaux* – Moses Saved from the Waters – with its theme of rescue, who delivers the anguished seeker at the end of *The Arrière-pays* from his life-sapping dilemma concerning representation and the science of perspective. Passages of colour, his blues in particular, deliver him from the conceptual, indeed from thought itself. The major essay included here, originally a lecture delivered at the Grand Palais in 1994, attends in great detail to a single painting, *Les Bergers d'Arcadie* – but Bonnefoy includes in his discussion the subversion and transgression of strictly Christian morality; the eroticisation, for example, in Tasso and Ariosto, of the bucolic tradition inherited from Virgil, but also graphically represented in the luxuriant Venuses of Titian. He registers a change in the climate of thought. In terms of the Catholic dogma then still dominant, Bonnefoy finds that Poussin, a man of strong sensual appetites, experiences his own 'fall', relatable to that of Midas, for gold, or Orlando, obsessed with Angelica; they must all break free from their desires for possession, 'which strongly reduce the field of perception'. This realisation – in short the necessity for self-control and renunciation – in the end allows the artist 'to grant a meaning to the theologians' recommendations, even if Poussin's ascesis is radically exempt from the Christian disgust for the flesh. Poussin the Platonist will be able to live in peace with many of the Christians of his era.' This is brilliant analysis, and once again it helps us to 'situate' Bonnefoy himself. In his Introduction to volume 1, John Naughton cites the love poems in *Pierre écrite*, and notes how the language is continuously ambiguous, and the address is as much to the woman as to the surrounding Provençal landscape and its scorched, stony, aromatic elements.[6] Like Poussin, then, Bonnefoy is careful that the 'field of perception' be not reduced; in familiar language, we could say he keeps his eye always on the 'bigger picture' even in his poems of erotic love.

The essays here on modern artists, and on photography, introduce into discourse the notion of chance – chance which admits details that the idealising painter would have filtered out. We have all been taken aback, have we not, by those worn and prematurely old faces, the scuffed shoes and stained clothes we see in late Victorian or Edwardian group photographs; 'accidents' of appearance that would have been cleaned up and smoothed away by the painter. The admission of *chance*, Bonnefoy argues in his original study from 2010, 'Poetry and Photography', into the universe of visual representation, was for some early photographers, like Daguerre himself, who

6   See Yves Bonnefoy, *Poems*, pp. xxi–xxiii.

was also a painter, considered 'a disaster'; and for Mallarmé it was a further proof – this admission of the purely arbitrary into the visual frame – yet again of his materialist conviction, frequently quoted, at times in agreement and at times in protestation by Bonnefoy – that 'nous ne sommes que de vaines formes de la matière' – we are no more than vain forms of matter. In Bonnefoy's remarkable account, again counter-intuitive in some of its conclusions, he is as always careful of 'being', and seeks its trace; and he finds it in 'the gaze', or more precisely, in eye-contact: in Baudelaire's poem 'La Passante', the speaker in the poem locks eyes for a second with the beautiful passer by, 'en grand deuil', the tall woman in full mourning: 'a gaze, a flash. And after the flash perhaps the night again, but during the flash, which is endless, are all the rivers and all the skies and beings of the world'. This moment of contact is rescued, or rather appears to 'rescue' Baudelaire, or his speaker, in Bonnefoy's account, whereas the narrator of Maupassant's story 'La Nuit', in which the lights go out forever on Paris and the city dies completely in the mind and experience of the terrified narrator, finds no such redemption.

It is human contact, the poet seems to insist, that saves; the early photographic portraitists, Nadar and Carjat, sought the gaze of Baudelaire, or Marceline Desbordes-Valmore, or Rimbaud: 'they did not want to speak to us of these poets, rather they wanted them to speak'. These early photographers, then, sought to reinvest being where other less scrupulous practitioners sought to steal it or deprive their objects of it. Giacometti and Henri Cartier-Bresson are two twentieth-century artists who rightly belong to this group according to the essay on them here, which is also an affectionate portrait of both artists, since they were all three friends. The sculptor and the photographer, the poet asserts, were both in their very different arts affirmative of being, in this sense of soliciting human contact. Bonnefoy returns to his overriding theme: Giacometti, through his endless, relentless attempts to solicit the presence of Annette or Diego, represents 'an extraordinary resurgence of the art that brings beings into the world'. He goes on:

> In his creations, sculptures as well as paintings, persons or things are not perceived by means of their visual aspects; they are evoked as presences. Nothing remains of them in the image he creates but

a sudden appearance which, coming from the inside of their very being, attests the fact of this being, signifies its mystery: Annette or Diego are there, in front of Alberto, they *are*; and yet it is necessary for the sculptor's gaze to be directed upon them, for them not to sink into the nothingness which surrounds everything.

The longer essay, devoted in part to Maupassant's story, draws together two signal events, the first daguerreotype, and the installation of electric street-lighting in Paris – both effecting a radical aesthetic change: visual representation underwent a tectonic shift in the first, and street lighting abolished the old, organic relation to the coming of darkness; by effecting a sudden artificial division into light and dark, the surrounding blackness was made blacker. This brusque 'surgissement', or emergence of an object or a figure, seen against pitch darkness, standing forth against a void, is something that haunted Bonnefoy in his childhood, and we shall return to it.

Poetics & Poets

The painter, deploying passages of pure colour, has recourse to an immediacy denied to the writer: 'To write – if it be only a word – and already a language is formed, busy with all the ambiguities, all the pretenses – all the past history – of language. The immediate does not exist for the writer, even if he is passionately attentive to what has no name, no definable image.' When it comes to considering Bonnefoy's poetics and his approach to verbal expression it is useful to contrast it with qualities available to the painter. In the same essay he writes this:

> It is by colour, by the violent red of a sun that is truly *seen*, beyond any consideration of symbolism or solar allegories, that Delacroix puts an end to centuries of narrative painting, a subordinated painting. And Poussin has blues which save him, as if in a flash of lightning, from reason in which he knows he will be lost.

If it was the immediacy of music – expressiveness but not expression – that haunted Mallarmé and that he wished to recover for his own art, then with Bonnefoy we might say it is painting, or colour itself.

He continues the insight quoted above, speaking of the writer: 'Intuitively, he knows that *other* quality of truth which is offered by the
flowering branch of a tree or a stone cascading down a ravine. But
to want to create in words the infinite density or the pure emptiness
of these things is from the outset a mad hope which poetry, drawing
its life from such things, must abandon page after page.'[7] We should
bear in mind, reading the early, foundational essays like 'The Act and
the Place of Poetry', 'French Poetry and the Principle of Identity' and
their 'historic' re-statement in his inaugural lecture of 1981 at the
Collège de France, 'Image and Presence', that these were written at a
time when literary art in France, especially poetry, was under attack
as never before, from political ideology and the linguistic sciences.
These essays are not for the faint-hearted: one does not just read them,
one undergoes them, with all their strange halting progress, complex
digression, passionate assertion, and as such they resist paraphrase,
even though they have been much discussed.[8] Bonnefoy's career ran
parallel, and in fact outlasted, the rise of Structuralism, and then
Deconstruction, the dethroning of authorial intentionality and the
proclamation of the death of the author. It is not surprising then, if
many of the essays here feel embattled. In the heady days of *Tel Quel*,
of Marxist ideology, feminism, and Lacanian psychoanalysis, with its
scrutiny of language as a ghostly system of signs, constantly a prey to
semantic slippage and pun revealing of the unconscious, Bonnefoy
can seem a lonely figure, even if his own work is in fact touched by
these things.

We need to understand his early credo, the first sentence of 'The
Act and the Place of Poetry', in this context: 'I should like to bring
together, almost to identify, poetry and hope (…)'. It is in this essay,
delivered as a lecture to the Collège de Philosophie in Paris in 1959,
that he sets out on his campaign against the concept, this time
framing it more academically, where the *Tombs of Ravenna* six years
earlier casts essentially the same insight in the heightened medium

---

7   See the essay 'On Painting and Poetry, on Anxiety and Peace' in Yves
Bonnefoy, *The Lure and the Truth of Painting*, ed. Richard Stamelman. University of Chicago Press (1995), pp. 169–74
8   See, for example, John Naughton, *The Poetics of Yves Bonnefoy*, University of
Chicago Press, 1984.

of poetic prose. The essay takes position against the whole tendency behind the nihilistic art of Mallarmé and the 'linguistic turn' his poetry announced, to prise apart sign and referent; Bonnefoy goes to war, so to speak, against Mallarmé's famous idea-flower, the pure linguistic notion, '*l'absent de tous bouquets*'. Bonnefoy's long struggle, involving as we have seen the visual arts, to escape the lure of idealism, and the sealed hothouse room of Des Esseintes, had no choice but to declare Mallarmé's art to be anathema, even though he returns to it unceasingly. The earlier poet is his *frère-ennemi*; Bonnefoy needs to keep Mallarmé in fact, in a war embrace, to give meaning to his own position, his own struggle. It could in truth be described as an Oedipal relation. As we shall see, just as he cleaves to Rimbaud as a poet who apparently retained hope, who wrote of 'une ardente patience' and who acknowledged the 'réalité rugueuse' – the rugged reality – of the world, so he abjures Mallarmé's renunciation. He declares flatly: 'Mallarmé's poetry represents the defeat of existence, impulse after impulse, desire after desire'. There is irony here, though, in that Rimbaud's renunciation was in the end more absolute than Mallarmé's, it was irrevocable: he simply gave up poetry.

Rimbaud and Mallarmé, along with Baudelaire, to whom he is devoted as, finally, a poet who rescues and defends reality, are constant reference points in Bonnefoy's essays – the phrases quoted above are used as a kind of shorthand, representing different spiritual states or intellectual points of view. Two essays here, published for the first time in English, contain the essence of Bonnefoy's mature thought about Mallarmé and Rimbaud. The first, on Mallarmé, 'The Unique and his Interlocutor', served as a Preface to a selection of the poet's correspondence. It was brave, or perhaps impercipient, of the publisher to entrust such a task to Bonnefoy – for after some more or less mild comments, he proceeds to launch a devastating attack, and claims to reveal 'Mallarmé's secret', that he could never reveal to his countless correspondents. This is a classic Bonnefoy procedure: *il avance masqué* , he moves with stealth and precaution, but as the proofs and arguments accrue, we realise that a powerful case for the prosecution is being set up. One might have imagined that the somewhat callow attack on his great forerunner, a necessary 'beheading', to establish a new poetics, would have mellowed in the forty years between the two pieces. Not a bit of it. He does acknowledge – and this is a major concession – the reality of Mallarmé's spiritual crisis of 1866–67, when he 'thought his Thought', when he died and rose again, 'an impersonal function of the Universe'; when he discovered the Death of God, and the possibility of Beauty. Bonnefoy says that, as a 'lived experience', the pages to his friend Henri Cazalis, in which he describes this crisis, 'go as far as those discovered sewn into the lining of Pascal's doublet'; an honour he accords, pointedly in the light of the different estimation he came to hold of the two poets, also to Rimbaud's 'Lettre du Voyant', written at around the same time.

The attack on Mallarmé's *notion pure*, is here increased, or shadowed by a scepticism as to whether even Mallarmé himself believed in his own project; or, more dramatically still, that after the tragic death of Anatole, his young son, the projected absolutely impersonal writing, in which the poet's self, his ego, would be 'perfectly dead', could not be carried out since that would be a betrayal of the boy's simple desire to live. As Bonnefoy says, with finality: 'One of the necessary conditions for the new writing had gone missing, forever'. Mallarmé's own lucidity on this matter, as Bonnefoy might have acknowledged less elliptically, is recorded in the painful fragments that were edited in 1961 by Jean-Pierre Richard as *Pour un tombeau d'Anatole*. The impossibility, the sheer madness of his own project, is what haunted Mallarmé, and in Bonnefoy's view this becomes the unavowed, guilty secret which explains why he eschews almost any discussion of his own work in the letters after 1871, when he arrived in Paris. The piece reads at times like an indictment, but there is compassion there, an awareness of tragedy in the 'perhaps increasingly dramatic relation of a monomaniac of the absolute to himself.'

What a contrast the long, arduous act of homage – 'Our Need of Rimbaud' – represents! We have, clearly, no 'Need of Mallarmé', though in the opening remarks of the Rimbaud piece, delivered as the 2007 Zaharoff Lecture at Oxford, he assures his listeners of the 'great affection' in which he has always held Mallarmé's work, 'despite the reservations I've raised'. This sounds strangely in the light of what we have just seen. What is not in doubt is the veritable drama of identification Bonnefoy projects upon Rimbaud, and which he sustained throughout his career, ever since his monograph of 1961, and his revised opinion about the poet's mother in 'Madame

Rimbaud' (1979). What he seems to respond to instantly, what still seems to stir him, in contrast to the metaphysical ordeal of the young Mallarmé – that he subjects to sceptical scrutiny – is Rimbaud's early restiveness, his social unrest, and his (barely focused) utopian vision; his empathy with others, his 'difficulty with girls', and more generally the relations between men and women – 'l'amour est à réinventer'. This is a side that affects Bonnefoy, and his later compassionate response to Shakespeare's heroines will tend in the same direction: it correlates with the here and now, with 'existing conditions', with the common lot. There may be some class solidarity involved here – Bonnefoy has described the 'chambres pauvres', the poor rooms in which he was brought up, in a modest house on a working-class street. But the political is never truly at the centre of his concerns, or not for long: the notions of 'hope' and 'lucidity', and 'plenitude', related to a more general idea of being-in-the-world, once more come to predominate. In any case, Rimbaud's later career scarcely corresponds to the idea of committed social reformer – adventurer, yes, restless soul, yes, curious intellect, yes, but not a political mover and shaker.

What links Rimbaud and Baudelaire is that 'le vrai du monde' – the veritable nature of the world – does not fade from their view. Bonnefoy then proceeds to trace the career of the 'lucidity', through its various vicissitudes, and despite the 'chimères', the chimeras or snares – the word recurs frequently here – laid in its path, in the body of Rimbaud's writing. Bonnefoy compares the two: 'Rimbaud had none of the disdain that this self-styled dandy believed he had for many of the men and women in whose vicinity he was obliged to live'. Again, this seems at first glance counter-intuitive – Rimbaud was not known for his tolerance, for example to the well brought up young poets of Verlaine's acquaintance at their club, the *Vilains bonshommes*; and he could be cruel to Verlaine. But on a deeper level Bonnefoy is surely correct, and this is borne out by one of the *Illuminations* that the poet discusses in his memoir, *L'Echarpe rouge*. In 'Royauté' a young couple, belonging to a gentle people – 'un peuple fort doux' – decide, in the market place, to proclaim themselves king and queen, for the length of a morning and an afternoon. And Rimbaud simply describes this, and would seem to assent, to the self-crowning of a beautiful young couple, emerging out of the people. Rimbaud is propelled 'towards men and women, all of whom, from the very beginning, will stand as plenitude offered and received, like gods'.

★

Such trenchant opinions as those we have just seen, concerning Mallarmé and Rimbaud, are inevitably controversial, especially when based on inconclusive psychological 'data'; and the whole thrust and project of Bonnefoy's poetics more generally considered is vulnerable to criticism. I have mentioned one obvious objection, which has has always been raised, that points out the apparently glaring contradiction between Bonnefoy's insistence on the primal, non-conceptual state of *présence* – which alone should be the preserve of poetry – and the remarkably abstract categories – *finitude, évidence, être,* often defined against *image, chimère, leurre* – he employs to designate this. In the important essay, 'Georges Poulet and Poetry' he offers a lengthy defense of his position, after the Belgian literary critic raised just this objection. Bonnefoy is always alert to such 'vulnerability', and to a great extent he assumes it, acknowledging at some places the inevitable 'vagueness' of his hypothesis, concerning *présence*, and the works that seem to him to manifest it or at least hanker for it. Let us not forget the passage quoted earlier, that speaks of the 'page after page' abandoned in the attempt to create in words the 'infinite density or the pure emptiness' of naturally occurring phenomena.

And yet he never lets go of his fundamental insight and conviction, and he argues it through with impressive tenacity in this 'reply' to Georges Poulet of 2004, presented here in English for the first time. It is a text in which Bonnefoy, facing a potentially grave challenge, feels called upon to make explicit his religious position, and although we had sensed it, it is still startling in its decisiveness: he believes in a transcendence 'already here, in our midst, a transcendence consubstantial with life'; and that even the art of a Shakespeare or a Mozart 'must need something to lean on in this world'; they co-exist with 'vestiges, in a birdcall, a child's laugh, a sob, at the very least, of a mode of being that does not let itself be explained and that solicits the mind in a mysterious way'. And so we are back once more with the non-conceptual or pre-conceptual phenomenon. And the apprehension of *présence* is, as we suspected, 'completely made up of immanence and certainly does not consist of anything personalised within a divineness for which I have no use, nothing that needs a theology of a Father or even of a Son'. These are important pages, and Bonnefoy advances to an explicitiness directly about his belief and intention as rarely elsewhere, where there is usually an object, a painting or a poem or a building, to mediate it.

In this passionately articulate defense of an art that would eschew that very articulation – after all poetry, this voice says – 'is the memory of a reality not yet undone by the work of concepts' – we are indeed taken far into the heart of a contradiction, even if Bonnefoy adduces a brilliant analysis of the existence of the signifier as *sound*, and how the word 'arbre' – the word 'tree' –, resonated when we were children, at the age 'when the concept is only beginning to establish itself in the youthful mind'. However, when he goes on to argue that the poem in fact is not only attentive to the concept, but must treat it with 'compassion' we may justifiably wonder if we are not at the heart of a riddle without an answer. Can poetry – should poetry – be described in this way? The essay labours to explain; it is a fascinating example of Bonnefoy thinking through as he writes. And behind it, I shall return to this, is the boy on his mother's knee, reading an ABC book of images, and learning with her the names of things.

At this juncture, I think we are justified in asking once more, we must ask, it would be disingenuous not to do so: can poetry be described, or defined in this way? At one point, Bonnefoy recruits Coleridge to his argument, with his great distinction between the fancy and the imagination: and imagination of course is claimed for the side of poetry, fancy is conceptual thinking. But Coleridge never sought to define poetry in quite the exclusive way the French poet does: his own poetry includes satire, light verse, pseudo-epic, ballad, the 'conversation' poem, exercises in hexameter etc. Does none of this qualify as 'poetry'? In two essays here, Bonnefoy writes about translating Shakespeare, and the particular challenges, and energies it releases, freedoms it offers, for the French poet constrained by the unaccented, 'timeless' alexandrine. But what should we make of this verdict on the *Sonnets*, recorded in an interview with John Naughton: 'Clearly, poetry has not yet accomplished its task. It should be the war against conceptual representations, the kind of war that would allow it to experience the immediacy of other beings and to free those beings from the stereotypical interpretations that impoverish them.'[9] Is that not seriously to underestimate, among others, sonnets 29, 94 or 116?

Nobody can predict how Bonnefoy's work, how his rhetorical position will stand in the future. It may be consigned to history as yet another attempt by a poet, notably a French poet, to explain and define poetry – Mallarmé famously divided the language into what was poetic and what was not, Reverdy offered further prescriptions, the Surrealists yet others. Bonnefoy's definition, like theirs, will take its place. He can be censorious: Mallarmé, Valéry, Eliot, among others, fall short in various ways. There was always a danger, when Heidegger's attractive and half-understood phrase 'Man is the Shepherd of Being' became applied, as it was, to poets, that it would instantly put both poetry and being to flight. Being cannot be thus shepherded; like truth, it must be stalked, and told slant, and in fragments, with the materials that come to hand. And mostly, poetry proves elusive, or pops up in an unexpected place, where the lawgiver may least expect it. This is as it should be. Bonnefoy himself is too scrupulous a poet, and too self-aware an intelligence to fall into this lure. The poets, the artists he admires most, in fact, are those in whose work the struggle against deathliness is most visible, even if the results are, inevitably, partial. This explains his devotion to Piero and Poussin, to Shakespeare, and Baudelaire, and Yeats. These are the poets who have 'gone on trying' and who display throughout, in their high sincerity, what Bonnefoy beautifully calls 'une mélancolie ardente'. This is his community. And before coming to judgment, we would do well to ponder anew Remy de Gourmont's famous remark: 'Eriger en lois ses impressions personnelles, c'est le grand effort d'un homme s'il est sincère' – to cast as laws his personal impressions constitutes the great effort of any man, if he is sincere.

★

9   See Yves Bonnefoy, *Shakespeare and the French Poet*, ed. John Naughton. University of Chicago Press (2004), p. 263.

The truth is, of course, that Bonnefoy's scope in the great sweep of his essays is much wider than his attempt to define poetry as such. His brilliant analyses of Byzantine, Renaissance and Baroque art and architecture conclusively prove that. In his advocacy of the visual arts, in his committed and prolonged encounter with the European tradition, he stands in a line of poet-critics that would include Rilke, Yeats, Pound, Valéry, Verhaeren, and nearer his own day, Zbigniew Herbert, who wrote on architecture and Dutch landscape painting. In France, there is an established tradition of poets writing on painters, starting with Diderot and passing on to Baudelaire; nearer our own time Breton, Aragon and Char have distinguished themselves, as have contemporaries like Philippe Jaccottet, André du Bouchet and Jacques Dupin. The cogency of Bonnefoy's discreet encounters with works, taken together, provide a formidable account of one man's spiritual and intellectual trajectory. He has contemplated canonical works, and he has sought out contemporary artists in their studios. The poems to the painter Jacques Truphémus, that are the final items in volume one, bear witness to this; and, typically, he supplemented them with catalogue essays.

Conclusion: L'Echarpe rouge

In concluding, it seems important to say a little more about the memoir I have mentioned, *L'Echarpe rouge* – The Red Scarf –which the poet completed shortly before his death. This is partly because we have been unable to find a place for it in this *Reader*, and I think it provides important 'inaugural' material that may go some way to explaining the single-mindedness with which Bonnefoy has pursued his vision of being, of presence, through his poetry and his essays on art and poetics.

A major theme of the book is the unequal relations between his parents, and his father's 'silence', and the anxiety the young Bonnefoy feels about this. Later on he comes to sense that somehow he and his mother, both more literary, and reveling in language, left Elie, the father, who worked for the railways, out in the cold. What is clear, concomitantly, is the closeness of the mother-son bond; his mother, Hélène, is described at one point – they lived near a railway – in a vignette that must rank high in the annals of a son's adoration for his mother: 'this gatherer-together of a world coming apart, this Isis of the little house by the railway line.' It is his mother who teaches him to read:

> The words of a young child in effect allowed the young woman who heard and spoke them with me to return to the never-forgotten intensity of her origins. And I believe it was this re-connection that led my mother, a few years later, to teach me to read. It may seem natural for a schoolteacher to want to instruct her own son, rather than to leave the task to someone else; but I feel that in her case this went beyond the usual possessive instinct. I can see before me now, on the dining table where meals were served after the hour of instruction, an ABC, a tall thin book, with worn, greenish covers; this contained the images that were, page after page, framed by a magnificent capital letter. Here were images of a cat for the letter C, or of a house fringed by trees for the letter H. Succinct and boldly coloured, these were line drawings that had no use for dictionary definitions, they were destined simply to show a cat or a house or a tree to the child bent over the book. And the child would re-live through them what belongs innately to being in the world, while at the same time discovering the existence of trees, of trees in general, but also of becoming attached to a familiar tree, and to feel it as a friendly presence.

This seems crucial, and Bonnefoy makes explicit what the experience meant for him: 'By revealing to me the great power stored in a few simple words, my mother inspired me, in my future life, not to give up on the child's gaze, which had helped her, in her own existence, to find her feet again.' [10]

We can set beside this intense memory, passages that involve memories of another, very different type, that he alludes to quite enigmatically in *The Arrière-pays*, but here again he expands on them, and their formative importance:

> But well before these thoughts, in my own childhood, I had already lived through experiences and emotions of quite another

---

10 The extracts from *The Red Scarf* are in my translation. The whole text is forthcoming in 2020 from Seagull Books.

nature. They were made up of instants, not the vague and floating time of dream. It was also in the here and now, where I was, and not yet where words called to me, beyond the horizon of the known world. And the context was all very ordinary, in the most familiar of settings, but added to them was a kind of standing forth (*surgissement*) that obliterated material reality: suddenly these events, these things, were nothing but the incomprehensible act of their being raised before me. [...] But the most striking of all these experiences, and the one which guided my consequent thinking about works of art, be it poetry, painting or sculpture, was this: night had fallen, we were returning from the nearby farm with fresh milk, and coming by the first house at the entrance to the village, there is a window open and a lamp burning within. And suddenly there I saw, all at once, a black silhouette against the light, a man standing, bent over some task or other. What a shock! A perception of the fact of being, and with it the fear of non-being, and to feel oneself swept towards a stranger by the surge of solidarity in the heart of an absolute, vertiginous solitude, only now fully grasped!

Bonnefoy goes on to comment: 'I had had an experience of nothingness, a scare, and after it I looked at the things around me with different eyes'. I have quoted at length, because of the central importance of these experiences. They stand for themselves; the young poet clearly experienced, from time to time, vertiginous visitations of the void, of nothingness which, one could speculate, fuel his later cleaving to all traces of Being.

Both passages recount foundational experiences, inaugural moments, and these are always central to Bonnefoy's thought and art. He never forgets them, and he is perhaps at his greatest, in both poems and prose, when alluding to them. To take one instance that runs through several texts, the encounter with cool whitewashed walls, and the smell of plaster. In the late memoir, again, he quotes a fragment he wrote about his visit as a young man to a painter he had befriended:

> An old house
> With deep recessed windows,
> With whitewashed walls. And I had drunk

Eagerly at that cup of whiteness,
I who came from the poor rooms
With their flowery wallpaper.

He will encounter these cool white walls again in Italy. In the early essay, 'Paintings and Places', which is a kind of love-letter to small museums or places that harbour paintings, he talks of the 'founding smell of plaster'.[11] Later on, such white-washed walls, and the smell of plaster, will provide the setting for some of his greatest poetry, composed at Valsaintes, the 'true place', the half-ruined Abbaye in Provence, whose echoing spaces he inhabited for several intense summers.

The essays that follow can be complex, but the experience they defend is grounded, founded on these intensities. As the poet says in the essay 'Second Earth', included here, 'there is no contradiction' between the humblest bowl 'carved out of knotty wood' and work of high art. This is because 'the most elaborated works of art, with respect to the most beautiful ordinary objects of archaic societies, are merely the same economy raised to a second degree of awareness, the same thirst quenched with the same kind of invisible water.' It is this invisible water that Yves Bonnefoy invites us to share.

11   *The Lure and the Truth of Painting*, p.25.

A Note on the Text

Yves Bonnefoy published some thirty substantial collections of essays during his lifetime. In addition to these he published, especially latterly, several freestanding shorter essays in volume form. Several of the essays, which often began as papers at conferences or colloquia, prefaces or introductions, catalogue essays or public lectures, went through various transformations in their publishing history, the poet frequently revising and expanding his thought. In every case, there- fore, we have adopted the final version of the essay, as published in the most recent available collection. Throughout the book, footnotes provide the publishing source, in which the original place and date of publication is given, followed by the most recent collection in which the essay is to be found. A number of the essays were originally delivered as public lectures, and we have maintained – as Bonnefoy himself chooses to do – the introductory remarks and modes of address that are usual on these occasions. At the time of writing, a volume of Bonnefoy's *oeuvre* is being prepared for publication in Gallimard's prestigious, 'bible-paper', *Bibliothèque de la Pleiade*. This edition (the number of volumes is yet to be dertermined) will contain the definitive versions and publishing history of the poetry and the prose.

A Note on the Translation: In a work of 'divers hands' such as this, in close collaboration with the translators, editorial choice has been exerted in the attempt to render as consistently as possible the abstract terms that Bonnefoy frequently employs, words such as *présence, évidence, plénitude, finitude, chimère, image*; since the poet applies different nuances to these words himself, depending on context, it was felt that a 'glossary' of some kind would be unhelpful and even misleading. As noted in the Introduction, it is only by reading Bonnefoy in depth, and absorbing these terms in each fresh context, that they can be fully apprehended. In this, as in all matters, the editors would like to take this opportunity to thank the translators for their patience and for their exemplary work.

A number of these essays first appeared elsewhere, and we are grateful to the publishers concerned for granting us permission to republish them here. Finally, and most importantly, the editors should like to thank the poet's daughter, Mathilde Bonnefoy, for her staunch support throughout the preparation of this volume.

Footnotes: It was rarely Bonnefoy's practice either to cite secondary material in any detail or to use footnotes. We have signaled the poet's own footnotes by appending the letters [YB]. All other footnotes have been provided by the editors, with contributions from the translators.

I.

PAINTING & THE VISUAL ARTS

Byzantium[1]

I think of the naive Byzantium of *fin de siècle* fantasies – like a fake gem, or one, at least, whose light has been dimmed by the heavy gold setting. All the signs of the ideal, rather than the absolute, of aristocracy, rather than nobility; but a pernicious immobility, like the heart that wants nothing to do with the joys and sufferings of living and turns away from what is real, though at the risk of experiencing instinct, in the passive anticipation of death, as a sudden and unintelligible violence. Thus the affirmation of the Beautiful became indistinguishable from the hatred of existence. The soul sought to survive in a room full of carefully chosen objects, but the choices were made on the basis of form alone and so were indifferent to the incarnation that forms take in life and in passing time; and thus the forms, left to themselves, grew and flourished demonically. Is it true that the historical Byzantium ever justified this specious perversity? Shouldn't we rather see it, with Yeats, as the place where the heart can find itself anew, sing when it might be tempted to weep, and reinvent hope? Yeats, it should be said, situated this pole of his passion in a distant region, far from a life he left to brilliant but fugitive couplings, and he set in opposition to the real and ephemeral bird that automaton of gold and jewels that signifies the autonomous reign of art.

I do not believe that art can be solely this kind of refuge without betraying itself. And yet, I, too, pay homage to Byzantium, feeling in my heart – doubtless like so many others of our time – that its call may still be heard. But has it, in fact, spoken the same word? That indistinct word, heard on the borders of lands not yet known, as yet poorly understood in its too subtle inflections. I, for my part, no longer heard in it Theodora in her gold but Mistra in ruins; no longer the peacock but the stone – and thus from the very outset I associated it with a desire deep within me that sought its homeland: the desire to confront our world in those aspects that are most fleeting, that seem the least charged with being, and to give sacred meaning

1   Originally published as 'Byzance', in *L'Arc*, no. 14 (Spring 1961). Reprinted in *L'Improbable*, rev. and enlarged edition, Paris: Mercure de France, 1992 and also in Paris: Gallimard, Collection Folio/Essais, 1992.

to them so that I might be saved with them. It's true: each time a bird cry has echoed in some forest far away, each time I have come to the threshold of a stony arena in which my own absence seems to reign, each time that the mortal and limited *here* has thus asked me to break the seal of the modem rejection of being, it was a ray of Byzantium I seemed to touch, as though by premonition, and from the very moment I first learned the name of the city of images. Here, too, it was a question of eternity, just as before; the dominant note of Byzantium, perceived in every era, could still be heard. But this eternity no longer presented itself as the negation of the land of what can he seen and felt; it was burning in its trees; it had to be drawn from the depths of the scattered reality we inhabit, for this eternity was its very substance, its glorified body suddenly visible. Every form of consummation and above all the voyage. If a boat left port at night, I seemed to sense the spiritual Byzantium glowing like a distant shore. I loved to bestow this name on moments of immanence and danger, on ruins, on cities one only catches glimpses of, on ploughed fields, on all things that cannot be named. Was I wrong? And yet I have also found places where, amidst the diversity of the signals of the historical Byzantium, an almost pure voice seemed to justify me. I remember Torcello, a few Greek churches – the walls in the sun, the paintings – and the Saviour of Sopoćani.

Sopoćani! I know of nothing more perfectly accomplished than this chapel in the mountains. And in this picture that I am trying to give, of the true country, I want to see in it the features of a threshold.

Already the nearby valleys, beneath the colourless light, resemble the far-off metropolis I had imagined. The mountains of Serbia are a rigorous elucidation. The spirit of diversion fades quickly away, and nature itself appears to rise above its own summit, and with all its silent ravines, its torrents, its elusive humanity, its dark roads, seems to lose itself like a flame in the sky. The monasteries are great circles of stone: the image once again of the sky. In these enclosures, where one or two churches grow old, where one can sense the immensity of the tumultuous horizon, one sees beautiful blue peacocks walking gravely over the brown earth.

And already, in the church itself, on the intrados of the great arch, beneath the capital, on the left, and intact in this field of so much ruin like a gift, like grace, there is the angel who speaks the words of welcome. But nothing can replace the most majestic of paintings. And when one turns toward it, in the October light, it is the true speech, so long sought after, that all at once resounds. How close he is to us, the man-god offered in this room that hereafter will remain empty! And in how pure a way he brings together, following the deepest wishes of our hearts, the two discordant intuitions of Western thought: what perishes – and is our fate – and what is eternal! There is the beautiful and pensive face, grave and as though wounded in the light of the nimbus, and yet all around him the army of this conqueror of the world is deployed – weapons, clouds, the clarified powers of what is human – and thus are effaced those excessive simplifications in which the dialectical ambitions of the Western mind have so often come close to ruin. The god of Sopoćani does not mutilate. He is not that Apollo of the Hellenic sixth century who, in all the brilliance of his force, remains like the unswerving trunk of a tree, like some pure and blind form of plant life, so strongly did Greece want to identify humanity with life, with its impersonal forms and with its harmonies, unaware of that other realm which is the finite existence of the human person who is conscious of himself. But neither is he, in his enduring vigour and nervous elegance, the Christian god who only reaffirmed the individual in order to separate him from his natural potential and turn his finitude into sin, as if the suffering finally acknowledged in man's twofold essence had to become an end in itself. If he knows the price of this suffering, he who bows his head like Jesus on the cross, the young god of the Serbian church never forgets that he is the sacred, in the essence of which strength and glory reside. And thus he bestows on us the secret of deliverance as well. The Christ of Sopoćani is the mindful son of the *Dormition* who, out of love, returns to the mortal condition. Before him lay the remains of the old woman, long and black: the real that seems destined to culmination and to death. But having loved, he transfigures what he loves, he raises in his hands the newborn child, fruit of his indomitable caring. In truth, he is our innermost future, what we might be if we could decide that death did not exist, if we could know how to see and to love. Never has a divine archetype more closely resembled the highest moment of subjective ambition, or been so easy to internalise for one striving to be a poet, or seemed so intimately related in its nature to the poetry of our time.

Byzantine art may have been the first in history to have spoken in the name of the individual who, though he remains obstinately attached to his particular condition, is yet anxious to return to the dwelling place of being. Furthermore, it is doubtless because Byzantine art has had this subjective side that the 'decadent' spirit and later Yeats have loved it; but it has never accepted exile; rather it has sought, experimenting always in the hypothetical field of forms, the conditions of a life that has returned to the heart of the sacred. It is its 'impersonal' aspect, unjustly criticised, which dreams for us – far off, of course, like some snow-covered peak – that our difference may, without denying itself, become the absolute.

And we must try to establish the history of this founding art – with all its contradictions, its denials, its forgetfulness – in terms of desire, paradox, grace, by first of all showing that form is a writing that in its simplification, its search for symmetries can suggest a complicity between the universal and being which mutes our presence; and by then discovering that these distorted, bent forms, these elongations are, in the Byzantine canon, so many refusals of this dangerous dreaming. In other words, these tendencies reveal an ambition beyond measure, one that is sometimes unavowed like the quavering of a voice and sometimes made explicit like a ritual. A certain splendor can celebrate the simple transcendence of a place. Similarly, a self-conscious stripping away can lead form back to its earthly reality – the circular contour of a cup, for instance, in itself revealing the materiality of the pewter. And midway between this reduction and this ritual pomp, we would have to define elegance, which is one of the daughters of sorrow, and which, from Ravenna to Mozart, from Botticelli to Tiepolo, haunts all the anxious works of Western art. It is Byzantium that first taught this paradoxical asceticism which demands that sumptuousness awaken all the powers of our senses, but swells in them only in order to reflect upon an absence. Byzantine art, which designated the absolute, also knows how distant the absolute is. It is not, as is sometimes the case in Venice and often in Rubens, the rather vain projection of an illusory triumph.

But I shall limit myself today to the evocation of great silver plates, gleaming and dark, whose only ornamentation is a cross inlaid in niello, or a slender line of foliage. Their whole art is contained in the relation of circumferences, sometimes as few as two – one of which is the outer edge, or rim, the other the crown which, marking the basin, is always a little uneven. And this relation never seeks to be the *perfect relation* to which Greek art aspired; it does not pretend to reveal, in shadowless light, the mathematical essence of what is. It achieves more simply a momentary equilibrium between moderation and excess, the harmony a soul establishes with itself and thus I would call it the *joyful relation* thanks to which one can live. When the experience of life is conducted honestly, even in the ebbing, or if you wish, the failures, a light is given. To know, to have felt one's own limits becomes, when all else has failed, a blessing, a freedom. In the best of Byzantine art, form is the very act of committed existence, and when form refuses what is in the domain of the miraculous, it remains what releases us from misplaced attachments, what gives us the unending freedom to exchange Possession for Knowledge and Desire. Byzantium holds out a cup to us – to us who are the infinitely personal consciousness, banned from the magic of sleep in the universal which we must see as a form of death. Here our lips touch for a moment the invisible water – finitude made presence – that flows in the depths of all things.

Translated by John Naughton

Art[1]

What view should we take of artistic creation? Though I may be wrong, this is what I believe to be a first simple and obvious truth.

Can we agree that our actions are motivated by self-interest? Compassion should open us up to more than life, yet compassion is in scarce supply, to say the least, and many of its doings are suspect. Visionary as a social programme or political project may be, rarely are those who instigate it effective or even sincere. Under that cloak lined with illusion, if not outright fabrication, our national histories, brimming over with disasters and false heroes, inspire precious little trust in what lies ahead. History is a dark place. One may be tempted to conclude that it had better come to an end before disclosing far worse.

Let us now observe these medieval sculptures: notice how, with a few simple knife-grooves carved into the wood, they conjure faces, decipher their short-lived joys and endless tribulations, and give voice to the resignation, or to the deeply touching naiveté of an irresistible hope. Understand, too, that if so many of these works are devoted to the figure of Christ, it is primarily for the sake of a head leaning on a bloodied shoulder – the real, ordinary man beneath the dream of divine presence. These works claim to express nothing more than what they see. Yet the concern for truth, the powerful affection with which they seek to do so, dispels any sense of factitiousness or all-encompassing vanity I might be tempted to feel. Art, great art, ought not to be chained to the wagon of triumphant pessimism. It is what restores confidence.

Which is not to say that artists are indifferent to accumulative urges that reify the world, replacing it with representations devoid of substance, which in turn enable fantasies and perverted actions to proliferate. There is egocentrism and delusion in even the greatest poems. Many of the painters we love placed their eloquence at the service of churches, both secular and religious. Rare are those

---

1   Originally published as 'L'Art', an essay on Spanish Gothic wood carving in *La beauté dès le premier jour*. Bordeaux: William Blake & cie, 2010.

who, like Poussin, refused to court commissions. Rarer still are the vehement ones who, like the late Goya – the Goya of the 'black paintings'– made a bonfire of their thwarted hopes and cast their entire life onto it, reproaching themselves all the while for remaining artists to the end in this regard as well. In their eyes, an artist is a person who remains in love with the beauty in the image, when what he should desire, and desire first and foremost, perhaps exclusively, is to intervene in the relationship with themselves of those others to whom his work refers, thus enabling them to reclaim their selves, changing their faces in images and eventually illuminating all other beings, all things.

But is the despair of these unquiet souls justified? Their chief characteristic is that, while aspiring to 'transform life', they harbour no illusions as to the invasion of ordinary appetites they observe in themselves; they don't lie to themselves, at least most of the time. Even when dreaming, they remember that they aspire to something more than the dream. This opens up an avenue for exploration, one they have no reason – no right, even – to judge impassable.

First, the fact that they are speaking beings is the reason they view themselves as prisoners of urges that reify and separate. For a landscape painter, the flower-laden branch, the river at mist's end, are words turned concepts; they generalise, produce abstraction and stifle the spontaneity of life. Following closely behind are greed that demands, fear that hoards, violence all around. Discourse obscures finitude, the only experience that enables us to shed our negative ways of being by revealing to us the certainty of unity.

Nevertheless, there is in each speaking being an underlying, if muted, prescience of the real – conscious coincidence, lived time – which the words of the concept obscure. Once explored, this insight is what gives a face – an open face, in the sense of trusting – to so many men and women who most often are victims, in contrast with the oppressor, who never ventures forth without a mask. But the painter has eyes; he has placed his trust in his eyes, and even when clouded by reverie, his gaze cannot but perceive the essential imma-teriality of faces. This incites the artist to take action, in a positive sense this time, an action that those who most doubt their 'charity' – in Rimbaud's awkward word – are best equipped to take, having already committed to doing so.

Once he has recognised the face – the necessary beginning of an art in the process of reclaiming itself – and perceived in it frustrated desire, astonishment and pain, the painter, the sculptor, can turn back to their work with signs and forms, which remain forever entangled in conceptual thought, but equipped now with memories that disrupt the rules of the game, rumpling or tearing at its fabric. They shall understand that the living form is not a collection of parts recomposed into beautiful harmonies, since these are born of exteriority and solitude always; it is instead what arises from the indecomposable, the teaching of the Other's gaze. They shall know that the indivisible transcends the divided, for it is presence beneath appearance, and they shall feel called to become portraitists who form with their model an alliance that is both being and meaning.

This first day together will pass quickly, no doubt, for knowledge is irresistibly exteriorised and all writing is blind, or almost, and night falls. Yet, in the work thus begun, a hope has taken root. A hope, or in other words a requirement, which subjects the former to a critique whose engine is the feeling that what exists exceeds the representation one makes of it; a preoccupation with truth, whose approach, though never-ending, is already a shareable place, already a part of being, insomuch as being is never more than what one can freely decide to create on earth with others than oneself. Signification becomes relative in the face of that critical insistence; meaning asserts itself. An intermittence in the artist's lucidity is thus created, perceived by him, acknowledged; it is the modest gift that begins an interchange of recognition with the other – an 'artist' himself, though unaware of the fact until this point – and enables one to move ahead, even in times of incoherence and turmoil. The poem is 'a handshake' Paul Celan wrote; that is how I understand this sentence.

Provided they agree to put their always illusory achievements back on the drawing board, art and poetry are what founds a society, what creates the world. Even when outside clamours repeatedly muffle their feeble voices.

Amid failure and disappointment, it matters not if the newly launched artistic venture is, at various times in its history, thoughtless, doctrinaire, or, more recently, tempted to embrace playfulness and derision as the only suitable response to the surrounding hypocrisy. What could be more natural than to revel in pure form and busy oneself exclusively with signs, signs that distract us from thoughts of death, as a way of 'shrouding the terror of the abyss'? Perhaps this temptation is one we need to experience, a mirror of self-discovery, offering moments of unexpected lucidity and ever more extreme revelations. There is a latent possibility in every work, no matter how aggressively intransitive it may appear at first glance, an accident waiting to happen, a fire ready to kindle. And then, the awakening: the more seductive or troubling the dream, the more wide-open our eyes.

Great art is always born of the disavowal of a dream. Masaccio and Brunelleschi dispelling the fantasies of medieval theologians. Manet – and even more so Van Gogh – rejecting the mirage of contemporary salons, with their stifling profusion of blazing mirrors and chandeliers. And today? Or at least tomorrow? The thousands of experiences that we have seen develop and disintegrate before our eyes since the Second World War may herald the accumulation of disquiet, anxiety even, necessary for a great awakening. I love those often-contradictory experiences, as long as they have intensity. Yet, one still hopes that a certain simplicity – not be confused with naïveté, for the call to denounce illusion is anything but naïve – may yet emerge and grow in assurance.

A remark on what I call 'great art'. I use this term just as I would 'poetry' as opposed, simply, to 'poem'.

Great art does not ignore that its relationship to itself and the world – the lived experience that is the true locus of the spirit – rejects all forms of speech that limit words to the expression of concepts, whether explicitly or not. And since concepts are what ensures the continuity of societies amid changing circumstances, great art – the art of Vermeer or Baudelaire, of Poussin, Kafka and so many others, who may appear minor – transcends the contingencies of history; it is the wave that buoys them up towards the scintillating fringe at its apex while the water below remains dark. The wave falls back, but the scintillation lingers in the memory of centuries. Or at least it has done until the present time.

Translated by Viviane Lowe

Humour and Cast Shadows[1]

I.

I am looking at those enormous hats that Piero della Francesca invented for the church of San Francesco in Arezzo in the most concerted and deliberate of his paintings, In the *Legend of the True Cross* especially, they become true edifices that first of all prolong, in cylindrical fashion, the shape of the skull, then widen, rising quite high like a kind of vase, before closing suddenly in a flat surface, a span or two above the hair. These hats are rather like a church constructed on a centralised plan, and also something like a hot air balloon. Precise in form and perfectly defined, they are related to those absolutely regular bodies, crystalline in proportion and symmetry, that the greatest of the painters concerned with formal harmony wanted to discover in almost all things. And to such a degree that one could easily believe for a moment that the bearded figure on the right, who absentmindedly touches his magnificent headgear, is thereby suggesting that the Cross is merely a new epiphany of the universal harmony. And yet something of the absolute is obviously missing from his gesture, just as it is from the headgear. The Pythagorean spirit could only be alarmed by them, sensing in them a sacrilege. And this is because Piero della Francesca has himself taught us to associate symmetry and stone, immobility and geometry: so that these tall volumes that move, suddenly change contour, become askew in the perspective; these scaffoldings we know to be hollow – a light frame hung with cloth – seem to exalt the virtue of the Intelligible only in order to deride it a little. Nor is it a good thing that these perfect bodies, which Plato considers in the *Timaeus* and which Piero himself studies in one of his own treatises, come too close – be it only in this less pure form – to those bushy eyebrows, to that dishevelment, to that hair that the *Parmenides* took, and not

---

1   Originally published as 'L'humour, les ombres portées', in *Preuves*, no. 129 (November 1961), pp. 38–41. Reprinted in *L'Improbable*, rev. and enlarged edition, Paris: Mercure de France, 1992 and also in Paris: Gallimard, Collection Folio/Essais, 1992.

without reason, for one of the most obstinate elements in the specificity of the tangible world. It is as though the Idea were exposed to
too great a risk – and anxiety overwhelms us. Could it be that Piero
let himself be led astray, in this case through overconfidence in form;
that he was unable to define with sufficient precision the mysterious line dividing the sacred and the profane, unable to adequately
protect his geometrical hypothesis from the shattering proximity of
the quotidian? Fortunately, the hats are placed in the very centre
of the work. The attention of the person looking at the picture is
thus irresistibly drawn not to the cross but to the hats. And coming
from a painter we know to have been schooled in the most rigorous
discipline of what the English-speaking world calls 'self-control': this
must have been an intentional act, itself of central importance, and a
reflection of the most difficult dimension of his thinking.

I believe in this intentional act, and I shall try to define it – asking
forgiveness for introducing yet another English notion into the
discussion of a Tuscan painter, but Piero has surprising resources – as
the idea of a kind of *humour*. Nothing burlesque, in fact, in this furtive
oddness, nothing tragic either, and nothing that might disqualify a
faith. And if there is irony, it is not at the expense of the forms but in
harmony with them, so that they might live more fully in an adhesion
that keeps intact the absolute they possess. There is humour when
values are examined without at the same time being destroyed; when
it is above all a question of testing one's resolution and one's courage;
and this is what Piero achieves here. In bringing into close contact
with one another the affirmation of form and the evidence of matter,
Piero is not seeking to destroy that vast rational dwelling he has so
solidly constructed. But like Plato in the *Parmenides*, he does want to
establish its limits, or more precisely, its mystery, and there are other
small signs, scattered throughout his work, that bear witness to this
cast of mind. Once again in the *Legend of the True Cross* I notice far
off in the distance, between the magnificent, peaceful castle and that
hat in the foreground which obscures it, an old man approaching.
He has one of those long, forked beards, at once substantial and
comic, which Piero loves, and for reasons that we are beginning now
to understand. And if he is late for the ceremony that is taking place,
it is because, smiling quietly to himself, his eyes half-closed in the
excess of his corporeal opulence, he represents for Piero, in the midst

of this deployment of the Idea, the resistance of matter, the incurable slowness of the lowliest element.

In his own easygoing, understanding way, isn't this old man a little like the stranger in the *Sophist* who has come to remind those bent on speculation of the insoluble difficulties inherent in their doctrines about being – and of the truth one finds in living?

What maintains this truth can be found everywhere in Piero's work, together with what recognises, without being fearful of it, the presence of nonbeing in the very centre of life: the oblique planes in the tranquil recession of the parallel horizons, a thousand tiny distortions that give life and depth to the apparent regularity. There is, above all, the *Madonna del Parto* at the cemetery of Monterchi. Against the perfectly symmetrical background of the angels and the curtains, in a space without depth, in the plane where the timeless has always haunted painters, the Virgin, with an astonishing irony – which is almost imperceptible and yet, I dare say, cosmic, and in this instance somewhat Chinese – points to the swelling of that most sacred life in her womb. There is nothing immodest in this suggestion that has been so precisely transcribed in terms of pure space, but there is nothing idealised either. And I recognise and honour this unswerving attention to the contradictions of what is – life or harmony, accident or law, darkness or the reassuring light in the distance – which is the vocation of the highest consciousness and the principle of the greatest art.

II.

And in order to better place them in the context of this vision, I should like to define the enormous hats of Arezzo, or the old man in the *Legend of the True Cross*, or the paradoxical icon at Monterchi, as aesthetic metaphors, since through them the painter has called upon certain aspects of the earthly object in order to signify an intuition of the mind: in this case, the refusal of the pretensions of the Intelligible. Another metaphor of this sort – which, while only permitted by the Form, is also in conflict with that Form – is found in the reflection of the morning sky in the murky water of Piero's *The Baptism of Christ*, which serves to indicate that God gives his love to the earth but that the earth also remains the earth, with all its dank clay in which the dead are swarming, even in the light of the new day. Furthermore, one can discern in the use of these metaphors by painters much more than the simple intellectual reminiscence of the existence of matter, of an ultimate element in the repudiation of the Idea, for such metaphors so obviously suppose an empirical reflection, and thus the most active intuition of what Rimbaud called '*la réalité rugueuse*', that 'rough, coarse' reality of life whose truths are discovered without any a priori assumptions. And, similarly, it is the richness and the freedom of this kind of concrete, and obviously personal, experience that allows great artists to enrich the questioning I am speaking of with the full weight of existence. How much is added, not only to metaphysical lucidity but also to our sense of the presence of the painter, when the ox's horn in Piero's *Nativity* is placed in such a way as to extend the line of the angel's guitar! In this case, it is true, the stroke is a sign of Piero's optimism, but it is still a reflection of his dialectical thinking, suggesting as it does that music and matter both oppose and collaborate with one another in that tension which in the final analysis Piero identifies with the real.

But let us not forget that this twofold intuition can take many forms, that it differs from one mind to another, that it can appear either as a decisive affirmation or as the involuntary play of dark forces beneath the uncertain skies of memory. And so the metaphor will tell us about the painter's frame of mind, about his courage or his scepticism, about his desire to bear witness to the truth or, on the contrary, to enclose himself in an attitude of passionate assertion, which Piero himself – in that serenity in which nonetheless something like a hint of sadness appears – seems to ask us to define.

What is the opposite of Piero's huge hats? What are the signs that have a similar resonance in other painters, but that no longer give expression to a tranquility of mind confirmed by pride but, on the contrary, to the more or less painfully endured confrontations between hope and despair?

I have no doubt that it is the cast shadow. In Giorgio de Chirico's work, on the horizon of the admirable paintings of his first period, are there not the palaces, the terraces, and the archways that at least evoke, if not achieve, that architecture of harmonious proportions in which the affirmation of the Intelligible has always been wagered and always been lost? But in the immobility of these places, there is a little girl who is running, and men who, far off in the distance, have met and are speaking to one another; there is an open cart that seems empty; and these figures cast huge shadows on the ground – shadows that one should recognise as conceivable, and even inevitable, in an 'absolute' art derived from the use of Symmetry: measurable by those squares and those compasses that de Chirico has solemnly represented but from the outside, as mysterious instruments whose purpose has been forgotten, since the aspiration toward salvation that classical art associated with their use now seems completely incomprehensible. De Chirico's whole art is this passage from the interiority of an earlier project to a meditation on the wreckage it has left behind and on the ambiguous categories that will have dismembered it as well as brought it into being: perspectives that tell of the Symmetry latent in things, but also of the relativity of the observer; petrified gestures which that heresy of fifteenth-century Tuscan art, the predella, also cultivated and that reinsert the moment into the effort to establish the timeless; and you, shadows, which, in the reign of geometry and the unity it seems to assure, bear witness to a resistant opacity. Born from the chance conjunction of light and volume, the cast shadow maintains the sense of this irreducible chance in structures built according to Symmetry. And one sees that the shadow also brings to life there, along with chance, the remembrance of time, the being of this furtive moment which the shadow marks with its length and direction in just the same way that it was required to do on all those sundials of a declining classicism. And it is not insignificant that de Chirico has often painted clocks as well, and those trains that can indicate what time it is the moment the place they are passing through is clearly defined. What the cast shadow designates, profoundly, like the pointer on the sundial, is *such and such a place at such and such a moment* and, beyond the impenetrable substance of this metaphysical pole of the mind, the reality of encounter, which has no name or place in the world of the Idea. In a word, finitude: the mystery of the presence of a being and our melancholy at seeing him or her excluded from the coherence of harmony and symmetry.

Like a demon in broad daylight, the ontological frailty of the human being haunts the category of space in de Chirico's work. And, in fact, it is only logical that the sun, which determines those shadows now so heavy with meaning, is often an evening sun, one that with-draws just as the Intelligible seems to disappear from this world where its vanity has been proven by the compass and the square. Alter the early morning light of Piero's work, where the shadows are subdued and transparent, and the Idea is thought to grow stronger with each passing moment, and after the somewhat vacant and colourless noontime of classical art, whose light is without source and seems to coincide with the envelope of things and to consume their matter, there comes an intuition of nothingness, the glory of a sun setting in the west.

With de Chirico, for one last time in history, the Platonic enter-prise – which so early had emigrated into an art that, in its concern both for essence and for appearance, gave this enterprise its energy and guaranteed it a language deploys all the levels of its power, but only in order to confess its abnegation. From now on, the road is overgrown and very likely closed. The soteriological ambitions of the spirit should now be shifted elsewhere, away from the seductions and the pitfalls of a thinking concerned with essences and toward the affirmation of the being of what passes. We must love the cast shadow, of course, even love it alone, but without seeing it as the proof of some sun. We must forget the mirage of the Intelligible and with it the *form* of the shadows, which is the daughter of measure and proportion. The new *hic et nunc* no longer appears in the prism of a metaphysics of symmetry, but rather in the immediacy of an emotional adherence. And perhaps de Chirico, who does not attempt, as does Piero della Francesca or Raphael, to construct essences on his canvas, who limits himself to suggesting them like a deserted city on the horizon, has such power over our modern consciousness only because he also concentrates on a glove, on a mannequin or a piece of fruit – on those brute objects where the reflection of the alignment of the archways fades and soon will vanish forever.

What power of invention and of poetry this tenacious Platonism will have represented in the history of the West, if it is true that the new intention has surged from its body, from a shadow suddenly become presence, from a form quivering with life, from a 'melan-choly' changed to resolution and rapture! The Platonism that fostered illusion also preserved hope. It imprisoned this hope, but gave it the chance to deepen and to seek a future of freedom in a thousand difficult situations – painful like the crises of existence – which both sap a life and offer it the great richness of new possibilities, and which thus become, ever more clearly between the great art of consciousness, be it Renaissance or Classical, and the Romantic art of passion – the necessary threshold of a new era. Pontormo, Parmigianino, El Greco, they are a founding foam on the shore. And neoclassical art, which is still so little recognised in its nonetheless powerful unity, is an art of exile and of the meditation on exile. It is this art that de Chirico has summarised in broad strokes through an intuitive act of Oedipal affinity; and he has legitimately done so, without anachronism or dishonesty, because the nostalgia that a later sensibility harbours is perpetuated more truthfully than the heroic illusion of what is called a great era.

I imagine an architect's study, perhaps at Bergamo around 1780. There are plaster casts that have been set on the floor, a pavement, precise and worn, of gray stone. There are diagrams and drawings rolled up beneath the tables. It is six o'clock in the evening, toward the end of the summer, and the room is empty. Somewhere else people are doubtless eating ices beneath the arcades. The music of Cimarosa battles as best it can against the layers of shadow in its depths. And I think as well of the first *Hyperion*, the one by Hölderlin, where Greece itself, dazzling Greece, is loved in the evening hour, and of Gérard de Nerval on the slopes of the Posilippo, trying to tear his eyes from the ineffaceable *black sun*. Neoclassicism was much more than an accident of history; it is not the weakening of creativity or the academic exercise it is often taken to be, since it is the necessary result of the eternal effort to make our reality coincide with form, and since it has known how to express, in this illusion that at last has become more sober, the movement of the soul that still remains captive to illusion. In the heart of the most objective art, a subjectivity declares itself. Men are converted to memory. The double star, the rising sun of the Intelligible, the setting sun of real man, has passed from its east to its west, and in its redder light has revealed that face which is surrounded by rays and whose eyes are half-closed – a consciousness prey to finitude – that has so fascinated alchemical imagery. Happy the men of the rising sun, if they know how to establish themselves in wisdom, as Piero does, but truer still are those who dwell in shadow. They sense another realm, a real one, lit up in the far distances of their night; and the opposite of those enormous hats of Piero della Francesca is perhaps above all that almost absolute moment in Mozart's *Don Giovanni*, when the masked figures draw near to the dark threshold of the party: *O belle maschere, cosa chiedete?*[2] This is an art that, no longer attempting the impracticable construction of being, becomes an art of existence and of destiny.

Translated by John Naughton

---

2 'O beautiful masks, what do you ask?' (Act I, scene 4).

The Strategy of Enigma[1]

I.

Just a few remarks about *The Flagellation*, which already has given rise to so many. For in order to explain this great painting historians, critics and even many pure and simple writers have not spared their efforts.

But it is just as true that they have not managed to resolve all of its problems, two of the most important being the work's date and what the meaning is of three figures painted in the foreground of a scene in which the torturing of Christ is portrayed only in the background, and in a rather unrealistic manner, as if he were of some other time or another place – another place of the mind – than the event of which the picture offers memory.

Of this second issue, which should not be separated from the other for meaning and date can only interact, very varying interpretations have been put forward, for almost two centuries now, and no one has yet been able to persuade anyone of the entirety of any one whatsoever of these hypotheses, although one may at times fade away only to reappear, somewhat modified, years later.

This is the case with the oldest hypothesis, which upon the faith of an equally old testimony would see in the youngest of the three men placed in the picture's foreground the murdered half-brother of the reigning prince of Urbino at the time *The Flagellation* was painted. I imagined this thesis had been discredited since the publication of Kenneth Clark's monograph in 1951, and that there had only been, since then, two or three historians – amongst whom, nevertheless, Eugenio Battisti – supporting it; but then on the occasion of the five hundredth anniversary of Piero's death, it resurfaces, justified differently, in the great catalogue of the exhibition at the Ducal Palace of Urbino. And there the conclusion is reached that the picture was painted in 1454, ten years after Oddantonio's death.

I shall not undertake a retracing of this long series of hypotheses,

---

1   'La stratégie de l'énigme', Paris: Editions Galilée, 2006.

some of which are very tenuous and even frankly aberrant. So is it, in the first instance, when Marylin Aronberg Lavin determines that the famous astrologer of Urbino, Ottaviano Ubaldini, is attempting to console Ludovico Gonzaga, the reigning prince in Mantua, over the death of a child the prince had adopted. And in the second instance, there is John Pope-Hennessy imagining, despite all his knowledge, that it is not Christ who is being tortured but merely Saint Jerome, the translator, who once dreamed of being flagellated. Whilst two scholars presumably were discussing with an angel the comparative virtues of classical authors and Church Fathers.

The main point, from my perspective today, is to realise that in this concert of discordant voices a certain amount of substantive proof has all the same emerged, which I must from the outset call forth, this being my starting point. It was Kenneth Clark who, if not quite the first then at least with most efficacy, supposed the painting to be alluding to the unfortunate fate of Constantinople in the middle of the century; and more precisely perhaps to the Council of Mantua, in 1459, which had sought a way of containing the advance of the Turks. The man with the split beard, dressed for travel, would presumably be one of those Byzantines the young Piero della Francesca had seen in Florence in 1439 when, astonishing Italians with, precisely, their beards, they had come to ask the Western Church for help. *The Flagellation* deals, one way or another, as Kenneth Clark lucidly conjectured, with the plan for a crusade that certain Westerners, including the Pope, were endeavouring to put in place. Subsequently, in 1981, Carlo Ginzburg took up this hypothesis, developing it along his own line of thinking, and in 1992, at the Washington Colloquium on the '*Monarca della Pittura*', Maurizio Calvesi added to this interpretation, which seems to me irrefutable in a broad way, certain significant further details.

A large question, indeed, and one unsolved by the reference to Constantinople and the projected crusade: who is the young fair-haired man standing at the centre of the foregrounded group? This very young, bare-footed man, wearing a simple old-style tunic, his head girded with the foliage of a laurel bush growing behind him and at once far off and close by, and so fair and his gaze so lost in invisibleness that we are ready to think, all commentators do, that there is in him something of the supernatural: an angel, some have imagined, a dead man, others have suggested? According to Carlo Ginzburg's theory, this young creature whose resolve and assurance are so clearly perceptible, and who is evidently in some direct relationship with the flagellated Christ in the middle of the other group, was Buonconte, the illegitimate son of the Duke of Urbino, cherished by him and loved and admired just as much by Bessarion, the great humanist: Buonconte already being well-read, an accomplished Hellenist, when he died of the plague at 17, in 1458. Buonconte, henceforth a simple remembrance but one still rich with promise, would thus be in *The Flagellation* alongside Bessarion, arguing the Byzantine cause in the difficult days following the Council of Mantua. But no portrait has remained of Buonconte. He is thus merely a simple conjecture. The interpretation that refers to the new crusade is in this point lacking – and yet it is the most significant point, we do not doubt – the support of a fact that would be determining.

It is to the establishment of such a fact that Clavesi gave himself, with very strong arguments in support of the idea that this strange, or strangely signified, being, is no other than Mathias Corvin, the Hungarian prince, still young himself, who with much enthusiam and conviction once suggested putting his great military means – and the advantages of the closeness of the Balkans – at the service of the Christian counter-attack, an offer spoken of throughout Italy. Christianity certainly needed a leader other than Pope Piccolomini, old and ill at this point in his life. Mathias Corvin appears in *The Flagellation*, emblematically of the difficulties the Church is suffering from, between the Byzantine, that must be defended, and the Italian, represented as a minister, indeed as a banker.

I am ready to be convinced, and so deem the game to be won for those who see in this work, that contains so few clues, an intent to put forward the plan for a preventive crusade: the task of supporting this intent via some striking image being then entrusted to one of the most admired painters of the time and his commission being decided upon in Urbino, perhaps even by Federico[2] – chosen at the Council

---

2   Federico da Montefeltro, (1422–84), Duke of Urbino and celebrated Condottiere. A renowned humanist, he oversaw the construction of the Ducal Palace, which houses the Galleria Nazionale delle Marche, where Piero's *Flagellation* hangs in the permanent collection.

to command the armies –, unless this was an initiative of Rome, where Piero stayed in 1459, so as to thank the Duke for having accepted this command – or to persuade him to do so. A meaning has finally emerged, in *The Flagellation*, from the thicket of diverging or contradictory interpretations allowed by the extreme rareness of explicitly meaningful elements and the no less great evasiveness of all the rest.

II.

I am ready to be convinced, but then only to see appear, by virtue of this very fact, a new enigma in the painting: for I am astonished that this proclamation of the need for the crusade – which is specifically an event in human history – has been entrusted to Piero della Francesca; and even more so that he would have accepted the task.

Piero as I understand him was, in effect, in no way one of those minds interested in the events of history, one of those painters who like to put them on stage: witness the clear ill-will – the provocative clumsiness – with which, in *The Legend of the True Cross*, he resigns himself to portraying Heraclius's victory over Khosrau. Next to 'The Invention and Proof of the True Cross', which has something of the absolute about it, we might say, in its rational organisation of space, this tangle of mens' and horses' bodies offers extreme confusion: as if, in his overall conception of the cycle, Piero had tried to show that what was real here, was the meta-historical, the epiphanic, the timeless, and not what is played out on the level of the randomness characterising lived time. How far we are from the easefulness, equally meaningful, with which Leonardo da Vinci will approach the same problem in his *Battle of Anghiari*!

But Leonardo, in this painting as in others, is ahead of his time; in Paolo Uccello the *Battle of San Romano* is, no more than with Piero della Francesca, the realistic evocation of a recent historical moment, and it would be an anachronism to interpret the first works of perspective, where Piero was a master, with the thought that their project involved visiting events in the space in which they occur, and thereby assisting our meditation upon their antecedents and consequences amongst the other events of the century. Certainly perspective immediately took up the task of putting into place a few profiles of buildings thereby giving spatial breathing to some scenes. But the latter are religious rather than societal, and the horizon which, within them, takes form, is much more that of the city here, invested with the signs of such hereness, than the conjuring up of some other place in Italy or elsewhere on earth: and this place, being identifiable, might lead one to imagine in the work some thinking concerned with events of the period. With all people in this remarkably homogeneous society – due especially to education, lay as well as religious – the most spontaneous and constant consciousness of the world revolves around other reference points.

It is a consciousness attached to the simple things of everyday living, and one remaining on the level of their mode of being. As Michael Baxandall has shown in *Painting and Experience in Fifteenth-Century Italy*, a people of artisans and merchants, geared to building houses, packing goods, assessing at a glance the weight or volume of objects of varying shape, and equipped for this with the teachings of an arithmetic and a geometry from the outset made for practicalities, has therefore in its primary gaze upon what surrounds them, in Borgo San Sepolcro, but equally in Florence, this interest in things *qua* things. And perspective is not a letting-go of this interest; it was wanted rather so as to assist in the production of this object very much of the here, a house – a church, too – with their numerous problems of an immediate technical order. As for Piero della Francesca, he thinks along such lines even more – or rather with more preciseness – than many others. Witness the manuals he wrote.

Piero knows how to offer perspective to paving, and he takes pleasure in doing so, but in his books we see him practise first of all on a vase, or a hat or even a head; he is alert to the relationships that exist between their various parts within a capital or a coping around a well, and his mastery of numbers is in fact remarkably tightly focussed on such internal relations, on that inner perspective the word *circumscription* so well evokes. Like Leon Battista Alberti, who uses this word, like Fra Angelico the Dominican, who influenced him, Piero della Francesca is interested in concrete things, considering that God did not make space but things; there are in his pictures no distant horizons – with one or two exceptions which offer only in appearance some sense of an elsewhere; we only see middle grounds belonging to the city close by, and his work as a geometrician and arithmetician, assuredly extraordinary, only offers heightened precision and casual harmony in the determining of sizes radiating about a centre. If such work is different from others, and it is, it is via the excessive care brought to bear upon such a manner of seeing and the spiritual ambition connected with it.

In the harmony that spontaneously the artisans of Borgo San Sepolcro, masons or carpenters, loved to feel in a work, it is clear indeed that Piero perceives the virtualness of a deeper harmony, of a rarer music, by dint of which the architecture of the simply human house might allow one to glimpse celestial architecture, thereby helping ordinary consciousness to shed many of the vain or wrong-headed thoughts which are the lot of disordered living. Thanks to prescribed proportions, thanks to his science of numbers, Piero della Francesca dreams of bearing himself up by way of the earthly city, and without in the least bit ridding himself thereof, towards a city spiritualised through art, a city that would be holy in some noon of the mind, noon being the hour when the sun, the *deus summus*, no longer casts any shadows: unless, shortly before this assuredly inaccessible hour, for those slight, fleeting shadows we sometimes see in this painting. Piero's project, his only project, is the consonancy unfolding, let us note, in the three-dimensional place of building, of human exchange, and not in the painted image to which he is clearly obliged to have recourse. His perspective takes no interest in the illusionism the painter of history will agree to, when it appears, and even find satisfaction in.

What holds Piero's attention? There is, for example, the city he offers us in the middle ground of 'The Invention and Proof of the True Cross', as if it had a natural place in this epiphany of the divine; but this city is Arezzo, the very place in which he is working at the time. If he is interested in the architecture of Alberti, his contemporary and most likely his friend, to the point of building into this same painting a typically Albertian facade, of irresistible beauty, like a manifesto of solidarity and sympathy, it is by situating this facade in relationship to other urban factors, which defuses Alberti's Platonic temptations – a source of many contradictions and fantasms, as with a certain church in Mantua – and privileges a play of exchanges and reflections developing from facade to facade, building to building, in a city that thereby pulls the absolute down to its own level of existence. And it thus follows that what Piero, the painter, is proposing – Piero showing in his pictures, as we truly feel he is doing, what reality not only is, but must be –, is that our holy city is something that must be built, and built here, even: the here, of Arezzo, of Borgo, of Urbino, being the necessary place of all deep searching. No need to enthuse over difference, over otherness, were the latter even Jerusalem or Constantinople.

And so, why, if this is the case, would one come to the support of a crusade? If there is a painting expressing forcefully such thinking, it is, even, it seems to me, *The Flagellation*, more than any other. In the picture the middle ground flows back into the foreground in such an obvious and natural manner, and by virtue of an art so clearly conscious of itself, that any notion of an elsewhere fades away: we are here, and this is indeed the appropriate word, here beneath real light, with real trees not upon the horizon but behind a simple garden wall. A here which is here, if I may put things that way, in our climate, our world; and the elsewhere – which has to be signified since it is a matter of bringing before us Christ's flagellation – is represented, in this pulling down of all that is into the bosom of what is close by, as a kind of dream, brilliantly suggested as such by its strange light, nocturnal in the midst of a diurnal space, with its inverted shadows. Whilst everywhere in this picture, which has an enamelled quality to it, colour reigns, colour that is the great contribution of thought born of things, in opposition to the Platonic valuing of numbers alone.

When we look upon a thing from the world below, in effect, one of those things we can touch as well as see, its colour strikes the mind as immediately as its form; this other register of perceptions lays before us its own intensities, its own capacities for harmony, as highly and as strongly as do numbers; and it follows that the elaboration of the music of everything can only involve, and it is essential to know this, a synthesis, from the outset, of form and colour. We shall note in *The Flagellation* the horizontal black line above the head of the figure on the left in the foregrounded group. This line has another function, to which I shall return, but it already has that of allowing colour to live all around it, raising it to a level of attention in which the relationships of its component parts intensify and deepen, and add to the harmony of the whole.

The Flagellation is a manifesto of Piero's thinking. How can it therefore also speak for the crusade? Out of simple painterly opportunism, a cynical decision to take advantage of a commission? Come now! At this level of seriousness in artistic work, everything is serious, and nothing remains outside of the artist's intent, even the opportunity offered him. There is surely another relationship between the picture as Piero has brought it into being and the ultimately external meaning he has agreed to inscribe within it.

III.

I shall try to clarify this relationship, this painterly intent, and offer firstly thereby an observation, and express an astonishment.

The observation. A great deal of attention has been paid, in past critical study devoted to *The Flagellation*, to the various enigmas one comes across, the meaning, by way of example, that the three foregrounded figures may have, but, too, the meaning of the gold, or gilded, statue, coming we know not whence in pagan culture to rest above Christ's head; and then there are many other such, as it were, gagged signifiers. Commentators have pored over such obscure points, perceiving their resistance, clearly stimulated by them, but they have not dwelt, in these enigmas, on their intrinsic nature as enigma, as if their content alone mattered, as if they were merely the current and momentary state of the painting, a mist destined to dissipate and about to do so, thanks to explanations hoped to be, in each case, decisive.

But such explanations, precisely, have not been quite able to convince us. Where, even, thanks to them, we come close to a meaning we may deem truthful, immediately we come up against a difficulty rendering impossible full proof and we realise the absence of some sign it would have been most natural, however, and even required, that Piero provide. It is as if Piero had enjoyed slipping free from our inquiry. And, having reached this point, I thus wonder whether such obscureness in a work as luminous in its colour is mere chance; or whether, turning the hour glass over, as it were, making the obstacle reflected upon its very purpose, we shouldn't think that Piero della Francesca deliberately sought in *The Flagellation of Christ* not only signifiers too particular not to be enigmas for us, but, too, in consequence of the latter, like an added factor of the image, an atmosphere of the enigmatical.

Why, you might ask me, would he have sought this? He who so spontaneously and deeply seeks in the human act what, through it, finds depth through its universalising; he who effortlessly caught, we never cease to realise, the attention of all minds, from the moment his name took up its place once more in history? But also, why would this painter of the absolute have agreed without some express intent that his painting be shadowed over with signifiers for the most part speaking merely to a few people in Urbino or Rome, a sad contraction for a work of such a great painter at the height of his fame, wanting to place within it, quite clearly, the best of his science and his art? Why would Piero have let this obscureness impede our reading, at the expense of our assent? Unless such obscureness had not been desired so as to solicit assent in some other way? Or, better put, to allow such assent to become for us a most specific, as well as, assuredly, new experience?

I believe, I can certainly say, that this is what Piero della Francesca wanted in his strange *Flagellation*. And that this intent and this project – whether they were completely conscious or not – explain why he painted this picture urging a crusade with no necessary relationship to his poetics and even his religion.

Why would the enigmas of *The Flagellation* with its enigmatical atmosphere be, as such, of interest for Piero della Francesca's thinking about what he had been asked to highlight? For a very simple reason, in fact, and subsequent to a reflection one feels any artist may spontaneously generate in his or her very work.

We must recall, at the point we have reached here, the period in which Piero worked. It is one in which the way of being we will later term humanist has begun to give weight to reason in human behaviour, to clarity in thought, intelligibleness in discourse; but this beginning of the Renaissance, this luminous moment of *pittura chiara*, comes about in an environment still cluttered with the pictorial production of a very different thinking, that of the previous century in convents and churches. Everywhere a theology as complex as it was dogmatic had installed altarpieces whose lateral panels and predellas offered scenes and figures at times far from obvious in their interpretation, even for the religious observer born to such offerings. Who knew, as well as would have been required, why heads were being cut off in a given torture, or what a young saint – yes, a saint, because he has a halo – was holding in his left hand? Obscurities which are potentially irritating for a painter of the new generation, a friend of colour and forms rather than the *Legenda aurea*, and encouraging him or her to aspire to a more immediately shareable art. But also, perhaps, allowing for a sensing of a particular experience.

For when we do not know what is happening in a scene, when therefore the men and women we observe are perceived in their essential humanness, amongst things themselves freed of meaning and thus present in their natural appearance, well, it is this visible appearance that rises up in what is figured; colours intensify, forms become thereby more immediately perceptible. The absence of meaning has helped us see reality as form and as colour. The painting so subjected to meaning that it had become unreadable has become painting in a new sense, and this sense, this potential, erases the old golden content in a growing manifestation of the data of perception. Perception of blueness or redness as they exist in nature and no longer as coded signs in a traditional structure with its abstract harmonies. An intuition of their free and infinite relationships in the real light of day.

This paradoxical effect of the obscureness of a narrative in some predella by a Lorenzo Salimbeni or an Antonio Alberti – or even, moreover, by older painters –, did Piero feel it, did he think along these lines in Borgo San Sepolcro or somewhere else between Arezzo and Urbino in his formative years? At all events, I become aware that looking at *The Flagellation* without understanding what, for example, the meaning is of the three persons in the foreground – all, let it be noted, in their posture and mass very much like the figures of saints or other biblical characters that fill polyptychs –, is to see all the more directly and more strongly what in the picture is not meaning and is, precisely, colour, form, the exchanges that colour and form have amongst themselves: to see in their specificity now the elements of perceptible being, and their musical potentialities which Piero, I recalled before, made into a resource for his spiritual development. Not to understand allows one to see. Allows one access to the unmindful and surface seeing of ordinary practice – that practice that truly wants to seek its depths but is diverted from doing so by its shorter term undertakings, those centred on meaning, precisely – at a secondary level where the innate music in what is can begin to be heard. Seeing, on this level, in order to listen, in a word.

To listen, let us observe, as the three characters in the foreground seem to be doing in a picture we are looking at without too much understanding. Is the figure on the left raising his hand so as to sanction, as has been said, an agreement he presumably has reached with the two others for some political action or military plan? Rather more clearly does he seem to be wanting – what do the specialists of oratorical gesture think? – the others not to speak, but to listen, this not belied by a gaze lost in things invisible, his gaze as well as that of the other two. An impression of suspended ordinary thought, requested in favour of something more than itself, spreads from the three figures over the whole scene.

And so I offer the hypothesis that there are in *The Flagellation* not only enigmas but, on Piero's part, a strategy of enigma, whose intent is to divert the mind from one level of consciousness towards another, in other words to lead it from common experience – that of the merchants and townspeople who love and admire what is, who deal with it in an already happily concrete manner, but without the depth necessary –, towards a level on which the elements of the perceptible world will henceforth be revealed with so much force that its essential music will have to declare itself.

Is that just dreaming? Not at all, for, on the one hand, it is difficult to imagine Piero was not conscious of the obscurities he left in a painting many uninformed viewers were going to look at, in astonishment, in the chapel or room in which this clearly antici-pated work would be staying in future. And many lovers of his art would also ask of themselves such questions, and even the few who had commissioned *The Flagellation* and knew why: for even if the Duke of Urbino or a few prelates of the papal court were able to identify the three persons we find enigmatical, they did not thereby know with certainty the logic behind the statue or that of the curious suspendedness – echoing the other one – of the act of those flagel-lating, each with his arm held back, the rods quite still, on either side of a Christ seemingly not in pain, even indifferent. Why would he not be suffering, being there as a symbol of the Eastern Church's distress? And why is the young man facing us barefooted? And why the man with his back to us, in whom the commissioners of this painting presumably would have recognised, and with reason, the rampaging Turk, is he gesticulating with his left hand, like the man in the foreground? It has been said that these two gestures were connected one to the other, but nothing allows us to believe this so; much rather it is on this occasion a sign of astonishment, incomprehension… In truth, Piero could not not know there would be a good deal of incomprehension over his painting. It even seems to me clear that in his strategy of enigma he took pleasure, at the heart of the image where meaning slips away, in placing details seeming to offer keys: urging the frustrated viewer to stick steadfastly to his searching, which can only veil everything over yet more.

On the other hand there is the fact that at other times of his work, so coherent, so unified, Piero gave himself to operations at once most subtle and very clearly intentional, operations with the same orientation as this strategy of enigma, though taking somewhat different paths.

In the first rank of signs he asks us to separate out from their meaning, the egg of the *Pala* in Urbino's San Bernadino, now in the Brera; the egg that has occasioned so much commentary, but which we see now in a new light. In the perspective I am proposing in our approach to *The Flagellation*, involving a suspension of meaning in favour of a heightened gaze upon the natural object in its immediate manifestation, it appears, in effect, that there is no reason to continue to become excited over what is probably an ostrich egg from the point of view of its meaning. Beneath the valve that wraps it round as its natural locus, it is true it has a meaning, or several, which were on this occasion clear when it was painted and shown, as a symbol of creation, fertility, birth, a symbol whose presence here is perfectly justified by that of Federico kneeling before the Infant sleeping in such a relaxed way – and with the red cross on its chest – that one senses death, which is to say, resurrection. Perhaps there is rejoicing in this great altarpiece of the birth of a prince; perhaps it is about the salvation of the father's soul; we just do not know today, but it is of little importance: everyone understood, at the time, and the egg that spoke of Incarnation had no enigmatical air about it for anyone.

But it is for another reason, to my way of thinking, that the egg drew the gaze of so many, and this reason is related to the strategy of enigma. What we must note is that Piero painted it paying the most extreme attention to its natural look, which bestows on it in the most direct and intense manner the quality of a seen thing. Now, he had yet wanted it explicitly as the symbol I was describing a moment ago, the undoubted proof of this design being the position he gave it, in the exact centre of the rectangle in which the work was inscribed before it was taken down and above all its height reduced. And so a dialectic is set up, in the following terms. Firstly, the meaning of the egg in its central place is clearly understood; the egg has become its symbol. But so much effort in painting it and this presence-as-thing that it assumes, involves a traversal of the plane of signification whose discourse is thereby suspended as in *The Flagellation*, although in a different, if not opposite fashion. This time it is not meaning that is occulted so that, in its place, the natural object in its manifest immediacy may be shown. It is the latter that has been directly grasped by the painter, but the intent is the same and the consequences similar: all around the luminous whiteness issuing from a perfect form, all the colours of the architectural décor, and even those of the clothing, or rather materials, let's say, eternal colours precisely coded by iconographic tradition, all recover equally their quality of immediacy, offer themselves to our gaze in the highest degree of their perceptible presence, where Piero spontaneously situates himself to begin, towards a higher level still, his spiritual ascent; and so such colours can now, in their solidarity with forms, lend themselves to his work as an architect of being itself, and become pure music. Meaning has not been suppressed, but it has been relativised from top to bottom of the picture. Even the coral necklace on the body of the infant Jesus is henceforth primarily colour.

On this occasion again, in the *Pala*, a work certainly coming later than *The Flagellation*, Piero della Francesca has, then, worked against discourse, a discourse of words, in order to bring forth the elements of perception in their fullness beyond words. One could say the same of *The Madonna of Senigallia*, that other marvel in the Gallery of the Ducal Palace, painted probably after *The Flagellation*: for there, on the left behind an angel, is a ray of sunlight so happily natural, filtering through the blinds, that it transcends any vague desire we might have to see in it another ray of light, that of divine power bringing about through the slats its mysterious act of immaculate conception. Yes, this symbolic meaning is there, we can agree, but the sun fills the whole room which yet is dark, shining a little still, on the right now, upon the basket of crumpled white cloths, behind the other angel; an entire interior, already somewhat Dutch, springs to life and we are on the earth which is in itself holy. A place of the everyday, on this occasion, and a mezza voce music whereas in *The Flagellation* numbers used several instruments, of high and subtle preciseness. But it is, as well, because the object of meditation, in this new instance, is no longer the destiny of society and world, but simply a small child.

And what shall we think of the old man who, in 'The Return of the Cross to Jerusalem', one of the frescoes of San Francesco, in Arezzo, is hurrying along, on the right edge of the image, because he is late, the procession is there, the Cross is moving forward majestically, the crowd is already on its knees? A mass of tall – very tall – hats from one end of the scene to the other. The cones and cylinders Piero knows all about, from all his trading or building contemporaries gauging bundles of grain or stone blocks, and having made of them one of the instruments in the genesis of his figures, but one normally hidden away, here he is showing them in their nakedness and, as it were, deprived, on these shifting heads, of the stability appropriate to the august character of their elementary, fundamental forms, the very mothers of regular bodies. What, at such a serious moment – the return of the sacred to its supposedly elective place – is the meaning of such disrespectful ways, such amusement in imagining the old man and sketching his mien? The same thing, in fact, as the ray of sunlight in *The Madonna of Senigallia*. The pretentious hats, the geometry comically brought to bear on the humble mop of hair, this is again ordinary reality, this time not in its natural, but its social aspect, where the unthought, the irregular, indeed the absurd are as implanted into being as the shadow from a venetian blind in the light, and seeing and showing the outsize hat of a young dandy from an episcopal court or the breathlessness of an old man, is to plunge into such reality ever in excess of the intelligible, a plunge from which our intuition of truth can only resurface breathing better.

IV.

The strategy of enigma in Piero della Francesca does not aim to draw us towards esoteric meanings other than those his usual patrons or commissioners might understand, but to see and reveal in the simplest of perceptions the intensity ordinary existence neglects to recognise, thereby to the detriment of its spiritual dimensions. Its function is to remove blinkers, to help us perceive what is there in the naturally given, then to construct with the latter, in its found depth, the most harmonious place humans have the power to build at the confines of divine transcendence. But it is thereby no less, and by virtue thereof, and this time in daily existence, an incitement to think. A given aspect of ambient society, an event, a political or ecclesiastic project, it can only, via the path it opens up, reflect on them with that increased lucidness guaranteed a great painter by his experience of the organising and saving power of Form.

And the moment has therefore come to take up once again the question historians have asked concerning the relationship of the picture to the plan for a crusade against the Turks, for it becomes essential to understand whether Piero's 'strategy' – perhaps after all my simple fancy – maintains meaning and function from this perspective.

Certainly, Piero della Francesca could have simply wanted to take advantage of a political opportunity to give himself over to his painterly research; but I have already suggested that a serious artist is generally incapable of such casualness, and it is a true interest in the Oriental question, and the mission which Piero has taken on, which I now believe we can uncover in *The Flagellation* precisely under the sign of this strategy its author conceived of as entailing assuredly much vaster ends. An interest so great and so specific with regard to this problem, to everything at stake in it, that it does not seem clear to me that Piero could have simply been chosen to convey with his widely known eloquence – confirmed at San Francesco in Arezzo on another already 'Byzantine' occasion – a certain thinking with regard to the crusade. He very well might have been capable of offering himself for the task, with the privately held design of slipping into the frame of his work a personal opinion.

In truth, what topic of reflection or even, let us put it rather, meditation, could better suit him than this discussion over what

Christian society had to decide to do in the presence of the Turks who had seized one of its holy cities and an Islam that held Jerusalem? Everything I think I understand of Piero della Francesca's instinctive thinking, an intuitiveness so profoundly open to transcendence, to an experience of the One, is that it boils down to the idea of – and the desire for – a city freed through numbers, through the music of their relationships, of all that blinds us in ordinary life, of the futilely multiplying fantasms of an exclusively sensual imagination. A city with only the slightest of shadows because the hour of noon approaches, when the unity of everything seems to be released in the advent of the forms of the simple. And from this great intuition it emerges that the ideal city, although only yet a mental vision, like the *Perspective upon a town*,[3] today in the Urbino museum and sometimes attributed to Piero himself – and which is certainly in his manner, at all events –, is not so much to be desired within a given place on earth, in opposition to the rest of the world. Pure reasoning set forth, pure music, the ideal city is the task of everything here in the bosom of this world, a task that can therefore be subdivided, and infinitely so, but which in return has no use for reveries subordinating it to towns become famous solely through their relationship to history, in the past, or even, let us risk the word, myths.

No, I do not wish to suggest that Piero della Francesca assimilates Jerusalem to a myth, an accident of religious thought; I agree he feels its presence as a mystery he does not have the means of challenging. But to reach the limit of his thinking or, he may imagine, of all human thought, does not prevent a great mind from elaborating his own vision and devoting his energy to it. And when it came to the problem of the crusade, that is, what was to be done to resist the religion of others, a resistance that involves the reconquest of Constantinople, indeed of Jerusalem, it appears to me legitimate to conceive of Piero della Francesca wanting first of all to verify his conceptions, his method, and then remind us that the true city of God is not to be taken back from the Turks, but to be built with what one is and where one is.

---

3   Also known as *La Città ideale*, or the 'Urbino panel'; it has been attributed, variously, to Piero, Francesco di Giorgio Martini, Melozzo da Forli, and Luciano Laurana, chief architect of the Palazzo Ducale.

And this is what *The Flagellation* does, since in the suspending of its meaning there appears not only strong form, pure colour, number, but a tightening of those elements of perception, understood as paths in our approach to unity, around an architecture whose meaning from the outset is beauty, and a desire for still higher beauty: a place for the mind. Whereupon it will have to be observed that this architecture even has as its framework, discreetly but clearly indicated by the trees in the garden, nature here, beneath the sky here with us; and that the buildings on the right, the large township palazzo and the tower in a quite different style, remind us of what exists, now, and which we shall have to add to so as to accede to purer form; this, as, in the Urbino *Perspective*, the lateral buildings, less developed than the central body, also tell us to do. By virtue of enigma, which suspends the discourse of the struggle against the Turks, a proposal for an ideal city emerges, and it is suggested, at the very least, that no sacrifice be made of this at once collective and individual pursuit to a military adventure doomed to compromise and other vain vicissitudes. At the heart of the discourse of his time, and by way of excavating its language so as to re-establish its full spiritual capacity, Piero introduces another thinking, and a quite different politics.

Build the absolute here, *The Flagellation* suggests, whispering but perhaps with some hope of influencing those men – and women too – of great sensitivity and culture who, in Urbino or Mantua or other small courts, made up the entourage of sovereigns. Is this so utopian, even in the short term? Let us look at the three figures in the foreground of the painting. Aware as they are of what Piero is pointing to, since they are, as we now understand, listening to its music. But placed by him between the ideal edifice and the simple ordinary town, so at the very edge of the scene are they and, in addition, out of scale in relation to what is being acted out in it. Who are these three men? We shall understand this in one case now, and we are going to speculate with regard to the two others.

The one case, yes, the man in the middle of the group: his forehead encircled with golden rays of light against a backdrop – the laurel beyond – of timeless nature and an equally timeless tunic, the bare feet of a pilgrim entering the temple, his gaze searching ahead with that curious unrealness which accounts for people frequently seeing in his face an angel, even a dead man yet one brought back to life, still interested in the moment and the place: well, this being, at once unreal and real, is the man to come, the one who will inhabit the city Piero has conceived. And so he places him in close parallel to the figures who are in front and on the column in Pilate's house: one, the Christ whose legatee he is and who already, thanks to him, is not suffering; the other, beneath his solar habiliment, the god of antiquity, Apollo or Hercules, whose worth, before Christ's, stemmed from embodying the energy of the *summus deus* and inciting Pythagoras, Plato, Euclid to break free from mere myth.

This young man, this man of youthfulness, certainly had another identity, and a clear one, one that a few notables or politicians aware of the programme placed in Piero della Francesca's hands knew how to recognise. For them, I am quite willing to believe, this was Mathias Corvin who wanted to raise armies, not however without, Calvesi has reminded us, presenting himself to Europe as, already, a solar figure. But upon the ascending path along which the strategy of enigma summons the mind, leading through form and colour beyond words, this mysterious presence is soon and henceforth that of the human being as he might become; it is the dazzle and the glory his divine origin enables him to attain. Although it is an allegory too, and why not, of the prince of the present place, or rather, in Urbino, the prince's heir, the son of the reigning prince, the child just born or about to be born and from which may be expected, in the future, certain actions of significance along the path of that building which is contemplation, which is being.

And around the future king of the world, around him to prepare his reign? On his right a man of religion, his clothing proves as much, but he is above all an intellectual, this time it is his face that tells us, and so we may think that he is the astrologer who advises the prince: astrologer as the time understood this word, that is astronomer as well, the witness to cosmic forms, to the divine proportion that is the meaning of God, and so the geometrician, the specialist in perspective, the close ally of the architect. Science serves the prince, dealing with the great task put to it. And to the left of the master the other of his great servants, who Piero well knows to be just as indispensable when it comes to building, and building with art: the financier. In his richly brocaded robe, his hand clenched under his sleeve as if holding in reserve a purse, this man on the right-hand edge of the picture, silhouetted against one of the buildings of the secular city, represents the society of merchants and artisans that creates wealth, managing it, and able to place it in the service of the mind's ambition.

Is all of this just dreaming? Whilst I'm at it, one more hypothesis. If I have spoken of an astrologer, it is because the split beard, rather like the one Piero gave to Solomon – the builder of the Temple, let us note – when he met the Queen of Sheba, is somewhat, if not very much so, that of the presumed Ptolemy who, on his knees, is rendering homage to astrology in person in one of the *Liberal Arts* that Justus van Gent had painted during his stay in Urbino at the end of the 1470's – that is, very near the time of Piero's *The Flagellation*. And this resemblance is not limited to the beard, it extends to the entire face, as Marylin Aronberg Lavin has shown in her study already mentioned. Now, this historian teaches us also that in the face of Ptolemy we should recognise Ottaviano Ubaldini, a man of very great humanist culture, a friend and protector of artists, principal minister of Duke Federico – who built the palace in Urbino – and at the death of the Duke in 1482 the regent of Guidobaldo, his son, still not of age. A prince for whom he remained for a very long time the closest counselor.

And in addition or, more precisely, firstly, Ottaviano was an astrologer, one of the most famous of the century; stars were in his skin, the poet Giovanni Santi said of him, more or less. Ottaviani Ubaldini, what a worthy counterpart to Piero della Francesca at the court of Urbino, himself a mathematician and architect! And how natural it would be for Piero to give him the role of advisor in a project involving the building of the city of divine proportionality. He has placed over the head of the wise man and man of science that strange black bar which might signify the need in architecture for a unit of measurement, a common denominator of forms; and the young man right next to him – his hand gestures before his arm – might then presumably be an all the more natural emblem of the future of Guidobaldo, the sole heir who came into the world in 1472, perhaps when Piero painted *The Flagellation*, a year after the accession to the pontificate of Sixtus IV, who so much wanted the crusade.

One hypothesis more and one too many, you are going to tell me, the thought that would almost have Piero asking not only to build

here, but, further, to build this specific thing: that is, the building
that the painting highlights, a chapel perhaps whose ground plan
and elevation a celebrated analysis has more or less demonstrated
The Flagellation to be displaying, and with considerable precision.
A request, in other words, made to the Duke of Urbino, Federico,
the condottiere become patron and a great and intelligent collector,
to devote his powers to art and metaphysics rather than to the war
people wanted him to wage as chief-in-command.

Let us not forget: this is also the moment, the decade, in which
Alberti, the close friend of Piero della Francesca, conceives and creates
for the Rucellai in Florence a palace whose chapel reproduces the
exact proportions of the Church of the Holy Sepulchre, measured
out in Jerusalem. And let us remember that Piero built the room
in *The Flagellation* by taking as unit of measurement Christ's size,
deemed perfect, brought this time from Rome where a relic is said to
stand as proof thereof. Christ's size is divided by a certain number.
But, thereby rendered proportional to the picture, this size is said to
be found everywhere in the building the picture represents, which
presumably brought home to Urbino the holiness of Jerusalem...
And this, not without some fundamental ambiguousness, and of a
positive nature: for this measurement, that is rooted in fact, in the
body of Christ incarnate, in its link with a place and moment in
history, is then going to be surpassed, transcended, through proportionality and a harmony that do not depend on it any more than
they might flow from some other unit of measurement. The potential music may perhaps draw from the divine body its inspiration,
but it will all the same depend upon the art the artist has charge of
and that the prince is able to finance.

V.

But enough of such hypotheses a little too risky all the same, and
even if I am not forgetting the touch of humour Piero della Francesca
has never failed to add to his most serious undertakings. And to bring
to a close my reflection upon this particular work, certainly one of
his most carefully thought through, rather I shall ask the question
underlying it, the place it is legitimate to offer, in the analysis of, for

example, a 'strategy of enigma', to the possible contribution of the artist's unconscious.

Piero della Francesca's 'philosophy' is perhaps, indeed, what I have suggested, but it remains that he did not live it in a way we could call conceptualised, spoken or even speakable; he did not render it explicit, it had recourse only to the agencies of what I like to call figural thought, the sort of consciousness that, as precise as it may be, only secures itself via aspects of the world perceived in a direct way, without the help of reflection and its concepts: analogies, for example, intuitively understood, and in Piero's case forms, proportions, whose possible music is sensed as having the capacity to 'change life'.

And the consequence, in this particular case, of this kind of approach to reality and existence, in other terms the desire that would have been driving this great painter – so as to demonstrate its value – to encourage first of all in his contemporaries a sense of greater intensity in the perception of such proportions and forms, well, this must have been, once again, just a barely self-conscious intent: and hence, today, in a century given to conceptual thought, the need for explanations it will be easy to challenge as unverifiable and even imaginary, and the product of the critic's unconscious much more than that of the author of the work. A step further and people will feel authorised to remind this incautious critic that it is permissible only to base one's argument on statements expressly formulated or, at the very least, on factors analysable from top to bottom by means of duly verified categories of thinking of an historical period.

And it is true that, in wanting to plunge further than the veri- fiable into the intimacy of someone's relationship with his or her self, one exposes oneself to many perils, and above all, one's own illusions, which justifies distrust. Isn't what seems to be outlined in a painting, a poem, merely the mirror image of the person investi- gating it? Let us not yet forget that a similar peril exists in reverse: by dint of sticking to the conscious thinking of the artist, when this is at times only his or her illusion too, out of intellectual inadequacy or some ruse of his or her desiring or some timidity, we shall miss things which, as we may very well put it, are blindingly obvious. In fact, no one truly doubts it, there is unconsciousness, it is in works, there in several ways, and if one of these is the intricate interweavings of our particular language that condition our speech and even disturb what we do – a whole burden of what is hidden that it is good to leave to the care of the psychoanalyst –, another unconscious exists, which is this time basic to intelligence and which it is appropriate to explore, for our consciousness of the world doesn't rest only on concepts. Beneath the readings concepts make, consciousness can approach empirical reality through perceived analogies and symbols, such perceptions being much quicker than speech and so absent from its outward discourse, but not yet without keeping alive within themselves an activity it would be dangerous to underestimate.

Now it is clearly this unconscious, the intellect's unconscious, that is most alert in the great works of poetry and art, those that aim primarily at knowledge and give themselves, in order to achieve it, the most effective means possible, whatever their source. And so it would be absurd to give up on hearing what the unconscious is saying via such means, on the pretext that one does not have available the conceptual tools to prove the unconscious has spoken. It is true one is often going to go astray in attempting to decipher it, but one can also reassess things, and in following clearly unsure paths one will at all events have crossed lands of which deliberately and exclusively conceptual thinking has no knowledge. Such thinking knows nothing of finitude, let us note firstly, being incapable, with its generalising categories, of understanding from within that life only lasts for a time, so that the choices we can make are not numerous and flow from a randomness we must think about instead of abolishing it, as Mallarmé dreamed of doing, in laws at great risk of being our worst illusion. And to adventure outside of one's territories, if only as an observer of artistic creation, is at least to meet up with that reality of existence which is all the same the most intimate concern, avowed or not, of each one of us.

Let us then take the risk, and ask rather the question, to which I do not intend to answer even so, lacking sufficient means, of the degree to which such artistic searching moving 'unconsciously' towards its truth – and so as to reach it having brought about in Piero a strategy of enigma – is contingent in relation to the moment in history in which the work has been produced. It is on this level, in effect, out of ignorance of certain categories of thought or sensibility of an era, that our attentiveness to what the unconscious element in knowing determines has the greatest chance of erring, even if such attentiveness comes from a love of the painter or writer observed and thus feels affinity for them. There are in human existence constant needs and intuitions just as constant, but historical circumstance and its particular language wrap such needs and intuitions in a veil of signifiers that render them murky and can lead us astray, today, for want of having been able to preserve memory of them. There is no doubt, to limit myself to one important example, that Christian morality at the time of Piero della Francesca impacted the thinking of the boldest innovators.

But why recall this fact? Because I know equally that these constant needs I am evoking are so rooted in one's relation to the world and so significant, relatively, in relation to those induced by the various moments of history's events, that they never cease being within us the true determining factors underneath the fables we recount to ourselves; and even if such moments bring about, over the centuries, a work of rectification, of reconquered truth, which may efficaciously transgress the successive censorings.

Who can doubt, for example, that even in the middle of the High Middle Ages terrorised by sermons, a simple gazing upon the fundamental beauty of the human body could be enough to dismantle the idea of original sin for at least certain artists and stone masons whom, thereby, we can understand: others remaining for us less opportunities for erroneous interpretation than evidence of beings we know we are not connecting with. – Unless, in the latter cases, pain, which contains something universal whatever its cause, natural or some sad fancy, becomes, in the ambient alienation, an experience of truth that opens them up anew to our gaze.

This is what I believe: a being-in-the-world ever the same has been at work since the beginnings of Western civilisations beneath the systems of representation and values most hostile even to certain aspects of its instinctive knowledge. And this sometimes manages to neutralise the discourse of these more superficial values, and then what comes about is a suspension of their readability which quite resembles that which Piero brought, in a manner I believe to be quasi voluntary, to the heart of the crusading proclamation that *The Flagellation* was supposed to be.

And the result of such work taken up repeatedly from one era to the next is that much of the past remains directly accessible to us, the constant needs of humanity being of diverse nature and very numerous. I have just referred to our thinking about the body, latent in the Christian Middle Ages, then suddenly reappearing when a few events – amongst which the rediscovery of the art of antiquity – took censorship by surprise. But to stick with my reflections in these pages, how can we not see too that our thinking about place and an intuition of its cardinal value in self-consciousness have always been maintained or have often reappeared even in the times when great myths lured the mind towards the mirage of holy cities, like Jerusalem, with its so very many crusades?

To observe the first shifting of our gaze away from the icons of Guido da Siena or Coppo di Marcovaldo's time – the progress made by Giotto, those before him and those who would emulate him – is to allow us to see that such still rudimentary perspective, a first draft of three-dimensional space, aims less to signify an elsewhere where our interest might lie, than to raise walls and place them in relation to facades, towers, in what thus becomes a place at hand, a measure of daily life. The here-and-now religious myth denigrates, with its dreams of paradise and holy cities, is born again at the very heart of scenes which are supposed to proclaim such myth. It is as if the need for truth seeking to foil censorship were, in such representations, lining their official meaning – made strongly evident, moreover – with a manifestation of forms that in turn bear a meaning and a project quite other. Exactly what we have found in Piero della Francesca releasing into his *Flagellation of Christ* forms and colour as such so as to offer them as paths to a construction of the absolute via an architecture right here.

VI.

It is the experience of place, of the value of place for living beings, the irreplaceable value of the here in which we live, which has been in this extraordinary painting the source of inspiration, the key mechanism of its work, and which thereby explains it and allows us today to understand it. There is nothing anachronistic in the idea of its strategy, because this struggle to find what is constant beneath the accidental has never ceased to be with us. And I shall observe in closing that in other painters than Piero della Francesca one can note at other moments in history the same associating of a strong thinking through of the place of life, its founding, essential value, with a strategy of enigma.

A single example, or perhaps two. We don't know what, in Vermeer of Delft, the young girl is reading so attentively in her room, or what, in another of his pictures, the lady and the gentleman drinking wine are saying, almost whispering to each other, and we shall never have the slightest chance of knowing. A suspension of meaning has come about at the centre of these paintings, spreading everywhere, shutting down the ordinary meaning of objects we perceive. But from this enigma as from that of the conversation of the three men in Piero's *The Flagellation*, there arises for the entire place, through the increased intensity of colours and forms, through silence in other words, a quality of absoluteness that reminds us of our own being-in-the-world. The finitude within us, that obligation to place, is plunged back into itself, and affirms itself. Enigma becomes mystery.

And the second example, certainly more complex, is that of Edward Hopper, a much more important painter than people seem to want to recognise. Hopper is manifestly of the family of metaphysical painters and poets to which Piero della Francesca and Johannes Vermeer belong. Like the first of these he opens himself spontaneously to the thought of space, the buildings met with in space, the light that rules there, now welcoming, now remote, and it is with the same suspension of the meaning of ordinary life's situations that he yet never ceases to offer his portrayals. As in *The Flagellation*, nothing in his pictures explains what is going on between the two or three people he likes to gather in places of their daily existence, with even the often insistent suggestion that what they are saying to one another, or thinking, is important, even essential to their lives.

And as for Vermeer, Hopper held him to be one of his masters and explicitly claimed to be in his debt. Painters, all three, of neutralised, chloroformed meaning, in favour thereby of manifest presence forcefully declaring itself in that immediacy of the sensible world whose features had been confiscated by such networks of signification. Painters of a silence rising up in places of urban society and amongst its dramas like the manifestation of a unity transcending such society and which it would do well to recognise in the light of those summer mornings, for example, that Hopper paints, in a profound and unforgettable fashion, upon the moulding of a poor house in a Brooklyn street.

But it can happen, with this new strategist of metaphysical enigma, that the suspension of meaning may not turn out right. The foregrounded chatting, amongst the few people, Hopper does not always, nor even often, moreover, manage to stop us from intuiting it, and there are signs, in gesture, attitude, clothing, or in still some other manner, so as to have meaning resurface when enigma ought to prevail. Thus is it that what the man seated on a bed and the woman standing very close to him, are saying to each other, we half-understand; it is a discussion over some problem of unhappy sexuality. And what the woman sitting on her bed is thinking, already quite old, before the window open upon the sky's indifference, we guess this too; it is a hesitant reflection upon the contradictory propositions of Western morality and Eastern wisdom. The concerns of being alone, alienation, ageing, ever present in the cities of our time, pierce through the surface of such scenes of modern life as they do not with the painter of the Quattrocentro or the artist of the Dutch golden century: two periods of coherence in social practice.

And what then is absolutely significant, from the point of view I have taken in these pages, is that Hopper seems to wish to express in a metaphorical way, in these same paintings, which are insufficiently enigmatic, a troubledness that thereby comes about in his consciousness of place. Did he have in mind Piero or Vermeer, here again? By way of the suspension of meaning place had become revealed in each of these two painters via the most radical mode of its spiritual capacity, as a field wherein what is, the things of society or nature, may lend itself to an elaboration leading mind to its unity. And it had appeared in their work as actually practicable, nothing having been encountered along the way that did not immediately contribute to its powers; as with the architecture in *The Flagellation*, so rich with potential universality or, with Vermeer, those beautiful objects whose silence resonates as if they were all musical instruments.

But in a painting by Hopper place is often an office with its abstract and interchangeable furnishings, or a hotel or even motel room – the car of those coming there still quite visible in front of the door which has been left open. And we quickly perceive that such locations or things, which have already helped maintain meaning in the scene needing silence, are equally what is preventing a full thinking through of place, and, in other words, of finitude. When Piero was feeding his intuition of the divine by dealing with the most naturally quotidian things, cut stones, for example, of a wall that his care over proportion was going to wed to other walls, fitting them into a building, in Hopper things – let's say objects, rather – show resistance, ever continuing to obstruct with pointless meanings the silence he is seeking to bring about: such is the witness of a painter of our time.

The faceless motel, less than a stop along the road to nowhere. Its close partitions, its empty chest of drawers and the reproduction hanging above, all that forgottenness already replacing the room of *The Flagellation*, a room so subtly constructed, a space in which the divine we can readily imagine becoming incarnate – much that is human urges this upon us – is tortured but without suffering, for a harmony has gradually been established, and aims higher still, through an architecture lived as a form of self-consciousness: what an allegory, such a difference in the two scenes, in the changes that have taken place and are continuing to do so in Western society! What lesson is there, in Hopper, one of increased lucidness? In Piero, is it one of confidence to be kept in the future of our gaze?

Translated by Michael Bishop

ROME 1630: THE HORIZON OF THE EARLY BAROQUE[1]

What strikes us first and foremost, when we survey the principal elements of art in 1630, is that the heart of its inventiveness does not lie in the work of a painter.

A great hustle and bustle at St. Peter's: and there can be no doubt that the hub of everyone's attention – the workshop of the most brilliant explorations – is this construction site where a new era dawns. We know that since 1615, thanks to Maderno's undertakings, St. Peter's has its facade, which perpetuates the name of Paul V. However, the latter died in 1621, and Gregory XV succeeded him for only a brief time, without many initiatives. In 1623, the highly cultivated Maffeo Barberini, the wealthy heir of Florence merchants, is elected pope: Urban VIII; and already, he ardently desires to eclipse his predecessors. Even before his election, he had ordered the decoration of his 'family chapel' in Sant'Andrea della Valle; and on employing the sculptor Pietro Bernini for that purpose, among other artists of the Florentine 'nation', he noticed the talent of his young son, Gian Lorenzo, and dreamt of having the means to monopolise his services. Less than a year after he takes power, his ambition is fulfilled. Bernini works at Santa Bibiana from 1624 to 1626, and then at St. Peter's, which must be stamped as quickly as possible with the glorious seal of Urban VIII. A construction site opens, and starting in 1629, following on the death of Carlo Maderno, the young sculptor will direct it totally. The 'Barberini artists' – the members of his team – are fully at work by 1630; in fact, they are already endowing the Baroque style, which they invent, with its most prestigious monument.

For they have started to build the Baldachin, which rises above

1 '*Bernini's Baldachin*': Chapter III of Bonnefoy's monograph *Rome, 1630*; first published in a large format illustrated edition, Paris: Editions Flammarion, 1970; reprinted in pbk edition Flammarion: Collection *Champs*, 2002; rev. 2012. A translation of the entire book by Hoyt Rogers, from which this extract is taken, is forthcoming in 2020 from Seagull Books, and printed here with kind permission.

Peter's sepulchre. This is the tomb that justifies the Catholic idea of the primacy of the Roman see, since it is the only true proof of the apostle's stay in Rome: so it was necessary to manifest its presence – and through a sign, of course, that the immense cupola would not crush. The problem was difficult; the solution, a stroke of genius. We know what it comprises: four gigantic, twisting columns, cast in bronze, ascend in unison at the crossing of the transept; four large angels surmount them, superbly graceful in their movements; behind each one, a vigorous volute thrusts forcefully upward, the four summits joining to support the orb and cross. The entire upper part hovers under Michelangelo's dome less like a dais than a kind of crown. We might also see it as a vessel that moves forward, in the limitless space of the basilica, with its crew from another world. A presence, in any case – an emanation, an authority – and that is indeed what is new. Let us imagine what Michelangelo's building would have been like, if times had not changed. Under the cupola, with its ultra-pure lines, in the perfect musical symmetry of the central design, an almost divine harmony would have sounded forth – but only for the mind. The Renaissance temple – such as Brunelleschi conceived it, and such as the great successor of Bramante desired it still – gives shape to the passage from the carnal condition to the intelligible; time no longer exists, place is more subsumed than solemnised by the dome, and reason prevails over passion and instinct. And thus St. Peter's, by fulfilling the cosmic structure, would have become the image, at least, of a Form finally delivered from its earthly ties. But was it possible, really, to embody a stance so contrary to the Christian idea – never wholly suppressed by the Greek vision of the world – of the incarnation *hic et nunc*? In a profoundly significant debate about the double postulation of Catholicism, partisans of the two crosses – the Greek cross of central design and of reason, and the Latin cross of suffering – had already confronted each other tenaciously, and the design itself had changed four times. At last, with Paul V and the endeavours of Maderno, at the dawn of the Baroque age, the Latin cross was imposed forever upon the great Vatican church. Accordingly, the tragic axis was recreated: that which runs from the visitor to the altar, from the believer to the personal god. Man, on the threshold of the last St. Peter's, has become an individual once more, a being who is known by God in his particular figure – and who will be resurrected in the flesh. The temple, in other words, turns into a church again. And yet the nave was too vast for the axis of welcome to align with it, and so it still required a kind of focal point where the divine could emerge.

The Baldachin was the answer. And of Bernini's work – started in 1624, though it assumed its shape and meaning around 1630 – we must say the following first of all: that he re-established the personal god, the god of anger and glory, in his house. But all the same, this is not a mere regression to a time before the Renaissance: even if the Baldachin makes us think of the *Pantocrator* of the Byzantine vault, how novel his visage appears! Certainly the Byzantine god – as opposed to the Renaissance god – is present, in a very personal and irrational way: but that presence is a perception of the mind; that figure is an idea; that figuration is an ascesis. By contrast, when we approach the Baldachin at St. Peter's – in such a haze of colours, before such sensuous angels, with the gyration of those whorls that powerfully sweep the reality of down-below towards the sky – what seems most excluded from the outset is the very idea of ascesis. No, nothing in that presence could be better or less good to us: form is equal to colour in its shimmering, just as the shadows in those heights are light once again. Similarly, there is nothing within ourselves – no urge, no desire – that still denies itself to glory, and cannot glitter there. All forms of love are redeemed in the heart of love. But the secret rigour that ensures their convergence is this: we find no trace of idolatry. For let us look at these angels again. With a foot, with the movement of a hip, they find a toehold in palpable existence, with its blinded entanglements; but their whole body already seems poised for a rebound. And here, in the spring their other foot affords them, the lesson takes shape: let us not stop at sensation as such; but let us not flee it. The moment that it lasts is necessary – if lived to the utmost, with all the links of acceptance this moment supposes – since it will resolve into pure *presence*, and cease to hold us back in what is no longer sin. Grace comes to those who expend themselves. In the intensity of earthly commitment, a conversion takes place, and its nothingness unmasks itself as a dazzling interiority.

But now a few clarifications, and first of all about the word *inte-*

riority: I want to emphasise it a bit – since in my view, it sums up Bernini's contribution; to that end, I will return to the art of the Renaissance, and to its latent drama. Is it absurd, in fact, before this Baldachin granted in one fell swoop, for our mind to reach back to Quattrocento painting, and its slow efforts to approach the figuration of the perceptible? For example, it took the Florentine innovators almost a century to achieve the fusion between the volume of the bodies in the foreground of the painting and the surrounding space, even though they already knew how to present it in perspective. Because as much as they were impelled by the demands of reason to recognise the laws of physical *appearance*, they also remained haunted by the religious feeling that their reality as human beings was spiritual, *interior*, not spatial – and this gave rise to the most insidious and dramatic of conflicts. In other words: Florentine art, insofar as it devotes itself to perspective – and by the same token, to analytical drawing and the scruples of *decorum* – regards the object externally, and thus reduces it to its appearance: a mere envelope which suggests to us that it is nothing, only a void. It follows that trees and hills, which are not at all non-being by nature, will become it – as soon as they are externalised into an image. The drama of the Renaissance is this risk of killing what it loved, with the very instrument that allowed it to be seen. And so it tried to save the figures of the saints or the Madonna from the ravages that instrument was causing. Even so, with Leonardo, then Raphael, continuity is established between the image of man and that of his surroundings. But then comes an uneasiness, even an anguish at times. In Raphael, for example, we see how this continuity, achieved with such mastery, becomes invaded from within by emptiness – hence the surfeit of *signs*, expressive or indicative (the sweetness of the gazes…), poured out by the painter to restore presence to this theatre of *nothing*. Whoever thinks in terms of objects, as perspective would have us do, only encounters phantoms. And this happens twice-over when the Tuscan mind, to grant being to so much exteriority, tries to manifest in forms a harmony that would join them to the divine. For that supposed perfection of the proportions of the real is only evoked at the price of excluding any happenstance – or in other words, any particular exist-ence. And since we cannot even truly reach this perfection, nothing is left to us but the double nothingness which racks Michelangelo:

that of the external, as to the soul; that of the imperfect, as to divine proportion. Surely the true path must lie elsewhere.

Indeed, it seems to lie with Bernini, since it is clear now that he has broken with a single stroke, through the wheeling of outer aspects, the pretences of each of them and the fascinating attraction – truly satanic – of appearance. The outer aspect had been 'invented' by the Renaissance; it was presented as rich with a depth all its own, independent of the existence that bore it. But here it is multiplied, superabundant, and by that very token it dissolves in a presence as total as it is immediate, once again. *Appearance*, that closed world of Renaissance paintings, that wholly spectral entity in the pursuit of which the fascinated mind can lose itself, has become *seeming* again: which only lasts an instant, yet which unites soul and body; which is everything, without claiming to be anything. None the less, form in Bernini will still have its beauty; he even drew on Renaissance conceptions a great deal, to such an extent that he is often seen as an heir to that classicism. But this new beauty is no longer the unstable evocation of an inaccessible essence, it is a simple fact of this world; and it is also the trusting adherence that brings the person towards it. For here is what has changed; here is the decisive point: what Bernini is considering is no longer such and such an object 'in itself' (that is, in fact, in its appearance), but our relationship with it, the figure of an encounter. Bernini achieved the transposition of the visual (that lure) to the existential, of the known to the lived – and I would say: of the object to the angel. Because we truly see now, in the authority of this epiphanic Baldachin, that *the appearance we freeze into place is evil* – is once again the substitution of knowledge for love. Evil, the secret meditation of all artistic experience... Indeed, Bernini assures us, evil arises not because man exists within time, condemned to finitude and obliged to die – but only because he fears this finitude and this death, and that he is petrified when facing them, as if overcome by vertigo; to such a point that these paroxysms of life will also appear like exteriority to him – like nothingness. Evil is nothing. Evil is just a moment that trust surpasses. That is why Bernini will portray the most material signs of death so often and so boldly – he knows how to step over an open grave without abhorring life. Not without a struggle at times, admittedly: and this is where sin comes in, which is never fully curbed. The transgression of a resistance has often been noted in the Baroque, which is none other than that of the person to abdicate self-love, even on the threshold of glory: Rome is not the Orient of Maya and shadows. And yet sin, in the art which will produce the *Transparente*[2] in Toledo, only exists implicitly: it is the 'happy' sin that allows our awareness to build its adoration.

Translated by Hoyt Rogers

2 'El Transparente' is an altarpiece in the Toledo Cathedral, completed in 1732; famed for its dramatic use of lighting, it was reputedly inspired by Bernini's Cathedra Petri at St. Peter's.

POUSSIN: THE SHEPHERDS OF ARCADIA[1]

Ladies, gentlemen, those who endeavour to reflect on *The Shepherds of Arcadia* ordinarily take Erwin Panofsky's study of this painting as their point of departure. But for my part, I have felt myself obliged to note that his essay says rather little about the work per se, and that on two points, at least, it must be reconsidered.

His contribution was to show that since the seventeenth century, two interpretations of *The Shepherds of Arcadia* have succeeded each other, or have even existed simultaneously. Each of them is founded on a differing analysis of the Latin phrase that appears in the work, engraved on the sepulchre, and almost at the exact centre of the canvas: *Et in Arcadia ego.* For Bellori, who commented on the picture, *Et* is related to *in Arcadia*, as the syntax would have it; and so the phrase can only mean: '*Even in Arcadia, I…*' After this, we must infer a verb; and according to proper epigraphic practice, it can only be one of the most common verbs, in the present tense: *sum*, almost certainly – *I am* – which would finish clarifying the meaning. On a tomb, who could say 'I am', or 'I am always there', if not death? 'In Arcadia as well,' Bellori comments, 'death occurs in the midst of happiness.'

A picture by Guercino painted around 1618, in which this initial segment of a phrase figures for the first time, seems to confirm that interpretation. Here as well, we see that several shepherds, moved and surprised, are looking at a skull set on a stone: and so it is of death that they become aware. Indeed, this time *Et in Arcadio ego* is not engraved on a tomb – which might give these words the function of an epitaph – but placed along one edge of the work, as a kind of title meant for those who might omit to pay heed. Thus we can plausibly consider – and in any case, Panofsky did so himself – that Guercino's *Shepherds of Arcadia* comprises a realisation of the fact that death exists. For the viewer of the work, it would be a kind of *memento mori*, one of those reminders of death that since the High Middle Ages, Christian art has issued so often.

1   'Les Bergers d'Arcadie' was first delivered as a lecture in Paris at the Grand Palais in 1994. Collected in Yves Bonnefoy, *Dessin, Couleur et Lumière*, Paris: Mercure de France, 1995.

But Félibien – Poussin's other biographer, and a friend of his – seems to have thought that we could combine *Et* and *ego* to say 'I also'; and from this he concluded that the being who pronounces the four words in Poussin's painting is (and I quote) 'he who is in the tomb': a being who is no more – 'he also', a being who has lived in the past, he like others – and not death as such. Certainly, in Poussin's *Shepherds of Arcadia* we observe a large tomb, which we do not see in Guercino's; and we also note that the death's head has vanished from the image. According to Félibien, Poussin did not intend to remind us that even in Arcadia, even amid felicity, death exists; he only wished to evoke a moment of elegiac meditation among these shepherds, on finding an inscription that reminds them of a being with a moral quality, no doubt, and an aptitude for happiness – like Daphnis in Virgil's *Fifth Eclogue*, and who, like him, had been obliged to die. What Panofsky finds intriguing, in the study I am summarising, is that Félibien's interpretation quickly took precedence over the other, the one set forth by Bellori. By the Romantic period, the former had become the rule. And this change is easy to comprehend, in my opinion, since the preoccupation with a dead man, and not death itself, reflects the focus of the eighteenth and nineteenth centuries on the enigma of the person: that reality which seems to be more than his physical condition as such, given his mental powers and his spiritual inklings, and which nevertheless – this is what they are beginning to understand, with the rise of atheism – does not benefit from any life in another world. Even genius must fade away without leaving a trace, except for a few words on what can only be a tomb… Undeniably, that would explain the melancholy some have thought they could perceive in Poussin's painting. But despite all that, has this picture been sufficiently – or even correctly – addressed? Have the questions it asks us even been framed?

I do not think so; and now I would like to dwell on the two points in the essay that seem debatable to me, as I have said. The first is the interpretation of Guercino's painting as a *memento mori*, nothing more. Is it necessary, in fact, to remind those who live in Arcadia that death exists? Any reader of Virgil's *Eclogues* – where the idea of Arcadia as a land of simple delights, in a woodland setting, took shape – will be aware that while life among the shepherds may be happy, thanks to the perfect accord between these beings and their

natural condition, it is still permeated at virtually every moment by
the thought of death – or by that second aspect of death which is, for
example, the irreparable loss of a loved one, either through absence
or through rejection. Mopsus and Menalcas do not discover that
Daphnis is dead: they have known about this for a long time. They
will do nothing other than celebrate his memory; they even evoke
the mourning that all of nature wished to wear at his death. Indeed,
we are fully entitled to say that the elegiac strain – the language
of loss, of absence, of mourning – is one of the two predominant
modes of Arcadian speech. Virgil has duly echoed the theme of the
shepherds' happiness – such as the Greek historian, Polybius, had
described it in the bygone era of his rustic, native Arcadia; but he has
added precisely that dialectic, between the capacity for happiness and
the knowledge of death, which gives to his great poem its admirable
light of late-afternoon, where shadows already lengthen. *In Arcadia*,
there is no need of the skull painted by Guercino.

As to Poussin's painting – and this is my other criticism – what
is the use of attracting our attention to its other reading, that of
Félibien and the Romantics, if we do not ask whether such an interpretation was acceptable to the painter, and whether his work itself
confirms his intent? Indeed, as Panofsky himself points out, Poussin
was a very good Latinist; we can assume he knew that Caesar, when
he was dying, cried out: *Et tu, Brute!* 'And you as well, Brutus!' And
we must add something of great importance, all the same: he knew
equally well that the use of '*et*' in the sense of 'also', but followed
right away by the principal word, is not just a mundane aspect of
the Latin language, a rule routinely applied, but one of the foremost
elements that characterises a high-flown style, the noble language of
artistic creation. Poussin could not have agreed with Félibien in his
interpretation of *The Shepherds of Arcadia*. But in that case, why has
his picture seemed to accommodate such a view? This is what we
should try to comprehend.

We have circled back to the work itself. But at this juncture, I
believe a comment needs to be made. Whichever of the two readings
we judge to be right, supposing the problem is framed that way,
we must not conclude that we would then have a sufficient translation of the four words – or, to put it another way – a meaning that
would allow us to proceed, without any further ado, to the analysis

of the work itself. Such an approach would reduce *Et in Arcadia ego* to a *topos*, a commonplace – a theme the painter may have agreed to treat as such, like a rhetorician who first chooses his subject, and then shapes his discourse. This would only have had poetic value in those archaic times when symbols and ideas constituted a structure of reality and of mind – objective, veracious, willed by God, and therefore sufficient. In the seventeenth century, after Galileo, in an era when the most diverse religious traditions begin to be examined, if not accepted, this authority of a few grand formulae is no longer extant – can no longer impose only their eternal verities on the artist's thought. And so even a Christian painter – though he may be depicting a scene from the Old or the New Testament – may henceforth, in expressing himself, give free rein to his personal preoccupations, his aspirations, his memories. The age of modern expression has begun.

Under these conditions, it is not just the syntactical function of *et* we need to weigh in *Et in Arcadia ego*, and whether or not this term may be shifted in the phrase. What also counts – what counts above all, perhaps – is the meaning the four words as such possessed for Poussin; and of course, first and foremost, the word *Arcadia*. What did they mean for Poussin in his own life, under the sign of his past, at the moment he was beginning his canvas? Strangely, the commentators who have pondered the *syntactical* structure of the phrase so assiduously have not dwelt on that *semantic* content. Yet can we dispense with trying to fathom it, when it may have determined the way Poussin conceived and realised his work? Far from it, in my opinion: and so I will now attempt to retrieve at least a part of what the inscription's words may have signified for him, taking into account that they appear on a tomb.

II.

The word *Arcadia*, first of all. Of course, there can be no doubt that for Poussin, this imposing term signified its major touchstone: the poetry of Virgil, in which the mind asks the pastoral condition – that is, the realm of the plainest, most natural satisfactions – to free it from the passions that prevail among those who inhabit the city.

In this perspective, death, as I have already stressed, was not at all absent; but one could be reconciled with it through the equilibrium, the serenity conferred by frugality transmuted into music. And at the deepest level, it was music – the experience of beauty – that formed the essence of what Arcadia offered: a noble tenet of Virgil's, and a tenet of the Renaissance as well. We come across it again, not without a certain enfeeblement, in Sannazaro's *Arcadia*, which renews the fashion for that age-old idea at the beginning of the sixteenth century. There is no better example of this than Titian's *Pastoral Concert* – the inspiration for which has been ascribed, incidentally, to a certain episode in Sannazaro's tale. In *The Pastoral Concert*, the city-dweller (already thinly disguised as a shepherd in the *Bucolics*), along with an authentic denizen of the pastoral domain, create a novel music together: a music that will be as natural, and yet as pure – as exempt from passions too vehemently sensual – as the sound of the water, poured into the well by the young woman on the left. In my view, that trickling sound, though only faintly suggested, is the central thought of the work: it provides the transition from the visible to the invisible. This suffices to show that Venetian art in particular had been able to preserve the spiritual implications of the Arcadian reverie, despite the sensual tenor of the portrayals that stemmed from it in painting – as in *The Pastoral Concert*, for that matter. It had been enough to understand, thanks to Neo-Platonism, that from the love of bodies we can ascend through music to the contemplation of the universal soul.

Nevertheless, Sannazaro's *Arcadia* was not without ambiguities which made it something other than an occasion for spiritual meditation. In a certain passage of the book, there is an *ekphrasis*, a description of a painting: it portrays sleeping nymphs, observed – or rather ogled – by satyrs. On the one hand, we have the chaste followers of Diana; but on the other, the crudest sexuality, which incites us to gaze upon the naked bodies as we would not do in Virgil – if there were any – or in *The Pastoral Concert*. The truth is that the *locus amoenus* of the pastoral tradition – the grove full of sun and shade, on the bank of a stream, covered with fresh grass and flowers – can be the silence where a shepherd-boy teaches the vast woods to resound with the alluring name of Amaryllis, his beloved; but it also furnishes an ideal setting for erotic reveries. And through the narrow entrance to this verdant bower, the lesser divinities of paganism were able to infiltrate the pastoral space with ways and habits that were not to be found in the *Bucolics*. It was Ovid who guided them, from now on; and it was painters and poets who revealed their presence and vaunted their charms. Hardly has the painting of Sannazaro been offered to the imagination of his readers in *Arcadia*, when Titian himself paints it in truth – for example, in his picture known as the *Pardo Venus*. And others follow, among them Tasso, who in his *Aminta* – a short pastoral play, still devoted to the myth of the (more or less) innocent bliss of shepherds and shepherdesses – does not hesitate to dramatize a coarse Satyr bent on raping Silvia, the heroine, whom he has denuded and tied by her hair to a tree. The *locus amoenus* has become the theatre of what – in this still very Catholic society – more resembles a revolution of mores.

To my mind, that is what yet another poet, the great Ariosto, wanted to underscore in an episode of his *Orlando Furioso*, in the most precise and conscious way. This poem is ostensibly a tale of chivalry, in which magic and the supernatural abound, but it is often underpinned by reflection. The heroine of the tale is the beautiful Angelica, who for a long time has been, in this lengthy poem, not only chastity itself, but extraordinarily scornful towards the number-less princes who have courted her. Still, one day, far from the places where all these others wage war, she passes through a little copse where a young man, apparently of humble origins, lies gravely wounded. And she, who up till now had only evinced her contempt for men, falls in love immediately, and ardently, with this Medoro. She nurses and heals him, and then she marries him, in the plain and summary manner of the shepherds who live in the vicinity. With him she will wander from one *locus amoenus* to the other, during an entire season; in the end, still with him, she departs from the book of which she had been the focal point, as much as the vanishing point. In these woods, in these charming places, Angelica and Medoro dedicate themselves untiringly and unreservedly to their mutual passion – and what is most remarkable – on each occasion they delight in carving both their names on the bark of trees, either juxtaposed or interlaced.

What does this mean? Ariosto was not unaware that among the shepherds of Virgil, the unfortunate Gallus was desperately in love with a woman, whose name he carved on trees – but who for him was only, and could only be forever, an absence. Hence in this case, the sign entrusted to nature was more of a challenge to nature – of the same sort as the inscription on the tomb, as understood by Félibien. And now, on the contrary, those two names – incised into the living bark – reveal a feeling of intimacy with that same nature, experienced by Angelica and Medoro each time they are joined. From the Virgilian pastoral to that of Ariosto the shift is thus immense, in regard to aspirations, ideas of life, and values; and since everything is played out near a tree – yet clearly without the least snake in the grass or foliage to trigger any fear – no one can doubt (and no one did, as soon as the book appeared) that Ariosto, in conceiving this passage, had thought of Original Sin, in order to deny it any relevance to sexual life. Angelica and Medoro are Eve and Adam, exonerated: the garden of Eden has been returned to them, to dwell there as God had forbidden them to do. Ariosto understood that what was happening in the woods of this modern pastoral, which we may call *eroticized*, imperiled one of the main aspects of Christian morality.

Are we asking too much from a poem and several paintings? Then let us go back to the picture by Guercino I previously discussed: it answers this question, while unveiling what seems to me its true meaning. Why, I had presumed to say, should shepherds in Arcadia need to be reminded of death – the fact of death? By the way, we should note that the year before this painting, which is from 1618, Guercino had painted some frescoes after *Orlando Furioso*, at the Villa Giovannina near Cento, his home town. Seven of them illustrated the life of Angelica; and at least one of them portrayed her carving her name and Medoro's on a tree: carving the names *herself*, which underlined the feminine initiative within amorous relations. However, Guercino was not without concerns of a spiritualizing vein, since at the time he painted his *Shepherds* he was was also working on an important *Apollo and Marsyas*. In it, these exact same shepherds – as Denis Mahon has shown – are witnesses to the torture of Marsyas: that flaying which marks the victory of the lyre, the instrument of the soul, over the flute, which ferments the passions and clouds the senses. Historians also know that Guercino undertook nothing without the advice, if not the instructions, of his friend and patron, Father Mirandola, a man prone to religious preoccupations. And from this cluster of facts, a conclusion comes to the fore. The

formula *Et in Arcadia ego* – employed here for the first time, as far
as we know – does not so much allude to the Arcadia of Virgil, or
even of Sannazaro, as to its subversion by the erotic imaginations of
painters and poets; thus it echoes the disquiet of churchmen, who
wish to recall that instead of seeking culpable pleasures, the shepherds should be far more attentive to dying a good death. Erase,
some ecclesiastics demand of painting – in this case, represented
by Guercino – erase these indecent inscriptions of lovers' names on
trees. Replace them with the skull, which signifies the true nature of
the body; with this owl, which will instil fear of hell; and next to the
skull, with this caterpillar that heralds the butterfly: the symbol and
promise of the soul's eternity, of its happy unfolding in the world
beyond. Yes, these *Shepherds of Arcadia*, as Guercino depicts them,
are indeed a *memento mori*; but one specifically addressed to certain
persons and artists in the society of his time.

Should we doubt such an interpretation of the word *Arcadia*, as
the object of a particularly Catholic indictment, let us examine now,
with this in mind, a picture that Poussin himself painted around
1627–1629, and which is now at Chatsworth, in England: *The Shepherds of Arcadia* again – or rather already, since for him it is his first
approach to the theme. That we are in Arcadia in this painting is
clearly evinced by the inscription *Et in Arcadia ego*, quite visible
here in turn – and doubtless borrowed from Guercino, whose fairly
sizeable canvas Poussin would have been able to see at the Barberinis'
palace, when he was painting his *Germanicus* for them. This Arcadia is
very different as well from the Virgilian setting, or that of *The Pastoral
Concert*; the contrast is revealed, even coded in, by an addition to the
shepherds: a young girl with a flushed face and naked breast, whose
leg is bared. Something of a bacchante, she resembles the famous
figure in the superb painting by Titian, *The Andrians* – a canvas then
in Rome, and which Poussin had studied closely. Morever, above
the tomb and skull which has made the shepherds and shepherdess
pause, Poussin has placed a large cross in a section of wall. This cross
is hardly visible in the painting, since it consists of indentations in the
masonry, between some of the stones; but it appears distinctly in early
engravings, as Milovan Stanic has recently pointed out. And in my
opinion, it can only be interpreted as an allusion to the refusal of this
modern, eroticized Arcadia by some representatives of the Church.

Consequently, Poussin's painting confirms my interpretation of Guercino's; and it also confirms that the word *Arcadia*, in the first half of the seventeenth century, bore an inflection (and perhaps even a polemical charge) that must be taken into account. This is especially true since Poussin himself would have belonged to those for whom that new-found sensibility – that suddenly explicit sensuality – held a great deal of meaning and attraction, at least during his first five or six years in Rome. For him – the creator of *Bacchus and Ariadne* or *Diana and Endymion*, to cite only works from this same period – it goes without saying that his spiritual exigency was straightaway immense, and that he knows as well as Titian how to distinguish between sacred and profane love. His *Death of Germanicus*, painted scarcely three years after his arrival, even discloses a moralist's way of thinking, which foreshadows the loftiest concerns of Corneille. It also bears witness to so much artistry, so much mastery of the most difficult resources of painting, and so much archaeological knowledge, that we cannot help but see here the effect of a veritable ascesis: in itself, a moral principle. And yet Marino – well-versed in such matters – on introducing Poussin to the Barberinis, had attributed to him a 'furia di diavolo,' a devilish fury. Looking at the battle scenes he painted quite soon after that, most likely on his own initiative, or *The Massacre of the Innocents*, now at Chantilly, we are struck by the ardour Poussin can bring to bear on the tension of muscles in bodies, the truculence of urges, the depths of cruelty or horror. In addition to that, in the same period as *Germanicus*, he painted some works that reprise the theme of the nymph spied on by satyrs – and indeed, with a sensuality more explicit and more heavily pronounced than that of any Italian in those years. Tellingly, the young woman is no longer – in a picture now in Dresden – a follower of Diana, but Venus herself; and these are not mythological beings who gaze at her, but shepherds, with whom Poussin can identify. In fact, in these paintings, as in his *Bacchanal with a Guitar-Player* at the Louvre, we feel the same type of insurgence of the painter's person against the image. Since it is precisely that – nothing but an image – it cannot fulfil his desire; and therefore it only deepens his frustration: to the point of throwing his connection with himself out of kilter, depriving him of his will, and almost blocking the continuance of his work.

This peril exists, to be sure – or certainly existed then, in that period between the Renaissance and modern times. To prove this, I need only point to the analysis made by Ariosto, whom I have already cited; significantly, it follows on the heels of his evocation of Medoro and Angelica. After they have left the scene, who should appear but Orlando, the eponymous hero of the tale, perennially in love with Angelica; and now, in a hundred different places, on tree-trunks or rock-walls, what does he see but the names of the two lovers, 'con cento nodi legati insieme', intertwined by a hundred knots? Though Orlando knows Angelica's writing quite well, he does not want to believe his eyes. But soon he discovers an entire poem written by Medoro; and alas, then he must read what these verses recount, with transports of the highest eloquence: the tale of what occasioned those emblematic signatures. Orlando is truly obliged now to know, to see, and this drives him mad – 'furioso' – with a madness such that for days on end it causes him to break the rocks and knock down the trees all around him. In a word, his madness lays waste to the *locus amoenus* and leaves him – the main protagonist of the momentous poem – annihilated, emptied of all awareness. – What does this second act of Ariosto's reflection mean? Quite a lot, from the standpoint of artistic creation. When Orlando discovers the inscriptions, and depicts to himself Angelica and Medoro together, with all the intensity that jealousy instils in him, he is on the plane of the imagination – with the means, and even the limitless capacities, it grants to desire in shaping its phantasms. But all the same, the place where he must remain, in his solitude and finitude, is then – as opposed to his dream – no more than existence such as we live it, with its limitations and its dearths. Thus Ariosto wishes to show that while the imagination has a positive value – since it has allowed him to conceive Angelica and Medoro, and therefore to set amorous relations free – it also betrays a negative potential. Does it satisfy desire, through its reveries? Imagination exacerbates desire just as much, then leaves it helpless before real-life situations: they run the risk of disconcerting, even shattering the kind of person who – as in the case of Poussin – is impelled by demonic fury.

For Poussin, indeed, such real-life situations were not always carefree. This is the period when at the end of the 1620s, a grave illness – almost certainly venereal – took hold of him, infringed on his work, and diminished his resources accordingly: to such a degree that in a self-portrait of around 1630, when he had emerged from the crisis, we still see him as overwhelmed, almost distraught. This is a *Nicollo furioso*, if I may be so bold, in striking contrast to the energetic, self-assured person who will appear in another portrait twenty years later. There can be no doubt that in the 1620s, Poussin was torn between the grandeur of his spiritual ambition and the virulence of his desires, all too well served by his means as a painter; and that he then traversed a crisis, to which certain paintings of that time lucidly attest. We have seen his first *Shepherds of Arcadia*, in which we discerned a cross. But the latter is decidedly less visible than the figure in the foreground, a river-god who lets the waters flow, a symbol of passing time – in a crestfallen slouch, almost prostrate: an indication that time is being wasted, and will be lost. Can we imagine a more faithful portrayal of Orlando in his despair? These shepherds, as I have said above, belong to the family of Angelica and Medoro, and signify phantasmatic images; and thus I am tempted to perceive in this supposed evocation of the river-god – not included by Guercino, and hardly germane to an *Et in Arcadia ego* – a projection of Poussin himself: the victim, in short, of the images he has engendered. Another picture supports my hypothesis. The Chatsworth *Shepherds of Arcadia* was probably conceived by Poussin as one panel of a diptych, of which the other half is *Midas Washing at the Source of the Pactolus*, in the Metropolitan Museum. The passion of Midas, which he strives to shed in this painting, is gold. But what are images, when they are lived with the hapless avidity that Ariosto describes in Orlando, if not a kind of gold: equally brilliant, and equally destructive? Moreover, in *Midas* we find another river-god, in the same crestfallen pose as in *The Shepherds*, and in the same place as well, between the observer of the work and the action it depicts: which makes these two figures of time the common element both paintings share. Poussin meant himself here, consciously or unconsciously.

And I would say: consciously – since yet another picture, of similar dimensions and workmanship, and most likely of the same period, is obviously an act of thought that tends in the same direction. It is *The Inspiration of the Poet* which is now in Hanover. Must we – as some have done – see in this young man, who drinks so greedily, the lyric poet as opposed to the epic poet? And in this god, should we discern

Apollo as much as Bacchus, fused into a single figure – as may be the case in yet another canvas of the same period, the *Bacchus-Apollo* of Stockholm? At any rate, this poet's eyes are lost in the bottom of the cup, where he is gulping down his drunkenness. And he has dropped his lyre. Perhaps the cherub holding the crowns may determine that it is no longer fitting to crown him. Rather than the lyric poet, I am inclined to see in this work a portrayal of the drunken poet, inebriated by images that are too beautiful: the poet or painter for whom Apollo has turned into nothing more than Bacchus, and who therefore runs the risk of losing both crowns, that of elegy as well as that of epic. This makes the canvas yet another symbolic depiction of Poussin himself at the end of the 1620s: he who 'in Arcadia' – in these woods too far removed from Virgil's by now – could feel that his grandest ambition and his highest spiritual aim have suddenly become imperiled.

III.

But we all know that after having painted this first *Inspiration of the Poet*, Poussin composed another, which this time is one of his most balanced pictures, one of his most masterly and serene: it proves that this truly great painter surmounted his crisis,' and emerged totally victorious. *In Arcadia*, in an Arcadia touted as the land of the freest imaginings, and where he had ventured quite imprudently, when all was said and done; in Arcadia, even in Arcadia, *et in Arcadia*, his connection with himself – his *ego* – had triumphed over the disintegrative forces.

And how did he achieve this? Certainly, I should take all the time required to tell you how; but time is precisely what I lack – even though we are approaching, as you must suspect, the painting in the Louvre. Thus I will limit myself, at this point, to the few indications that will let me arrive at my goal.

I will do so by looking first at *The Inspiration of the Poet*, in fact. Manifestly, this canvas could only have been painted by an artist who, like the great creators of the Renaissance, identifies the Beautiful with the Intelligible, and the Supreme Good with a unity that can only be attained by the transmutation of sensory givens, of colours and forms – through the grace of a music which opens the mind to the soul of the world. The god of this picture is surely not the one Caravaggio loved, and whom the Baroque will take up once more: that Christ of mercy who disparages nature, in order to reserve the absolute for human beings alone, even if this means they must first be redeemed from a flaw innate to their earthly condition. Though it is true that shortly before 1630, Poussin painted two or three works that bear witness to a certain emotion before the sufferings of Christ – his *Deposition*, at the Hermitage, or his *Lamentation over the Dead Christ*, in Munich – these remain unique, or nearly, in his entire life as a painter. Confined to his sickbed, or distressed about the conflicts that undermined his spiritual ambitions, did he ponder, for several months, the words of the Gospel? In any case, it is Apollo who takes precedence over Jesus in *The Inspiration of the Poet*, with his stringless lyre – a programme of music on all planes of perception. And the cross that we made out – with such difficulty, moreover – on a wall of the Chatsworth version of *The Shepherds*, must have figured less as an affirmation, even fleeting, than the sign of a temptation overcome. It is not by turning towards the cross, with all it portends of sweat of blood and tears of joy, that the downtrodden man in the foreground of that canvas has stood erect again. It is by conceiving, in the wake of Marino, a *deus pictor*, a painter god: and at any rate, if he is Christ, he has become flesh only in order to open human eyes to the absolute beauty of the world.

All the same, this conception that we may well call *aesthetic* – since the contemplation of forms is both its cause and its consequence – does not imply in the slightest that Poussin denies existential experiences; nor that as a result, he has lost all contact with the categories of thought that Christianity suggests to him. No, the crisis he has gone through has even allowed him to realize their import more fully: if human beings are blind to the beauty of creation, it is because their desire to possess – whether gold, as with Midas, or an Angelica, as with Orlando – obliges them to focus on only a few aspects of the immense discernable reality, which deprives them of the perception of its other facets; and this instils in them an alienation – exactly what will doom them to phantasm, to the shoddy image, to groping along in the dark. Indeed, we can truly call this alienation a sinful condition: and in any case, a fall. Thereafter, to get a grip on themselves, to open their eyes again, Midas, or Orlando, or Poussin will have to break free from those desires for actual possession, which so strongly reduce the field of perception; and this will lead to ascetic practices that allow the artist to grant a meaning to the theologians' recommendations, even if Poussin's ascesis is radically exempt from the Christian disgust for the flesh. Poussin the Platonist will be able to live in peace with many of the Christians of his era. Indeed, we should grasp that his artistic theology assures him a vantage point within the spirit from which he will observe the diverse religions his century is learning about – and most notably, the myths of paganism, from which he will draw such important lessons.

Still, he must truly accomplish this slaying of the ordinary self: that is, in practice, he must analyse the passions that affect it, that snare it in desire – analyse them in order to shed them more effectively. Yet nothing could be more false than to imagine, upon viewing *The Inspiration of the Poet*, a Poussin girding himself to seek in some direct manner – by banging out a few chords on the keyboard of colours, as it were – the beauty, in essence divine, that lies in the things of this world. That beauty is surely not accessible to those who abandon themselves to the passions – to those who extinguish their gaze with the fake jewels of their reveries. And so, to gain access to that beauty, one must first accomplish a *negative work*; and we can easily see that Poussin undertook such an effort from the time of *The Inspiration of the Poet*, if not before. That severe analysis is certainly attempted by *The Plague at Ashdod* starting in 1630. In this picture, and a number of others from the 1630s – for example, the two *Abductions of the Sabine Women*, or *The Gathering of Manna*, from 1638–1639 – Poussin will study the effects of fear, greed, and covetousness; he will ponder cruelty and violence. He will also acknowledge selflessness, and the capacity for affection; and he will highlight – which is something new in painting – the moral and spiritual potentiality of women, as when Erminia binds Tancred's wounds. Poussin will observe, will reflect. And before some of his canvases, we may conclude that he was working more in tandem with the historian or the sociologist, than as a disciple of Orpheus or a devotee of Apollo.

Yes: but from the depths of the sublimation that doubtless transpires within him, there arises little by little a clearer vision, a vaster gaze, that will make from the colours and forms of the world the timbres and rhythms of a music, wherein the relationship between the One and the Multiple, which has always eluded the musings of philosophers, patently unfolds. In the scenes he portrays, it is as if the horizon became more and more harmonious, despite the restlessness of its peaks and clouds. After this, in 1640, we will suddenly have the first landscapes that Poussin painted as such – as landscapes: the one with St. John on Patmos, and the one with St. Matthew. Two superb paintings, which carry the great golden light of *The Inspiration of the Poet* to the three dimensions of real nature. And now Poussin has arrived where he ultimately wanted to be: a *locus formosus*, let us say, a place of beauty at the centre of an earth with more veritable delights – 'delectation', that will be his word – than the *locus amoenus* of the erotic pastoral. In 1640, Nicolas Poussin is finally himself.

IV.

And this is also the moment when we can look at *The Shepherds of Arcadia* with a better chance of understanding the work.

The moment, because we have established the meaning for Poussin of the words: *Arcadia... Et in Arcadia ego.* But also because the picture itself was painted in the same period as those two great landscapes. To discuss a painting aided by the meaning the painter has given to certain of its elements, we should obviously know its date; and in the case of *The Shepherds of Arcadia*, this may seem to pose a problem, since no document has been linked to the work. But in fact, the solution is easy: we need only compare the cracked blocks of stone in either of the landscapes with the stones of the sarcophagus in *The Shepherds*; or scan with our eyes the horizon's line in each of these three canvases. Clearly, the kinship is close. Moreover, we have recently learned that the landscapes, which constitute a diptych, were paid for by their purchaser in October 1640. Consequently, *The Shepherds of Arcadia* is from 1639, perhaps – or at the latest, 1640.

At the latest, I emphasize, since at the beginning of November, Poussin will leave Rome for two years. Thus we discover that *The Shepherds* dates – not from some ordinary juncture in his painterly career – but from the months that were probably the hardest to bear of his entire existence. It was then, in 1638 already, and in 1639 above all, that the superintendent of buildings, and soon the king himself – who wrote to him personally – summoned Poussin to come to Paris to work for them. And he tried, as long as possible, to refuse; but one day, the flattering invitations turned into orders. And now he must leave – or in other words, leave behind his wife, and his house in the Via Paolina, and his studio, and the city of Rome; and above all, the countryside he loves, whose magnificent light has become the catalyst of his alchemy. He must also face the risks of the trip, which will be daunting; and furthermore, his health, which has remained unstable since his first bouts of illness, and his age, already forty-six years – no small number for the period – may also make him fear that his departure will be definitive: that it is only a foreshadowing of death.

In short, here is one of those moments in life when we think about drawing up our will; and if we have desired, hoped for, and attempted a great deal, we take stock of what we have succeeded in doing, or failed to do, or abandoned. – My hypothesis, then, which will not surprise you, is that *The Shepherds of Arcadia* – for which we know of no patron, no buyer, as if Poussin had painted it for his own use – is precisely this testament, this assessment, meditated upon and composed in that language of forms which was natural to him.

What subject, in fact, what *topos* could have been more suitable to his present situation than *Et in Arcadia ego* – which, as Bellori says, reminds us that 'in mezzo le felicità', amid satisfactions and contentments, 'la morte ha luogo', death may be present? Especially since ten or twelve years earlier, Poussin had already taken up the theme – but in order to denote another kind of death, that which can reduce to nothing the mind's ambitions. Did Cardinal Rospigliosi, or Cassiano dal Pozzo, or some other member of their society of Roman literati – which entitled itself 'Arcadia', by the way, and was not unversed in rites of mourning – suggest this idea to the painter, whom they saw constrained to depart? But that kind of prompting was hardly needed. His past experiences concerning Arcadia and the self – the *ego* – suffice to show that at the time of this second crisis, the phrase that had in effect summed up the first one could only assist Poussin in reflecting upon himself anew.

And yet, it is not as if in undertaking the painting, Poussin wanted to break completely with the commonplace inherent in the phrase – that is, with the generality of an idea, and a manner of giving it shape, that everyone could grasp: from which follows that art-lovers were able to consider, with Bellori, that here was indeed a moral allegory. At face value, everything is in place for such a reading. Here is a sepulchre, obvious proof that we must die. Here is a phrase which – correctly decoded, as they knew how to do in that period – states the *topos* in no uncertain terms. On a tomb, it can be explained as one of those maxims often inscribed in such places, of the type: *Vita brevis, spes aeterna*. As for the shepherds, why would they not ponder it, instead of showing surprise? The prevailing taste has become more classical in 1640 than ten or fifteen years earlier, and the art-lover has learned to find significance in calm gestures.

Nevertheless, beneath this treatment of the theme that I would call *rhetorical*, we can easily recognize other signals and clues. To begin with, the gravity of the shepherds, justified by the subject of their reflection, and which balances their gestures and attitudes: let us note that it forms a continuity with similar balancings on the horizon, which is very close by now – we might even say that it envelopes the foreground. On Poussin's part, this gravity comes down less to an oratorical invention – on the level of discourse, of rhetorical construction – than to the act of a painter, who thereby exercises his mastery, and lets us perceive his self-assurance. I would even say that he expresses his serious satisfaction, such as he must have felt before the landscapes with St. Matthew and St. John – the first, let us recall, of that long series of evocations of the earth which he will pursue until his death. I, Poussin, he must have said to himself – even in the *locus amoenus* so easy to evoke through painting, and so dangerous for the spirit – I, Poussin, have known how to preserve that spirit, my overarching project. I am still here: having succeeded in transforming the dream-scene into an earthly place, at once real and divine – let us say into the *locus formosus*, the place of beauty. *Et in Arcadia* 'I am'; and thus the missing word is simply *sum*, which is compatible this time with the rules of syntax and the habits of epigraphy, since they only allow us to infer a simple verb, in the present indicative. As we shall see, only slightly does a hint of the optative tinge that absolute present.

In the end, as we have grasped, Poussin was only able to survive in such a way by 'dying' to his personal desires, to his existence as an individual. And this explains why the proud declaration now appears on a tomb – and all the more so, on this one. For the sarcophagus in *The Shepherds of Arcadia* displays well-defined hallmarks. First of all, in a land of shepherds, poor and ignorant of architecture, it is uncustomary: and this comprises a meaning. In fact, it is a monument such as art creates, though this one is handsome only owing to its proportions; and yet, for a Poussin, this constitutes the essence: such is art itself, since proportions are music. From which it follows that this tomb, where the former self of Poussin lies sacrificed, is his art, is his creation, born precisely of that sacrifice. We think of what a poet had written who was very dear to the Barberinis' milieu – and very dear to painters as well, since it was he who had pronounced the equation *ut pictura poesis*. Horace had declared, he too with pride: 'Exegi monumentum aere perennius' – I built a tomb for myself more durable than bronze. There is a real difference here, nevertheless. Horace saw in his poem a 'monumentum', a funerary memorial, only because he deemed that it would ensure his glory through the centuries. Poussin made the tomb into the very possibility of his oeuvre – and in order that it would grant him, not glory, but a direct, clear-eyed gaze at the divine within the depths of the external world.

The tomb in *The Shepherds of Arcadia* symbolizes the art of Poussin; rather, let us say it is the fact of art itself, the self-reflection or 'abyme' of art in the painting. And that is why the painter, in order to erect it, had recourse to the fissured stones we see in *The Landscape with St. John* and *The Landscape with St. Matthew*. In them, they are the tumbled elements – though obviously reusable – of Greek or Roman architecture. St. John, St. Matthew, seated among the blocks of stone, compose the writings that proclaim the new law; yet it is not without antecedents in the world of Antiquity: Poussin has denoted this by having a cross appear on the remains of a pedestal. But here it is a cross of pure and beautiful geometry, the sign of a *deus pictor, architectus, opifex* more than of the god of the Apocalypse. And by reusing these stones for his own artist's tomb, as Poussin clearly does – realizing a conjunction with the Platonist art of Antiquity – he counters the exoteric tradition of *caritas* with the idea of divinisation through the pursuit of harmony.

With merely a few inflections to the obvious givens of the *topos*,

Poussin has already said many things that are his own; and it is not surprising that some inhabitants of this land, which he may henceforth call his, have assembled there in order to reflect. But apropos these four young people, now I must make a fundamental remark: inhabitants of this land, they inhabit Poussin's painting first and foremost, since he is the creator of this place – and thus we must understand them as aspects of himself. So let us eschew a priori hypotheses about their meaning; first let us seek them in the previous pictures, where he has always projected so many of his own modes of being.

Let us start by looking at the figure of the Alpheus River in the first *Shepherds of Arcadia*, in whom I had recognised the Poussin of then, anxious about time, which was going to waste in his life: we will find that his crestfallen pose resembles that of the shepherd who, to the left, leans his weariness against the tomb. This figure is somewhat reminiscent of a faun; he is the only one in the work who suggests to us the life and vigour of eros. Here we have a gaze that rests on what the other shepherds are doing as from afar, without our being able to know whether he understands them or finds them of interest. And therefore I recognise in this shepherd to the left the Poussin of the late 1620s, who did not know whether he was truly committed to the momentous art for which he had such ambition. The Poussin of the unquiet beginning of the great oeuvre is here; he takes his place in the self-appraisal. Indeed, he may have a meaning, in the future, for many young artists who will contemplate this picture.

And near the man he was, we now have the one he was able to become. Bearded and thick-haired, like the figure who already deciphers the tomb in the Chatsworth *Shepherds*, he continues that work – but with more attention, one knee on the ground, struggling, we might say, to read. And it is true that he casts a rather irksome shadow on the inscription. It is as if his body had had to be pulled aside so that his finger might attain the truth, by reaching right to the edge of the light. Let us understand: this shadow of the mortal body – this body that is desire – is the dream inherent to that desire, which can hide the true meaning of existence. And do we not make out a sinister warning, a scythe moving toward his head? We will not decipher the inscription, we will not attain the idea of the *ego*, of the universal self, still halfway in shadow, unless we unceasingly get rid of the encroachments of that shadow. Separating shadow from light! At the extremity of this hand, what is his gaze fixed upon? And he is kneeling, or almost, as if he were pointing out a bas-relief in the Forum! It is enough to say that this shepherd is Poussin at work, Poussin always at work, and teaching his potential disciple the difficulty of the task.

Luckily, to help them both, there are those two young beings on the right-hand side of the work – clearly the side of certitude. And we recognise them, too, without having to search too far. That shepherd who turns toward us to designate the tomb, to tell us that here there is a meaning, and who says this with self-assurance, his foot firmly placed on the rock – which in good iconography, codifies certainty – have we seen him in Poussin? Why of course, he is the poet in his splendid *Inspiration of the Poet*. This is the same face, not at all singularised but archetypal, since it must reveal the purity of poetry, its interiority, as well as its classical beauty and eternal youth. The shepherd is near the one I call the painter, his hand quite close to his – which calls to mind the Sistine Chapel vault – his body, his head, his limbs in perfect correlation, in perfect symmetry and complementarity with his: here is the poet under whose sign Poussin had placed himself in that founding picture, circa 1630 – knowing that he is Orpheus, who receives from Apollo the secret that everything is music. *Ut pictura poesis* is one of the secondary meanings of his *Et in Arcadia ego*.

Along these lines, let us recall that in the 1620s, Poussin had gone astray by painting with too much ardour – and above all, by regretting the sleeping Venuses and other Bacchantes, with too much spite towards his own life. At that time, it was a poet, Virgil, who had been there to remind him that the pastoral, the natural place, only has a meaning that is fundamental, and a value which is literally infinite – as in the *Eclogues*, as in this Arcadia forewarned by evening shadows – insofar as it resounds, unendingly and from every side, with music. And it is truly Virgil to some degree who is here, under the appearance of this young man, who also resembles the idealised portrayals of the poet of the *Bucolics*. Which is why we find ourselves dreaming, for the first time in this analysis: the beautiful young woman, so noble, and whose gentle smile, attentive and free of disdain, signifies she harbours a knowledge – is she not that Muse of the *Fourth Bucolic* to whom Virgil appeals: 'Let us elevate our song somewhat' – whereupon he pronounces the ten or so verses that shook the foundations of the West. The woman has her hand on the shoulder of the poet, as if to inspire him, to bolster him in his intuition: and so, do they not both understand, before this tomb that is a life, before this life which is that of art, always waiting to be born, that a *magnus ordo* can arise? One that would reestablish the happy reign of Saturn through the grace of music, of sounds, of words – and of colour and forms as well? In this composition, at the exact antipodes of the shepherd who is still faun-like, the Muse of Virgil would promise that this Arcadia – which has always hesitated between hedonist reverie and the yearning for a higher reality, between the erotic and the ontological – will ultimately comprise, in its essential poverty, yet which signifies plenitude, the threshold of the golden age.

But do we ever have the right to dream – to dream for long – before a painting by Poussin? On the contrary, must we not remember, as we look at this one, that the three other figures are less allegories here than quintessences of what Poussin bears within himself? And accordingly, rather than an allegory of poetic inspiration, must we not sense in the figure on the right a being of the same kind as Poussin-the-painter or Poussin-the-poet, such as they are portrayed here: that is, a generality, but also – nonetheless – a being truly of this world? I believe, once the moment of our dream has passed, that it is Poussinian to think in such a way – at least for this picture, which has to do with its creator above all. And so I recognise, in this attentive woman, simply woman in the end: woman when she ensures a man's relationship with the world. Certainly, let us not doubt that in this case that role has always been decisive, in fact: at once eros and love, peril and inspiration, dream and ultimate reality. Poussin could not help but acknowledge this, particularly during his crisis of the 1620s. And it is thus unthinkable that he would have omitted to raise the issue once more, in this moment of a summing up. The young woman in *The Shepherds of Arcadia* embodies woman in general, resuscitated, reborn like a Gradiva rising again from the ruins of the erotic imagination, henceforth vanquished – or rather, tamed. Here we should obviously pinpoint her meaning in the picture more precisely: that is, we should reconstruct her history, through the reflection carried out by Poussin in the preceding canvases – where we encounter her, of course. Is she not already present, looking just about the same, in his momentous *Inspiration of the Poet*? Or as the daughter of Pharoah, an Isis who is also smiling, in his *Moses Rescued from the Waters*? In a noteworthy coincidence, Poussin has just painted this picture in 1638, as the first of a series he will continue to develop till very late in his life.

But I have only enough time left to assess the way these meanings that we understand, or that we sense, are incorporated into *The Shepherds of Arcadia*, are uttered by it – to consider, in other words, that impression of mystery, which has forcefully struck so many observers of the work. Spontaneously, they have not seen it as a moral allegory, knowingly calculated and magnificently painted, but rather as an epiphany. As if before it, we were the initiates at Eleusis, looking at the ear of wheat silently revealed by the celebrant; as if we felt something surface through the image that mere thought could never say.

For that very reason, it is certainly not easy even to seek the framework, the basic framework, in which this mystery manifests itself; yet *The Shepherds of Arcadia* has a remarkable particularity that will allow us to gain our bearings. This characteristic is what I shall call the *precariousness of significance*. At first glance, everything in the painting appears motionless: made to last without end, like an allegorical scene. The gestures, the attitudes – those bearers of meaning – seem stable to us; they seem ready for the time – which will be long – that observers take to ponder them. But this is only an appearance. As has often been noted, someone within us begins to say that the hand resting on that shoulder will not remain there. This finger pointing at a letter will shift towards another in a moment, carrying with it that shadow which the sun, in tracing its arc, will also cause to move: thus conferring another figure, which will suggest another sense. And the shepherds themselves – we realise, all of a sudden – will soon leave this scene, where the tomb will speak no more. So everything has only been said through the suspense of an instant; nevertheless, its configurations will come undone, evincing the randomness of the world. And so the picture suggests that reality, if we went there, would contradict, would annihilate the image – and therefore the image avows itself as such, despite its unbreakable core of truth. It is as if the River Alpheus, the river of forgetfulness, the river of Arcadia – which Poussin had evoked in the Chatsworth

Shepherds, but not in this new work – had figured here nonetheless: flowing, invisible and scintillant, through all points of the human condition.

But why did Poussin want to display so cruelly, in a painting that must say the truth, its nature as merely an image? Why did he want to stress the precariousness of truth's formulation, even though he has lived and ripened a part of it – verified it, at least – while becoming aware of his mastery of so many means to express it? This is easy to understand. In 1640, Poussin has surely arrived at various certainties: he has the right, and even the duty, to indicate them to others besides himself – which he did. But despite that, he is conscious that the work of his maturation has not been completed. He also knows that his lifework as a painter, starting with the two landscapes, has only begun to exercise its new-found powers. And this is precisely the moment when he must depart, must interrupt his work, must leave the place of his reflection and ascesis for another, Paris – where the passions reign, threatening to absorb him again, and cloud his vision anew. What he was discovering, will it not cease to appear to him now? Much as Poussin feels sure of the validity of his recent quest, he can still worry about his future, about the destructive effect of the time to come: it is the precariousness of the means on which he has relied that betrays this disquiet. To the face-value meaning, that which shapes a poetics, he has added another: the indication that the mind's lucidity is only assured for an instant – in other words, in the flux of the real, it is merely an image.

But this is not all he says; and it is only now that we can grasp what touches us in the work – what grants it, in our eyes, that quality of mystery. In Poussin there is a spiritual self-assurance, and also a disquiet; but even if he is worried, and afraid of the near future, *he still does not lose hope*. At this point, I would hypothesise that through these signs and this mode of thought, which trust in the instant and play with fire, he admits his fragility to himself – of that there can be no doubt. But he embodies it in such a fashion that this fragility – who can tell? – may well be surmounted; and by him once more, by Poussin, in this an 'ego' more vigorous than he knows. This hand, this finger, this shadow will move? Yes, in the external world, but not in the image. And here, are they going to evince that this immobility is just an unreality, an insufficiency, a lie? Or, under the striving hand of the painter, possessed of sympathy and delicacy, will all these meaningful elements not reveal instead the necessity of their interconnection, its mysterious organicism? A reciprocity so strong that it bids time in the outside world – time that passes – to stop? The image that is most openly an image then asserts that it is truer, and more real, than the teachings of ordinary wisdom, itself lured by appearances. The instant, which is fugacious, but which is also the place of finitude, declares that it is the place of true awareness; and Poussin ventures to paint that instant – in part because he doubts himself, and in order to admit that doubt. Possibly, he also sought to disclose that truth, through an act of profound attention to himself which would prove to him, if achieved, that he henceforth has nothing to fear. What is the golden bough of Virgil? Perhaps simply a brief glimmer of sun on the branch of a tree. And what can pluck it from that branch? Not iron, as we know, but only a hand that has the same delicacy, the same intelligence of the world – of life, of duration, of the instant – as the wind that passes through the tree.

What did Poussin think, on finishing his picture? Did he feel, far down in his depths, that he had less expressed his thoughts than succeeded – beyond that – in this supreme experiment? Or that he had only implied it, while continuing to doubt? Be that as it may, I imagine that he painted these *Shepherds of Arcadia*, in the months before his departure, in order to leave them in his empty studio, where they would await his return. The sun would rise each day, would trace its arc, and would withdraw, having swept its play of shadow and light across the painting. But perhaps the shadow and light of that picture – having remained the golden bough, with its gleam that is truth – would still seem vivid upon his return to the voyager, whose eyes had remained undimmed.

And a last remark. In this picture, everything is entrusted to the instant – to an instant. Accordingly, it goes without saying that Poussin – who neglected nothing, as we know – could only have given a literal meaning, and an important one, to the sign that stands at the centre of the work, where the shepherd's finger rests: the letter R. Moreover, it lies at the exact midpoint of the letters in the line that says *Et in Arcadia* – or in other words, speaks of a place.

R? Why R? Is it not simply because that is the first letter of Rome, the city Poussin is leaving; and does he not denote in this way that he wants to return? A future indicative, valid for him personally – an indicative, or an optative – would thus emerge in the eternal present of artistic accomplishment. And hope, which has sustained Poussin in this work, and from which it draws its mystery, would find here the sign that can say it, without reducing its scope.

Translated by Hoyt Rogers

POETRY AND PHOTOGRAPHY[1]

I.

'Poetry and Photography: Daguerre, Mallarmé, Maupassant and the Surrealists' – this was the theme I initially set myself, but when I began to put the different parts of the argument together, it soon became clear to me that I had first to lay out the hypotheses, few in number, that will underpin the central idea. This is what I am going to do first, reducing correspondingly the space I would have devoted to Mallarmé and Breton, but not that which I shall accord to Maupassant. The reasons for this will become evident.

This research I am beginning – on the impact of the earliest photography on the experience of the world and the conduct of existence in the nineteenth century and up to our own day – must necessarily also be a reflection on poetry, since the study of what I shall call 'the photographic' enables us better to understand both how poetry has developed and the tasks that confront it. The kind of – historically unprecedented – act the photographer has accomplished, and continues to accomplish, in fact exerts its influence directly on what poetry is seeking to be. And poetry, in its turn, must therefore examine what that act is, and what it asks of, or imposes on, contemporary society. And it mustn't hesitate to express its reservations, concerns or, indeed, its approval when presented with the diverse and perhaps contradictory forms which that activity has taken since its earliest times, in the days when Baudelaire's intuitions were beginning to dispel the – once again so feverishly religious – illusions that had encumbered Romantic poetry.

But, first of all, these few preliminary remarks on poetry, the fundamental nature of which ought properly to be recalled, even if I can do so today only very summarily. Poetry is what evinces unease at the constructions erected over the centuries by conceptual thought, that thought which bases itself on aspects of the empirically

---

1   *Poésie et photographie*, Paris : Editions Galilée, 2014. The present translation first appeared as *Poetry and Photography*. Calcutta : Seagull Books, 2017. Republished here with kind permission.

given – from which it deduces laws – but not on the totality, the compactness which we nonetheless perceive spontaneously in things when we encounter them in the here and now of our lives. That kind of conceptual approach, which proceeds by choosing among those aspects – and, hence, simultaneously simplifies and generalises – deprives the mind of recognising, within what it perceives, the unity that is the way its various parts breathe together or, in other words, that quality which makes of it a particular, finite thing, even as it opens itself up to that other whole that is reality as such. And this is a blindness that also affects the self-consciousness of persons, who can no longer fully think their belonging to the being of the world. Poetry is the memory of that loss, an effort to re-establish the lost contact with that which is.

How poetry goes about achieving this task isn't my subject today, though let me make one comment on what it is aiming to re-establish. This is a relation of persons to their environment that would provide the needs and intuitions of the body – as much as those of the mind – with their place in consciousness: a body that is both alive and destined to die. Freeing itself from the many systems that conceptual thinking is only too ready to build as a home for those who accept its simplified representations – churches, for example, armies, sets of values peculiar to commerce or industry – poetry's role is to examine, in a critical or supportive spirit, the ways in which the men or women of our time combat the alienation they undergo.

These ways are many and varied, but they are unified, nonetheless, by a procedure they have in common. Conceptual thought develops within an overall idea of the world, within what I shall term a world-in-image, a schematic world, both underpinned and explicated by a certain use of language that congeals utterance into its categories and projects. And the persons stifled in this way often believe it sufficient, if they are to recover their difference, simply to work on the signifiers of that language 'in image', to appropriate them for their own stand-point, apportioning to the main figures this thinking offers them characteristics that ensue from what they are in their particular exist-ences. For example, for the idea of a tree in general, they substitute the evocation of some tree that they love, this being brought to mind by certain of its aspects. This is to personalise the collective image. But we should beware here of the following danger: operating with the words of the grand image shared by all, this work on the part of the individual can only be the production, once again, of a similar schema; confinement again within just one image. And poetry has to be aware of this trap, into which it falls too easily, and has to learn, in order to expose it, to recognise its nature and characteristics.

What are these characteristics that distinguish the image from fully lived life? The first is that every image requires a support – wall or stone or canvas or paper, or at least the idea of such a support. And this is so because the support immediately means a delimitation, a framing, which suggests that the things and beings the image seems to evoke are situated in an authentic place, with its own space and even its own light. The frame confers a semblance of reality on the image, and it is from the frame that this illusion derives its capacity to endure beyond the moment of reverie. It confers credibility on it, but first and foremost it confers authority, at a level we might call ontological – the level at which decisions are made regarding what is and is not. From which it follows, indeed, that the usual complement of the frame, in the image that it renders credible, is a certain point among the figures which seems to provide the foundation for the *being* the image claims to possess. This is the case with Pharaoh's daughter in Poussin's *Moses Saved from the Waters*: she is a beautiful, standing figure, full of authority and the very centre, we might believe, of the harmonious proportions which present themselves as reality in the conception this picture has of it.

The fact remains that no image structure is complete reality. This schematic representation may gather up a great deal of the appearance of things, but, first, it inevitably leaves outside itself, for example, that which conceptualisation suppresses and wishes to forget – namely, the finitude within what is, and the way of seeing the world and life of those who haven't forgotten their own finitude. The image cannot express this inwardness of existing beings, which is, indeed, essentially temporal.

And it is a fact that in many images the hint of a level – their unconscious – peeps through, at which there is still an awareness of that limit, and the idea that a world exists outside those images. We even see them attempting to ward off this 'outside' by heading off the encounter with it and striving to convince themselves that nothing in it will elude their idea of the real: that nothing in it will manifest that element of chance which is what they fear most. There is, in fact, no room in images for chance. What might seem to signify such a thing has been surreptitiously removed. The folds in the Virgin's gown in an altarpiece, the cat that seems to be present by chance in an *Annunciation* by Lorenzo Lotto are, in fact, the product of the needs, desires and fatalities inherent in the painter's dream. There is no element of chance in the field of the image! This particular throw of the dice has truly abolished it. Yet chance exists, nonetheless, at the margins of the work in the daily existence of its creator, and, as a result, the image, however affirmative it may be, always has an underlying disquiet to it, which, we might surmise, may even be what lends some paintings their restless, fevered beauty.

II.

And I shall now observe that this disquiet of images, this foreshadowing within them of the ineradicable reality of what remains outside was, more intensely than ever, the experience of some great artists of the Age of Enlightenment.

Why was this? Because this project of submitting the knowledge of the world and existence to reason was also a project of dismantling the myths that had built, explained and justified worlds without the aid of that reason. Yet, with myths disappeared also what enabled religion to exert its control over all the regions (even the most nocturnal ones) of reality and life, and which set thought at the edge – or almost – of the abyss, with a sense of vertigo or anxiety that the great art of the age was able to express; the dizzying sense that there was no longer any foundation for the moral values that had, up to that point, been buttressed by the divinity; and the sense that, henceforth, genuinely human responsibility would have to be assumed. This is what Leopardi and Goya experienced; it is what shows through in the works of Sade.

Then, in the Romantic period, the darkness simply grew and spread – and the vertigo with it – even if the poets of those years attempted to recover their poise by way of religion, with representations and forms of belief of their own private devising. This effort is what Keats and Hugo or Nerval have, more or less, in common, together with Novalis and Caspar David Friedrich. It is not enough, however, to deliver Delacroix from his 'lake of blood' obsession, as Baudelaire rightly saw:[2] in vain would that tormented painter claim to be a follower of Apollo. Around 1840, everything was ready for the development of a more intense – and also more resolute – awareness of the vast 'outside' of the image: of non-being. A crystallisation such as Stendhal expressed in 1822 in respect of love, perhaps seeking in that way to deflect attention.[3]

And it was indeed in these same years of the middle of Baudelaire's century that a crystallisation occurred that was quite different from that of the thinking of the lover – or self-styled lover. The precondition was an event which, we should note, was immediately celebrated with astonishing – both secular and religious – solemnity. It was on 7 January 1839 at the French Academy of Sciences that François Arago announced to the world the invention of what would be termed the daguerreotype, a procedure by which representations of things from the world around us were permanently fixed on a support – in this particular case, a copper plate. Fixed! This was not yet, therefore, what photography would make possible. It was merely direct image-capture, affording no possibility of reproduction – that wouldn't come for another ten years. But that is of little consequence. What constituted an event was that there was to be found on the copper plate a full, exact reproduction of what could previously only be met with in three-dimensional form. And hence the 'outside', the realm of perpetual change, has been ensnared and is going to remain here, immobilised, in this very singular new image.

Why is fixing so important? Why am I going so far as to say that this immobilisation was as crucial an event as the transporting of external reality into the image? Because it is what enables things which might each merely be considered in itself and on its own to cohabit on a sustained basis with others captured in the same way and hence leave their plane of shifting, temporal existence and come to exist on the plane of images – that is to say, at the level where

2   See Baudelaire's 'Les phares' : 'Delacroix, le lac de sang hanté des mauvais anges' […]
3   Stendhal develops the famous notion of crystallisation in his essay *De l'Amour* (1822).

images assert their claims. We should note that seeing something at a point other than where it actually was wasn't absolutely novel in Daguerre's day. There had for many years been situations in which an 'outside' had been captured without the intervention of an artist; the surface of the moon, as it could be seen through Galileo's telescope, is one example. But the representations produced in that way weren't immobilised in a frame; they couldn't, therefore, compete with traditional images, which possessed such a frame and hence the power, as I have remarked, to suggest that the scene they showed had reality and being – indeed, a higher nature of being than our own. And now, with the daguerreotype and, shortly after it, the photograph, which were fixed and framed, these representations had slipped in among the images.

Now – and here, as I see it, is the important, indeed essential, element of the event hailed by Arago, who, like Galileo, was an astronomer – these new images take their place among the others only when they have in them something the old images knew nothing of and never wanted to know anything of: namely, chance – an element of chance that was, in this case, wholly unfettered and fully, rightfully itself.

III.

How could this be? First, it was not at all intentional. Daguerre had been a painter and composed his photographic shots as he would have composed paintings, not wishing to leave anything 'to chance' and indeed making copious references to the artistic tradition. But let us consider what will inevitably appear on the little copper plate. A particular tablecloth and an article of clothing are going to be there, before our very eyes, with their actual folds – those ordained by the chance arrangement of their material, not the painter's art. A person whose portrait is taken holds his arm in a way that hasn't totally been decided by the photographer either: hence an element of chance shows through. In group photos, which proliferate once snapshots can be taken, that element becomes even more marked by the random arrangement of other bodies and their reciprocal positions, with no one now attempting to create harmony among these in a manner alien to existence as it is lived. And it won't be long before some cat the photographer neither planned nor wished for would walk into shot, which isn't something that could occur in any painting, despite the suggestion of it in Lotto's *Annunciation*. Chance is active in the photographic image; it deflects the mind from what the composition is saying, if there is composition; it shows that things exist as such, in a 'being-there' irreducible to mental activity. In painting, chance is sometimes simulated – by the very people who are trying to be rid of it. In photography, there is no need to simulate it; it is present from the outset.

It is legitimate to ask whether this really represents an invasion. But let us look reasonably closely at the most ordinary of photographs. Look at this pile of stones in it – most certainly there by chance – or the fabric of the jacket of someone who wanted to have their picture taken. In the photographic image, we see not only how these materials represent a complement to the idea of stones or jacket, but also the grain of these objects, if I may use that term – that accumulation of irregularities in the brute fact of the thing, the blotches, embryonic forms, folds or cracks that are indeterminate and practically infinite in number. In painting, an artist, guided by his idea and composing meaning, instituting it, would have controlled these details and might even have erased them with his touch and brushwork. In photography, by contrast, a free play of forms and forces, clearly beyond our laws and indifferent to our wishes, shows on the surface of things – a profound, deep-seated refusal that *what is* levels against our pretensions to control it in the interests of a higher, entirely mental, reality. The element of chance here arises from the detail of what the camera perceives in the matter of the world, as much as it does from the relations that existed between the components of the work at the moment the photograph was conceived and taken. And, as such, it addresses the level of the intentions, plans and thoughts of the photographer and says to him what Mallarmé was shortly afterwards to admit to himself – namely, that we are 'but vain forms of matter'; that, in fact, we *are* not.

This is frightening. And it is also new. For the intuition of non-being was already in the air, most certainly – philosophy had always spoken of it or formulated it as a hypothesis; it had even, on occasion, asserted it as something self-evident – but it was so

merely in the realm of thought and on the margins of actual existence, whereas this plain fact was now being registered as close as could
be to the creations of those who painted and drew, whose most stead-
fast intention had always been to deny it. Awareness of chance was
henceforth most acutely present in our looking and at the heart of our
thinking. If one perceives the element of chance in the lawyer's jacket
and one then looks to the composition of his portrait, that composition, that product of the intellect, will appear as only one accident
among others in entanglements of trifling events that are entirely
unrelated. And this is sufficient in itself to relegate the image from
providing an impression of reality to producing a record of unreality
in an unlocatable, spectral dimension. This photographed room is no
longer within the world of our actions, our acts. The drawers in its
furniture cannot be opened, the vase on the table isn't there for any
of us and these two people together, smiling....It becomes clear why
the first photographers erased what they saw as useless detail from
their work: they felt it to be dangerous. With Daguerre's invention, it
was non-being that entered the previously closed field of the image.

In 1842, barely three years after Arago's announcement, just as
long as it took for Daguerre's new invention to reach a wider public,
Edgar Allan Poe, always in the forefront of the thinking of his day,
published *The Masque of the Red Death*. In that story, in a castle
shut up to prevent penetration by the plague, a cause of death and,
to an even greater degree, evidence of nothingness (a castle that is,
moreover, the scene of a masked ball – a clear symbolisation of what
I term the image), the sickness still gets in beneath the external form
of a mask or, in other words, of one part of the means deployed to
combat it, now revealed in its true nature. The rejected element has
just insinuated itself into that which was trying to keep it at bay, thus
testifying to its radically illusory character.

And what consequences immediately follow! For what becomes of
the person who looks at the photograph, as he is now able to do? Like
all the men and women around him in the castle where the orchestra
falls silent, he is going to have to understand that he is merely one
montage among others of those images that vainly reject chance, to
understand that, right down to his most intimate sense of himself,
he is this non-being. For if one of these images deconstructs, is it not
obvious that all the others are together going to unravel? The looker

empties himself out, ontologically speaking; if he allows himself, as indeed he must, to see the element of chance in the image, he cannot but register this emptiness within himself – though not, we should say, the emptiness of the night (in the positive, full sense of the mystical experience, in which the *nada* is an excess of being) but the fact that the things of his days are now bereft of meaning and have each become a cupboard whose drawers don't open, a pure enigma, the inwardly collapsed outside of the inside of *here*. In that space of the self which, deserted by meaning, has become a stranger to itself, has become an *other of the self,* divesting it of selfhood. Hence the fear of going mad described in Maupassant's famous short story 'The Horla'.

IV.

'Really?' the reader will say. Does this disaster really happen each time you view a photograph – or even a daguerreotype?

No, of course not. That wasn't the reaction of many of Daguerre's contemporaries or many of the first photographers, who even welcomed the new technique with enthusiasm. But I shall say, presently, that not all of them did so and I shall remind the reader here and now of the nature of a certain mode of communication called *insinuation* and of its history over the centuries. This involves ideas – or information – formulated in such a way that we may fail to form an awareness of them, or may refuse to do so. But they lodge themselves in interstices of the great systems of representations and ideas that predominate in our conceptions of the world and of ourselves, and hence get through to our sub-conscious, which is precisely where these systems have their – never very firm – foundations. At that level, they act on us in a way that is initially little noticed, yet may in some cases be very intense and disproportionate to their apparent effect. When, as is the case here, such ideas function somewhere short of systems of thought and their associated scales of values, then distinctions of large or small cease to be operative. The tiniest sign or indication may be the thing that is most destabilising.

Think of the person who is speaking – and growing frantic – in 'The Raven' by Edgar Allan Poe, to whose short stories I have already referred. Think, as Poe intended us to, of that student awake in a dark chamber of the mind, seeking in his books – the bulwarks of a religious tradition – to allay his already deep doubts, who hears a scratching at his door, a very faint noise which nonetheless overwhelms him with unprecedented, unimagined terror. How disproportionate the relation between cause and effect! And think of that other insinuator, who has his place since the dawn of time in the everyday world of Christians, that Devil who slips almost imperceptibly into the world willed by God, with the destruction of faith as his chief goal. In each of these cases, it isn't some demonstration or argument, but a tiny flaw in the structures in place that leads to their collapse. Now, it is an event of the same, apparently imperceptible kind that occurs within traditional images when matter shows up there in all its brute nakedness as a result of photography. And one might even fear that this emergence may be of greater effectiveness than the Devil's insinuations, since the latter, as is well known, is only allowed to attempt to lead astray. His cloven hoof shows beneath his duplicitous clothing. He hasn't actually gained access to the very idea of the world he wishes to discredit.

Insinuation is that tiny element that threatens beliefs and certainties with collapse. And, in case anyone is possibly not minded to follow me in these thoughts, I shall go beyond these long preliminaries and mention a number of facts which seem to me to provide evidence for them, since they can only have been effects of the night that daguerreotypes and photography instilled into the image. Effects at the collective level, affecting the whole of society, and, consequently, for the most part, unconscious but perceptible and measurable in artistic creation or moral conduct. I believe it essential to take account of these events, some of them still ongoing, from the years that followed Daguerre's invention. They will enable us to gain a fuller understanding of the disruption of which they themselves form a part, once we attend to what certain literary narratives, for example, say of them in their figurative way – that is to say, in a mode both conceptual and symbolic, and fuelled, as dreams are, by metonymy and metaphor.

V.

With this, I begin the second part of my argument, though I am already quite a way through this essay and I shall only be able to indicate the broad outlines of the study I believe should be undertaken, a study of the effect of the photographic in various areas of human activity.

First, we should pay particular attention to the thought of Edgar Allan Poe and the work of Mallarmé, which, from this angle, develops and extends that thought, opening a whole, previously unexplored dimension within French language and literature. I have already mentioned 'The Raven', the great poem of 1845, the impact of which, as I very much believe, can be partly explained by the way it transcribes into language the image as refashioned by the hand of Daguerre. But I shall not go back today over Poe's 'nevermore' or a number of his stories that, in various ways, reflect his dread of nothingness, nor shall I even turn to Mallarmé's 'Sonnet en -yx' or *Igitur,* even though these latter works are, for intellectual understanding, extremely important effects of the photographic. For it would take a whole book to gauge the significance, for example, of the phenomenology Mallarmé was attempting in *Igitur* of that announcement of nothingness that had just been made to the Western world.

Then we would have to note a number of situations in the context of social life which attest to this impact, such as the following development, which the first great photographer Nadar noticed as soon as it occurred, with the critic Jérôme Thélot subsequently producing a remarkable analysis of Nadar's account. The event in question was a murder and the role played in the public indignation at that murder by the photograph of the mutilated body. The idea of nothingness to which the photographic phenomenon gave rise within self-consciousness expanded its scope in these photographs by their presentations of the corpse, the dark underside of life, the epiphany of non-meaning. And, in return, the fascination aroused by the new kind of image showed up and made manifest this particular kind of consequence with as much curiosity as horror: we are at the beginning here of that lifting of visual taboos that would characterise the twentieth century. A disaster which would, literally, become one body with a press photography replete with scenes that even Assyrian or Aztec art would have censored; and also with pornographic photography. A disaster which would, nonetheless, assume a genuinely artistic form in certain practitioners of the photographer's art. We ought to go back to see what was done by these gnostics of photography, who fully exploited the hint of darkness within it, though less with the aim of fighting it than of dreaming of worlds more luminous than our own – ways of taking up once again, with the new image, the metaphysical ambition inherent in the traditional one – and doing so openly this time.

Above all, however, we ought to take heed of the wave of resistance that arose – in this case openly and directly – against the denial of the experience of being, as constituted by photographic technique and the images it produced. It would be impossible to produce even a rudimentary history of photography if we failed to recognise the importance of these – in this case, wholly and fundamentally poetic – decisions which, from Nadar to Cartier-Bresson, and in many places since, have sought to provide being with a new kind of foundation in that very place where the thinking of being was deconstructed. And to set against the nothingness that may be discovered in photography, when it deploys chance, the will to being that stands out clearly in that other apprehension of reality it makes possible, namely, the gaze, which was never previously perceived so fully and frontally in portraits as it was after Nadar's day. It is in reaction to its own pernicious insinuation that photography has been capable of works that entirely justify its being ranked on the same level among the activities of the mind as painting, which was in fact affected and deflected from its course by it at a very early stage. Not because photographs are able to reproduce objects with a precision and completeness which the most realist of painters cannot attain – that capacity is something that has interested only mediocre painters – but because they suggest we look elsewhere than on the paths of mimesis for ways to think the human condition and its true needs. This was the case, for example, with Giacometti, obsessed as he was by the photos that lend weight to identity cards.

We should, at this properly ontological level, write the history of invention in photography, that history at times becoming a battle against the fascination that lures people down into its abyss. This history would follow the crest-line of the new times, doing so all the more – and all the better – for the fact that cinema has come to form absolutely essential links with this resistance. But this is much too enormous a field and I am going to confine myself today to a very tightly defined example, though one that shows up the primary effect of the photographic in a striking way.

VI.

I am referring to 'The Night', a story Maupassant published in 1887, at around the same time as 'The Horla'. It is, in other words, a work from his last years – years that saw him descend into madness. The year 1887 may seem a very long way from 1839, and even from the beginnings of photography, but that is merely superficially the case, given that this new date is also the date of an event which is itself of great metaphysical significance and on almost the same plane as the earlier one.

That event is the use of electricity for public lighting at certain locations in Paris. And we need to pay attention to this under-examined aspect of modern life – how the streets are lit, and with what. Public lighting plainly affects our relation to the world and our anxiety towards it very directly, since it confronts that darkness which the image – the traditional image – has always had the function of keeping at bay. And it does so in the name of our interests as civilised human beings – that is to say, at the heart of our cultural investments, and at the centre of the cities which, as such, are also products of image-based thinking. Battling against the darkness of the outside, it is fighting the same battle as the world-images of its age; it is, so to speak, in the front line in this ever-incomplete repulsing of nothingness.

Now, for a long time it had provided relatively effective protection in this regard. These were the days when lighting was done with candles. These latter, carried in the night-time, threw up shadowy figures, jerkily moving figures that could easily be regarded as threatening or even frightening but were nonetheless interpretable using the knowledge, beliefs and, also, hopes available. Though arising at its edges, this was all still within the image society projected on to earthly locations. And, moreover, that light of candles and torches was too weak to eclipse the light shed by the stars or the moon, which had their place in this ancient experience of the world, connecting with the likes of draughts of air, fragrances and even colours. Which meant that the night, the fair night, could be appropriated to the truth of the day, and one might even be encouraged to find refuge in it, as Leopardi does with regard to the moon, imagining it as a friendly young girl who is all gentleness and understanding. The candle's flame throws a bridge between the unknown and the known; it is as reassuring as it is disquieting. It extends towards the outside world the myths by which convictions and beliefs are strengthened.

And this ambiguity didn't fade when gas made its appearance in the lighting of towns and cities, for its weak flame remained responsive to the wind; it had a life to it, animating shadows in which lovers or prostitutes concealed themselves with no great fear – all of which fuelled a very specific imaginary, present even in Mallarmé: in his 'Le Tombeau de Charles Baudelaire', the wick of the gas lamp is *louche*, which means that it looks to both sides of the mind.

But electrical lighting was something quite different. First, electricity isn't a flame, such as would respond favourably to entreaties from the immediate environment, nor is it a form of combustion which could be ranged unhesitatingly among the natural processes from which image-worlds build up a part of their meaning. It is a modern substance, shorn of all myth and, similarly, remote from age-old thinking on the elements of water, earth, air or fire: all in all, a positive denial of the light inherent in what was an overall conception of the world in which light was both the light of thought and the light of being. Moreover, by its intensity, both bare and decentred, electricity effects a violent but clean break between the world here and a night outside that is now felt to be entirely black, even though, on our avenues, that 'elsewhere' is very close by and is, indeed, almost *here*. Electric light offers up the night to our thinking as truly the other of *here*, of this being that is ours; it enwraps us in nothingness. And, in so doing, it corroborates what had been revealed by photography.

It is, we might say, as though it lifted the revelation out of its original frame, the photographic plate, and as though the city became the second frame, becoming itself a photograph and showing up now in three dimensions the same suggestion of exteriority, brute matter and chance. With Paris having indeed changed, even before Daguerre's day. As I have tried to say elsewhere[4], in Baudelaire's century the Parisian crowd lost its vesture of signs and emblems that made it, before the Revolution, a manifestation of the image of the world in its hierarchy of functions and figures. The human environment became anonymous there; it was something neutral now, something sadly unknown and, similarly, the network of church porches and statues ceased to be instructive and overflowing with meaning: there was everywhere, if not a declaration of non-being, then at least a disposition to listen out for such a declaration. Paris, which would soon be photographed magnificently – think of Marville, and later of Atget – was already, in that new age, the pendant to the upcoming insinuations of the photographic plate. And electric lighting merely confirmed those insinuations by making them more immediately perceptible.

1887–88 is, then, the second time the photographic makes its impact, the time it spreads into the streets and society by way of electric lighting. And that lighting, we may note at this point, is mainly installed on some of the major boulevards, in precisely the places where a kind of perpetual party atmosphere had been established – in the cafés and the theatres – for those who wanted, as they say, to deaden their senses. This is in some ways the situation of *The Masque of the Red Death*. Paris and life in Paris became both scene and message. They are something to ponder over, these dialectics of the so-called City of 'Light'.

VII.

And pondering, pondering over Paris, pondering over this 'Now that is the Night'[5] is what Maupassant did in the short story I am going to address next. In 'The Night' (where they are virtually made explicit), we may follow both the successive moments and one of the possible

---

4   See Bonnefoy's essay 'Le poète et le flot mouvant des multitudes', Paris : Bibliothèque Nationale de France, 2013.
5   The reference is to Hegel's phrase 'Das Jetzt, welches Nacht ist', that occurs in his *Phenomenology of Spirit*, (1807).

conclusions of this development of an awareness of non-being experienced as non-meaning.

To begin with, these few pages are a reminder of the characteristics of the night as it used to be experienced in cities that had, as yet, little lighting: the 'gentle night' of Baudelaire's poem[6], where fears were more calmed than aroused and where the – at times light and enveloping – shadows could be regarded as benign; a night for which Maupassant, at least, expresses a very great liking. We are looking here at 'yesterday', in particular ('was it yesterday? – yes, surely, unless it was before that, another day, another month, another year'), and we may take him to mean a time that is now finished, since which point 'the sun hasn't reappeared'. Yesterday everything was, indeed, clear in the mild night air and 'I gazed up at the black river flowing above my head, the black star-studded river framed in the sky by the roofs of the buildings in the winding street.' At this beginning of the story, we are in the presence of night such as it was shaped by the all-embracing image of the world produced by conceptual thought – a margin within being, not its denial.

Then – and this clearly runs in the same direction as my present thoughts – Maupassant begins to rove around the boulevards, where the cafés are 'ablaze', where people are laughing and drinking, singing or shouting, and at that point he becomes aware of the excessive intensity of their lighting – the lighting produced by electricity. Beneath the 'electric globes, like pale but brilliant moons or lunar eggs fallen from the sky or monstrous living pearls [...] the chestnut trees, smeared with yellow light, seemed painted'. A very discerning vision of the starkness of these new perceptions which disperse into the mere appearance of things what it was that made them analogies for human life; and which strip the colours from them, as though these weren't the simple, happy emergence of their particular natures, but that pure exteriority that is blindly registered by the photographic machine.

And, quite logically, the narrator of 'The Night' then leaves the city to take refuge in a place that is unlit and hence still natural – in this case the Bois de Boulogne, where he stays for 'a long, long time'.

6   'Recueillement' in *Les Fleurs du mal.*

Yet he fails to recover his peace of mind. 'I had been gripped by a strange thrill, a powerful, unexpected emotion, an intense mental excitement verging on madness.' Are not this excitement and this madness, presented here as the consequence of electric light, the effects on the mind of the revelation of nothingness effected by photography and confirmed by electricity – that effect that will also be expressed by the 'horla' of the other story at almost the same time? We have here an 'emotion' that was definitely 'unexpected' at the beginning of the evening. An agitation of the mind writhing in horror at the catastrophic loss of its bearings.

I feel justified in believing that a sudden awareness of this particular kind is at issue, since, just after it happens, there comes the return into Paris, where the most astonishing event conceivable by which to represent that horror to oneself occurs. The narrator passes through the Arc de Triomphe and is now on the Champs-Elysées, but first – and in a more pronounced way than before he left the city – we have once again this impression of colours acquiring a life of their own and reducing to nothing things whose colour actually specifies their identity. On an avenue, there is 'a line of vegetable carts on their way to Les Halles'. And Maupassant observes: 'They were moving slowly, laden with carrots, turnips and cabbages [...]. At each pavement light, the carrots showed up red, the turnips white and the cabbages green. And the carts went by one after the other, red as fire, white as silver, green as emerald.' Appearance has become detached from life, and form dissociated from meaning. Sufficient grounds already to see the buildings as mere facades with nothing behind them.

And then there are streets, more streets, avenues, which are extraordinarily – even incomprehensibly – empty, completely empty of passers-by. Space, which is simply itself and which, in itself, is nothing, has invaded life through the insides of its words, of its attributes; it undoes life, dissipates it. What the man we are listening to more and more attentively discovers, what we see him moving into, is an entirely deserted Paris, where at first he encounters just a few stragglers hurrying home, after which he will see only unlit cafes, extinguished street lights, places with not a single person in them in a night growing darker and darker, where this sole remaining living being has to grope his way along. And he goes along haphazardly, continually getting lost but realising now that there is no re-finding his way, no safe haven to return to. Places he recognises as he passes – the Château d'Eau, the Crédit Lyonnais, the Stock Exchange – are eyes that are closed, but clearly not closed in dreaming. And he is amazed, so natural is it in this world to want explanations for everything. But terror rapidly overtakes him and he yells, though no answer comes; he utters a cry for 'help' which he knows to be laughable.

And now he is suddenly asking himself, 'What time is it?' Won't time, which is memory, thought, project and properly human reality, save him from this drifting and anchor him in a reality? All remaining hope is now located in this point outside of space – his watch. 'I listened to the gentle ticking of its workings with a strange, unfamiliar joy. It seemed alive,' writes Maupassant, 'I wasn't so alone.' It is quite natural that it should be time that helps him extricate himself from this lifeless space which renders even the starry sky black – 'blacker even than the city'. Feeling his way along the walls with his cane, as a blind man might, he rings hopefully at a door.

But the sound of the bell in the house is such as to suggest that there is nothing but that noise alive within. And ringing once more without getting an answer, he is afraid, very afraid, and runs to the next house. And the next and the next, their doors remaining closed to him despite his shaking. And so the hope his little watch had brought him subsides. Moreover, 'No clock struck the hours, either on the church towers or the public buildings. I'll open my watch-glass, I thought, and feel the hand with my fingers. I pulled out my watch… it wasn't ticking… it had stopped.' With this discovery, we feel that his end is nigh. Except that now he is down by the river and feels a 'glacial chill' rise to meet him. And he asks himself, this assuredly being the most anxious of all his questions: 'Was the Seine still flowing?'

VIII.

Let us pause over this question. It seems to me that the whole experience of 'The Night' is condensed in it, but with an additional element not formulated there, though I believe that is something we can recognise and ponder over.

What is the Seine here? It is alone in having the better part of its life outside the city. And when we have noted the destruction of meaning in Paris, don't we have to ask ourselves whether that urban *here* isn't just a kind of bad dream – a 'nightmare', the subtitle of the story – from which we would awaken if we travelled upriver? Our network of mere surface thoughts is perhaps just the nocturnal flip side of being in the world. And *out there*, in a place that is purely natural, a truer meaning perhaps has currency, which would restore life to the *here* that is now merely a place of vain imaginings. It was already with this idea that Maupassant – the fiction he invents scarcely provides him with a veil – had sought refuge, instinctively, in the Bois de Boulogne. In short, doesn't nature have resources that are forgotten in those places where the café-concerts, for example, are 'like so many hearths amid the foliage'? It is certainly true that nature herself has been infiltrated and corrupted by our late language. But it may also be that at some crossroads in a wood a path may yet open up with a true light still burning in the distance...

Sadly, the river's reply to the question from the man who is now down by the waterside merely seems to confirm what this empty, silent Paris around it is saying. And it actually does so in a way that is as terrifying as it is, once again, unexpected. Is the river flowing? 'I wanted to know,' writes Maupassant. 'I found the steps and went down... I couldn't hear the current roiling beneath the bridge's arches... Still more steps... then sand... then mud... then water. I dipped my arm in... it was flowing... flowing... cold... cold... cold... almost frozen... almost exhausted... almost dead.' What is signified by the river running dry like this, by this great chill? That the absence of meaning prevails as much in the realm of nature as in language. That there is nothing to be hoped for from this universe plunged in the darkness of night. And for the narrator it means understanding that he won't have the strength to come back up from the quayside. It means knowing – these are the last words of the story – that he will die there 'of hunger... fatigue... and cold'. Words that seem, indeed, to form the basis for the totally pessimistic intuition that has led, through surprise and horror, to these waters whose flow is coming to a halt.

Words that are the ending of 'The Night'. But do I, its reader, have to come to the same conclusion? I am, in fact, amazed. The

Château d'Eau, the Stock Exchange, the markets of Les Halles had risen before us, frozen in their mere appearance, pure exteriority, though none of the details of their ordinary form were lost. It was even this completeness which, gathered there to no purpose in the general silence, had provided the heart of the horror. And if the green and red of the carrots and cabbages seen at first had, indeed, a kind of autonomy, their light rays turning all these vegetables into simple though terrifying images, they nonetheless preserved their minutest features in the market-gardener's cart. 'The Night' is essentially this collapse of meaning in something which retains its appearance. So why is it not the same with the river? So close to all these places and things 'frozen' in their *being-there*, why is the Seine itself not also complete in all its – transfixed and yet preserved – appearance? How terrifying it would be to see it both flowing and not flowing, its whole great regular flow frozen to a standstill! This would be both the climax of the ever-expanding vision in 'The Night' and yet, as we may note in passing, also what photography – mere run-of-the-mill photography – does to the vibrancy of life.

At the end of 'The Night', the Seine isn't the ghostly entity that Daguerre and the first photographers presented us with as a substitute for lives. The author wanted nothing of this vast flow, this foaming swell against the arches of the bridges which, mysteriously muted like time in the watch, would have been the great horror in the story; instead, he replaces it with the running-dry of the river, which at this point expresses, as though in words, what the Château d'Eau or Les Halles or the colours green and red had themselves demonstrated against a backdrop of silence.

But this substitution is highly meaningful. Does it really bring confirmation, in this new way, of the declaration of nothingness made by the rest of the city? No, we should rather see matters as follows. This water, which signifies non-being rather than showing it, is therefore an instance of signification – one further signification, at the farthest end of this world which had ceased to have any. It is speech amid the aphasia that seemed to be the basis of everything. And though this signification, admittedly, bespeaks death, we are talking this time of ordinary human death, the death to which a man suffering hunger, tiredness and cold resigns himself. What are we to conclude? That Maupassant, despite his terror, has succeeded by means of a metaphor – that constant resource of human speech – to wrest from non-meaning a scrap of meaning. Now, that meaning is entirely negative, it is a cry of despair. But, black as it may be, it is a signification nonetheless. Even at the last moment, speech will not have abdicated its role.

Might it be that we cannot step outside of meaning? That the only experience of a withdrawal of meaning comes in and through an ever-continuing life of language? But if that is how things are, must we really accept the clear fact it believes it registers, because of the accumulation – 'vain walls' said Mallarmé; 'Unreal City' echoed T. S. Eliot[7] – of so much damning evidence?

IX.

I ask myself this question and, in doing so, I find myself back with photography – if, indeed, I ever left it.

This Maupassant who writes 'The Night' is someone I can properly call a photographer. These streets and monuments, as they unfurl themselves in silence, are nothing more in his eyes than their inscription in space. And that is precisely what the photographs of his day presented us with – those photographs printed in white and grey with no hint of colour or atmosphere. Reading Maupassant, even when he speaks of the carrots or turnips in the market-gardeners' carts, we think of such work as Eugène Atget's, who was barely thirty years old that year. Atget, who also shows empty streets, silent 'vain walls', ghostly displays of wares in a light that may be the light of dawn, of misty day or of endless night – of day worn down by night.

And Maupassant is also a photographer in the way so many professionals were in his time, because, for all that his novels and stories abound with evocations of men and women wrested from the whirl of life by his psychologist's and sociologist's eye, they are nonetheless as deserted as a daguerreotype is on its silver surface. This singular body of work teems with figures but, for want of affection for his characters on the part of the storyteller, we don't meet

7   Mallarmé, 'Toast funèbre' ; T.S.Eliot, *The Waste Land*.

any presences in its pages. Arriving from his native Normandy the way the narrator in 'The Night' arrives back from the neighbouring wood, with a ready-formed mastery of language camera-like in its precision, he too entered Paris without encountering a living soul. His experience of human beings is the perception of the grain of their skin and a magnification of features which mean that his supposed realism veers towards that same withdrawal of meaning, that same latent fantastical vision as the monuments we come upon in 'The Night'. And on all this there falls, like a night-time chill, a pessimism that rendered him familiar from the outset with fumblings forward in the dark. The sky is empty above him; values seem mere fancies, lives mere solitudes.

But is this actually true? Wasn't Maupassant capable, deep down, of another way of seeing and, by that very token, of an anxiety about others – other human beings – which his existential choices failed to allay? We are entitled to believe so, since his last writings speak of the experience of a presence, even if that presence – the 'horla' – is inaccessible, hostile and negative, and even if it prompts in him such desperate horror and renunciation as was felt by the narrator of 'The Night' as he ended up down beside the river. Maupassant hasn't met the gaze of the 'horla'; he is going to die. But in that absence he felt a foretaste of, and a sense of regret over, the presence he hadn't been able to desire earlier in his life.

And what comes back to me, in the light of that other tale from his last days, is the feeling that I haven't understood everything about the last lines of 'The Night', the impression that, in this river running dry, a reality of a quite other nature is surfacing and yet eluding me for a reason that is perhaps as crucial as can be. What was this weak current, this growing chill, this sand and silt mingling as they did, with that already 'almost dead' water the way that, in Goya's *The Dog*, the same silt and sand put a final end to a life whose astonishment is entirely summed up in its last gaze?

Well, this water, of which Maupassant asked whether it was still flowing, this water which would run dry without ever having ceased to be the water we so needed – eternal water – is, as I now understand, life which, like the dog in the great painter's thinking, perceives, at the moment everything is falling apart, that it could have had being. And how could that be, in such utterly dark night, except by way of a gaze that would have recognised it and welcomed it in – and as – shared time? This almost dried-up flow is an existence which, becoming aware of itself, is essentially that gaze which seeks to encounter and hold another's – something which would at a stroke establish another reign than that of mere matter. And in this Maupassant, who dies from not having known this earlier, there is, as in the more lucid Goya, the sudden memory of that human being that he ought to have encountered at least once, instead of constantly wandering aimlessly in the crowd – that human being who was mortal like him, thus making the meeting that failed to take place an irreparable loss, a death-in-life more real, destructive and hope-sapping than the death that puts an end to him.

What is Maupassant doing in the last words of 'The Night'? In the unreality of everything, he is at last becoming aware of the reality of the Other's gaze. Aware, in this world emptied of self by the apprehension of nothingness, that there is a possible being: to be convinced of this and to accede to it, it is enough to move to empathise with those who share with the person one potentially is the condition of the dog buried deep in the sand in Goya's painting. What have we to do with nothingness, since we are mortal? Since, out of infinite astonishment, which could become despair, we can create the site of a decision to recognise and to share? At the darkest point of 'The Night', Maupassant spotted this glimmer of light – that we may recognise the powers of finitude and, employing this key, move on to new ground. Alas, for him it is too late; he feels he lacks the very bodily strength to do so.

But in his way he bears witness, and to do so is also to shed light on that photography of his time which, like him, allows itself to be overwhelmed by the false proofs of non-being, but might, in its case, recover itself, if indeed it hasn't already begun to do so here and there. In the century of Daguerre and Atget, which was also Nadar's century, 'The Night' is what best enables us to understand the events of the first photographic era in their future-laden dialectic. First, we should ask what else these eyes did – the eyes which, in the work of Daguerre and then of others, perceived chance, the outside of things, the vanity of metaphysical dreams and the death of God – other than enter the darkened, deserted city, like the Maupassant of 'The Night', and stroll around in it for hours. But, again like him, perceiving that in this frozen world water still flowed, in the case of some of the photographers of that age, those same eyes, which had nonetheless remained human, opened up to a deeper level of reality.

How were they able to do so? Well, I now see on the photographic plate another kind of first, deeply moving apparition than that which put an end, in Edgar Allen Poe's story, to the eternal masked ball of what I call the image. What did we see in so many paintings by painters such as Titian, Franz Hals, Rembrandt, Goya, even Van Gogh and Giacometti, who came upon the faces of so many men and women and turned those faces towards us? The eyes in those works are full of thoughts and emotions and we can read intentions in them; often the painter even succeeds in rendering the pain and compassion visible in those faces, but the look in their eyes isn't real, because when our eyes meet real gazes in our lives, in the street, they contain not only what we can read in them but also an obvious unknown element we cannot fathom. What is this person exactly, what is he planning, what at this very moment is he just beginning to grasp? It is a whole excess element in the person which we sense with our own eyes, but cannot fathom in the slightest, and which it will be impossible to depict in a painting – even a portrait – since works are, to their very depths, only what their creators know or feel or wish to make. Some artists have understood this and tried to push beyond the mysterious limit, but to no avail. In their works we find at best the idea of a gaze, but not that unfathomably individual gaze that emanates from a real person. The image as we have known it over the centuries is incapable of opening itself up to the gaze, that expression of finitude.

But what of the new image, the photograph? Here, very much to the contrary, it is the real gaze that is captured and presented in the least significant photograph we take of someone, the moment they turn towards us. No longer is this something imitated, the outcome of an incomplete analysis that would lack the knowledge of finitude; it is a real presence, and a presence all the livelier for the fact that this time there is perceptible in the image what the photographed individual has in them that is unbeknown to us or even that remains unthought in their own relationship to themselves. The photograph, which expresses non-being through its perception of chance, is also – and it is unique in this – what puts us in the unmediated presence of beings other than ourselves: in the presence of their presence. And the fact of the great saving exchange (or even the need for it) which Maupassant seems ready to recognise at the end of 'The Night' – an exchange he is regretfully unable to experience in his own life – is something photography can remind us of through its own particular resources. It can even attempt to bear testimony to it itself.

And this indeed did occur. What were Nadar and Carjat doing but seeking out the gaze of Baudelaire, of Marceline Desbordes-Valmore, of Rimbaud? It wasn't that they wished to speak to us *about* these poets; they were intent, rather, on speaking *to* them. It wasn't their aim to discover what this sorrowful man was, or this aged woman, or this young boy at the stormy dawning of his self-awareness; rather, they registered the fact of their existence, they detected the – anguished or confident – summons which existence always is. And, in that way, they were beginning the resistance which, as time went on, ranged a number of photographers – clearly, the greatest of them – against the pernicious promptings of their practice. Promptings and incitements to spiritual abdication, which were veiled – and yet rendered even more dangerous – by the snapshot and by colour. This is the standpoint from which the history of twentieth century and subsequent photography should be written.

In conclusion, I shall simply mention a poet who criticised photography solely from an intuitive sense, as I see it, of the destructive effects of that realism which his contemporaries liked about it. When one thinks of 'The Night', Baudelaire inevitably comes to mind. He too walked in Paris with a certain inclination not to encounter real existences. When he presents himself as the observer of the passers-by he spots in the crowd – and as able to read their cares and their dramas – he actually manages only to project his own cares and categories of thought on to them; he substitutes a schema for what might have been a fuller presence, in which case the person concerned would have had an opportunity to respond to the other's idea, to react. And it is doubtless this subservience he desires, out of a lack of courage to confront what he calls 'the tyranny of the human face'. All things considered, he employs his intellect to override his truest need. And he can dream then of a Paris that would help him soothe his painful fear of the other thanks to the night, with its sparser throng, a night he even sees – 'At One O'clock in the Morning' – as somewhat similar to the night Maupassant imagined. 'Alone, at last!

Nothing to be heard now but the rumbling of a few belated, weary cabs… At last! I am able to relax in a bath of darkness!'[8]

Yet is the 'gentle night' he desires as beneficial as he wants to believe? Is it not, as such, a dream that exposes him, in its very bosom, to some terrible awakenings? I am struck by the analogy that exists more deeply between Maupassant's text and some pages from Baudelaire. In 'Parisian Dream' ('Rêve parisien'), that dream of Paris in Paris, the issue is no longer the desertification by rigidification of the streets and facades that was so overwhelming in 'The Night', but the multiplication to infinity – in a world of nothing but stone and metal, with no vestige of sun or moonlight, in a 'silence of eternity' – of the colonnades, the 'sheets of water', the cascades; and it is, further, the disintegration of the ordinary sites of life, the same triumph of space over the time inherent in real existence. The bad dream has merely increased the fear at having to live. And through these 'vast buildings' and these labyrinths, there can be heard the creakings of an imminent collapse. 'How to warn people?…' Baudelaire wonders in that other dream narrative, 'Symptoms of Ruin', which he planned to add to his *Spleen de Paris* – though it is undoubtedly he himself who needs the warning. He is the one in danger of sinking into non-being by dint of his – recurrent – temptation to 'double lock' his door and cherish loneliness.

The fact remains that Baudelaire is a poet; at every moment, in his voice – and in the words that voice conveys – there wells up, to surprise him and also to send him back to life, the thought of evening sunlight, of 'the glow of coals' in the hearth, of the 'mother of memories', with a woman present beside him for better or for worse.[9] And it is this unshakeable attestation of the Other – poetry, great poetry, the kind that eschews dreaming – that will, remarkably, change his relationship with Paris and, down beside the Seine again, lead him back from the passion for the night to what Karl Jaspers calls 'the norm of Day'. I shall not dwell on 'The Swan' again here, inexhaustible as that poem may be, but I shall simply note that time, which had evaporated from Maupassant's empty city and

8   Both quotations are from Baudelaire's prose poem 'A une heure du matin', in *Le Spleen de Paris* (1889).
9   Baudelaire, 'Le balcon' in *les Fleurs du mal*.

had returned only as something black and terminal in 'Symptoms of Ruin', has resumed its course in 'The Swan' – and in its social being – since we are told there that 'Paris changes'. And it is a change that troubles Baudelaire: the end of 'old Paris', a building-site of soulless avenues, an inert mass of scaffolding and stones with a further risk that time will freeze. With it, Baudelaire stokes his 'melancholia', but self-conscious melancholia is a lesser evil than death installed in the heart of life, and Baudelaire, re-born to himself, can achieve a genuine encounter, whereas Maupassant in 'The Night' will only be able to dream of that deliverance.

I shall turn from 'The Swan' now to another poem. In 'To a Passer-by'[10] Baudelaire is again walking in Paris, as he did so often, perceiving instinctively that this progress around the city was the ordeal he had to conquer. And Paris on that day too is in danger of merely being a tableau of nothingness, since the street mentioned in the first line is 'deafening' and even 'roars' – the roar of a noise that makes it as much of a desert as the tomb-like silence of Maupassant's night-time city. But it is at this point that Baudelaire rises, directly and explicitly, to the idea of meeting, of exchange and also, and perhaps most importantly, the idea of the conditions in which that event occurs. The other, in this instance, is that which, the moment before – and as ever – might simply have appeared veiled by the prejudices of the dreaming self, substituting the – fundamentally aesthetic – flatness of the image for the three dimensions of lived experience: and, indeed, the woman who is the poem's passer-by is described as 'agile and noble' with a 'leg like a statue's'.

But she is also 'in deep mourning' and we are not to make a work of art of her but to get up close to her life, sense the suffering in it, recognise it as a finitude; it is on this level that real encounters take place. Now – and this point is at the heart of the poem – Baudelaire reports that this meeting was an exchange of glances, which was sufficient to 'bring him back to life', to gather up within him the real, which is never anything other – or anything more – than the desire to be in the world. A glance, a lightning flash. And after the lightning flash the night perhaps once more, though for the duration of the

---

10   See 'À une passante' in *Les Fleurs du mal*.

lightning, which has no end, all the rivers and all the skies and all the beings in the world.

The glance a lightning flash. The light in which this world appears, which only the moment before was in darkness. Nadar was quite right to seek out and respect the gaze in the man or woman he photographed. That gaze, brimming with its unknown element, was enough to remind us of the potential that remains alive in a seemingly dead reality. It was enough to preserve the invention of the photographic from exerting its potential deleterious effects. It was no longer the ghostly exterior or the nothingness entering the masked ball, but the fresh air of morning, as the – so often ineffectual – lights of the chandeliers were going out.

Translated by Chris Turner

GIACOMETTI AND CARTIER-BRESSON[1]

I.

There is much to fear when it comes to looking. Indeed, it is language that enables us to take our bearings among the things of the world. Language teaches our eyes that a tree is a tree, a stone is a stone, and that this man walking along the street, well, he is a man walking. Such knowledge is useful, without any doubt; it can even be enjoyable. Action is possible as a result, but so is dreaming, on which all kinds of artistic creation depends. Let your eyes lock onto nature, and a landscape is likely to emerge, asserting its beauties, its harmonies. It is not even necessary for those aspects we have retained to possess continuity or coherence. We can content ourselves with selecting among them fragments of sensory perception, scraps of events; this permits unforeseen combinations, of interest for their suggestiveness or their disorder: a game which can be pursued without risk of entering into conflict with the claims of ordinary existence.

For such is indeed the danger of looking, beneath the apparent advantage. Given the fatal necessities of language that govern looking, our eyes only perceive the exterior aspect of things, not the mystery of their presence in the very site of our existence. They cannot understand the extent to which chance is existence itself, so that the more we rely on words to differentiate what is – in that respect every word is a concept, conscious simply of the generalised aspect of the thing – the more we are induced simply to slide across the surface structure of the visible, without ever meeting ourselves. But fortunately we are blessed with more than eyes. Found in our eyes, of course, but coming from somewhere deeper within us, there is the gaze, which involves a completely different preoccupation. This gaze pays no attention to colours, to forms, to the characteristic aspects of the things named by words; it aims directly at an object

1 Catalogue essay for the exhibition 'Une Communauté de Regards: Alberto Giacometti/Henri Cartier-Bresson', shown in Paris then Zurich in 2005. Collected in Yves Bonnefoy: *Le siècle où la parole a été victime*, Paris: Mercure de France, 2010.

which it thus separates from its environment and chooses whether to cling on to it, or to argue with it; and then, at once, the facts, sites, fears and hopes of existence awaken into consciousness. The gaze, if I may say so, does not see. Around what it fixes on, it traces a halo, outside which everything is blurred. But it creates; it brings its object into the very heart of being.

We can say that the gaze substitutes the experience of presence for the order of representation; it sets up or can set up speech – which never ceases to ask questions – in opposition to language, which differentiates, classifies, forgets real states of being; it sets up the truth of the instant in opposition to the timelessness of scientific formulas or the experimentations of play, and it discovers the powers of the instant, which are immense; for conceptual thought, which requires extended time for its deployment, is caught unawares by the suddenness of the instant; in other words, conceptual thought deprives us of a full encounter with other people, and therefore of the means to understand how to act in finite time. Conversely, the instant possesses the keys of intimacy in our relationship to others and, as a consequence, those of our self-awareness.

This is well known to the arts that involve the eyes: sculpture and painting; from the beginnings of civilisation there have been works of art that know the gaze well and serve that great cause. Epiphanic statues from Greece or Egypt, Byzantine or Roman vaulted roofs, this is the art that – at times of the triumph of conceptual thought – the project of representation via appearances, known as mimesis, entered the scene to contradict, but which for all that has never ceased: during the Renaissance, troubled by geometric perspective, it simply transported itself under cover of the visible, intent on remembering what 'the eyes' hide from view: and this was the 'great' art, so specific to the West, like a certain sort of music that was inspired, I might add, by the same intuition. Vermeer: could this be mimesis carried to the limit? Of course not, for the curtain trembles, presence is apparent beneath representation. See how many gazes are directly evoked in paintings, even in sculptures, as if in reply to the fundamental and foundational gaze of the artist himself: the gaze of the resurrected Christ at Borgo, the gaze of Poussin as he finds himself, in the self-portrait of 1650.

All the same, ever since the fifteenth century, science, technology, journeys of discovery, with their eternal curiosity for new aspects of the world and societies, have turned attention away from this great ontological design. And, moreover, we cease to believe in supernatural forms hidden beneath appearances; we have come to believe that every formulation is a fiction, which allows us to dream that we are only fictions ourselves and therefore non-mortal, and to disengage from self-responsibility, leaving the coast clear for the necessity of play. *Les Demoiselles d'Avignon* is a victory for the eyes over the gaze. This did not prevent Picasso from remaining fascinated by great art, in particular that of Giacometti.

II.

In a century of unstable representations, as though a tidal wave was arriving from many places, inundating everything, the work of Giacometti was indeed an extraordinary resurgence of the art that brings being into the world. In his creations, sculptures as well as paintings, persons or things are not perceived by means of their visual aspects; they are evoked as presences. Nothing remains of them in the image he creates but a sudden appearance which, coming from the inside of their very being, attests the fact of this being, signifies its mystery: Annette or Diego are there, in front of Alberto, they *are*; and yet it is necessary for the sculptor's gaze to be directed upon them, for them not to sink into the nothingness which surrounds everything. The artistic effort of Giacometti coincides completely with the fundamental act that is the gaze; and he does so in such an intense and total way that it permits the observer of his work to become aware that the gaze is the only path to whatever has reality for human beings in their essential finitude. In doing so, he has given new life to the archaic tradition.

With one difference, however, a difference which marks Giacometti out as a modern. In ancient art, what is lived as presence is also lived as evidence, the archaic Kouros or Theotokos are epiphanies as obvious as they are overwhelming for the artist, while with Giacometti presence in the figures results from his own efforts: we might say that his gaze has plunged in, to bring presence to the surface when it was on the point of drowning, and it still breathes although we cannot know if it will survive. And what risks carrying off being into its darkness is the very body of the sitter. Because it is perishable, and therefore part of nothingness, but above all because, in relation to the fact of being, which is invisible, it is a surface which the fascination for nothingness can use, in the same way that the devil would do.

Whence derives the constant fear of Giacometti, a fear that, for example, explains what he does with the head of Annette or Diego, those intimates he never ceases to try to keep standing in the ebb and flow of passing things. It is indeed from the head that whatever manifests being flows, through the sitter's gaze met by that of the painter; but the head is also the skull, that box of pure matter, which the devil can take in his hands, laughing derisively. And it follows that the need to grasp the distinctive traits of the face involves a contradiction. It is certainly necessary that there is sufficient likeness in the portrait for it to be a real meeting with the person, in that individual's essential particularity. All presence of the self is, moreover, a unity, transcending the material aspect of eyes, nose or mouth, to release a face. But these components are also something material, an outside where nothingness loiters, and likeness is therefore a trap: we must look for its invisible background, we must destroy likeness as well as question it. Giacometti never ceased to be fascinated by the absolute photographic likeness that mediocre portrait painters are capable of; but this was because he sensed these portraits brought him to the brink of an abyss, that is the false absolute where the devil was waiting to destroy him. The more he is tempted, the more it follows that he resists, and he resists through the working of his gaze upon the propositions of his own eyes, which resemble those of the 'negative' theologies that signify the divine through the effacement of everything claiming to manifest it in natural reality.

Why this fear of losing contact, this doubt concerning what one feels as the only reality? Did the child Alberto fear losing a mother whom he felt was being itself, perhaps because in his mind he was guilty of a transgression against her that the work of the artist, if he consents to mimesis, only repeats? But it is also – and it is here that Giacometti is modern – because the myths that used to sustain the experience of presence have collapsed. The artist concerned about this fundamental experience can no longer rely on religion; he has to substitute himself for God in relation to the act of giving reality to other beings and thence to the world itself; when accomplishing this task he cannot but escape the feeling that such ongoing creation instant by instant rests entirely on his intuition, on his personal will: whence, inevitably, angst.

Giacometti lived this angst to the full. Every single gesture in his work experiences it and expresses its paradoxical nature, and the fact that the gaze, at every instant, can renounce the task. This painter who brings forth flames from the halo with which he surrounds his faces, gives no indication that, for all that, their transcendence, observed by him, is a light that comes towards him, like a grace, a delight. This contradictory nature of his great art has been marvellously emblematised by Henri Cartier-Bresson in the famous photograph of Giacometti crossing the rue d'Alésia towards him, on a dark and rainy day, when the light seems to survive only in the puddles. So, it is raining, and Alberto has raised his old mackintosh above his head, which, in a face thus reduced to its essentials as much as in any of his portraits, re-centres his entire being on a gaze that points straight ahead of him, without any interest for the surrounding space, as if he was pursuing an interior vision. So difficult is the attestation of presence, as well as being so desired, that with Giacometti it is never anything but a flowing back towards his origin in the debate he has with himself, amidst his obsessions, his memories, his fragile but enduring affections.

III.

Henri Cartier-Bresson had only one second at his disposal to understand that this place, this gesture, this movement expressed, in a striking way, the essence of the art and personality of his friend, but he knew how to seize it, and our reward is this icon of spiritual quest such as it can be lived in our time. But doesn't this homage that Cartier-Bresson, with his customary generosity, renders to Giacometti, contradict his own spontaneous way of being, in his own life and in his activity as a photographer? At first sight, it appears like that; and that these two great minds who were such good friends had very little in common. Given that he had a completely different kind of early childhood, Henri Cartier-Bresson clearly has an instinctive

faith in being, which ensures that he does not doubt that it is incessant, that it won't cease, that it cannot be escaped, that death itself is
simply an accident within this continuous state, an epiphenomenon;
whereas life is one of the manifestations of being, but not the only
one. And the instant, that communion in being which two humans
can share, the instant which for Giacometti is the only reality but
equally represents something inaccessible, is for Cartier-Bresson
the immediate datum of his consciousness, always at his disposal,
with the endless capacity for him of coinciding, without ceasing to
be itself, with successive objects: other people, but also things and
places. This aptitude for being present at the presence of the other is
why he loves and enjoys quoting a famous Zen Buddhist text, which
teaches that the art of archery must open out to the experience of
unity, through the intimate reciprocity of the archer and the target.

And it is this gift that generated his love of photography, in the
manner permitted by mastery of the snapshot and above all the
Leica. There is no doubt that Henri Cartier-Bresson would not have
become a photographer if, behind a box and tripod, he had had to
drape his head with a black cloth, which he might have recalled on
seeing Giacometti raise his old coat above his head. And he has been
a great portraitist, but in unusual ways. Assuredly he goes straight
for the most intimate aspect of his model, and that is an intention
that might be supposed to benefit from a frontal approach to the
face, with a potential reciprocity of gaze. And yet, as soon as Henri
finds himself in this situation, facing someone sitting quite still, he
is disconcerted – he does not hesitate to use the word 'intimidated'
– and can become the witness of the truth of the other person only
if he or she moves around, offering the photographer a range of
instants to seize. Being, for Cartier-Bresson, is always being on the
move, is always being active. He needs the unforeseen for his gaze to
soar, and immediately the capacity for love.

It is this soaring that the Leica permitted him: the Leica, an
instrument as quick-fire as his mind. This tool, which was his exact
contemporary, has been the intimate complement of his gaze, and
he welcomed the immediacy and offered it the chance to deepen its
responses, to intensify them thanks to the experiences undergone
with its aid. Leica photography resembles a ray flowing from the eyes
in the direction of the object to elect it, to bestow being: being which

is the real light. And the Leica also brings support in the battle you must fight, at the very heart of any photography, even the snapshot, against what I would call its *dark side*.[2] Indeed, this danger does exist, for a photo grasps not only the central object, the observed being, the simple object that becomes being through the gaze, but also, pell-mell all around, the entire content of the visual field, that is a mass of things whose disorder risks petrifying the scene, sweeping up the instant in its net, allowing it to founder into nothingness. The snapshot can thus seize simultaneities between events, making them clues for an investigation by a detective, quite the opposite approach to the Zen archer's. And since the body, the clothing and other accessory meanings of the person deployed in the image, now take precedence over his gesture, his gaze, another risk appears, that of stealing from this other, who has become his own outward appearance, some unforeseen but still exterior semblance which will feed the conventional and too easily malevolent idea that the photographer can happen to have of it. There are photographs that, entering opportunistically into an instant for reasons quite remote from a full and immediate sympathy, can only be looked at with unease and disapproval. It feels as though an intimacy has been violated.

Nothing of that in Cartier-Bresson; none, absolutely none of his photographs shocks or alarms, and this is clearly because his spontaneous adherence to the presence of others delivers them from the weight of their own appearance; they are seen and shown in the light of this fullness of being which springs from their depths, always mysterious; and when, faced with morally questionable people, Henri sometimes becomes indignant, he photographs them in such a way that, while incriminating them, he also allows them the right to reply, to defend themselves. Even here, the reciprocity of the Zen archer has come into play. And across his entire body of work, which is huge, the immediate has therefore always triumphed over a priori thoughts, over meanings that distract from the essential: his ways and means being what Cartier-Bresson calls his 'geometry', a word which might cause surprise.

But in this case, by 'geometry' we must clearly not understand a

---

2   In English in the original.

concern for the relationships of forms or meanings established on the plane of flat images, which photography can certainly entail. If these sorts of proportions and equilibriums interested Cartier-Bresson he would not forbid himself, as he does, from reworking the photo once it has been taken. Certainly, he aims at relationships, at interactions between the components of the photo, but these relationships are neither on the plane, as in abstract painting, nor in the spatial aspect, as constructed and inhabited by perspective; they are in the movement of wholly interior apprehension through which the gaze is centred on its object and, throwing itself towards where the object is, perceives laterally events that help it to elect the object, to understand it better, and therefore to take their place in the very instant of the photograph like a current which amplifies its efficacy, like a circle of converging rays. This geometry, this clear and strong organisation of the data of apprehending is characteristic of certain African sculptures that, I imagine, have influenced Henri but in a way quite different from the lessons in plastic form it offered the Cubist painters. Geometry, in the snapshot photography of Cartier-Bresson, is what releases the mind from the opaque simultaneities which burden the events it gazes at, bearing it, like two wings, towards what it loves and asks us to see; geometry triumphs over what I've called the *dark side*, comforting this will to love that Cartier-Bresson calls the 'heart'.

In sum, an art which gives life to the world not in images but in its actual existence; an art which seizes the event on the wing without lingering on a consideration of the thing; an art which one could call, as Cartier-Bresson does himself, reportage, in the highest possible meaning latent in this word: art attesting to universal presence as something open to simple, everyday existence, art therefore radically different from the quest which other artists and poets are obliged to engage in when their relationship to themselves remains enslaved to the aporias of language. An art that seems in any case to be at the opposite pole to Giacometti's *Head on a Stalk*, for example: that is, this time, a fascination for nothingness still active in the very place where the intuition of being is seeking to reaffirm itself.

IV.

And yet! When Cartier-Bresson photographs Alberto crossing the rue d'Alésia, it is a gaze his own gaze fixes upon. And this focus means that, for Henri, Giacometti's art has the gaze as its origin, as is the case with the one who is taking the photograph. Henri is not unaware of – indeed he underlines it – the darkness from which Alberto's gaze rises, and within which this gaze is in danger of disappearing; but he insists, however, on saying that gazing at another person is, for Giacometti, an essential experience, thus recognising between himself and his friend a very close kinship, even a connivance. And who can doubt this! Whatever might be the differences in their temperaments or in their early development, this primacy they allow to the gaze, this sentiment that what is real is the person in his time and place, is sufficient to keep them on the same side in the contemporary debate between representation and presence. 'Negative theology' on the part of one, 'positive theology' the other, but always paying attention to whatever in the object transcends materiality, transcends the level of meaning, and does so in a way which is not less mysterious or less satisfactory because today we no longer have to relate this transcendence to God. An art that, as a consequence, does not simply reduce itself to what we call a work of art, does not conceive of works as an end in themselves.

And with Giacometti it is clear that his quest is burdened with the chains the Christian past has imposed on him: inhibitions, feelings of guilt, obsessions and fantasies which are the heritage of the West and explain why it makes sense, even today, to refer to them when one plans on making any real change in society. The art of Giacometti is modern through its need for liberation, which the new century reveals to be as urgent as ever; whereas Cartier-Bresson, unusually liberated in his relationship to bodies and people, could entrust the beautiful needs and aspirations inherent in life to an intuition which this time is not Western, and indeed is mainly Buddhist and less anxious to incite historical progress than to dissipate alienation; which had been Rimbaud's desire when he tried to leave 'this continent where madness prowls around'. Alberto Giacometti and Henri Cartier-Bresson were two very different people, but in both of them I see the same fundamental affirmation, which I believe truly beneficent and necessary; for society will perish if we, users of language, are no longer able to perceive a secular transcendence – an absolute beyond all mythologies – within every man and woman on this planet. In other words, if we are not able to understand that our relationship to the other is the ordeal that has to be overcome. As Rimbaud wrote: 'My friends, I want her to be a queen. 'I want to be queen!' She was laughing and trembling'.[3]

Let us come back to the photograph of Alberto crossing the rue d'Alésia. I have cited it because it demonstrates the attention that Cartier-Bresson was paying not only to the person, but also to the poetics of his friend. And because it reveals Alberto's gaze, so concentrated that it seems to re-enter itself and no longer encounter anything ordinarily visible; but also because of the sculptures that Cartier-Bresson had certainly recognised in the chiaroscuro of this road: men walking, slightly stooped, inhabited, it seems, by a single and irreducible thought. The Giacometti of that rainy day reveals the extent to which he was projecting his own desire into his great post-war statues, before devoting himself to portraits. While his face in the nimbus of the old raincoat could almost come from one of those portraits.

But is this all this remarkable photograph says? Doesn't its meaning have another level, a *sub-plot*[4] that matters because it interferes with the main action? In fact, it should now be observed that what Cartier-Bresson seized on the wing Giacometti too must have been aware of while he was crossing the street, walking along the row of studs, with the road sign of the two children behind him, warning of the danger of crossing a road. Walking straight towards his friend, his head under his coat, he knows that this approach front-on and the way the rain effaces colours and many other visible aspects of the world make him resemble his statues; it tempts the observer with thoughts of his work as a sculptor, and recalls therefore the extraordinary project underlying it. But Alberto knows something else too. He is not unaware that when he wraps himself in his rain-soaked coat, he is amusing those who admire him, but he is also engaging in

3   From 'Royauté' in Rimbaud's *Illuminations* (1886 first edn.). YB returns often to this text, notably in his late memoir *L'Echarpe rouge*.
4   In English in the original.

a seduction. After all, is he not the one who has no furniture in his studio, very little in the way of heating, who has broken with any idea of precautions at any level of life or artistic ambition? It is therefore quite natural that he has no umbrella, no hat; it's merely one more aspect of his heroism. How could this rather unexpected aspect of Giacometti – assumed and lived so lightly, and lending itself to joking – not arouse attraction for the man himself as well as for the artist?

Now, Alberto had this desire to seduce. To compensate for his anguish when working or because his life, beneath the affections and friendships, was fundamentally and irreducibly solitary. And there are plenty of indications that he was aware of this desire. When he crosses the road, under the gaze of another person, with his head hooded, this thought is in his mind, and it troubles him. It reminds him of his childhood ways, which made of him an object of wonder, of fascination, for everybody, without this affecting his inner feeling that he was remote from other people, that he would never truly offer himself to somebody else.

But that other person in the rue d'Alésia was not just any acquaintance, close or less close; it was Henri Cartier-Bresson who, he surmises, will notice his gesture, bring his desire to light, but who, he is also aware, knows him in depth, him, Alberto, him Giacometti, and appreciates him for what he really is, this time on the most serious level of all, that of the greatest exigency both artistic and moral. And thus the game with his coat takes on another meaning. Putting his trust in the trust of his friend, he indulges in the game to elicit from him not admiration or subdued astonishment but rather a connivance, the one which he knows that the deeply intuitive and sympathising art of Cartier-Bresson can grant him, and at once; let Henri photograph not only the gesture but the meaning that Alberto invests in it, and reveal what it contains: good humour and courage but, in equal measure, sadness.

And as he always does, Henri has caught the ball on the rebound, and he responds to the trust placed in him; he reveals that this man who says that he is playing and thinks that he wants to seduce is also a great sculptor and even more a weary man, advancing anxiously into the mystery of being.

Translated by Anthony Rudolf

SECOND EARTH[1]

Dear Norbert Pierlot, when you offered to let me use the rooms of the Château de Ratilly for an exhibition this summer, wishing to open up to poetry what you had provided in previous years to painting and to sculpture, a word immediately came to mind, a word that I mentioned to you and dreamt about for a few days: civilisation. To gather into one place that I sensed was favourable a number of objects or works of art from various countries and periods of time, yet, as one would have noticed, possessing the same spirit or, I could almost say, the same blood in that they would each have, in their primary condition, responded simply to simple needs – to those for which subsist only the experience of belonging to the earth, of living according to its rhythms, of having its Being for their Being. I well know that 'simple' and 'earth', not to mention the idea of 'experience' that is today dismissed as subjective, are notions that cannot be more uncertain; nor am I unaware that such imprecisions, such remote gleams, create the danger of golden-age nostalgias, of pastoral reveries, through which one loses the taste of truth. But a certain relationship to life, to Being – let me insist upon these words, which weakly express but do designate – a relationship including both non-illusion and plenitude, ripened in oneself like heavy grape clusters on vine arbours at the end of summer, indeed existed in societies whose light still comes to us, a relationship that is still present here and there in the world. The exhibition would have had the precise task of showing the virtue of this relationship without further resorting to words, by showing nothing but the straightforward relation that certain functions, long meditated on in the forms and the materials used, would have suddenly established between themselves. Vases so pure in contour that no hiatus is possible between the beverage and the thirst – or so, at least, one is tempted to believe. Bowls carved out of knotty wood but earthenware objects as well,

---

1   'Terre seconde' (1976) served as the preface to the Catalogue published for the exhibition, with the same title, held at the Château de Ratilly in summer, 1976. Collected in *Le Nuage rouge*, Paris: Mercure de France, 1977; re-issued in *Folio collection Essais*, Paris: Gallimard, 1999.

fragile like a plant sprouting from sand. Photographs of peasant walls, of trails among boulders. And, without contradiction – on the contrary: a Bodhisattva of Japan, a Romanesque or, otherwise, Baroque Virgin with Child, and a painting by Poussin, even an oval painting – towards 1913 – by Mondrian, because the most elaborated works of art, with respect to the most beautiful ordinary objects of archaic societies, are merely the same economy raised to a second degree of awareness, the same thirst quenched with the same kind of invisible water. From the humblest to the most deliberately pondered works of art, if one passes over the hasty fruits of fantasy, only one question resonates, only one response is sketched. And this unity, which our predecessors on earth therefore sometimes understood as the only reality among the shadows, would thus have been rekindled in the depths of your silent summer.

But soon I had to resign myself to thinking that bringing together in this way a few figures of trueness would also have created a falsehood: the too beautiful presences would have tended to hide, by means of their apparent facility – by what was 'natural' about them, one could say, at the moment when they were produced – the terrible obstacles that our age runs up against when it takes similar paths. Forms as balanced, vibrations as vast in only a few rhythms or pigments could encourage, in our age of reduced plenitude, repetitions from the outside, imitations of the result and not of the act that gave birth to them. And rather than meet up with a purity of times past in shimmering reflections that one cannot grasp, I thought that it would be more suitable to our present preoccupations to try to determine if the source, murky or not, is still within hand's reach.

It is so easy to harbour doubts about this. It has even clearly been the great concern of many people in these recent years.

For example, a young critic[2] recently wrote that any attempt at poetry is henceforth burdened by a contradiction that cannot be resolved. He knows, as he must, that poetry is 'incarnation', in other words that it must, in order to aspire to its truth, be sought out and experienced in the indefinitely recurring situations through which the earth speaks to us: suffering and joy, birth and death, but also

---

2   Georges Formentelli, *'Une poésie juste'*, in *Solaire*, No. 10–11, 1975.

simply walking, questioning the sky, lighting a fire and watching its lively flames. And poets, he observes, have also and in all times meditated on fire, have nourished from its manifestation their own experience of duration, their knowledge of what is good. 'But', he specifies just as soon, 'this is something that we, the youngest, know only through memory'. Fire and a good part – he also cites trees, clouds – of what once ensured an intimacy with the earth, a prescience of what is immediate, would not only be for those new consciousnesses a lesson no longer listened to, but also what has vanished, or is going to vanish, in the most material sense of the term, from most lives in the suburbs that sprawl over everything. And from this it follows, as this witness to our penury logically adds, that the only poetry which, in a sense, is still valid – a poetry that insists on recalling, with increasing abstraction, those necessary conditions of a well-founded existence, an existence that seeks to practice them, and can do so sometimes because of some last chance – has become, despite itself and as if countering its specific intuition, a kind of idealism. Poetry designates a place, indeed, but one that cannot be found; it is a new form of transcendence. And although it genuinely bears itself toward one of the accesses to Being by reformulating the meaning that there is to building a fire, to keeping it going, to thinking about life and death, and about the needs, true or false, arising within its precariousness, its resistance, it immediately betrays the vocation of the concrete, of life here, of this experience, because it forgets that fire, 'real fire', the 'familiar god', has vanished from this world. One notices that this accusation is not aimed at some works of poetry as opposed to others, as ordinarily occurs as poetics evolve over time; the accusation does not pinpoint an inconsistency that could be repaired elsewhere; instead, it incriminates a period of time, in the human condition, when a forever insurmountable obstacle has seemingly risen in front of every poet. And of this break between two periods of history, the accusation states that it destroys even the ability to hope and makes all spiritual ambition vain. 'Are we perhaps going to lose the 'thirsts', the 'hungers', the old desires?', we hear him asking with anguish. Along with bread and wine, hunger and thirst are also seemingly vanishing, along with what the earth offered as human presence: a request, and within this emptiness in which only a vague desire to desire remains, only a hunger for forgotten hungers, only this joyless game of signs is presumably going on at the end – signs of our languages, of course, no longer the star, the illuminated stained-glass window, the cloud – a game which, as we know, increasingly attracts so many human beings and which, in any case, is valid as testimony.

I listen to this, knowing all too well on what real facts this anxiety is founded. It is true that a world is ending, before our very eyes, which still has no apparent alternative. I am walking through the last coun- trysides, but I see everywhere that the paths that followed the slopes, contradicting them only by understanding them, appropriating the ground for our needs, making it speak in our legs, ferment in our fatigue, making in us the wine of presence, the depth from which the light comes, disappear one after the other beneath the asphalt. And houses, for millennia so authentic, also emanating from the ground, the advent of the earth, are now either hideously embellished or destroyed; grimacing masses and colours increasingly take their place and resemble masks like those worn on a Day of the Dead. A relation- ship with animals, with vegetation, with the horizon, with different kinds of light, a relationship that perhaps emerged in the Neolithic period and lasted, while sometimes deepening, until yesterday, if not this very morning, falls apart. There is no remedy. One cannot travel across France – whose genius was everyday life, silence, low walls always repaired – without harbouring an impression of disaster. And elsewhere and everywhere the links come undone, in the chain of species, when it perhaps already suffices that one link is missing for the terrestrial sentence to become meaningless. What's the use of setting off reserves or fitting out parks when only working in a field, the apprehension of a storm, the roof that one raised for goats, the tool rusting in the grass – life, in other words – made the place that made Being for us: and when the entrance ticket has been taken, and even if those strolling along occasionally toss their garbage into baskets, one no longer meets up with the earth in those wastelands, but rather, instead, wax representations of a tree, its dead leaves, and blackbirds hopping among the berries. Lost is a music we thought of as an ever-present mother. And she is lost at the very moment when the evil that we asked her to heal, or at least explain, increases so madly in the world that we begin to doubt that she, even intact and understood, would suffice to sustain a hope. I certainly understand how being haunted by the fear that the fire has been lost increases one's anguish. But I do not draw the same conclusions – not yet.

First of all, this does not mean that the wounded, ravaged depths have ceased letting themselves be heard. I admit that one no longer knows what a tree is, and that, at best, forests become parks, and that parks are falsehoods: yet if one follows suburban roads in the evening, within the maze of dipped headlights, at the edge of nowhere towns – there, suddenly, amid the infinite concrete, is a dusty tree standing at an intersection; in its heartrending situation, it is the whole lost earth, intact, an absolute pacifying beauty. A black bend of a branch fastened by a few leaves, and the One comes to life again amid the multifariousness, and even in a more violent and compelling way since the solitude is greater here, the precariousness more pronounced. And if there were no longer a single tree in its natural state, in the endless urban network, then the dawn, observed from an end-of-the-world window across the flow of windowpanes in the distance, would remain a physical presence in its reddish glowing haze until the very last day, setting ablaze a background fever of life on the dismal facades, the hard edges of the rooftops: in such a way that there would be teenagers up there, in flats, still moved, and listening, on whatever audio cassette then exists, to the ancient *raga* of the rising sun. Crimson clouds will always slowly move across in the sky. Reflections will always speak of appearance and goodness even in murkiest oily waters. As to fire, how can one say it has vanished from our lives? I agree that it is rather dishonoured in our fireplaces – in his poem, Mallarmé pokes at a fire 'desperately' one last time in history,[3] and the fire is no longer but theatre – but it flares again with the rigour of an exploding star on any vacant lot where children with neither hearth nor home, as one used to say, gather cardboard packaging to light up their loves, to make their violence serene again. Like the last desire, fire will be the last force among the seaweed and the wood of shipwrecked boats, on the shore of the sterile sea. Its *joyful presence* has been lost – by this, I mean its ability to speak to us at leisure, to speak, in silence, its analogies to other things of the world, to motivate us to make metaphors. Its *tragic presence* remains.

---

3 Stéphane Mallarmé, 'Mes Bouquins'.

To my mind, this is already a more accurate assessment. It's true that we once seemingly had the privilege of an earth leaning over us, patient to signify; one could say: loving, maternal. And it's also true that the book on her knees is being ripped apart, burning, curving into rolls of ash page after page, the reading suddenly interrupted, difficult. But things, words, signs – how to put it? – are not yet effaced. I see them as being less coordinated, less transparent; they are like inscriptions in a language from which much has been lost, and this is irritating, discouraging. However, although they speak less to us, they come back all the more immediately, harshly, all of them now possessing the intensity one once sought on the edges of clouds, in the evening, where pure colour is ablaze, or in the infinitude of scree. As worried as I myself am about fire or trees, or about any other hieroglyph in our book, I do not forget that I have also often experienced that colour, that stone, even in their indefinite quality – over there, outside of our places, down there beyond words – as the fullest expression of Being. For I love the things of this world, imagine nothing else, wish for nothing more, and even hear, at least sometimes, their speech. But at other times, it also seems to me that the meaning that comes to me through them is muddled, an enigma, beneath this remote intensity. It is as if even presence, our only good, had been wounded at its origin. And doesn't one discern as much anxiety as confidence, as much fear as joy, in our poetry across the ages? One has surely much wandered, and doubted, amid the signs. Even in regard to periods of time that were better aware of the earth – Greece, for example, or the Romanticism that reawakens it, Hölderlin, Nerval – I would hesitate to speak of this voice from the depths as being fully listened to, without echoes mixing in, without painful obscurity.

Isn't it in fact true – and isn't this what is dramatic – that where this voice expresses itself, where its words become articulate, perhaps utter meaning, it is our words, and how relative they are, that immediately transcribe its words? One speaks to me of fire, with nostalgia. But if, today, we were an ancient poet intensely calling fire by its name, even attentive to giving birth to it, literally, on some cold winter's eve, well, we would blend with our thinking about the fire a fear of nightfall, the nearby arching walls, the idea of a hearth with its legends, that of evening gatherings and their wisdom, that of hope-rekindling dawns. What would remain of the blind flame, of the primordial destructor in this little god of vigilance? A representation, an image, have refashioned the unknown. We speak and by doing so change the aspects of the world, even create them. We have words for knowing, but they refuse just as intensely, and this kind of tension is more or less as primitive as the first utterance. And if societies have attempted to keep alive in their practices – in their language, it is the sacred – a sort of reverence for the anteriority of Being over speech, how many other people soon came, and we are still them, to listen instead to the propositions of the image? There are so many good reasons to attach ourselves to what we dream! After giving oneself a place and wishing it to be coherent, one can quickly be shocked at useless suffering, at the erring ways of chance: the idea of evil flares up, hopes awaken. Reality that is rejected, reveries that one wishes were real. Doubt, henceforth, and violence to repress it, in oneself as much as in others – the first genuine violence. And religious speculations, the idea that this land surrounding us is a mere envelope that is going to be torn apart through an epiphany of another world: yet a turning away, in return, from the depths of Nature, which one abandons to science… Even if today the crisis grows, which is our fall from unity, our forgetting of the depths of the earth, let's not imagine that this crisis is new. Conversely, let's not fear that poetic consciousness, long accustomed to these contradictions and these sorrows, can be so brusquely thwarted and forced to resign.

Instead, I believe, simply believe, that the moment has come to offer it a task, and not so much in regard to our worsened conditions as with respect to the events that caused them and that one should henceforth, all the same, better understand so as to avoid re-experiencing. Earlier, I recalled the fact of objects, in however dissimilar societies, and tried to evoke their simplicity and silence. I will now speak of their distrust of languages and of their dream. That these beautiful taciturn objects have another relationship to the earth than the one we are subjected to is not doubtful. The proof is that, if the dangerous evolution has recently occurred so rapidly, it is because peasant civilisation, whose presence we still can spot, is now coming to a complete end. The objects were the expression, if not the very act, of the sacred, which does not forget that the earth is more than our words, from which it follows that the experience of the One, which I call meaning, calls on the body as much as the mind – a respiration, an experienced equilibrium – to pay attention. Dance is going to express this. But let me finish up this argument by pointing out that to recognise in objects this quality of memory is to notice now, with this illusion, which is also one of the forms of dreaming, that they were, in their day, a facile response to the incitements of the earth, a gesture that would seem self-evident, that one can spontaneously make, a first stable solution which, God knows why, then went out of kilter. Today, when one sizes up the high moral quality of so many Romanesque churches, and the pure intellectual quality of so many Renaissance chapels or palaces, one is tempted to believe in golden ages of the mind or the heart; but other testimonies remind us that foolishness, pride, sin, and miserliness shaped and occupied, as much then as for all other human beings in other periods of time, those who lived in that light. Similarly, the 'simplicity' that we recognise with joy in a two-coloured cloth, in the vibration of a bowl, the shine of the Multiple that speaks to us of the One, which makes an appeal beyond words, indeed takes place among words in their very birth to speculation, to chimeras; and those weavers and potters had to have the wisdom to struggle against speculation, to relearn a thousand times their own ever-threatened truth, to act alone, in the final reckoning, in the fatal drifting away. Spontaneity? No, self-mastery, which is always what is needed in our divided condition. The simple, in its natural effusion? No, a teaching: that one must simplify. And this apparent peace in fact calls for a struggle – which later, or elsewhere, other artists understood.

*

Poussin, as I was saying, or even Mondrian – from the period before his years of anguish. The consciously created work of art next to a peasant bowl, an oeuvre emanating from the most exceptional moments called on to last in daily life… I will be criticised for underestimating the importance of elaborate, difficult languages, which obviously distinguish what one calls great art from a craftsman writing on the level of ordinary words.

But how could painting and the other arts, which have 'represented' so much, either directly or indirectly, and thus work on an image of the world, an image that their day and age favoured, not be concerned about the Being specific to the image, that is, its ability to flee, where what I call meaning vanishes? And cannot one conceive that, at the very least, some lucid consciousnesses have wanted this alienation to end, during certain moments of their quest, which, as there is every reason to believe, were the richest, most decisive ones since they already demonstrate the most truthful thinking about the problematics of Being? As far as I am concerned, I believe in this finality of creative work. I even perceive, from one end to the other of its history in Europe, a lineage of artists who – this appears obvious to me – as inventors of images who were all too aware of their own immoderateness, nonetheless tried to heal the image, to dissolve what is imaginary in it, to revive in their mediations what seems to be the origin, which then takes shape as a sort of simple sacredness diffuse in the main aspects of what anyone can experience. This tradition, in its essential diversity – since it depends on gaps that the tradition must reduce – comprises the Greek icon; Piero della Francesca mastering the perspective of the Florentines, through which appearance is externalised and will take on phantasms; Bernini who dispelled the lasting *acedia* of the mannerists from the beautiful élans of his robust joy; just yesterday, it was Bonnard in his little morning garden, leading all the work of modern writing into, simply, presence. And at the limits of this endeavour that can be called alchemical – a transmutation, a dissolving of the invisible that coagulates – one must still hear all the desiring clamour – 'those maledictions, those blasphemies, those laments'[4] – of those who sense this good, desire it, but cannot carry out the endeavour because of too much secondary, incurable hope lingering in them – too much anger: hence Delacroix, Goya, already Michelangelo, the majority of those whom Baudelaire designated. A 'testimony', says the latter, an anguished cry that confirms the accomplishment of the greatest artists. A quest gone astray, except that it can encounter, by dint of desperately founding grace on its very lack, moments of a kind of grace where the lost simplicity suddenly gives itself over, all clarity of

4   Baudelaire, 'Les Phares'.

dawn and freshness, in tears of appeasement. It is a kind of peace – I wish to retain only this word – which forms the unity, at the highest level, of Western art ever since it has gone in search of itself. And this peace has been so assured and seemingly vast, at certain times, that one wonders why unhappy societies have not come back to it like a homeland, have not gathered together under its cloak of light.

And I can now attempt to formulate what comes to mind whenever I hear words of anxiety and doubt – the thought that also initially motivated my desire to silently bring together a few, almost random, examples of eternal civilisation.

Cannot one hope that those missed opportunities, those great moments of artistic creation, announced that at least once, in the future, the opportunity would be seized? And that the earth, ever betrayed by the image and today even attacked by it, will reacquire meaning from this fact, and this, in short, because of still another image, yet one transmuted by poetic intuition – let's put it better, because of a poetic meditation that is suddenly at last convincing, suddenly recognised as true thought, true experience, a true religion without gods, the true generalised work of makers of icons, mandalas, altarpieces, of frail infinite paintings, in our age beyond myths?

It will be said that this is a utopia and bitter to hear: all the same, I cannot prevent myself from making a few more remarks or, if you like, from dreaming about this utopia further if one can bear with me. First of all, this is, after all, the first time – this period of time in which we are living, and tomorrow – in which terrestrial presence is, I won't say altered by verbal immoderateness – I specified that this has always been the case – but *evidently* altered, wounded and, in this respect, it is more brutally eloquent, more apt to recall, even obscurely, that it has its own unrecognised truth. Fire becomes tragic, truly, this voice again becomes irrational, savage: conceptual thinking is thus weakened at the very moment of its victory. And this fire or tree or wind that we regret and for the same reason seek out, here they are, in their censored being-there-ness, as if suddenly pointed out to a mental approach which, this time, would no longer be an externalising ideation. Secondly, the very threat could permit a return to lucidity. Although poetry and what it awakens in art have always tended to have this aforementioned function, it took a long time for poetry to know how to assert it, let alone be aware of it; but it will henceforth be forced to understand, to announce, to insist on: helping the silent arts, finding the true meaning of 'ut pictura poesis', that long-obscure adage calling on painting and poetic creativity to each share its consciousness with the other... And as this shared consciousness thereby becomes deeper and its words more eloquent, energies will be liberated, the voice of meaning will be able to make itself stronger, alliances more efficient – human action change its pole. A dream? But the illness from which we suffer is a spiritual fact, and we will thus be able to fight it only where it originates, which is our most intimate relationship with the sounds that come from things. The only response to the depredations of the concept lies in practice at the same mental level, a practicing of the other life of the sign, the poetic sentiment. And even if this alarm resounding everywhere in the mind can be insufficient – so many societies suffer from the illness borne by words – at least this alarm, which never reigned, is necessary, and we must subscribe to it; in fact, there is no alternative.

Who knows if everything does not actually happen, in our day, despite the devastated grounds, the undone symbols, the pollution of the elements and of the heart, at an innermost, very secret – and dialectical – point of consciousness? And if, for an entire season, we must not approach the worst, which is also an unveiling, so that goodness emerges, perhaps opens up? And if it is therefore not the moment to stand firm against the 'evidence', taking back up, in favour of the terrestrial dwelling place in danger, the 'insane' demand of immortality formerly proclaimed by Chestov while facing the resignations of conceptual thinking? After unpredictable episodes, it will perhaps be only one word in only one poem, only a harmony of colours on a single canvas of flowers and fruits, which may just divert the scourge that we sense, hesitating above us.

Unless, perhaps – and this is actually my most intimate reason to believe – the breaking down of peasant labour – that endurance while making an effort, and with hope, an endurance which alone took on meaning where reality is 'rugged' and which loved the earth, which obliged it to comply beneath the plough and the seed, which delivered the earth as well as it eternally gave birth – can only be countered, in our needed countrysides, by a kind of work, true work, that is, risky, unsure of the future, factual in its grip of things: so that beyond the parks whose falsehood I have denounced, it needs to be understood one day that the only possible inheritor of the labourer is the artist, who will be able to find in the life of stones and plants, and in animals if some still exist, the vastest and ever-virgin of canvases on which to attempt the form that vibrates, place the harmonies that keep alive. Art is the only work attuned to the horizons that need to be refashioned. On art thus depend the future territories, which must be reconsidered in their very Being and their manifest nature held high, as has rarely been attempted up to now except for colours and forms: yet as Poussin and other landscape artists nevertheless sensed for the earth from the onset of their exile in the image. Here, the seeded furrow in its ochre brown colour that is life; there, new chapels for the dances and strange cries of the still unknown feast day; and the factory that will poetically enter the telluric depths, as Nerval – Poussin's brother, as it were – indicated with such lucid force in *Voyage to the Orient*. Ah, the 'natural' park that photographs nothingness would be all over: the intervention of art that reveals, that no longer hesitates to mark the ground as harshly – like a saint – as ancient labour or medieval spadework did… Once nothing seems practicable any more, everything remains to be done. And the time is nigh to wonder if artists from our age have not already experienced worries, needs, varieties of intolerance, and alchemies that would put us on the right track. All in all, this question is the best response that I can imagine, for the walls of Ratilly offered this year to poetry.

Art, today? Must I say that a good share of what art dreams moves me only intellectually, like an invention or by means of a daring gesture, but on levels where I see only nothingness being stirred as waves stir sand, so as to capture us in its torpor, to push the desert still further on. Oblivion increases, for example, every time an artist prefers the signs at his disposal to the referents that they were designed to make known, and lets them play, giving up the idea of meaning. Does he sincerely believe that only language is real, he who will sooner or later be covered by some of the outdoors – isn't he only amusing himself? This is what Plato condemned, and he needs to be reread in this light; to realise this, it suffices to better understand that, for him, it was a question of words, that he was attacking fiction, not poetry, which is enamoured like him of anamnesis. And when one resorts, as often in recent years, to random forces, to the foam frolicking above matter, it's intoxicating to set one's gaze on an endless swirl that might lead to some profitable illumination; all the same, I believe that one actually betrays random chance by doing so, and it can be the key. For it is not in the abyss where nothing remains of us, on the almost molecular level, but rather where what is unpredictable enters our projects, thwarts them, frees us from our pride, re-situates us in the indifference of Being, unseals this indifference for us like an ultimate secret, that random chance truly teaches and delivers. To turn away from that field of potentiality is to refuse the true tasks.

But there are other resources in contemporary artistic research, insofar as allusions to nearby things, to the human beings who fascinate us, or simply colours, rhythms, lines that can vibrate, help the painter's writing to safeguard the memory of the world where the writing bears its fault line. Such signs of attachment are time experienced, life lived, and this is not without virtue. Should one bring together two colours, or simply an intense black and white on a blank page, and if one is sensitive to quivering foliage, to that moment when a continuing fire becomes motionless, to how rocks are scattered on a peak, this consonance or this stormy contrast will be able to bear much more than the representation of an object: one will perceive the enigmatic light. Meaning is prefigured in materiality. In the image as it is born, the absolute that bears witness against the image is signified.

I actually know of artists, in our time, who seem to have wished, in one way or another, to call into question this pleasure that the sign takes in itself – soon becoming a concept, soon a dream – and that I see as having always deprived us of the nearby earth. Such and such an artist, whose eagle eye swoops down on the details of rocky valleys, brings the detail back alive to the nest of the geometric space – up there in what one might believe is the most reckless ambition to re-create the world, in the lineage of Quattrocento perspectives – and in fact intensifies the tension of the aforementioned black and white in the image, the tension of nothingness and being, whence thunder and a zigzagging lightning bolt, it's the 'hour of superior lightning bolts'[5]: a lightning bolt that is going to scatter the infinite

5 Rimbaud, 'Michel et Christine'.

herd of signs while the absolute rises in the evaporating figure. 'Figuration', as one says, obviously does not tend, when it attains a poetic
quality, to repeat what our language has already done with perception; as much an iconoclast as it is an idolater, it meditates on this
entrapment that is guilty when it accepts itself and dangerous when
it dreams. And such and such an artist who seems at peace with the
image also works to bring it down – a body sleeping or staying up
late near a fire, motionless fruit in baskets – for he has embraced,
as one immediately senses, what he loves, what he has experienced
as the true and the good, from which it follows that the idea of the
sacred or even its voice vibrates in his figures. What is imaginary is
dissipated, we become silent, we listen to the meaning, veiled by
form, as it breathes.

After which I will also express my gratitude to and affection for
painters who seem to take as the onset of their thinking – as the
non-designated yet pervading object – a radiance beyond the image
that the former mostly tend to join into a dialectic which, as we
have seen, is that of representation and presence. These new, reticent,
even silent witnesses appear unaware that these figures already exist,
that others have questioned and worked on them. Such painters
seemingly stay upstream of that, embracing rhythms and colours
still untroubled at their birth by the notion of things. They thus
let their own being respond, less by the employment of something
that is represented than by their harmony, a musical harmony with
these colours, these rhythms: it seems that the world and the mind
are in consonance, in such cases, with a harvested meadow or a tree
branch. I thus once again notice that there are indeed two kinds
of music, even among painters, and this would be just as true of
poets. A music which, from the onset, imposes a phrase upon the
orchestra, for it is all the horizon, all of experience, all of thought
that is suddenly grasped by intuition, by means of the project of an
earth on which to live; and it is Titian and Rubens, and Carracci's
inheritors as much as an oratorio by Monteverdi, a mass by Haydn, a
symphony by Beethoven or Mahler. Then those approaches, through
silence, that push back the beyond of sound, that spread out in
circles to infinity, beyond time, the moment when they participate
in the invisible: from a few quartets, in Europe, born of pure sound,
to strings that vibrate in India and play with noises, yielding to them,

enveloping them and dispersing them, at last letting the absolute cover everything with its grassy, insect-teeming water. And in that other intuition, which actually has two poles, who are they closest to? Is it the remote cithara player, the late Mozart, the late Beethoven, painters who want nothing of space, but who are not abstract – our friends?

May I restrain myself, all the same, from now raising a historian's or a critic's questions, thereby turning art into an object of study and soon thereafter one of aesthetic appreciation, transforming today's exhibition into an apercu of an era. Is it necessary to point out that I have not thought in these terms? For example, I have by no means referred to all the painters whom I love. As if by an evening habit, I have gone to those whom I have learned to love while watching them work, sometimes even while collaborating with them. What is essential, it seemed to me, in this age of a well-founded doubt, is to show that there are also responses. And that the earth that is taken from us has even begun its second existence with them.

Translated by John Taylor

2.
POETICS

The Act and the Place of Poetry[1]

I should like to bring together, almost to identify, poetry and hope; but to do so indirectly, since there are two sorts of poetry, one of them chimerical and untrue and fatal, just as there are two sorts of hope.

I am thinking first of all about a great refusal. When we have to 'take on a burden', as is said of someone smitten with misfortune, when we have to face up to a person's absence, to the deceitfulness of time, to the gulf that yawns in the very heart of presence or maybe of understanding, it is to speech that we turn as to a protected place. A word seems to be the soul of what it names, its ever-intact soul. And if it frees its object from time and space, those categories of our dispossession, it does so without impairing its precious essence and restores it to our desire. Thus Dante, having lost Beatrice, speaks her name. In that single word he evokes the idea of her and solicits rhythms and rhymes and all the solemn devices of language to raise up a pedestal for her, to build for her a castle of presence, immortality, returning. One kind of poetry will always seek to detach itself from the world, the better to grasp what it loves. And that is why it so readily becomes, or seems to become, a form of knowledge, since the anxious mind, separating what is from natural causality, immobilising it in absolute form, can no longer conceive of any relation between things except by means of analogy and prefers to stress their 'correspondences' and their remotely envisaged harmony rather than their obscure mutual antagonism. Knowledge is the last resort of nostalgia. It emerges in poetry after defeat and might confirm our misfortune, but its ambiguity – its fallacious promise lies in maintaining our awareness of the situation in which we were defeated, and even of its future, from which we expected so much and which has vanished. Such is the theme of *Mémoire*, the most 'daydreamlike' of Rimbaud's poems:

1 'The Act and the Place of Poetry' ('L'Acte et le lieu de la poésie') was first given as a lecture at the Collège de Philosophie in Paris. It was subsequently published in the revue *Letters nouvelles*, 4 and 11 March 1959. Collected in *L'Improbable*, rev. and enlarged edition, Paris: Mercure de France, 1992 and also in Paris: Gallimard, Collection Folio/Essais, 1992.

Jouet de cet oeil morne, je n'y puis prendre,
o canot immobile! oh! bras trop courts! ni l'une
ni l'autre fleur...

Plaything of that eye of dull water, I cannot reach
o motionless boat, o arms that are too short!
either this flower or that other.

O motionless boat, arms too short! I can hear this fervent voice regaining control even as it makes its admission, and separating a concept of itself that it thus knows or feels to be its essence, its divine part, from the degradations of lived experience. In the castle of the poetry of essence, when some weakness is admitted it is in so archetypal and pure a fashion that instead of a desire accepting failure we find a soul breaking free of its earthly fetters and thus seeking salvation.

Such poetry is forgetful of death. And so it is often said that poetry is divine.

And indeed when there are gods, and when man believes in his gods, this spiritual impulse may bring some happiness. That which we have loved, and which has died, finds its place in a sacred order. Nymphs are bearers of earth's waters. All that has shocked and disturbed us in this world is resolved in a wise acceptance; or, if one chooses death, or rather the anguished anticipation of death, one will die with the god who is dead. It is easy to be a poet among the gods. But we come after the gods. We can no longer have recourse to a heaven to guarantee our poetic transmutation, and we must inevitably question the seriousness of the latter.

Which brings us to the question: What are we concerned with? What are we really attached to? Are we entitled to reject the contamination of the impermanent and to withdraw into the stronghold of speech, like the king in Poe's tale, far from the plague-stricken land? Or did we love the lost object for its own sake, and do we want at all costs to recover it? Of course. I don't think there has to be an answer. But I have no doubt that modern poetry – poetry without gods – has to know what it wants in order to judge the power of words with full knowledge. If we only want to save ourselves from nothingness, even at the cost of possession, then perhaps words are enough. Mallarmé thought so, or rather he suggested such a hypothesis. But his unbounded honesty contradicted his attempt.

Yet he had taken enormous precautions. Through intransigence of mind, and doubtless also as a deliberate method, he had consented to abandon almost everything to the nothingness he saw everywhere at work, to finitude and chance. Appearances banished, pleasures and feelings disdained, no part of reality is required to found the new domain except the form of things, which is above suspicion, which outlasts their death and even the obliteration of their memory – the *presque dispariation vibratoire*, the all but disappearance of what is vibratory, that the word, by chance, seems to have the mysterious power of inventing. Mallarmé seeks to preserve only the kernel of being, but since the word seems identifiable with this he really believes he can do so. Should some demiurge have abandoned this world to be undermined by darkness, speech would undertake to restore the lost creation. In spite of halting syntax, speech will endeavour through its lucid patience, through its discretion, through the gradual elimination of what is risky and irregular, to convert those essences that were mere flotsam of a great vessel into the Idea become at last immanent, and the Book into the holy place which will retain that Idea amongst us. Poetry must save Being, which in turn will save us. Was it from blind pride that Mallarmé undertook such a task? Of course not; it was from disgust with illusory satisfactions, from love of poetry, from the feeling that someone must at last assume responsibility for restoring poetry, at least to truth.

For it was only to truth that Mallarmé attained.

Language is not the Word. However distorted, however transformed our syntax may be, it will always remain merely a metaphor for the unachievable syntax, signifying only exile. And what a sentence reveals is not the Idea, but our aversion from facile speech, our reflection so to speak, the confirmation of exile. And there is worse: the corpus of Ideas, being self-contained and self-sufficient, can only be born of itself; without contact with emotional vagaries and errors; and such purity, such coldness oblige the poet not to tolerate at the inception of his work that 'inspiration' that, in the poetry of the past, did at least bring passion to sustain the concern for intelligibility. This is the meaning of Mallarmé's well-known recourse to the pretext, a significant renunciation which binds us entirely to poetic invention, sacrificing pain, the poet's 'illustrious companion', for something almost non-existent which vanishes as soon as it is stated, which ceases to concern us, frivolity or perhaps scatology being the bleak conditions of that will to break the initial impure link. Mallarmé's poetry represents the defeat of existence, impulse after impulse, desire after desire. 'Fortunately,' he writes to Cazalis when initiating his great plan, 'I am perfectly dead.' We have here, indeed, the ancient baptismal concept that one must die to this world in order to be reborn in a higher, holier one. The fact remains that Mallarmé could only hope to gain a foothold on the threshold of being by silencing the original desire within him toward anxiety and understanding. What is the value of a gift conferred only on one who is already dead?

Stéphane Mallarmé demonstrated the failure of the old impulse of hope. We can no longer ignore the fact that it is impossible to escape through speech from the nothingness that consumes things, ever since *Un Coup de Dès* celebrated this irremediable fact. And those of us who have sought to evade it, such as those to whom I referred earlier – those seeking to retrieve from nothingness not their own lives but the object, those who are anguished at the thought of losing rather than of being lost – we are all tossed out of the safe harbour of speech into a land of dangers, where, moreover, the premonitions and the dissatisfactions of many great poets will recover their meaning and their authority.

*

For poetry, despite its great design, has always preserved within its closed dwelling the sense of an unknown existence, an alternative way of salvation, a different hope – in any case, of a strange and inadmissible pleasure.

How indeed can we forget the fascination exercised on poetry by blood and death, the wounding of Clorinda, the dying of Eurydice and Phaedra, situations of misfortune, dispossession, farewell? How can we fail to recognise, behind all its idylls, poetry's predilection for something sinister wandering among eternal woods like the ghost of the limit one would like to forget? The truth is that there is something ambiguous about all great works. And this makes them more deeply akin, among all edifices, among all mansions whose eternity is assured, to a temple, to the dwelling of a god. For the temple, through the rules of proportion and number and the essential economy of form, seeks to establish in the dangerous region the security of a law. Here we escape from the shadowy and the indefinite into the crystal clarity of the timeless. But in the secret heart of the temple, on the altar or deep in a crypt, the unforeseeable is present. Just a gleam on a stone face – but it reawakens all the storm within the symmetry, as though a well had been pierced in that luminous enclosure to reveal the unknowable depths of the place.

It is the destiny of every work of art to create a ceremony from that which is obscure. But often poetry does not admit this to itself, does not know itself, does not consent to release and name the mysterious powers it celebrates. This is the case with Racine, whom I take as an example of that central region, of those high places inhabited by incessant thunderstorms, where the symmetry of the facade tells nonetheless of the impossibility of rest.

What admirable coherence there is in Racine's capacity for denial! Never has prosody been so strictly confined, the vocabulary so lofty, meanings so pure and so controlled. Nothing can be said unless it conforms to the inflexible economy that the word sets against reality. Racinian man is by divine right remote from things. Or rather, nothing remains on his diurnal stage but a specimen of each thing, which has been assigned to him so that he may accomplish, outside of space and time, the essential actions of his immanent royalty. Here death serves only to punctuate great actions. It takes place in a single moment, without defilement, by means of poison, as one slips into the wings – and when something dark and formless, like the thought that obsesses Phèdre, is revealed, death is seen not as annihilation but as the victory of being, since the dying Phèdre cries out that she restores 'all its purity' to the light of day. The Racinian hero dies, it seems, to simplify the universe, to give greater weight to being, offering sacrifice to an aulic conception of the sacred in which the smallest possible number of figures are set out in the glorious sunlight. But this highly abstract death assumes a terrible importance. It seems as though by reducing it to pure act we merely precipitate its rhythm; it seems as though the quintessence of man, freed of its lees, has become an unstable substance which vanishes as soon as it appears; it seems, in a word, as though the essences cannot cohabit without eternally destroying one another and that if Racine is led intuitively, and by a supreme yearning, to that garden in the evening sunlight where characters stand motionless, these will only be able to move again for immediate death. Thus, in *Bérénice*, the opening words of those lucid, generous, and faultless beings give free rein to disaster. Thus, *Iphigénie* or in *Phèdre*, we find that doom-laden heredity, that incestuous blood, as though, on the one hand, even the splendid background of the great ancestral figures were marked by disquiet and guilt, as though, on a deeper level, the dimension of time inevitably revealed the existence of a material element where poetry had thought to attain the inaccessible empyrean. Within the transparency of his pure crystal Racine recognises a shadow and cannot cease seeing it. And this may well be one reason for his notorious silence. Had he not undertaken to portray Alcestis on the stage, and then failed to triumph over death?

Meanwhile, however, he had consented, with an absorbing passion he doubtless considered sinful, to the dark night that terrified him. He speaks with voluptuous decorum of that which kills the thing it loves. He brings it almost to the daylight of speech, with what would be unparalleled lucidity, were it not that the death he contemplates can only be expressed negatively, as an inconsistency in existence, a privation dissociated from the deep eternal object which is man dying *under our sky*. From within the world of essences, death is imagined as the unseen, as absence. That, I assume, is how in that supposedly sunlit century, passing over the rustling sand, one drew near to the closed orangeries. For I consider these the emblematic key to the period, its latent conscience; their great windows under admirable semicircular arches let in the daylight of being; they have no dark areas, and housing as they do choice specimens of plant and flower they prefigure Mallarmé's garden of the future – yet night, or the memory of night, fills them with a faint odour of sacrificial blood, as though some deeply significant act had once taken place there. The French orangery is the index of darkness, one of the 'thousand open ways' that Racine admits, and even more that *vacant self* that is classical French poetry itself, almost self-aware but inactive, waiting for an intuition to complete it, and which doubtless for that very reason was to exercise an irreducible fascination on later poetry.

★

One must go to the orangery and press one's brow against its dark panes. I can see Baudelaire as a child in the garden of essences. I mean that Baudelaire accomplished what classical prosody had always required, or rather what it had inaugurated. For on the way toward what Kierkegaard has called *purity of heart*, one inevitably encounters the classical concern for unity, even when it does not represent the most essential intuition. The Racinian concept of speech also means simplifying consciousness, confining us to certain thoughts which are indeed the most serious ones, and looking beyond the irrational light shed on everything in this world by false romanticism Baudelaire recovers this decisive poverty. His prosody has the same spiritual monotony as Racine's. Simply, however, whereas the latter conceives of unity as an ideal sphere, infinitely separate, Baudelaire brings it – or seeks it – within the physical world, outside of consciousness, outside of the self. I take *Le Cygne* as an example. Whereas Mallarmé, with *Hérodiade*, was to make a last attempt to suspend human action, to unite it with the stars, to transform the Racinian heroine – still too shadowy – into an Idea, Baudelaire substitutes for the classical archetype a real woman seen passing in the distance, not really known but respected for her essential fragility, her contingency, her mysterious grief. Baudelaire does not create this Andromache, he 'thinks' of her, and this means that being exists outside one's consciousness and that this simple fact, with its hazardous basis, is of far greater importance than the stable dwelling place built by the mind. For all around this wounded woman, and through the sympathy she arouses, the world – rather than being abolished as it once was, or proliferating senselessly as in picturesque poetry – suddenly opens onto the plight of all lost beings, the 'captives', the 'vanquished', as Baudelaire calls them, all those whose very exile renders their presence still less explicable, less reducible. The swan, a bewildered castaway, an enigma to the poet as much as to itself, destined to die and yet capable, in its extreme distress, of giving life and expression to the paradoxical song, represents individual existence recognised for the first time in sovereign manner in a poetic tradition that was dying. It is the *here and now*, our limitation; which poetry must ceaselessly rediscover in a pure and violent crisis of the feelings and of the mind. For this act which we expect of poetry, and which was finally achieved by the poet of *Les Fleurs du mal*, is primarily an act of love. Baudelaire speaks:

A quiconque a perdu ce qui ne se retrouve
Jamais, jamais!

To whoever has lost what can never, never be recovered!

and declares with that sufferer that the one irreplaceable reality is this particular being or thing before us, and if he dedicates himself to words with unchangingly impetuous passion, he never forgets that while they enchant us, they rob us and that they are not our true salvation.

★

Thus Baudelaire, ascribing supreme value to that which is merely mortal, showing human beings against a background of death and through death, can indeed be said to have discovered death, having understood that it is not that simple negation of the Idea that Racine secretly loved but one profound aspect of the presence of individual beings, in a sense their only reality. And Baudelaire seeks to make his poetry express that absolute exterior, that great wind against the windows of speech, the *here and now* on which any death confers a sacred character. A new and a thankless task. For as Hegel has shown, seemingly with relief, speech can retain nothing that is immediate. *Now night has fallen* (*Maintenant, c'est la nuit*): if by these words I claim to express my sense-experience they promptly become merely a frame from which presence has disappeared. The portraits that have seemed to us the most lifelike turn out to be mere paradigms. Our most private words become myths once we have let them go. Are we then condemned to be unable to speak of what we love best? At any rate, Baudelaire endeavoured, by means of those *chevilles* for which he has been so much blamed (though they, are surely the only valid response to the traditional closed prosody), by those muffled blows struck against the wall of speech, by the shattering of formal perfection and the collapse of Beauty which, in spite of himself and perhaps of ourselves, he envisaged for the poetry of the future, to suggest the way in which words dedicated to the universal are brushed by the wing of real life.

Baudelaire did more than that. I maintain that he chose to die – to summon death into his very body and to live under the threat of it – the better to grasp in his poetry the cloud looming on the boundaries of speech. Dead, already dead, already the one who has died in a here and now, Baudelaire no longer needs to describe a here and now. He is within them, and his works carry them.

And, I believe, that almost satisfied desire to attain to presence in language means that intelligence must efface itself in love, which is greater than intelligence, even if love can only take the form of pity or regret, *amer savoir*, that bitter knowledge, ineluctable and despairing.

But if poetry has to be this son of stoicism, what is the meaning of the strange joy that often surges up in Baudelaire's work when it is closest to the doomed object? In *Un Voyage à Cythère*, in *Une Charogne* or *Une Martyre*, it is unquestionable that when dealing with the most horrible things, the most cruel degradations of humanity in existence, this poet displays an ardent joy devoid of sadism and not exclusive of the most earnest pity – with all the energy of an initiation. Indeed, there is nothing in this sudden, feverish excitement that recalls the lamentations of Dostoevsky or a Chestov faced with intolerable truths. Baudelaire, who wrote *L'Irréparable*, *L'Irrémédiable*, and so many other poems in which he admits defeat, who lacked all resources of strength and was always acting and thinking on the very verge of exhaustion and anguish, seems to glimpse a gleam of light and to identify the perishable object, in spite of its profound precariousness, with something precious. This is what he so rightly called the *new sun*; and we could trace its rays through the twilight of his work – yet it is better to note that he did not seek or dare to understand it fully nor to probe the problem, rather enduring it as a kind of enigma, a secret forever lost and a source of remorse. I am sure – and I want to put this statement at the centre of my remarks – that Baudelaire sensed at the very core of that which exists, through its death and because it must die, that it may prove our salvation. And for the sake of poetry we have to ask this question anew, trying to found a gnosis of passion, to invent a way of knowledge. Baudelaire himself left the privilege of that mysterious act to a legendary past or to the paradise of childhood.

Je n'ai pas oublié, voisine de la ville...

I have not forgotten, nearby the town..

The house described in one of the most beautiful poems ever written, is it not the crystal of some beneficent reality, steeped as it once was in 'the streaming splendour of the evening sun' ('le soleil, le soir, ruisselant et superbe') that all day long has witnessed everything and now comes to settle on the 'frugal cloth', the purest inclination of our hearts, the place for welcoming what is substantial. Here, or at that time, the servant is the *desservante* or officiating priestess, and in another poem of *Les Fleurs du mal* which forms a diptych with the one I have just quoted, *La Servante au grand coeur...*, we see that priestess of a bygone rite bring against poetry the grave indictment of forgetfulness.

In the dawn of consciousness there is the promise of a good which is later submerged by reason, as though by sleep.

And the muted prophecy we find in Baudelaire, once uttered, was to spread its message unceasingly. It is surely to Baudelaire that Rimbaud owes, if not his uncompromising exigency, at any rate the notion that poetry has the power to satisfy it. Rimbaud is convinced that poetry can be a practical action; he has no use for the traditional sort that is bewitched by illusions, that is content to lament the poet's sufferings, the sort of poetry he calls 'subjective' – he believes that a place and a formula, in poetry and, if need be, beyond it, will bring about the transmutation of dispossession into a benefit. Rimbaud was less savant than Baudelaire, less the cunning chemist, being less close to reality and less able to gauge it in its deep transparency, because he had been deprived of love at the most vulnerable moment of his childhood. But for that very reason he demanded more. It is thanks to Rimbaud that we know, we *really* know that poetry must be a means and not an end, and we owe him the immensity of what we might ask for – those demands, that thirst that have proved so alarming.

*

For it is not true that the poets who followed Rimbaud and Baudelaire understood their problem or maintained their attitude. It seems, on the contrary, as though they had taken fright and chose rather to listen to a message of pessimism that may be found in Mallarmé and that exists, in any case, in the great space of our modernity, under the 'dead sky' – a twofold or perhaps just a single crisis, which offers the legacy of an empty world. And if it is true that no god any longer sanctifies created things, that they are pure matter, pure chance, why indeed should one not seek to escape from them? The end of the idea of divinity may bring about a revival of puritanism, of the fear of existence, since it completes that dissociation of the human being from nature which a certain form of Christianity had inaugurated. And among the most brilliant poets of our time we find, at the same time, a certain pessimism and scepticism, and the wish for a discipline by means of which to withdraw from the world as it is. The useless dwelling that Baudelaire had abandoned is inhabited once more. But this time it is not, it is less than ever, in order to save one's existence; it is rather to save oneself from existence in a purely formal act, secret and immobile, what I might describe as the wrong sort of death (*la mauvaise mort*).

Indeed, as I must now admit to myself, I mistrust those disciples of Mallarmé who in different contexts, with contradictory intentions, have also turned away from their master's conclusions. Valéry, who for his own peace of mind and in order to forget the tragic awareness of the Greeks, spends his time seeking rules for the making of a poem. Claudel, fettered by orthodoxy, with his list of things. Great minds, certainly, profuse and subtle personalities; but in fact personality, with its marked features, its authority, its latent mannerism, is the basic resource of a negative idealism. Absence here appears creative. Such poetry achieves a moment of glamour at the cost of true passion and real experience. On the other hand, what is valuable in our age has often been characterised by its distaste for the rights or privileges of a markedly personal intelligence. There was the impossible Surrealist dream of collective invention. And in some of the best poetry of our century – I think of glaciers, of deserts, of forgotten crafts, of moments of dry stone or mist – we find that the object has become hollow like a wave, separate from its body like a flame in the light, to imply the essential fluidity we share, both it and us, when we meet. Then there is the attention that speech pays to its most obscure strata. And finally, above all, we find younger poets scrupulously examining with an almost moral end in view, the pretensions of that ego that had so often asserted without proof, written without believing, and misled. They will not accept without extreme prudence and reservation, and after careful verification, the necessary impulses of their own minds and voices. They have made a clean sweep of self-confident gestures, and then reinvented those few elementary gestures that unite us to things, in the ceaseless cold dawn of a life anxiously seeking the absolute. Thus poetry is today returning to a profound realism. This, needless to say, is not that self-styled 'objectivity' with its precise inventories, of those 'new novels' in which the authorial voice is muted. When there are no more desires, mistakes, or passions, even wind and fire lose their reality; the whole world becomes the home of absence. And it is the final result of the shattering of Providence, but also the dangerous contradiction of atheism, that we should have destroyed divine machinery only to deny all subjective life to things or happenings.

Already in *The Castle of Otranto* the strange sight of a huge helmet or an enormous iron arm in courtyard or hail implied man's bewilderment, confronted with a world abandoned to itself and with the mutely enigmatic presence of a real object. And possibility – that most precious of our assets – suddenly deprived of its religious dimension, was degraded into a mere vicissitude. The difficulty facing modem poetry is that it has to define itself at one and the same moment through Christianity and in opposition to it. For Baudelaire's discovery – to return to the truly decisive moment – of the *individual* person or thing is indeed Christian insofar as Jesus suffered under Pontius Pilate, endowing a particular place and moment with dignity and every human being with reality. But Christianity only affirms individual existence for a brief instant. The created thing is brought back to God by means of Providence and thus deprived once again of its absolute value.

Thus in order to complete Baudelaire's revolution and strengthen hesitant realism we must also carry out a criticism of the religious thought we have inherited. The duty of giving a meaning to existence and to all that exists – the private destiny of every work of art – is intensified today by the urgent and imperative need to rethink the relation between man and those 'inert' things, those 'remote' beings which the collapse of the divine may lead us to think of as mere material.

In other words, we have to rediscover *hope*. In the secret region of our contact with being, I believe there is no true poetry today that does not seek, and will go on seeking to its last breath, to found a new hope.

★

T. S. Eliot in *The Waste Land* expressed the real myth of modern culture. But he ignored, or sought to ignore, one paradoxical resource of that culture.

We now know the meaning of that desolate land, where a spell has dried up the springs, disrupted the harvests: it is reality, if I might so put it, *realised*, concluded; a reality endured by the spirit without a quest for possibilities. A realm of essences and the knowledge of essences. Man has embarked on the wrong path. Is it from despair at the lack of a higher life? But suppose the contrary were true and metaphysical sterility only the consequence of a bleak lack of curiosity? Was it not said at the castle of the Fisher King that a single question would be enough to break the spell?

The honour of conceptual thought – of all thought – lies in asking rather than in answering. The West began badly with Oedipus.

However, I have in mind a very different question, and the most fundamental one, bearing on the presence, not the nature, of things. The Percival in each of us, the consciousness that is to be, would not have to ask what things or beings are, but why they are in this place we consider our own and what mysterious answer they might give to our call. He would have to wonder at the chance on which they depend; he would have suddenly to see them. And of course this would mean, in the first stage of this groping knowledge, recognising the death, the anonymity, the finitude that dwell in them and that destroy them. ... I suggest today that we should once more follow Baudelaire in his love for what is mortal, stand once again on the threshold he thought was closed, facing the most distressing proofs of darkness. Here all thoughts about the future, all projects vanish. Nothingness consumes the object; we are caught up in the winds of that shadowless flame. And we no longer have any faith to sustain us, any formula, any myth; our most intense gaze ends in despair. Yet let us not abandon this blank and empty horizon; let us hold our ground, *le pas gagné*, so to speak. For it is true that already a change is taking place. The mournful star of existence, the elementary Janus, turning slowly – but at this instant – on itself, reveals its other face. A possibility appears on the wreck of all possibilities. And the horror of *Une Martyre*, or the 'green gloom of moist summer evenings' ('les ténèbres vertes dans les soirs humides de la belle saison'), or anything else that is real, whether tragic or pacified, will emerge in the sacred heart of this instant for an eternity of presence. I resent using this approximative language when I should really be *telling*. But what words would henceforth not betray us? Here – and it's still the same here – and at this moment – also still the same – we have stepped out of space, we have slipped out of time. All that we had once lost is restored to us, still and smiling at the gates of light. All that passes and never stops passing pauses, postponing night. It is as though sight had become substance, and knowledge possession – but in fact what do we possess? Something has happened, something of infinite depth and gravity, a bird has sung in the ravine of existence, we have touched the water which would have allayed our thirst, but already, the veil of time has wrapped us in its folds, and as the instant draws near we are exiled anew. Something was offered to us, we are sure of that in spite of Baudelaire, but we were unable to grasp it. Were we so ill-prepared? No doubt we were like Lancelot in the *Quest for the Holy Grail*, who, having come to a closed chapel and fallen asleep on its threshold, suddenly sees it lit up by a great fire, sees the Grail issue from its gates and hears a knight cry out, as he suddenly, emerges from the darkness: '*Ha, guéri suis!* I am cured!' – while he himself remains sunk in the lethargy of his fatal sleep, remote from God.

And yet, in spite of this missed opportunity, we are no longer the same, we are no longer so poor, some hope remains. Although indeed the question of what might save us remains unanswered, although we have had to doubt insofar as, and almost at the very instant when we were given to believe, we have nonetheless received the boon of certainty; and, even as the view of the purpose of man is revised, we know on what basis we can build. Henceforward we have a reason for existence, which is that sudden act. And a duty and a moral goal – at any rate provisionally – which will be to recover it. And all our actions, lost, crippled creatures that we are, should be a call to this; or rather should recognise that this is what they have always been, in depth, else why do we love those lighted lamps in empty rooms, those statues whose faces are obliterated by sand, those lifeless cloisters? Is what we are seeking there some sort of beauty, as we are told? Of course not; it is rather something eternal which we share with these things.

And of speech, too, this is true. Speech is the same quest, without knowing it. Has it not waged a long war against nothingness? Perhaps the act of presence – that lost light of Baudelaire's poem – may be its origin too. And I myself am prepared, envisaging the future of poetry, seeing speech as invention or recovery, and pursuing the path which is the only possible one, to affirm passionately this *here* and this *now* which, indeed, are already an elsewhere and a past, which no longer exist, which have been stolen from us but which, eternally in their temporal finitude, universally in their spatial limitation, are the only conceivable good, the only place that deserves the name of place. In modern French poetry we see the Grail procession passing – the most vividly perceptible objects of this earth – a tree, a face, a stone – and they must be named. Therein lies all our hope.

But the difficulty confronting language, its well-known incapacity, to express the immediate, has not been solved, as I well know. At best it has been clarified or emphasised, since I have only asked of words that they put their trust in silence. What can they retain or say, when presence is offered to us *in* the universe of the moment? Speech can indeed celebrate presence, sing of its being, as I am doing now; it can prepare us spiritually for encountering it, but it cannot in itself allow us to achieve it. Speech implies forgetting; it may even explain our fall. At any rate, it is denied contact with being. Must we not, yet again, condemn the pretensions of poetry?

★

I think rather that we must recognise its limitations and, forgetting that it may once have been an end, take it merely as the means of an approach, which, given the limitations of our perspective, is actually not far from being the essential thing. Deficiency has one virtue, which is to recognise itself as such and thus lead us to a passionate knowing. And if language is as incapable of the Idea as it is of presence, if the reflected light of the one hides from us, in the words of poetry, the finitude and death that are the steps to the other, we are still able to recognise this and to direct our anxious lucidity of mind against the facility of speech. I should like poetry to be above all a ceaseless battle, a theatre in which being and essence, form and formlessness wage strenuous war. This is possible in a number of

ways. Poetry in the past has taken risks where truth is concerned.
And the fervent empiricism we shall need will have to admit that
in any serious work all the 'devices' of poetry are maltreated and
almost destroyed. Thus we shall learn that words can above all be an
action. Their potential, their infinite future of associations, considered merely verbal and assumed to be gratuitous, will turn out to be
only a metaphor for our endless connection with the slightest thing
that is real, for the subjective nature of everything that is profound
– and in a moment of unreality, of free decision about the physical
world, we shall be able to release what is from the sleep of its stable
forms, in which nothingness triumphs. Thus, too, the facile delight
of rhythms will be denied. Formal beauty, is the dream on the edge
of an ideal world. It found expression in regular verse with an even
number of syllables, but it was here, *in* the realm of abstraction and
forgetfulness, that Rimbaud dealt the fatal blow of the irregular line.
He made possible a conflict and, beyond it, an understanding, of
which the silent 'e' is the secret link. Moved both by desire and by
clearsightedness, he made it possible for the thoughts nurtured by
poetry to be realised at last. The myths to come will tell of death or
will admit that they are concealing it. The adventure of meaning will
begin at last. Or rather, *the hypothesis of meaning*, our frantic need
to organise our knowledge within the space of a poem, to formulate
the myth of what is, to construct the concepts, will be subjected
to diffraction by the formless. And this poetry which cannot grasp
presence, dispossessed of all other good, will be in anguished proximity to the great accomplished act, as its *negative theology*. When, in
relation to what is, all landmarks, all frameworks, all formulae have
been questioned or obliterated, what can we do but wait, hoping in
the substance of words?

And it is true that in authentic poetry nothing remains but those
wanderers of the real, those categories of possibility, those elements
without past or future, never entirely involved in the existing situation, always ahead of it and promising something else, which are
the wind, fire, earth, the waters – all the indefinite offerings of
the universe, concrete but universal elements. Here and now, but
everywhere beyond the here and now, under the canopy and in the
forecourt of our place and our moment. Omnipresent and alive; one
might say that they are the very speech of being that poetry draws

forth. One might also say that they are words, being no other than a promise. They appear on the confines of the negativity of language, like angels telling of a still unknown god. A negative 'theology'. The only universality I recognise in poetry.

A knowledge, negative and unstable though it be, that I may perhaps call the *truth of speech*. The very opposite of a formula. An intuition, complete in each word. And a 'bitter knowledge' certainly, since it confirms death. It knows that the healing power of presence evades us. It rediscovers and relives past failures. It has brought no proofs to the reawakened hope. Yet is it true that it does nothing toward that salvation with which we are obsessively concerned? And is poetry merely one appeal among all the others, with no privilege, no future? We must ask ourselves, and this is a distinction that is surely not useless, since here lies perhaps our only recourse – whether in addition to the negative intuition which a poem is *for all of us*, poetic invention brings nothing to the life of the writer other than aimless desire, unrest, and futility.

★

I should like to show, by way of conclusion, that this is not the case. To think so would be to misunderstand this world of expectancy in which, having reached this point in the invention of speech, we are involved. Here, where nothing is considered, sought, or loved but the act of presence, where the only valid future is that absolute present where time evaporates, all reality is still *to be*, and its 'past' as well. We conceive that the past event, that apparent proof of death, is only an action initiated or veiled, possessing its glorified body in the depths of the future; and that it is thus a test for us. For its nothingness is definitive only if we betray our hope. Out of respect, I speak thus curtly of that which exalts the spirit at the highest point of poetic experience. For it is true that the past and death, however manifest, however acutely present to our minds, no longer overwhelm the lover of what has been lost. He can contemplate the traces of them. And although these are nothing, having failed to present presence and being unable to restore its scattered essence to our inert memories, he will understand why he guards them so jealously as being the key to an unknown future. He may meet with words; they, too, are what remains of what has vanished. Let us take them as tokens of a good and not of a quiddity. And let us try to understand that they, like the past, are a test for us, since, given the recurrences of the future, they require us to act instead of merely dreaming.

They require us to act. And first of all to imagine what is very deep, to remove the contradiction between the lightning flash and our night. Logically (if I may use the word) to conceive of a true place. For if it is certain that here, in the everyday world, the only good worth wishing for is evanescent, so that we are in disarray and divided within ourselves, why should we not ask some other place in this world to restore us to our law? Another place, beyond other encounters, beyond the war of being alone. Having now discovered that travel, love, architecture, all the efforts of mankind are only so many ceremonies to summon presence, we have to bring them to life again on the very threshold of that deeper region. And in the changing light of its dawn, to fulfill them absolutely. Is there not somewhere a true fire, a true face? I can almost see those stones in the daylight, and for a whole day of this world, a day redeemed, after which, if the word still has a meaning, one will only have to die. This is, if you will, the blessing of the torn ivy leaf, given and possessed at last.

The true place is a fragment of duration consumed by eternity; in the true place time is annulled within us. And I might equally say, I know, that it does not exist, that it is only the mirage, against the background of time, of the hours of our death – but has the term reality still a meaning, and can it free us from the engagement we have contracted toward the remembered object, which is to go on seeking? I maintain that nothing is more authentic, and thus more reasonable, than to go wandering, for – need it be said? – there is no method for returning to the true place. It may be infinitely close. It is also infinitely far away. So it is with being, in our moment of time, and the irony of presence.

The true place is given by chance, but in the true place chance will lose its enigmatic character.

And for the person seeking, even if he is well aware that there is no path to guide him, the world around him will be inhabited by signs. The least object, the most ephemeral creature, because of the good they do him will arouse the hope of an absolute good.

The fire that warms us tells us that it is not the true fire. Its very substance proves this; it is here, it is not here. We recognise again those wanderers through the great space of reality, those promise-bearing angels of which I spoke. In the true place, elementary realities reveal that they are not confined to place and moment; that they partake less of the nature of being than of that of language; that they can compel whatever appears beside them to speak to us, in a whisper, of an unforeseeable future. I have rediscovered the point at which, by the grace of the future, reality and language have united their powers. And I say that a longing for the true place is the vow made by poetry. Having conferred the energy to undertake the journey, poetry provides the path. Words appearing before us in the space of our waiting, words being only a matter of waiting and knowing, poetry will know how to dissociate, at the most important moments, quality that is ephemeral from meaning that is vigilant. It will search the horizon according to the wish of our hearts. It will question all that pass by. And when certain things reveal themselves to be *openings*, signs consumed by the close proximity of the good they have called forth, poetry will keep these keys in mind in its strictest economy; it will establish the word *lamp* or the word *ship* or the word *shore* in the stronghold, this time, of a memory that is striving between dispersal and recovery. These things are, in fact, the buttresses of the true place, and their names will come together in poetry to form what is intelligible, *subjectively intelligible*, or a necessary hypostasis before the unity we desire. Thus speech is the sense we make of our involvement in the obscure possibilities of earth, of our relation with what is. And certainly, in our twofold journey, speech is likely to lead us toward an increase in consciousness rather *than toward* a place. But the whole spirit must keep watch, waiting for the decisive, chance moment... The poet is the person who 'burns' with expectation. The truth of speech is a proximity – when essential realities are so clearly the threshold of the true place, and yet all the more opaque and strange in that they always conceal, through their chance dispersal, the next step, which remains a secret. There is a cloud in the light; something elusive, dark, and formless in the purity of the crystal. This is why words offer to the anxiously questing mind of the poet not only the clarity of the concept but also their material opacity, their arbitrary and fascinating letters. I say a *flower*, and the sound of the word, its mysterious figure brings back the enigma. And if opacity is joined with transparency, if a poet is able to write 'Le pâle hortensia s'unit au myrte vert', there can be no doubt that he is as close as possible to those elusive gates. Of such a poet it will most frequently be said that he is 'hermetic'. For his only object, his only lodestar is beyond any expressible meaning, even though his quest requires the full richness of words.

The process of poetry takes place in the field of speech, but each of its steps is verifiable in a world newly affirmed. Poetry brings about the transmutation of the finished into the possible, of the remembered into the expected, of the waste land into a journey, into hope. And I might speak of it as an *initiatory realism* if, in the end, it gave us reality. But how can one answer that question, which is the first one I asked? This poetry will prove to have been our destiny. For *in the meantime* we shall have grown older. The act of speech will have taken place in the same space of time as our other actions. It will have given us one kind of life rather than another, amidst the perils of poetry and the contradictions of exile. What indeed shall we have had if we do not reach the true place?

I think of that poet whose hope was the clearest, whose suffering was the keenest; the most secret of those who, in nineteenth-century France, formed that sort of quadrangle in which all thoughts are lost and then recovered in endless refractions. Purely, like poetry incarnate, he became totally absorbed into the hopeless love that is love for mortal beings. But his desire remained desire, and his impulse toward plenitude maintained in honesty of heart the sense of the unpossessable. This union of lucidity and hope is what I call melancholy. And in the world of Justice nothing comes closer to Grace – whether truth or beauty – than this ardent melancholy. This at least is the gift that a true poet can offer. And in his poverty, giving remains his wealth.

For a long time, poetry sought to dwell in the mansion of the Idea, but, as it is said, was driven out and fled, uttering cries of pain. Modern poetry is far from its possible home. The great four-windowed hall is permanently closed to it. The repose provided by form in poetry can no longer be accepted with honesty. But the opportunity of the poetry that is to come, its good fortune (and I can admit that good fortune now) is that it is on the point of realising, in its enduring exile, the issue offered by presence. After so many hours of anguish. Was it so difficult, then? Surely it was enough to glimpse, on some mountainside, a window gleaming in the evening sun?

Translated by Jean Stewart and John Naughton

SHAKESPEARE AND THE FRENCH POET[1]

How might we evaluate French translations of Shakespeare? Do we have a truthful image of him in French – or at least a compelling one? Have we, for instance, a French equivalent of the German translations by Schlegel and Tieck, which have enjoyed such favour and renown since the Romantic period? No, there is nothing comparable in French, and I believe it is useful and important to analyse this astonishing absence.

It is not that Shakespeare is unrecognised in France. We read him, as best we can; we evoke him; for quite some time we have had a general idea of his greatness, if only because an army of adapters, coming at Shakespeare from all sides, have managed to point out this or that aspect of a body of work whose essential feature is precisely its extraordinary diversity. In one sense, it is probably an advantage that we have no French translation comparable to that of Schlegel and Tieck – a 'classic', beautiful and powerful enough to constrict us within the limited perfection of its own particular vision. The Romantic age, in any case, was incapable of truly understanding Shakespeare. The fact remains that to this day we still do not have in France a complete translation that is both faithful to the original and great literature in its own right – one in which the reader can get more than an abstract idea of the dramatic elements of the work and something of the substance of Shakespeare's incomparable poetry. Perfectly good translations of particular plays there are. I would mention, for example, those of Jules Supervielle, Pierre Leyris, and Henri Thomas – but they seem piecemeal and inconsistent when what is needed is an organic whole, a single profound vision combining anew all the aspects of the Shakespearean world – and this could only be attempted by a single poet working alone with authority and decision.

1   'Shakespeare et le poète français' was first published in review in 1959; re-published as an Afterword to Bonnefoy's translation of *Hamlet* (Mercure de France, 1962). Collected in *Théâtre et poésie. Shakespeare et Yeats*. Paris: Mercure de France, 1998; and in *Shakespeare: Théâtre et Poésie*. Paris: Coll. *Tel Essais*, Gallimard, 2014. An English translation of the essay was published anonymously in the magazine *Encounter* (1962); the present version is based on that translation, but considerably revised.

In other words, the French have only been *told about* Shakespeare, and if translating means catching the original tone of voice, that fusion of personal vision and word which makes the poetic dimension, then he has not yet been translated at all. Why is this so? I have no doubt that it is worth looking at the problem from a somewhat theoretical angle and trying to find out if there is not some basic, essential cause for this persistent failure. But in order to do this I shall first consider the earliest translations. What strikes me most about them, apart from any individual shortcomings, is one serious weakness they all have in common.

II.

Although, historically speaking, the idea is absurd, it is a lasting pity that no one thought of extemporising a translation in Shakespeare's own day. At the beginning of the seventeenth century, before Malherbe's influence turned the scale and while the impression of Garnier's breathless verse still lingered, something of the essence of Shakespeare could have seeped into our poetry and modified it, perhaps profoundly. But the taste for classicism soon barred any genuine understanding of Shakespeare. In an age dominated by Racine, one can hardly imagine anyone translating *Macbeth*. And when Voltaire takes it upon himself to initiate the French mind into what he calls 'English Tragedy' (after Corneille and Racine even the word *tragedy* is charged with overtones very remote from anything English), the rendering he offers of Hamlet's 'To be or not to be', for instance, is a complete travesty of Shakespeare, and precisely because of that facile and totally unpoetical alexandrine which was then the principal cause of the vapidity in the theatre:

> *Demeure, il faut choisir, et passer à l'instant*
> *De la vie à la mort et de l'être au néant*

What is surprising is that Voltaire, with the intention of giving some idea of Shakespeare's 'woodnotes wild', should have followed up this doggerel with a literal, line-for-line translation which has a kind of beauty of its own and, in its freedom and flexibility, is related to what we might welcome today. In rendering 'Or to take arms against a sea of troubles' as 'et de prendre les armes contre une mer de troubles', he shows a fine audacity, and in my own translation of *Hamlet* I have paid the unwitting forerunner of all modern translators the compliment of taking over this line. Voltaire, however, put it forward only to cut it out, as if he meant to show the kind of excesses from which the French genius had to be protected. And in the age of Louis XVI, when Ducis in turn composed 'imitations' of *Hamlet* and *Othello* that were widely read and often reprinted (I remember they were still to be found in my grandfather's small library), it was from Voltaire that Ducis had learned to cut and rearrange and simplify Shakespeare's text so that the end product was a 'five-act tragedy' of the utmost regularity and inanity. 'I don't understand English' – this is how Ducis begins his preface, and he distorts the original plot to such an extent that Claudius, to take one example, is turned into Ophelia's father, and we can be fairly sure this is done so as to face Hamlet, like a character in Corneille, with a choice between revenge and love. From the neoclassical point of view of the Age of Reason, Hamlet's procrastination had to be justified on rational grounds that were *perfectly clear and distinct.*

Nevertheless, Ducis's clear-cut line is occasionally fuzzy; he has a touch of the *roman noir*, and I must confess that I do not find his renderings altogether intolerable, if only because they illustrate with such perfect clarity the difficulties of translating Shakespeare. Indeed, after Ducis, the problems were more often shelved than solved. Between the Revolution and the Second Empire, Shakespeare was continually being translated, but in the spirit of a vague Romanticism. Letourneur (between 1776 and 1782), Francisque Michel, Benjamin Laroche, Guizot, François Victor-Hugo, and Montégut all published *Complete Works*, with some progress in accuracy (though Letourneur had no compunction in cutting out complete scenes and bowdlerising passages he thought coarse), and even in felicity – but with the same defect that is present in Ducis and is so subtle and elusive that it defies easy description.

Here is a famous passage from the first part of Henry IV, the one where Falstaff is in a black mood, repenting of his evil life: 'Why,' he says to Bardolph, 'there is it':

Come, sing me a bawdy song, make me merry. I was as virtuously given as a gentleman need to be; virtuous enough, swore little, diced not above seven times a week, went to a bawdy-house not above one in a quarter of an hour, paid money that I borrowed three or four times, lived well and in good compass; and now I live out of all order, out of all compass.

In these few lines, and in the background they suggest – a world of authentic bawdy houses and taverns – we are confronted with a real human being talking about himself; and any feeling of unreality arises only from the jocular way he himself contrasts his actual way of life to the impression he would like to create of it. Falstaff is fully there in the flesh, and for whatever universal meaning he attains, his starting point is the same as that of any other mortal: his individual reality, which persists in vivid unpredictability throughout the entire play. Falstaff is an archetype only because he is primarily a complex and mysterious being that we cannot fathom any more than we can really understand any other real human being. And the words seem to lend themselves to this total *thereness.* They seem to be one with the puffing voice, and even to be reabsorbed into the world of sense they evoke, so that we are left with nothing between us and its raw assertiveness, its undiminished complexity. But let us now look at a translation, a very meticulous one, by François Victor-Hugo:

> *Oui, voilà la chose. Allons, chante-moi une chanson égrillarde. Egaye-moi. J'étais aussi vertueusement doué qu'un gentilhomme a besoin de l'être; vertueux suffisamment; jurant peu; jouant aux dés, pas plus de sept fois … par semaine; allant dans les mauvais lieux pas plus d'une fois par quart d'heure; ayant trois ou quatre fois rendu de l'argent emprunté; vivant bien et dans la juste mesure; et maintenant, je mène une vie désordonnée et hors de toute mesure.*

Certainly, it is the same passage: the ideas and the references are the same. But there is a world of difference between the original text and the translation. Whereas Shakespeare's Falstaff seems actually *in the room*, in the translation he appears distant, insubstantial, dimmed, *as if we were looking at him through a windowpane.* He is no longer a living being, he is a character in literature, but one striving, by his exuberant language, to resemble life too closely and hence all the less convincing. In all these translations, all Shakespeare's characters lose their roundness in the same way. Even where Shakespeare's 'excesses' – the puns, the bawdiness – are scrupulously preserved, the characters seem insubstantial and their speech lacks life. 'I have immortal longings' is what Shakespeare wrote at the end of *Antony and Cleopatra.* 'Je sens en moi l'impatient désir de l'immortalité' is Letourneur's version, while 'Je me sens pressée d'un violent désir de quitter la vie' is Francisque Michel's. Where are we? The words create neither reality nor myth. This is the ghost of Shakespeare.

And yet we can be confident that these translators chose a prose rendering so as not to be led into the unreality, the unnaturalness and lack of body, characteristic of the Voltaire and Ducis versions. They used prose because it served the Romantic aspiration to lay hold of the real in all its heterogeneity – local colour and the picturesque, as well as the truth of beings as different as possible from ourselves – in short, to bring language and real life as close together as possible. Admittedly the earlier Romanticism (I mean that of Hugo and Musset) had no very profound grasp of this reality. But since Shakespeare could hardly have been less concerned with the picturesque, it is likely that one of the reasons why nineteenth-century translators missed the mark was just that they had lost touch with what is the real source of Shakespeare's truth – that vital force of human creation, that passionate depth of feeling, that his verse directly expresses. Even in the most recent efforts, that sense of looking through a windowpane is painfully persistent, so much so that in André Gide's translations (unfortunately very poor) we are left with the effect of a puppet theatre – literary, artificial, and affected. Surely we cannot attribute this defect to a mere accident of literary history. It seems to be an inevitable misfortune of the French language when it tries to translate poetry without being able to escape from the hidden principles of its own very special and peculiar verse.

What I wish to do here – and this is all that I am attempting to do in these few pages – is to contrast Shakespeare's poetry with this unspoken assumption about the nature of poetry. For I am convinced that, quite apart from all the particular illustrations (I should like to have quoted more but nothing would really be adequate or decisive), the essence of this failure in translating Shakespeare lies in the opposing metaphysics that govern and, sometimes, tyrannise the French and English languages.

III.

If I had to sum up in a sentence my impression of Shakespeare, I should say that I see no opposition in his work between the universal and the particular. In spite of scholastic tradition, he does not envisage these two poles of thought as contradictory because, in his plays at least, he doesn't focus his mind on them. Is Macbeth an archetype like Antigone, or even Harpagon, or is he rather an individual caught in a unique destiny, the product of pure chance? Is Othello the type of the jealous man, or the incoherent victim of blind and senseless forces that could not be further from anything 'clear and distinct'? These questions cannot be answered because they are wrongly stated. For Shakespeare deals with people's actions, which are never 'particulars' because they participate in the universal categories of the consciousness that conceives them, but which also never – not even in the case of Brutus and Julius Caesar – reach the fullness and clarity of the universal because they have to compromise with raw contingency. Human action cannot be fitted into the framework of logic because a person acts only in order to contradict his or her own nature, to be at once both individual and universal – and the essential ambiguity in Shakespeare means that his theatre is the empirical observation, without literary or philosophical preconception, of people as they actually exist. The apparent subject of his tragedy is simply a means of capturing a possibility of human existence so as to examine it. The seemingly abstract setting of the action does not so much exclude the real world as concentrate it, like a framework within which all the variations of action that human passion might conceive could be instantaneously evoked.

And Shakespeare's language too is a means rather than an end; it is always subordinate to the external object, which is something English allows. Nouns fade before the real presence of things, which stand starkly before us in the actual process of becoming. The uninflected adjectives snap qualities photographically, without raising the metaphysical problem of the relation of quality and substance, as the agreement of adjectives and nouns must do in French. English concerns itself naturally with tangible aspects. It accepts the reality of what can be observed and does not admit the possibility of any other order of reality; it has a natural affinity with the Aristotelean critique of Platonic Ideas. And if its words with Latin roots to some extent unsettle this philosophical choice and grant a more abstract handling of experience to an intelligence shaped by this 'devotion to the realm of things', they do not undermine the natural realism of the language so much as simply make it easier to express those moments in life when we are guided by a sense of the ideal. To quote once again that moment of the purest poetry, those sublime words of Cleopatra, 'I have immortal longings': on the one hand, this phrase is capable of seizing hold of the living actuality at its most concrete, immediate, and instinctive, while on the other hand, by using a word like *immortal*, which is pure Idea, it retains the capacity to reveal in this same concrete action the timeless and the universal, which are our purest aspirations. At a deeper level, the English language tells us that immortality, this pure *Idea*, in some sense really exists and that it is a noble and veridical part of speech but also that its activity and life depend on our will to create them. English poetry, Shakespeare's at least, rejects archetypal realism but only in order to follow the inalienable liberty of man with greater flexibility.

And the greatness and richness of English poetry come from service to this liberty, as if offering it at every moment the entire range of its possibilities, so that any given word can open up a world, a 'brave new world', to our perception. With French poetry it is a very different matter. Generally, with this more cautious, more self-contained kind of poetry, the words seem to state what they denote and immediately to exclude from the poem's field of reference whatever is not denoted. The poet's statements do not set out to describe external reality but shut the poet in with certain selected precepts in a simplified, more circumscribed world. For instance, Racine rejects all but a few situations and feelings in his plays. By stripping them of all the contingent or accidental details of real life, he seems to raise them to the dignity of the Platonic idea, as if he wished to reduce his dramatic structure to the bare relations of congruence or opposition which hold between those ideas. A more coherent world of intelligible essences is substituted for the real world. Yet it is not an abstract world, for the Platonic Idea is profoundly double-natured, in the sense of taking on the life of sensible appearance in its most intense and specific form. But this world is nonetheless a *place apart*, where the bewildering diversity of the real can be forgotten, and also the very existence of time, everyday life and death. Poetic creation, in short, is hieratic; it makes an inviolable place, and while the rite of reading continues, it draws the mind into this illusory communion.

Not all French poetry, of course, can be identified with the art of Racine. Indeed, in Baudelaire's case it goes counter to Racine's design for poetry, but even then without moving out of this magic circle by which words circumscribe the mind. In rediscovering and reaffirming for himself the notion of poetry already implicit in the work of Villon, Durand, and Maynard, Baudelaire – in contrast to Racine – is asserting the very existence of sensible things, the particular reality as such, the stubborn entities that people our mortal horizon, as if surrendering totally to the phenomenal world and abandoning the hieratic use of language. Baudelaire is the most consistent and determined opponent of the Racinian theory. And yet this *principle of exclusion* I have referred to still governs his poetry. Even though he is dealing with *this* particular swan or *that* particular woman rather than with swan or woman as such – with the idea, that is, of swan or woman – what these particular entities are like are not what matters to him. What matters is simply this mystery – that the idea should have strayed into the very marrow of the sensible world, that it should be willing to undergo limitation and death, and that, while retaining its absolute status, it should have entered into this world of shadows and chance. Baudelaire is not trying, at any level of penetration, to describe things as they are: he is trying to convey the act of being, and the passion and moral feeling that can be based upon it. An intense, narrow aim that restored to poetry the almost obsessional detachment from the phenomenal world that seems to be the fate of our main body of work.[2] It is as if words, in French, excluding instead of describing, always encourage the mind to shake off the disintegrating diversity of things; it is as if they always make the work of art a world of its own, a closed sphere.[3]

2 If Baudelaire, for instance, calls up the image of a woman with black hair and green eyes, these are not so much personal characteristics as a definition of his own kind of sensibility. [YB]

3 And that is why English poetry 'means' so much more than French poetry. The former, whose words have no pretension to be Idea – principle and origin of the world – can put the world into words, interpret and formulate it. The latter can only reveal the Idea, manifest beyond words and concepts. From this contrast, the profound divergences of Anglo-Saxon and French literary criticism can also be deduced. [YB]

I should like to conclude by saying that in English the word is an opening, it is all surface; and in French it is a closing, it is all depth. On the one hand, we have the kind of word that can call upon all the other words (more than 21,000 in Shakespeare, according to Jespersen) to aid precision and enrichment; on the other hand, we have a vocabulary as reduced as possible, so as to protect a single essential experience. On the one hand, unlimited dissociation, receptiveness to every dialectical or technical possibility, so that an alert awareness can penetrate always further into the phenomenal world. On the other hand, all these evocations of sense entering into poetry as one enters into an order, to be completely transformed, dying to the world, becoming one with the idea that is constantly being realised in the poem. English poetry is a mirror, French poetry a crystal sphere. The French poet who, according to many, is least like Racine and most like Shakespeare is Paul Claudel. Yet in *L'Annonce faite à Marie*, not only Violaine but Mara, not only Pierre de Craon but Jacques Hury, speak with the same deliberate and highly stylised speech, a uniformity that symbolises the unity of creation in the bosom of God, the nonexistence of evil at the heart of God's world. In spite of its richness, there is no poetry more organic, more closely knit than Paul Claudel's; it is still a sphere even though Claudel, with a medieval, pre-Copernican sense of the cosmos, thought he could succeed in making it into a correlative of the Sphere of Created Beings.

IV.

English poetry, as I have said, can be represented by a mirror, French by a sphere. How can these contradictory forms of poetry be translated into each other?

It may be easier now to see why so many French translations of Shakespeare are mediocre: they are nothing more than a compromise between two linguistic structures. The French poetic vocabulary irresistibly tones down and dims the particular reality, that stubborn compound of the essential and the contingent. How then could we expect it to preserve Falstaff; who is singularity incarnate, emancipated from all forms and laws, even moral law?[4] It is easier, too, to see how the majority of these translations came about historically. Romanticism thought it could be free of that inner law of the French language which I have tried to isolate. But the Romantics, who sought to revolutionise the old dictionary and multiply its references to the real world while still producing poetry, never achieved more than a shallow exploitation of this new territory. They were no more sensitive to the deeper stirrings of instinct and passion than they were to the dialectic of essence and existence, which had engaged both Racine and Baudelaire.

How, then, is Shakespeare to be translated? If I wanted to end on a pessimistic note, I could easily make a list of all the forms this fundamental opposition might assume, or, in other words, all the points of fidelity that a translation should realise and that French structure makes difficult, if not impossible. Thus the alternation of prose and verse in Shakespearean tragedy is true to reality; it witnesses to the opposing forces – the heroic and the commonplace – at work in the world: at the end of the cobbler's scene in *Julius Caesar*, the abrupt return to verse is a dramatic assertion of the will to nobility in a boorish world. But this plurality of perspectives is not possible in French poetry. Not only in Corneille and Racine but also in Hugo and Claudel, the minor characters speak in verse and, like the chorus in Greek tragedy, the less they share in the nobler dimensions of the action, the more strictly they are bound to formal poetic expression. Another difficulty is that wordplay has to be translated. Shakespeare's punning is genuinely ambiguous, reflecting the complex nature of the real world, but French does not take kindly to the pun, and it is unlikely to be anything better than a nihilistic (sometimes subversive) assault on rational mind. Indeed, the least significant word in a poem has latent within it the entire structure of its language. Mere literal translation of the word is not enough to break down the structure. Take that one word 'Sortez!' – Roxane's cry in *Bazajet*. How much of its implication would we expect to survive, once translated

---

4 Of all Shakespeare's characters, Falstaff is the least understood and the least appreciated in France. In a country where the problem of good and evil is approached conceptually, dialectically, Zarathustra, who is *beyond* both good and evil (showing that he has at least considered them), is better understood than Falstaff, who remains, if you will, *beneath* good and evil. [YB]

into English? There is a great danger that this tremendous word by which Roxane severs herself from the world of sense, this word that implies a whole metaphysics, would wind up a mere theatrical effect.

But is there much point in making a long list of difficulties? It would be more useful to take note of the one remaining possibility that may, one day, give us the chance of solving the problem of Shakespearean translation – or at least of raising it to a new level.

If, as I have tried to show, every language has an individual structure, and the linguistic structure of French poetry is Platonic while that of Shakespeare's English is a sort of passionate Aristotelianism, then every true translation – and this quite apart from accuracy of detail – has a kind of moral obligation to be a metaphysical reflection, the contemplation of one way of thinking by another, the attempt to express from one's own angle the specific nature of that thought, and finally a kind of examination of one's own resources. From that point, translation goes far beyond the rendering of explicit discourse and the meanings that can be grasped directly, and penetrates into indirect ways of expression (prosodic usage or the handling of imagery, for instance). Translation becomes the struggle of a language with its own nature, at the very core of its being, the quickening point of its growth.

Now I believe that French poetry today is much better prepared than it ever has been to wage this struggle with its own language. In general terms, we may have reached a point in Western history where the major languages have to emerge from their naïveté and break with their instinctive assumptions so as to establish themselves in a different kind of truth, with all its contradictions and difficulties. And without attempting to deny the existence of its ever-present structure, recent French poetry is undergoing a revolution which, by disturbing this metaphysical tendency, and curbing it, could at some time or other allow us to better convey Shakespeare's artistic intention.

What is the real point at issue? I have contended that a French word, in its 'classic' usage, designates what it refers to only in order to exclude the real world of heterogeneous existences. I have contended, too, that Baudelaire affirmed this reality of existences but that it was not so much these real entities as our relations with them that he took as the focus of poetic contemplation; and so once again he made a

closed world out of language – the world in which a soul struck by
the mystery of presence is doomed to speak only obliquely of a reality
he could never truly make part of his life. This kind of poetry is still a
subjective account of the soul, it is a *psychology*; but there is another,
more recent kind of poetry, which aims at *salvation*. It conceives of
the real object, in its separation from ourselves, its infinite otherness,
as something that can give us an instantaneous glimpse of essential
being and thus be our salvation, if we are able to tear the veil of
universals, of the conceptual, to attain to it. Whether this ambition
is well founded or not is of little importance. The essential thing
is the demand it makes on language – to be open to what is most
different from us and most external to us, to what is most difficult
to capture and express, the being of things, their metaphysical *thereness*, their pure presence before us, in all of its silence and night.
While it continues to exclude conceptual descriptions, this poetry is
an attempt to lose its identity, to go beyond its own nature, to the
point where the universal *becomes* the particular (the ontologically
unique), an ecstatic plunge into what is. This pursuit of otherness,
of absolute exteriority, is surely not so far from Shakespeare. Is it not
an attempt to contemplate what Shakespeare lays bare in particular
beings as their secret source and background – when, for instance,
he weaves through Macbeth's whole destiny the irreducible element
of chance, which is the presence of the witches; or shows Hamlet's
mind haunted by the voice coming from the shadows; or reveals, in
The Winter's Tale, the hope – absurd but still triumphant – of a real
resurrection in the flesh? After all, a mirror that truly reflects life must
of necessity reflect an experience of being as well. Always a rational
universe is given the lie; it melts away before the void, and human
action projects itself into an obscure and incommunicable region.
There is no great difference between the Hamlet who realises that
the rule of law has passed away (and that justification is to be found,
if anywhere, in a subjective choice without ground or warrant) and
our contemporary French poetry, which has abdicated its age-old
kingdom and taken its chance, like the prince of Denmark, with
anguish, impotence, and silence.

To put it another way, it is at the level of their deepest, most
immediate intuitions that the realism of Shakespeare and the denial
of idealism in recent French poetry may henceforth communicate.

For the one presents, describes, what the other asks to live. And what can be *said* directly by Shakespeare may, perhaps, be indirectly suggested in a language of translation that, while honouring the explicit content of each work to be translated, can now contribute a profound feeling for the very being and presence of things, which will be an unremitting testing of all its poetic resources. Thus the necessary surpassing of classical forms, of closed types of prosody (which is not inconsistent with a concern for the real laws governing the verse), can become one, in translations of Shakespeare, with the need to preserve the poetic line and its tragic quality, but without giving the impression that the English poet believed in a hieratic and unreal world. In fact, Shakespeare and many other Elizabethan writers have become immensely instructive for French poetry in its process of finding itself. We ought to give them our most serious attention. And if we still fail to translate them properly, we shall certainly have less excuse than translators who have gone before.

The confrontation of two languages in a translation is a metaphysical and moral experiment, the 'testing' of one way of thinking by another. Sometimes it is sheer impossibility, indeed vanity. From time to time, however, something may emerge that will add another level of interest to the mere fact of translation, raising a language to a new level of awareness through the circuitous ways of poetry.

Translated for Encounter, *1962;*
Revised by John Naughton

TRANSPOSE OR TRANSLATE?[1]

In a special issue of *Etudes Anglaises*,[2] Christian Pons proposes a new method of translation for *Hamlet*. He suggests that there be intentional transpositions, done in the broader rhythms and the unimpeded abundance of the *verset* – the long verse line favoured by Claudel. He writes: 'In the particular case of *Hamlet* – I would not say the same for all of Shakespeare – it would be better to transpose, that is, transfer into another movement that would be the equivalent in our language ... We should not hesitate to be more ample than the original wherever the French language requires a logical breaking up or the development of what in Shakespearean imagery is either implicitly stated or else concentrated in a few words.' And, having legitimately criticised me for an inadequate translation of 'to watch the minutes of this night'[3] from the opening scene in *Hamlet*, Pons unhesitatingly 'develops' the meaning he sees contained in these words. His translation becomes: 'Afin qu'il surveille avec nous les ténèbres, et cc lent écoulement des heures, tous les moments de la nuit l'un après l'autre' ('To watch over the darkness with us, and the slow passing of the hours, all the

---

1   A version of this essay was part of the 'Afterword' to Bonnefoy's translation of *Hamlet* (1962). Collected in *Théâtre et poésie. Shakespeare et Yeats*. Paris: Mercure de France, 1998; and in *Shakespeare: Théâtre et Poésie*. Paris: Coll. Tel Essais, Gallimard, 2014.
2   'Shakespeare en France', *Etudes anglaises* 13, no. 2 (1960).
3   The full passage in Shakespeare reads as follows:
      Horatio says 'tis but our fantasy,
      And will not let belief take hold of him
      Touching this dreaded sight, twice seen of us:
      Therefore I have entreated him along
      With us to watch the minutes of this night;
      That, if again this apparition come
      He may approve our eyes and speak to it.

moments of the night one after another').[4] More oratorical than the original text, as Pons himself admits, this adaptation is nonetheless the way to true fidelity, through a movement 'analogous to the Claudelian *verset*'.

Let me begin with a comment that is not crucial and that has more to do with the psychology of translation than with its geometry. It is true that when an English word is rich in ambiguity, it is a thankless task to have to choose between meanings. To side with the principle of 'developing', however, would mean having constant recourse to solutions through abundance, at the cost of breaking with the poetic tension of the line. The translator may have forgotten that the Claudelian *verset*, especially in his plays, can be quite short. I am convinced that constraints are necessary in the prosody itself in order to translate well, if not with ease.

More important still, what really is 'meaning'? And doesn't the sort of 'explicating' recommended by Pons lead to a kind of betrayal of meaning, since it might fail to recognise the duality, at the heart of speech, between what is formulated and what is held back, or, to put it another way, between the conscious and the unconscious? These oppositions, moreover, are themselves significant; they are a part of everything that has to be considered when translating. When Marcellus asks Horatio to stay with him and 'to watch the minutes of this night', it is possible that these words mean all that Pons's translation has them say and would immediately he apprehended by the audience as such. Yet it is also possible that Marcellus is unaware of all that, or is unwilling to express it quite so fully. In fact, he is probably saying much more. But to 'develop' almost to the point of exhaustion what is only one aspect of the meaning is to turn the mind away from its deeper reaches. One can no more deliver a word from its meaning than one can transport the density of a symbol into

---

4   Bonnefoy's translation of the passage reads as follows:
     Horatio dit que ce n'est qu'un rêve,
     Il ne veut pas accepter de croire
     A l'horrible vision que deux fois nous avons eue.
     Et c'est pourquoi je l'ai pressé de venir
     Avec nous, pour épier ces heures de nuit.
     Si ce spectre revient,
     Il pourra rendre justice à nos yeux – et lui parler.

a concept, or cast the tragic dimension of immediacy into discourse, or put into a flat formula those indistinct stages through which the assertions or implications of the manifest meaning join the mysteries of what remains unconscious.

I would say that such ambitions sin through intellectuality; they presuppose the primacy of the idea in the act of writing, and even of a precise program of significance to be communicated, over every other function of the word – for instance, to *invent* a meaning rather than to say it; to *constitute* a world rather than simply to mirror it; to approach, while at the same time holding them at a distance, obscure and dangerous realities in a moment of conjuration. The rationalist view is not the best philosophy with which to approach the Elizabethan age. And I'm afraid it has little claim on Claudel, whose *verset* never had anything analytic about it, even in his translation of the *Oresteia*. A line of verse is always more than what it says. And a 'developed' analysis of its meaning will always tend toward prose.

II.

But I still have to formulate what strikes me as the most important reason for not translating *Hamlet* in *versets*. Pons presupposes that Claudel would have been a good translator of Shakespeare, but I disagree. It is a fact, after all, that this great dramatist, who did translate from the English, never tackled the Elizabethan theatre. It is true that there is both a tragic and a comic breadth to Claudel that makes his plays perhaps the only body of work in French drama capable of competing with Shakespeare's variety. But on so vast a horizon a similar vision is not necessarily cast, and in order to translate *Hamlet* or *Macbeth* (this would have been less true of the history plays), Claudel would have had to abandon a good part of his own being and, in any case, his *verset*. For the *verset* signifies immediately, organically, an astonishing optimism, at once dogmatic and congenital, shot through with darkness and light, which is very far indeed from Shakespearean thought.

Listen to this line: 'The time is out of joint: O cursed spite!' Nothing could be more pessimistic than *Hamlet*; nothing wanders quite so far from the security of faith. An intuition of nothingness

darkens and fragments all of Elizabethan consciousness. Hamlet
seeks but does not find the foundations for a viable order. And it is
remarkable how well the Shakespearean line is able to express this
torment. It identifies with the voice, breaks with its anguish, picks up
with its newfound hopes, hardens when it might have come undone
in the distress of the moment. The pentameter in *Hamlet* is by no
means a secondary or negligible fact. And this is because it bears
– like the decasyllable or the alexandrine in French – a power of
metaphysical receptivity that is a good deal more specific and precise
than is often thought.

Can we honestly believe that this length – five feet, six feet – has
been imposed on Western languages by chance? It is the length in
which the long and short syllables that make up each word can,
in the midst of a visible ensemble, either come together or clash
– creating this or that rhythm – with the greatest intensity, thus
allowing the poet's relation to himself and the world to be expressed
with a maximum of richness.

When the line is shorter, this activity at the heart of its sonorous
reality is diminished; it tends to disappear, invariably at the expense
of a whole dimension of feeling and thought. It is all too easy for
the very short line to play, or to affirm; it risks losing much of its
capacity for intuition. When it is longer, much longer – well, I
will come back to this. In its average length – in English, five feet;
in French, ten or twelve syllables – it helps to create between the
various sounds of words, and also between their meanings, a system
of reciprocal relations that is the very life of speech, and this fact
has certainly contributed to its development, as evidenced by the
history of poetry in recent centuries. And it has done more: it registers and expresses the structure of the world that the poet, at various
moments of his relation to society, has had the power to create or
the destiny to endure. An example? Doesn't the classical alexandrine, with its rhymes and its caesuras, require that clear and distinct
ideas, a perfectly transparent form of intelligibility, replace the dark
night of empirical reality? And isn't the one who uses such verse not
aware of this metaphysical demand, and in a better position to think
deeply about it and to refute it than he would be were he to use any
other form of language? It is in the hollows of Racine's verse that the
horizon of the truer intuitions and the new illusions that will preoc-

cupy Chénier, Nerval, and Mallarmé can already been seen taking shape.

In short, the line of five or six feet, or ten or twelve syllables, is the boundary between the mind's inner workings and the world outside on which that mind must work. It makes note of the order of things thought true by an era; it perpetuates that order, keeping thought fixed on it. But it also brings thought into contact with the unknown and with the unconscious. It is thus a form of speech that not only helps to constitute a society but enables it to visit the most distant regions of perception or the most hidden recesses of the psyche. This is why, historically, poetry has known a whole development from orthodoxy to revolt, to discovery, along paths that are sometimes direct, sometimes roundabout, and among which are the metaphors prosody itself can create. If the pentameter begins to 'limp', it is not just because an actor in *Hamlet* does not know his role; it is also because the human being, the speaking being, no longer wants to play the role that tradition has assigned to him or her – that is, can no longer have faith in a myth, an ideology, a dogma, preferring doubt and confusion to the endless repetition of forms now devoid of being.

And this is also why the *verset*, be it Claudel's or Pons's, cannot be faithful to the truth of works written in the kind of verse practiced in Elizabethan England. For a line that is too long does not have the same constraints as do more tightly constricted meters; it therefore cannot create the same experience. In the longer line, form weighs much less heavily on the substance of the word, and the word is perceived less strongly as a resonant presence. It tends to be reduced to the notion it carries, and this encourages an entirely different relation to the world. I would say that, in contrast to the line of 'average' length, the *verset* seeks from the outset to pass over that boundary in consciousness which is the idea of order, concern for the intelligible, so as to reach that happy state of plenitude and variety in which naming things and listing places takes precedence over the need for mastery and coherence, over the understanding of rules. And this can seem to be freedom itself, a perfectly appropriate welcoming of the future, and much superior to the 'limping' I mentioned a moment ago, which is as much a prisoner of the past as a sign of changing times. But let us beware! Can this kind of fervour be called an authentic transgression when it has not known constraint? Is it not more likely to be the utopia that conceals a habit of thought we are unwilling to submit, in the line itself, to the test of the depths of the relation to oneself? The *verset* defers the examination of traditional forms rather than actually attempting it. After his series of words, in the aftermath of his wave, the poet appears to have settled on a shore decreed new and propitious, with the energetic, if debatable, self-assurance of a conqueror or a missionary. This seems to be the case with Claudel, whose verse for conquistadors hardly seems suited to the melancholy prince who gives up even his Denmark. To translate *Hamlet* with Claudel's methods would be to abandon the space of the question – which has value to the extent that it exceeds the resources of the intellect and must even, at times, be recognised as insolvable – for the arrogant genius of the answer.

Translated by John Naughton and Stephen Romer

FRENCH POETRY AND THE PRINCIPLE OF IDENTITY[1]

Of what value is the French language to the experience of poetry? We know that Baudelaire and Rimbaud, among many other witnesses, were sometimes given to fits of anger against it. Baudelaire writes, for example: 'I am bored in France because everyone here resembles Voltaire.' And in a letter to Ancelle, dating from the last months of his conscious life, a letter that is in truth his spiritual testament, Baudelaire again writes: 'And you were enough of a CHILD to forget that *France* ABHORS poetry, *true* poetry, that it admires only bastards like Beranger or de Musset.' Some years later, Rimbaud spontaneously finds similar words: 'French, that is to say, detestable ... Yet another work of that odious spirit that inspired Rabelais, Voltaire, Jean La Fontaine explicated by Monsieur Taine! ... French poetry will long be savoured, but only in France.' These insults, I admit, are aimed more directly at society than at language. But can one truly make a distinction between civilisation and its mode of expression? Is not the latter, at least, one of the causes of the former and thus of the difficulties of its poetry?

But listen to how Baudelaire, and Rimbaud also, correct themselves. 'French, not Parisian!' the latter exclaims, referring to the 'odious spirit'. And in the draft of a preface to *Les Fleurs du mal*, a book, incidentally, that is dedicated to a 'pure magician of French letters', Baudelaire writes: 'Like the languages of Latin and English, how mysterious and unappreciated is the prosody French poetry possesses.' There is thus a city of poetry in the land of prose, a rhythm in our language whose quality, cannot be squandered by so many ignorant 'bourgeois'. In truth, it is to a certain esoteric quality, rather than to a deficiency that Baudelaire and Rimbaud allude. French poetry should exist, but it hides itself or, in any case, keeps its distance. What it most hates is what is called poetry.

---

1 'La Poésie française et le principe d'identité' was first published in review in 1965 and then in a signed and limited edition by the Galerie Maeght in 1967 with two watercolours by Raoul Ubac. Collected in *L'Improbable*, rev. and enlarged edition, Paris: Mercure de France, 1992.

Therein, however, lies a problem. If our language is capable of poetry, why does it make contact with it only in these obviously reciprocal misunderstandings and deprecations? Is this the fact of all culture since Romanticism, perhaps? Or is it a characteristic peculiar to the French language alone?

I believe it is the former; but in order to explain why, I have to define what seems to me one of the initial movements of the poetic intuition. This is also its first contact with language: namely, its reaction to the most simple reality, that of the word.

It is important to stress that this approach differs radically from what is ordinarily considered the only conceivable explanation of the sign. In fact, this difference is so decisive, and so consistently unrecognised, that there may perhaps appear one of those persistent nodes of dangerous certainty that for many authors makes the *reason* for poetry so difficult to understand.

From this perspective, moreover, how little progress has been made in recent critical theory! Saussure and his followers have shown that the sign is determined by a structure, thus adding a new dimension to meaning and consequently to the knowledge of literary works. But they assign to the word the unchanging task of merely signifying, and the very richness of their discoveries has become a danger for a meditation on poetry.

For all linguists, so it seems, the word *horse* represents what is, let's say, neither donkey nor unicorn. Its content is a quiddity, nothing else; thus, in its destiny to evoke, as a proper noun can evoke when one shouts it out, it does not express the actual existence of the 'horse' that is here before me.

That seems obvious. What would 'the horse' be if not a concept? A horse, yes, before me; and 'the horse' as its idea, by whatever means this idea may be determined. I admit that this point of view allows one to describe correctly the way language is available for most uses. But poetry is, precisely, not a 'use' of language. Perhaps, it is a madness in the language, which we can understand only through its eyes of madness – only through poetry's way of understanding and taking hold of words.

This, I believe, is what initiates poetry. If I say 'fire' (yes, I am changing examples and that already in itself means something), poetically what this word evokes for me is not only fire in its nature as fire – what there is about fire that suggests its concept – but the *presence* of fire in the horizon of my life, and certainly not as an object, analysable and usable (and, therefore, finite, replaceable), but as a god, active and endowed with powers.

But I fear I am becoming unclear, so I will use another example.

And I shall imagine or remember – we will perhaps see later that the two ideas are equivalent – that one summer's day I enter the ruins of a house and suddenly see a salamander on the wall. Surprised and frightened, it remains motionless. And roused from my reverie I, too, am ready to be held captive. I look at the salamander, I recognise its distinctive features, I see the narrow neck, the gray face, the heart that beats softly.

So, several paths have opened before me. I can analyse what my perception has shown me, and thus, profiting from the experience of other beings, mentally separate this small life from other realities in the world, categorise it in the way the prose word might, saying to myself 'A salamander', and then absentmindedly continue my walk, as if I were only superficially affected by the encounter. But other, more profound reactions are possible. For example, I can keep my eyes on the salamander, pay particular attention to the details that had enabled me to recognise it, think about continuing the analysis that makes it more and more into a salamander, that is to say, an object of science, a reality structured by my reason and penetrated by language – but with the immediate result that in these appearances that have been abruptly separated one from the other, in this contour of an absolute, indisputable, barren leg, I no longer perceive anything but a terrifying bundle of enigmas. These things have a name, but suddenly become strangers to that name. And these concepts, these definitions, these appearances are for me no more than an empty coherence, unresponsive to any question.

What is a salamander? *Why* this salamander rather than the hearth, or the swallow, or the cracks in the wall? *Where* is the origin of what lies before me? In sum, I have just discovered the agonising tautology of language by which words only speak themselves, having no real hold on things – which can move away from words, remaining distant from them. I shall call *bad presence* (*la mauvaise présence*) this latent muteness of the world. And I am even tempted to call it the devil, for there is a power, a strange appeal, hidden in the depths of this void. It is as if nothingness mimicked our most familiar realities and by the darkness of its night penetrated the closed form of being. I experience the idea of death. I am fascinated, as surely as if by a snake. But, fortunately, at this moment I find in myself the freedom that denies it.

For here is the third path. By a sudden act, this reality (*ce réel*), which has divided and exteriorised itself, *comes together again*, and this time in a plenitude where I am taken up and saved. It is as if I had accepted, *experienced*, this salamander. Henceforth, rather than having to be explained by other aspects of reality (*le réel*), the salamander, here present as the softly beating heart of the world, becomes the origin of what is. Let's say – although this experience is barely describable – that it has revealed itself, becoming, or becoming again, *the* salamander – as one says *the* fairy – in a pure act of existing where its 'essence' is contained. Let's say – for one must also save the word, above all from the fatal desire to define everything – that its essence has flowed into the essence of other beings, like the flux of an analogy by which I perceive everything in the continuity and sufficiency of a *place* and in the transparence of *unity*. The wall is justified, and the fireplace, and the olive tree outside, and the earth. And having again become one with all that, having been awakened to the essential savour of my being – for this space arches in me as the inner world of my existence – I have gone from accursed perception to love, which is prescience of the invisible.

How, indeed, to express true reality (*le vrai réel*) through another word? This *invisible* is not a new appearance that will be revealed beneath other imperfections. Rather, it is that all appearances, all coagulations of the visible, have dissolved as particular figures, have, like sloughed-off scales, fallen into knowledge, *have found the body of the indissociable*. The salamander has freed itself from the world of objects created by an analytic reason that runs the risk of remaining on the periphery of things. And before me, in me, it is no longer anything but pure *countenance*, although its features remain material. It is the *angel* that drove devils away, the angel that is unique; for the One is the great revelation of this limitless moment when everything surrenders itself to me to be understood and bound together.

'Mine the sun,' writes St. John of the Cross, speaking far ahead in the distance on this faintly traced road, 'mine the moon and the stars, mine the mother of God'.

This reestablished or, at the very least, emerging unity I shall call *presence*. And now I can return to the subject of words and better define their appeal for the consciousness of poetry.

What I have briefly tried to show is that in unity, or in any event under its sign, there is no longer a salamander at odds with this hearth, or with one, or even, a hundred swallows, but *the* salamander, present at the heart of other presences. The idea of a creature on this path – it matters little whether it is illusory or not – implies its existence, and this defeats the concept, which must abolish that existence if its forms of expression are to flourish. In the expectation of presence, one does not 'signify'; one lets a light disentangle itself from the meanings that conceal it.

But that does not mean that one turns away, from language. For language, and this is the other point I wanted to emphasise, is naturally continuous with the experience I have described – in one as well as the other of its aspects. On the one hand, there is dissociation, which occurs when words become concepts. In language, especially analytical language, there is certainly this potentiality for muteness, against which feeling, desire, humour – the beginnings of poetry – rise up. But since language is a structure, it can become – even before any form of expression has begun its work of death – a *cipher* for the unity that every form carries within itself. In this instant when everything is decided, it can thus return with me to an encounter with being. Language – and this is why one spoke of logos, of 'Word' – seems to promise the same unity beyond its conceptual moment as life offers beyond the fragmented realities of its presence. It seems to invite us to carry in its depths the word that will give being to what it names. And the word, a flashing of unity, will henceforth suggest that I no longer assimilate existence to language but, on the contrary, assimilate language to my participation in the real. Every language is thus the field for the elaboration of a kind of order; for the establishment of the sacred in the destiny of the person who speaks; for, at least, the efforts of a poetry.

For I can now define what I mean by poetry. It is by no means, as is so frequently asserted even today, the creation of an object in which meanings are given structure, whether for the purpose of capturing moments of revery or for the deceptive beauty of having fused into the mass of these meanings – into their elusive particles of 'truth' – the appearances of what I am. This object exists, of course, but it is the castoff skin of the poem and not its soul or intention. To attach oneself only to it is to remain in the world of dissociation, the world of objects – of the object that I, too, am, and do not wish to remain. The more one seeks to study the subtleties and expressive ambiguities of the object, the more one risks overlooking an intention of salvation, which is the poem's only concern. Indeed, the poem aspires only to interiorise the real. It seeks the ties that *in me* unite things. It must allow me to live my life in justice, and sometimes its finest moments are notations of pure evidence, where the visible seems to be on the verge of being consumed in a face; where the part, devoid even of a metaphor, has spoken in the name of the whole; where what has been silent in the distance rustles once again and breathes within the open, the whiteness, of being. The invisible – it needs to be said again from this perspective of the word – is not the disappearance but the liberation of the visible: space and time dropping away in order for the flame to arise where the tree and the wind become destiny.

I recognise that the paths leading to this liberation will in fact be quite different. Language is not the same as word. The most important word, since it is at every moment involved in acts that analyse and dissociate, can only share this alienation; and thus it must run the risk of exhausting itself in perhaps endless preliminary work. The clearest danger the poem faces is to let itself be mastered by an exterior vision that may contain a great deal of 'art'. But there is another, even more profound, danger. Recalling the phenomenon of 'bad' presence (*la mauvaise présence*), I believe I am justified in fearing a specious imagination that, while captured by appearances and terrified by the nothingness that dwells within them here, in proximity to us, is going to delight in giving them another life, a *raison d'être*, a plenitude 'somewhere else', continuously endowing them with qualities of exteriority that are all the more alluring for being somehow touched by enigma. Thus, chance, space, multiplicity surge into existence here as magical powers that keep appearance from dissolving into presence. The good, for which one always dreams, is assumed only to exist beyond this curtain of matter. And this dreaming, since it is passionate for being, will therefore appear 'poetic'. But compelled to imagine the interior with the exterior – whether through the idea of some illusory perfection of measurable form, or the idea of the distant lady of medieval imagination, or the idea of a Faustian depletion of the possible – this dreaming, deprived of the unique threshold of the absolute that any ordinary thing, truly loved for what it is, can be, is the evil inherent in poetic intuition: the burning, 'luciferian', highly pernicious form of its innermost and, perhaps, fatal flaw.

One should perhaps name this flaw 'symbolism', because of the naive confidence one finds in the 'hard lake'[2] of the visible, in the gold and pearls one encounters there, and in the beauty of appearances, this illusory marble. These played a large part in fin-de-siècle poetry; in its shimmering surface and its ever so narcissistic and sterile essence.

I will have to come back to reconsider, from the point of view of the French language, this aberration of poetic intuition. But for the moment I will content myself to show the change and significance that it introduces into our relationship with language. In the form of poetry that I consider the only true one, fundamental words – they vary of course from person to person – bear the promise of being. They preserve the idea of a voice, in which an order will be clarified that, as Mallarmé would say, 'will authenticate' our life. But in the same instant the inward character of this experience of order, of the sacred, dissipates any feeling by which this voice, imminent in the substance of words, can organise itself into forms of expression. The most intense sentences speak of our proximity to transparence and of something like its savour – the taste of fruit dissolving in the mouth – but nothing more. They evoke order, yet without revealing its structure. And this is because true experience, which only searches for the absolute through the threshold of finitude, is in any event only our necessarily relative consciousness, experienced to its innermost depths as such. On the contrary, he who, like Mallarmé, has dreamed of an 'elsewhere', where certain aspects of this world can at his pleasure be resignified in keeping with another order, in itself

---

2   An allusion to the frozen lake in Mallarmé's sonnet 'Le vierge, le vivace et le bel aujourd'hui'.

more 'true', more 'real', will opt for rare words or even rarer sensations and will seek the form of expression best able to make this secret order reveal itself to the mind. His prescience of the *logos* is that it might be absorbed into a speech that is at once utterable and definitive, and is stronger than the chance that governs this bleak earth. We know about these plans for the *Livres*.[3] They are only one of the ways to seek presence by means of appearance, which is, however, the salt that eats away at it.

But from the perspective to which I would now like to return, this may not be important. To summarise, then, I will say that what poetic consciousness has hoped for in words – in some words at least – is that unity, divinity shine in them, that there be true presence. And this should be enough to catch a glimpse of certain of the relations existing between poetry and languages, in particular, the French language.

It will seem perhaps obvious to remark that not all the words of a language lend themselves in the same degree to poetic intention.

Wind, stone, fire, Rimbaud's 'mazagran coffee',[4] Baudelaire's 'train carriages' and 'gas', or any other name for the most banal realities can become radiant with light – as long as, through these realities, we have experienced in some small way our attachment to the world. But from this very fact it follows that the call will be heard all the more intensely when words will speak more clearly of 'essences' – and by that I simply mean those things or creatures that seem to exist per se for the sake of our naive consciousness in ordinary life. Thus the word *brick* speaks less clearly to the spirit of poetry than *stone*, because the calling to mind of the manufacturing process prevails, in the reality of this word, over its own being as 'brick' and all the more so because it is the opposite of *stone* in verbal structure. It is

---

3   Mallarmé sought unsuccessfully for most of his career (especially after 1866) to make possible the creation of *Le Livre*, which he envisioned as the orphic explanation of the earth. The writing of the Book, transpiring without the active intervention of the author, who surrenders himself to the power and initiative of words, would occur only when the real world, the individuality and personality of the authorial self and the role of chance were reduced, until they ultimately disappeared. See below, 'The Unique and his Interlocutor', for YB's critique.

4   See Rimbaud's 'Après le déluge' in *Les Illuminations*. 'Le mazagran' is a coffee served in a glass and mixed with water or brandy.

perhaps only a nuance. But *silicate* has less appeal than *silex*. And the verbs *to grimace*, *to sneer* will lend themselves less well to the poetic process than *to cry* or *to laugh*, because those words take hold of the human act too clearly from the outside; they only describe it; their only signified is an *appearance*, which is difficult to maintain through the interiorisation that is poetry's task to accomplish.

Of course, numerous words that seem to express this appearance can be taken up again and redeemed through poetic interest: one will have learned that such words can name something that 'is' and that lies beyond external appearance. From the verb 'to grimace', Laforgue could have created one of the fundamental, *irreducible* components of his existence in an ambiguous world, between irony and desire. But finally, if I want to rescue the word *to sip*, for example, I will have to struggle long against the winds of exteriority, whereas *to drink*, since it expresses an essential act, will surely maintain its capacity for the absolute, even during life's most disillusioned moments. In spite of the caricatures presenting Rimbaud prostrate before the glass of absinthe – caricatures that he provoked and sought – Rimbaud *will drink*, he will not *sip*, because as a poet he dwells within the gravity of destiny. Poetry desires words that one can make part of one's destiny.

But if that is the case, then one of the points linking the intention of poetry to the fact of language becomes clearer. In this encounter one will be able to tell whether language abounds in words that express appearances or in words that name essences. From the comparative relationship of exteriority (which language on the whole imposes) to interiority (which, despite an habitual decline in use, language accepts), one could derive a sort of poetic coefficient that has steadily and significantly influenced the development of poetry.

And if there is some doubt about the import of this point of view, allow me – in order to show the gap it reveals between two kinds of poetry – to stop a moment and consider the English language.

What strikes me the most about English is its great aptitude for noting appearances, whether they be of human gestures or of things. A host of expressions allows one to grasp precisely and quickly the way in which the event – everything becomes event – proposes itself to immediate consciousness. And as a great number of words also express 'realities' that apparently differ from other realities only

by the slightest nuances – for us, this would be different appearances of the same essence – one quickly has the feeling that English
seeks to describe what consciousness perceives, while avoiding any
preconception about the final being of these referents. It may be
true that languages are structures, but this is hardly felt in English!
The words are there, so numerous, so unclassifiable, so difficult to
define, and so elusive in their usage. Often as related by their form
as they already are by their meaning, and without an obvious deri-
vation or an etymology that could be called meaningful, they press
against each other in opaque continuity, like the crystallisations of a
dazzlingly beautiful substance – in fact, like the flashes of intelligibility extracted from a real that one has deliberately approached by
empirical means. The power to photograph, so to speak, is boundless, but the capacity for hyperbole is less apparent; and yet, a few
great essences – the sea, the bird, the springtime, which are at the
universal heart of our relation to the world – are there to reveal the
radiance of an epiphany, which they alone keep pure.

So, it is very probably from this tension that English poetry has
drawn its remarkable energy. The consciousness of the One is alive
here; this is what Blake's poetry proves with a violence and a clarity
of purpose that have no equal in our own language. And it is Coleridge who has given us the most poetic definition of the Beautiful,
asserting that Beauty is that by which the many becomes the One,
even as it is perceived as the many.[5] From Marvell to Wordsworth to
Hopkins, this prescience is constant. Yeats can oppose it only with
rage, overwhelmed as he is by its irrefutable reality. But if poetic
intention is the same in English as everywhere else, then, in order
to develop, it will have to follow paths that, as one now perceives,
will be unique to it alone – even if, in doing so, it were to provoke
Voltaire's incomprehension. The contradictory metaphors, the
images that were sketched and then abandoned, the interrupted
verses, the obscurities, all this chaos by the 'erratic' author of *King
Lear*, what does it mean? Simply that Shakespeare wishes at one and
the same time to interiorise the real (as *The Tempest* will come so

---

5 'The Beautiful is that in which the many, still seen as many, becomes one'
(quoted in English by YB).

close to accomplishing) and to preserve the richness of a language that has so many words to express the appearance of things. As a result, the assertions of the exterior consciousness are simultaneously silhouetted on this stage and shown to be inadequate, like the figures of God in negative theologies. It was necessary for image to annul image so that the invisible could be felt.

Thus, in fact, Shakespeare's 'barbarity', constitutes his greatest seriousness. And, evidently, it is the same paradox, the same 180-degree turn of the compass, that permits John Donne as well, though he is very different from Shakespeare, to lift up the stone of appearance in order to revive the absolute. One sees the absolute – a scandal for Racine almost as much as for Rimbaud – clinging to the anecdote, this 'exterior' vision of human reality. But this is to show – such is the secret irony of Presence – that it is in our reaction to the inessential that our essence is revealed. It is also through existence, through being, that we must *by indirections find directions out*,[6] that is, by roundabout ways discover the way; and from this there are two consequences that ensue. On the one hand, English poetry enters the world of the relative, of meanings, of ordinary life, in a way almost unthinkable in the 'most sublime' French poetry.[7] Its gaze at the object, at least at first, fixes on the outside appearances that our literary tradition refuses to see; for the inattentive reader it is sometimes hardly different from the gaze of the moralist, the humorist. But, on the other hand, placing itself at this common point and pursuing its own ends, poetry in English will all the more forcefully leave the mark of its difference and truth. Who has ever doubted that an English poetry exists?

But I will end these imprudent speculations here. I have offered them only to put into clearer relief the very different characteristics of French poetry.

From the outset, what seems to me obvious in our language is that its words connote for the most part not empirically determined appearances but entities seeming to exist in themselves as the props on which to hang attributes that different kinds of knowledge will

---

6 These lines from *Hamlet* (II.i.66) are quoted in English by YB.
7 Laforgue and Corbière, so admired in England and America, do create this kind of poetry, but only by resigning themselves to being 'minor' poets. [YB]

have to determine and distinguish, unless – and, in fact, this is what we seem asked to believe – these attributes are already revealed in the idea of the thing. For example, we readily say 'A spade is a spade' ('un chat est un chat'), and this proverb makes us think that there is a well-defined quiddity (*en-soi*), an autonomy, a permanence about the spade in a reality which thereby, and without much difficulty, becomes intelligible.

It follows that what is true in English of only a relatively limited number of words becomes in our language a kind of rule that tends to identify reality and reason and suggests beyond a doubt that in its structure language itself accurately reflects the Intelligible. This fundamental reality of our way of looking at words I shall call the *principle of identity*. I believe that it is profoundly accepted by the naive consciousness, for which the fact that a spade is a spade (and remains so and cannot be anything else) always seems so easily verifiable that one could not deny it, except through dishonest intentions. There is a moral corollary to the principle of identity, and it is the imperative that Boileau states – 'I call a spade a spade' ('J'appelle un chat un chat') – but not without revealing almost in the same breath the dialectic of our language. From the primary evidence, two consequences follow and may appear to be in opposition. On the one hand, the intuition that there is an order to the world makes us want to preserve it and to be united with it: in French society we quickly and constantly rediscover the fundamental *word of identity*, barely transposed into oath, cry, or slogan. It is '*The king is dead, long live the king!*' of which, from the point of view of identity, a not very dissimilar variant is '*The Republic is one and indivisible*'. Like everything else that exists, institutions are perceived by the French as substances. But this sense of their being will by no means exclude a critical spirit and even a revolutionary project, since by its overall evidence the Intelligible can call into question those of its parts that have deteriorated.

Let us turn to our polemicists, and we will see that for them it is certainly not a question of empirically improving a state of society but rather of rediscovering the *true order* and of denouncing the lies that have succeeded in taking its place. Yes, this can only have been deception; intellectual error is not a convincing excuse, and we reject it. 'Dissolute monks, leprous bigots, snail-like hypocrites, dissemblers, false zealots, debauched priests, self-indulgent friars, and other such sects of men, who disguise themselves like maskers to deceive the world!' Rabelais exclaims in *Pantagruel*. The order of being or of nature is obvious: to him who wants it, it is there for the taking. It will be necessary, therefore, to denounce continuously the liar, the 'good apostle', the person interested in spreading confusion. And from the loyalty to essences represented by the 'I call a spade a spade' will come as much an implacable psychological lucidity as the political necessity of *calling Rollet* [sic] *a scoundrel*...[8] It is always the same equation, triumphantly solved. '*There is nothing like these Jesuits ...*', Pascal writes, here pursuing the devil in one of his avatars, a devil who must have been up to his old tricks again, since what could only be clearly evident has for a moment been hidden from view.

But what meaning does the principle of identity have for poetry?

To answer this question I believe that I have to examine it again in a more historical way: for, if since Boileau or Voltaire it is associated – and if I must, from the outset, in order to simplify, also associate it – with a rational, potentially materialist vision, it is clear as well that from the very beginnings of French it has had to fluctuate in its apprehension of essences and has had to change its metaphysics.

In these beginnings, for example, who could doubt that order was experienced as a religious reality – that is to say, as an interior and even mysterious relation between forms of experience? If French is so forcefully dominated by the thought of identity, it is because as a late language it developed out of linguistic and social givens – the Latin language, Rome, Christianity – that were already clearly impregnated by the idea of a world order, with distinct essences well-established in the great chain of being and thereby all the more sacred. The priest who taught the Credo also taught essences. The belief that bread is the body of Christ may be conveyed only insofar as bread is already

8   Rolet was a seventeenth-century lawyer and prosecutor who lived at the time of Nicolas Boileau, the poet and critic of French classicism. Rolet's dishonesty and lack of probity, for which he was severely punished in 1681, were so blatant that his name was used eponymously during his lifetime to designate any notorious thief or scoundrel, as in the expression, 'He's a Rolet'. He is remembered thanks to Boileau's celebrated, now proverbial, line: 'J'appelle un chat un chat, et Rolet un fripon' ('I call a spade a spade, and Rolet a scoundrel').

bread, which is to say, a clearly identified and stable reality and not some obscure and changing apparition indefinitely prone to taking on new forms. The fact remains, however, that this bread, if given its clear and distinct image, is experienced in God and under the sign of the One.

'*Clear is the night.*'[9] This order is magnificently radiant in the *Chanson de Roland* where everything is simple, shadowless and perfectly mysterious. We are not surprised to discover this very 'objective' decasyllabic line, whose four-initial feet firmly involve consciousness in the permanence of a knowledge, while the second part of the line, through its natural ternary rhythm, accepts human time in an act of sympathy but only in order to return it to the eternal. We are not even surprised that the poem is anonymous. When poetry becomes personal, it is because the individual, so far as he is concerned, has had to free himself from a collective forgetfulness of being, which is not initiated here. And we can observe finally that, by means of words opening themselves to presence, poetry as such, in contrast to other words, has as few distinctive signs as possible. The poetic line is undoubtedly necessary so that consciousness can find its level of greatest importance. But beyond this, the simplest reality appears in its familiar expression and countenance. And the greatest poems of the French Middle Ages will perhaps be the plainest songs, where it is clear that the sacred can be experienced with astonishing familiarity and playfulness. Order, here, is given by the nightingale, figure of origin; by the garden, figure of place; by lovers, figures of the eternally renewed human effort toward Presence; by the 'deceitful and jealous husband' (*le faulx-jaloux*), figure of the opposite of communion and sharing and expression of the possessive instinct by which the beloved is debased and transformed into an object. And all this is 'natural', but not because one has dreamed of 'nature' as later one will create it; rather, it is a question here of an experience of the whole which encompasses the sufferings and recognises the limits of the human being, as illuminated by Christianity and as enlightened also by words.

9 'Clere est la noit e la lune luisant' ('Clear is the night and the moon is shining') is the first line of *laisse* 184 of the Oxford text of *La Chanson de Roland*.

Never better than in these poems could one glimpse how a language, by constructing itself, can construct a world and, by becoming transparent, reconcile us to the universe. From the Strasbourg oaths to *green boughs* (*la ramée*), to the *nightingale* (*l'oursegnol*), to *may songs* (*reverdies*),[10] what has grown within the substance of words is light. And I would like to assert that for my part I have always found French words, as they have grown in the past, to be half transparent, so much does the structure of the consonants (inherited from Latin with its air of erudition) seem to bear the faded imprint of an absolute root, while the vowels, which become apparent through this structure, are either like the shadows of tangible existence or, as in the case of the mute 'e', like the light that comes from the One. Thus, it is in the deep spaces of the word, and not in some conventional form of expression, that the tension between finitude and presence can be resolved in a mysterious affinity. The word seems to suggest of itself the always virtual crystallisation of being. Poetry can be made, as Mallarmé will say, from words. And it is this potion of furtive reflections that Rimbaud also contemplates when – at the end of his most exhausting decantations – in the new 'songs' of a rediscovered communion he writes that eternity is the sea gone 'with the sun'.[11]

I will say, therefore, that in these first moments of poetry in the French language, identity is at its highest point of substantial saturation, and that poetry is, in its almost invisible difference, above all a work of simplicity, and seriousness. But in the original state of our language an ambiguity had already embedded itself, the consequences of which will be very grave. It is from Latin and its civilisation that French received the vocabulary and syntax of an order. But, for all that, it did not receive along with this propensity for essences the legacy of a great myth that might explicitly designate earthly things

---

10 In the lyric poetry of the Middle Ages the *reverdie* was a song in which the poet celebrated the return of spring, the singing of the nightingale, and the greening of nature.

11 In the first and last stanzas of the poem 'L'Eternité' of 1872 Rimbaud writes:

Elle est retrouvée.	It is rediscovered.
Quoi? – L'Eternité.	What? – Eternity.
C'est la mer allée	It is the sea gone
Avec le soleil.	With the sun.

as spiritual realities, since religion continued during all this time to express itself in the only existing language, Latin, and in terms of transcendence. So there ensued, first, the loss of a creative energy, since all theological or mystical minds had to abandon French; then, the absence of a belief that might lastingly ensure the sacred meaning of green leaves and the nightingale; and finally, even the condemnation, vigorously pursued, of the vestiges of paganism. All that could not but render extremely precarious, and in any event unprovable, this direct experience of the absolute in the French word.

And therein lies the ambiguity, and sometimes the drama, of our language. This principle of identity, which was so intensely experienced in medieval poetry as the axis of participation, as the certainty of being, has merit only, because of an intuition that nothing in our tradition or knowledge justifies or evokes. Thus, it can at any moment lose its substantial virtue, which, in truth, it did very early on for a great many people. France could become the country of simple and rigid certainty, of 'good sense'. The French gaze could find satisfaction in a certain, almost shadowless picture, in which objects are clearly visible in their logical relationships and are few in number (relatively speaking), because they were carefully drawn within lines rigidly enclosing them.

But – conversely and in a totally sudden way – this picture, or one of its variants, which I will soon describe, becomes for certain minds enigmatic and nearly terrifying.

This is a fact to which Rimbaud par excellence bears witness, and, recalling the emergence and evolution of the initial gaze at the salamander, I should like now to speak about the considerable importance of some of the notations of 'Alchimie du verbe' for the understanding of poetry, of French poetry, that is. In the 'Lettre du voyant' Rimbaud had already with the greatest violence condemned the entire poetic tradition, and it is quite evident that he blamed it for this simple, inharmonic clarity about which I spoke a moment ago. In 'Alchimie du verbe' he says, in this vein, that 'he found laughable the celebrated figures of modern painting and poetry' – but he adds, as if to counterbalance his assertion: 'I liked stupid paintings, the upper parts of doors, stage scenery, canvas backdrops for acrobats, signs, popular prints in colour, old-fashioned literature, church Latin, erotic books deficient in spelling, novels of our ancestors, fairytales, little books of childhood, old operas, foolish refrains, naive rhythms.' And further on, he writes: 'Poetic obsolescence played a considerable part in my alchemy of the Word.' And finally: 'The title of a light comedy caused tenors to rise up before me.' We can well imagine what these readings might have been. In the country of Favart, of Mme de Ségur – can I add, of Raymond Roussel? – all of us have encountered these stories and these descriptions, in which, because the power of intelligence presented is weak, the picture of the world is reduced to a few realities, in principle simple and obvious, but so schematic, so devoid of contrast, that a fascination is in effect revealed, and, I will even say, a strange hope comes into play. Now, here is how I understand this feeling of 'being on fire', this presentiment of meta-morphosis. These essences, so poorly developed and so reduced in number, are seemingly stripped of the usual system of reciprocal rela-tions – of what one could call the 'depth' of conceptual description. It follows that the things these essences show reappear there before us in this 'quiddity' (*en-soi*) that the concept appropriates, wears, conceals; and they reappear in the same way that, presently, in one's glimpse of the salamander one will vaguely sense the surging forth of a presence, either auspicious or inauspicious, along with 'the terror' that the proximity of the sacred awakens in consciousness. In short, the mediocre text or the weak image has played the same role as the object that is *seen* suddenly, either before its meaning hides it from view or as soon as this meaning, once disintegrated, abandons it. And for an adolescent, lost here or there in the desert of the concept, all of external identity at its most empty is abruptly transformed. As for me, I felt during my childhood 'the terror' of those gardens that are aptly called 'French': a clarity possessed of frightening internal forces. And now I understand quite well that it was above all an event of language that transpired there. Yes, it is in a single stroke, invisibly, sometimes at the moment a simple word or a name is uttered, that absolute identity surpasses conceptual identity – that the spirit that leads toward poetry begins anew.

Moreover, it would be worthwhile for the historian to study it again from this point of view, replacing the usual descriptions of the chains of influence or of the supposed meaning of themes with an examination of the tensions that oppose or render dialectical the intuition of presence and the necessities of the concept. Thus, the same Rimbaud who, in his 'delirium', which is simply the rejection of conceptual identity, wanted to see a mosque in the place of a factory, a drawing room at the bottom of a lake – that is to say, the other through the same – ends up in the poem 'Bruxelles' – where in a single stroke he comes close to achieving immediacy – by declaring apropos of reality that 'It is too beautiful!' which one must take to mean that 'It is too present!' Poetic modernity, in every period has its origin in this return that frees the object from hackneyed rhetoric. It is true that poetry, moves in advance of action,[12] since it is the power by which the concept that governs action is depleted and renewed.

But it is, above all, in itself that poetry born of 'terror', French poetry, is an act, and this is how I understand it. First of all, because of the very fact that in its absolute gaze poetry initiates the appearance of presence; it does not have to demonstrate it, to express it through myths – it does not even have time for this – it is compelled only to live it. And immediately, therefore, it is the effort by which, in the midst of 'things-as-nullities', poetry will attempt to dwell in the light of being and thus assimilate it to the realities of a destiny. I believe that the poetry of a language of essences, like French, has therefore, as its most urgent task the constituting or the rediscovery of the profound, infraconceptual order at the heart of which the poet can live his being as presence, having verified analogies, having undone impenetrable appearances, having reopened the path that leads inward. This is a matter of discontinuous, silent experiences, but from them will emanate the energy that enables a few important, revitalised words to exist together and to open themselves to endless rays of light. And the true subject of the poem is a life that recovers its form – a finitude that becomes limitless. As far as meaning is concerned, one is well aware of its ambiguities, considering the importance of this enterprise. Sometimes, it is true, the author of a poem has *spoken* a sensation, has formulated an idea. And one could discern there a will either to describe what exists or to express what one is. But, in fact, of what is it a question here? Of evoking in a

12   In 'La Lettre du voyant' Rimbaud writes, 'Poetry will no longer give rhythm to action; it will be in advance.'

savour the deeper savour of the unity one desires. Of summoning in the palpable fruit the supreme fruit. Of loving; or, again, of refusing – as in an act of purification – to serve the interests of nothingness. Poetry is an oath that both differentiates and confirms itself in the textures of spoken things. It is that which *brings together*, like the mason who selects his stones – and who can certainly comment on them, or even speak about them, apparently at random, but against the background of the silence where he already sees the emergence of the future threshold.

And as the mason demarcates the place of life, at first abstract, so the poet, reenacting the ancient beginnings of the word – of the word as *founding act* – changes Presence in building his poem, so as to rediscover reason, that site in the Universe of the most humble realities. It is frequently said that English poetry 'begins with a flea and ends in God'. I would say that French poetry moves in the opposite direction and begins 'in God', whenever possible, only to end up by loving the most inconsequential thing.

But I would not want to close without anticipating some objections.

I imagine, first, that the reader, if he has followed me up until now, must be surprised by a definition of poetry where not much place seems to be given to the subject with which I began: the aversions and impatiences of Rimbaud and Baudelaire that so many other poets can identify with, because of the suffering, and sometimes the doubt or the despair. What does this reconciliation with the real or this 'poetically inhabited' earth have to do with Vigny's scorn, Verlaine's renunciations, Antonin Artaud's cries of horror? When Baudelaire, stricken with aphasia, is brought back to Paris and sees Asselineau, who had come to meet him at the train station, he lets out a long, shrill laugh; Asselineau is frozen with terror. Does one find in that, and in the *cré nom* of the final months,[13] the plenitudinous silence

13 On July 2, 1866, after two-and-a-half years of self-imposed exile in Belgium, Baudelaire returned to Paris. Since the previous spring a series of strokes had completely robbed him of the power of speech, except for two words, *sacré nom* (an oath not unlike 'goddamn it' in English), frequently abbreviated and pronounced as *cré nom*. Until his death in August 1867, these were to be the only words Baudelaire spoke.

to which the greatest perhaps of our poets would certainly have been entitled, according to my definition? And despite everything, if the French language, in its ever so formidable essentialism, holds the key to the idea of what is sacred and ordered, how is it that our country gives the world its most celebrated *poètes maudits*?

I fear, in fact, not having sufficiently emphasised – and not only in what has preceded (which can be easily corrected) but at other times as well – that in this movement toward unity there is, alas, nothing idyllic, nothing determined, nothing that could even imagine being freed from a false life, nothing that could put its faith in dreams. To interiorise the real does not mean bypassing what prevents us from living; rather, we must reduce or transmute it. And often fire does not catch in such intractable matter, especially considering that the alienation of the other is intimately involved with ours, and it will therefore be necessary – an undoubtedly impossible task – to clarify both at one fell swoop. Poetry, or the remission it brings, is not a form of repose. What value would poetry have, for example, without union or justice? And does it not raise questions about the enigma of evil, which its own intuition cannot answer? This can be seen in Rimbaud: 'I want freedom in salvation', he writes. We must take this to mean: the right to uphold my values, which are equality and justice, in the very experience of Presence. And this contradiction is not readily forgotten – as Hugo's work reveals – in a language where the universal can show that it is as much the universality of right as that of being. French has no words for evil: nothing except abstract expressions that already rationalise it. Yet, the existence of evil will for that reason alone be all the more harshly felt. It can prevent the French from finding happiness.

In truth, the word that seems to me to lend itself best to defining our poetry, in its sudden depth, in its hindered momentum, is *contre-jour*. For the light I am talking about will be discovered in the darkest poetry, in images of 'vibrant violins', of 'child days'. Yet, the world of dissociation and evil remains present to cast a shadow; and so it is in this *clair-obscur* that wanderings and fits of anger occur – an order simultaneously building and demolishing itself in the often proclaimed persistence of hope. 'Can one light up a black and muddy sky?' Baudelaire asks, while Rimbaud writes: 'And at dawn, with a burning patience we will enter the shining cities.' The metaphor of the *spiritual dawn* is common among French poets. It aptly corresponds to this gleam, this *lustre* of language. And if it rarely has the chance to transform itself into the truth of noontide, except perhaps through dream – or maybe through deceptive illusion – it is sometimes possible for it to be recognised in that most ardent *contre-jour*, the red light of evening.

The other remark I will make will relate to what I had earlier called the flaw inherent in poetry. Perhaps in reading the preceding pages, one will think that I was not sufficiently concerned about it or that I consider it absent from French poetry. That is not the case, and I will even say that, to my way of thinking, this 'flaw' is more common in our language than in many others. This is because, if in the words we use there is this virtuality of presence, this great hope, it will therefore follow that we will speak under this sign, as if intoxicated, without having critically examined, as we should, our experience of things. To name the tree too easily is to risk remaining captive of a weak image of the tree, or in any case of an abstract one, which in the space of the absolute could only grow from one of the inadvertently remembered appearances of the object. And thus, Presence is no longer envisioned except as a fabulous unfolding of this appearance, as a profusion of marble. No longer anything but a décor, from which the *I* also is absent, it is soon nothing more than a convention and a refashioning of a rhetoric. This is what Romeo unwittingly reveals when he thinks he is in love with the 'beautiful' Rosalind, the symbol of appearance, of what one has imagined and not experienced, and of the object that disappears, therefore, beneath the myth. Fortunately, he has Mercutio close by – Mercutio, that incarnation of the English language – to remind him of the obligations of 'triviality'.

French poetry has no Mercutio. In our language it falls to the poet alone to regain self-control in this beauty of words where so often he has placed the ghost of things. And our poetry also has, as a dimension of its history and diversity, moments of deviation and return. Some – the moments of recovery – are found in Baudelaire's 'Le Cygne', in Rimbaud's 'L'Eternité'. The others, sustained by pride, are found in Racine's tragedy, in Mallarmé's 'pure idea'. Between the *exterior* identity of good sense and the *interior* identity of presence, there was for a long time – from, let's say, the poets of the Pléiade to Paul Valéry – this proud and very alluring appearance of the flaw: the claim of the Idea to be its own proof and the illusory materiality of the dream's figure.

Translated by Richard Stamelman

'IMAGE AND PRESENCE'[1]

Monsieur l'administrateur, My dear colleagues, As I appear before you now, let my first words be to tell you how much I appreciate your confidence, and how grateful I am for it, for myself personally but also and especially for the great cause which you have called on me to represent. I extend this gratitude, entirely, to each of you, since I have already had occasion to notice that, in spite of the extreme diversity of your research, each of you takes an interest in poetry.

And since through your various researches you all manifest an exigency and a rigour – those which characterise science in its concern for method, in its passion for truth – allow me to tell you as well, and this is my second wish, that I take on the task that you have defined with the keenest sense of a new responsibility which is both distinct from and related to my preoccupation with poetry. There is a point, in fact, about which I no longer have the slightest doubt and which I feel it necessary to stress at the outset. Although I place above all the kind of thought characteristic of the great poems, which strives to base itself on nothing if not on the purity of desire and the fever of hope, I know that our questioning of it is fruitful, that our teaching about it has meaning, only when they ripen in the midst of the facts which the historian has come to recognise, and when they are formulated with words in which are heard, in echoes more or less distant, all that has been acquired by what we call the sciences of man. The impatience of intuition, but close beside it the preciseness of careful study – these are the 'loyal adversaries' which must be reconciled if the statements of an epoch are not to fall as quickly as dying embers go out; and I am the more convinced that they are in fact reconcilable, in the case of poetry, and that it is therefore worth the trouble to attempt this exalting synthesis, as I know of

1   Yves Bonnefoy made his inaugural address to the Collège de France in December 1981. A slightly revised version of the address was published as *La Présence et l'image: Leçon inaugurale de la Chaíre d'Etudes comparées de la fonction poétique au Collège de France, 1981* (Paris: Mercure de France, 1983). Collected in *Lieux et Destins de l'Image: Un cours de poétique au Collège de France (1981– 1993)*. Paris: Coll. La Librairie du XXe siècle, Editions du Seuil, 1999.

several examples of these achievements in this very assembly where, to my joy, are active some of the great scholars who encouraged me to think in this way.[2]

But is it enough to aspire to this double postulation to guarantee that one will be capable of it? And is it not imprudent to hand over to someone who writes poetry – and even if he knows the value of scientific reflection – the problem of analysing the very act he is in the process of performing? Many critics claim, as you know, that the author knows less about what he is doing than his writing does; that writing possesses a finality and follows paths which the writer as he writes cannot but misunderstand: and so, if he happens to formulate some statement about poetry, this evaluation should only be considered at best as another dimension of his own creative work, as a further manifestation of the forces which are brought to bear upon it – in short, as one of the byroads of a creativity whose totality is best grasped by those standing on the far shore, looking from a distance. This is a fact: the observations of the author are somewhat casually collected in the laboratory where over the last few years particles of written material have been analysed, particles whose minuteness rivals the fragments of matter explored by the physicist or the biologist; and perhaps, indeed, it is simply good method that the writer of this new era ask himself, on occasions such as this one, if it would not be more rigorous to devote himself to creative passivity rather than to judgments which might prove illusory.

My dear colleagues, I am not forgetting that it was here in this room, not fifty years ago, that an idea was initiated, and with what authority – which signs of personal sacrifice made only more intense – the idea that poetry in its greatest specificity does not allow for self-knowledge, and that one can therefore only deal with it through a discarding of beliefs, where what the author takes seriously, if not sometimes tragically – let us say his feelings, his values – is reduced,

---

2   André Chastel: One of you was my guide through the world of Renaissance studies, and I owe to him irreplaceable moments of growth as well as of discovery. And as for Georges Blin, who proposed the project of this Chair, is it necessary to recall, since all of you know his great books, the first of which virtually reinvented Baudelaire, what a model of clear-sightedness but also of scrupulousness he offers to all who are attentive to poetry? [YB]

under the watchful eye of an algebraic and almost ironical witness, to the level of a simple variable in the equation of the mind. This was not the way the first poets who frequented the future Collège de France thought; and when the 'King's Lecturers'[3] gave new life to the great poems of the ancient world before these enraptured listeners, Ronsard and Du Bellay had no doubt that to be, if only for a moment, the *Vates*, the poet blessed with enthusiasm, was to attain to truth. But when Paul Valéry was called to the first Chair in Poetics at this college, he had already decided that the content of the poem – which had been regarded, doubtless with too much facility, as a veridical cry of suffering or as a premonition of the secrets of being – is in fact only another element in a play of forms and has value only insofar as it is discarded, forgotten on behalf of a more serious study, of the laws of writing. A development had begun, summed up by the fact that sometimes Roland Barthes was among the young people who came to hear Valéry – Barthes who did so much thereafter to deconstruct the illusions of self-possession and of self-knowledge which beguile writers when they work; and who, consequently, carried further than anyone else the formalist exploration of writing, but not without turning away for many years – and this was no accident – from the direct study of poets. It is true that a contrary evolution began little by little to make itself felt in this lucid consciousness – you were yourselves witness to it as colleagues and friends of Barthes. After having wanted only to describe the functioning of language, of which literature would merely have been a partially unconscious intensification, he came to the conclusion – through an experience of grief which involved his whole being, which was an intuition as much as an act of reason – that all language is as such an order, that every order is an oppression, that every act of

---

3 The 'King's Lecturers' or 'Lecteurs royaux' was the name given formerly to the professors of the Collège de France because, in the beginning, all read lectures written out in advance. Originally called the Collège du Roi, the Collège de France was founded by François I as an academic body independent of the Sorbonne, whose power the king wished to uproot. In the beginning, there were two *lecteurs* appointed by the king, one for Greek and one for Hebrew. In 1534, a Chair of Latin Eloquence was created, and the name of the body was changed to Collège des Trois Langues. Ronsard and Du Bellay, the most famous poets of the so-called Pléiade, were friends and followers of the *lecteurs*.

speech, be it even of scientific truths, is consequently an act of power, and that therefore to recover our freedom, to place ourselves 'beyond power', we must cheat with words, make light of them while playing with them, and that this identifies the free act – and therefore true lucidity, this time apprehended as an act – with the practices of the writer who knows how to evade every formula. It was a writer who took the floor here in 1977, a writer filled with the sense that literature is a consciousness; and his last book, *La Chambre claire*, would soon show – and this touches me under the present circumstances – that he was drawing close to poetry.

The question of the author's right to claim to know some sort of truth about his own work remains, nevertheless, a valid one; for some it is even an issue already settled in the negative; and it is this basic controversy, this dispute that is sometimes violent and always secretly anguished, which I feel I must examine first of all, raising questions in this first lecture about the categories involved, which should perhaps be modified or made more complete if we want a more intimate understanding of poems. In the calculations today which attempt to situate exactly the significance of poetry, it may be that one component has not been taken into account. In the doubts certain poets themselves feel about their capacity to know, it may be that we should see nothing more than a sudden moment of vertigo, brought about by the perception of the abyss which is writing, but which a more courageous decisiveness could dispel. And is not doubt itself, in this situation as in so many others, the area in which what is obvious – although veiled for a moment – can take shape again in still more striking fashion? From which it follows that doubt, in this deep sense, was also a necessary moment in the history of poetry, where it functions as a test, where it offers us a chance. I am going to try to put these ideas together and to find my way through them.

★

Ladies and gentlemen, My friends, One of the great contributions of our era has been the importance placed on what is called the activity of the signifier, and, correlatively, the denunciation of certain illusory aspects of our consciousness of ourselves. Where the critic or the philosopher once thought to find in the work of literature or in common speech the unequivocal and direct expression of a subject to whom fidelity to the truth would have been enough to feel present to other presences, and by degrees through these fundamental experiences the master of the world's meaning or even a divine emanation, we have learned to better perceive a maze without beginning or end of transitory representations, of fictions without any authority, where what seems to remain most worthy of being called real is this mass of words, ceaselessly changing their meaning and often their form, a mass which rolls down through the ages like a huge river across languages and cultures. Where once spoke what were called geniuses – because they were thought to have gone straight toward a higher truth – galaxies called the text have begun to glitter, more complex and resonant spaces than what not long ago was found formulated in them, but where one searches in vain among the constellations and the shadows for the being who nonetheless, in the boundless abyss of the white page, had brought together or thrown out these signs. A 'hollow nothingness', said Mallarmé, and which is the more an enigma as it is sometimes a husk indeed.

And consciousness has seemed, in this perspective, to have a new task to assume. Rather than evaluating in the discourse of the person speaking a statement of truth, based upon facts about the world which will be reputed to be knowable, one should analyse the way in which verbal states – signifiers briefly enclosing unreal signifieds – produce themselves one from another, using rather than expressing the universe. It is here that one encounters at their origin, and with a weight of proof it would be idle to deny, the impressive programs of recent research: first, that archaeology of cultural events which seeks to unearth from our age-old neglect the interlacing strata of the concepts of a time such as they really were, that is to say, other – and yet more active, more determinant of practical behaviours than the carefully meditated notions of philosophy and science; and, second, a completely renewed method of analysing literary creation. For there is just as much concern as ever with literature, in the new thinking, since it is in the writer's work that the life of words, constrained if not even denied in ordinary practice, achieves, with the help of dream, a freedom which seems to be the avant-garde of the world. Often without the author's awareness, but clear to the critic's scrutiny, the constant flow of change which takes place in the relationship between meanings and words pushes forward its meanderings throughout the text; one might say that it opens there onto the unknown, to such a degree that the witness to this burgeoning of anagrams, to this unfolding of polysemies – which are so many shatterings, so many centers of fleeting iridescence in that mirror where once one followed the eyes of the artist – comes to ask of avant-garde authors to finish smashing this reflecting water where Chateaubriand or Baudelaire, and Rembrandt as well as Van Gogh, sought with an anguish now considered outdated either the refinement of their attitudes or the devastations of their torment. Criticism just renewed the pact it makes every generation with the obscure need to create. But the old idea of the creative act, which had drawn so close to that of a sovereign subjectivity, is only the more severely denied thereby.

And yet, if it is easy enough to verify, in the quiet of a study, that, in the ruins of the cogito, nothing remains but thousands of levels of the fleeting clouds of this language of which, for our passing moment, we are only a slight ruffling of the structures, a mere crinkle which we cannot pretend to entirely understand, it is nonetheless true that when we speak we say 'I', and we say it in the urgency of our days and in the midst of a condition and of a place which remain, whatever may be their false pretenses or their groundlessness, both a reality and an absolute. We say 'I', and thanks first of all to this word, we give direction to our existence, and sometimes to that of others; we decide upon values; it even happens, strangely, that beings die for the latter through what seems to be a free choice, while others, and we know what a misfortune it is, others who are many in our time, suffer at having lost a clear and coherent relationship with something in them they might call their own being and prefer from then on, in so many instances, to simply let themselves die. This capacity to acknowledge and to accept oneself, through the agency of a few values which may be shared with others, would have been a simple fiction – we can accept this last word – but this is also what would have given to those lives a reason for lasting and to the world around them a meaning, with a little warmth. And I notice moreover that this era, which has disqualified all inner experience, is also the period which, for the first time in history, turns with nostalgia toward the arts and the poetry of those times when the relationship of individuals and an asserted meaning of life or the universe was the unique concern of collective thought. Unless preference is given, beneath the withered leaves of 'cities without evenings',[4] to the proliferation of erratic acts whose violence seems gratuitous but in fact reveals in the desperate incendiary the ever-human desire to be a responsible subject and thus to gain access to freedom. If the deconstruction of the old ontological ambitions seems, on a certain level, an imperative of consciousness, their weakening, in any case in concrete situations, is accompanied by a risk of decomposition and death for society as a whole. And this seems to me, in the final analysis, much more the aggravation of a problem than a gain made in the direction of the truth. At best, we have become conscious of the divided character of our being-in-the-world, but we now run the risk of falling prey to its catastrophic consequences through forgetfulness of the action which once opposed this division. And while we must continue to study how the signifier ceaselessly fluctuates within the signs, it seems to me that we must also search for the way in which this élan that we are can affirm itself, in spite of being adrift in words, as an origin. What must one do, in other words, so that there still may be some sense in saying 'I'?

What must one do? Well, in any case, ask questions again about poetry, which we left a moment ago in that position of tutelage where the philosophy of language, the moment it is a question of veracity, would like to keep it today.

Ask questions about poetry, which in my destiny furthermore is only the most natural reaction, since it is in the experience of poetry over the course of the years that the contradictions and the misgivings I have just tried to indicate have become clear to me, as well as the persistence of a certain hope, and of the very idea of hope. In fact, poets themselves were the first to have sensed what criticism has stressed recently concerning the role of the signifier in writing and concerning the part played by the unconscious in their decisions, and, on the threshold of our modernity, which began as a breakdown of the Romantics' absolute idea of the self, they had already made this

---

4 See Mallarmé's 'Le Tombeau de Charles Baudelaire': 'Quel feuillage séché dans les cités sans soir.'

role their principal preoccupation. Rimbaud was not unaware of the autonomy of the signifier when he was writing his sonnet 'Voyelles', nor was Mallarmé when he put together his 'Sonnet en yx'. And this excess in words over meaning is precisely what attracted me in my own case, when I came to poetry, in the snares of surrealist writing. What a call, as if from an unknown heaven, in these clusters of lawless tropes! What energy, it seemed, in this unpredictable bubbling up from the depths of language! But once the initial fascination was over, I took no joy in these words which I was told were free. I had before my eyes another kind of evidence, nourished by other poets, the evidence of running water, of a fire burning peacefully in our daily existence, and of time and chance of which these realities are made, and it seemed to me fairly, soon that the transgressions of automatic writing were less the desired surreality, existing beyond the too superficial realisms of controlled thought whose signifieds remain fixed, than a reluctance to raise the question of the self, whose richest potentiality is perhaps in the life that one takes on day after day, without illusions, in the midst of what is simple. What are all the subtleties of language, after all, even turned upside down in a thousand different ways, next to the perception one can have, directly, mysteriously, of the movement of the leaves against the sky, or of the noise fruit makes when it falls into the grass? And always throughout this whole time I kept in mind, as an encouragement and even as a proof, the moment when the young reader opens passionately a great book and finds words, of course, but also things and people, and the horizon, and the sky: in short, a whole world given all at once to his thirst. Ah, this reader does not read, be it even in Mallarmé, as the theoretician of poetry or as the semiologist asks him to read! If he understands everything in the polysemies through comprehensive intuition, through the sympathy that one unconscious can have for another, it is in the great burst of flame which delivers the mind – as formerly the negative theologies rid themselves of symbols, and as, when one raises one's eyes at Tournus, one sees unity spring forth from what is elsewhere only space. Words are there for him, of course; he can feel the vibrations of the signifiers which lead him toward other words in the labyrinths of the signifier, but he knows that there is a signified amongst them, a signified which depends on no one of them in particular and on all of them at once, which is intensity as such. The reader of poetry does not analyse – he pledges to the author, his brother, that he too will remain in intensity. And soon he closes up his book, anxious to go and live out the promise. He has rediscovered a hope. And this is what gives us the right to think that one should not give up hope in poetry.

And yet it is not that I am trying to deny the capacity for self-deception, for spreading unreality which exists in the work of the greatest poets; and, come to this point, I even feel the need to denounce this vanity myself, convinced as I am that true power is found only where weakness also lies, and that power can only grow and have merit if it has first of all recognised this weakness through careful study.

This study of the illusory in works of poetry seems to me all the more necessary, furthermore, in that recent criticism has rather neglected it, given as it is to an emphasis on plurality in writing. Fascinated by what takes place on the level of the signifier, recent criticism fixes on what violates, in the writer's text, some previous or more ordinary state of common speech; it therefore seeks out the work of art in its deviation, or in its becoming, which thus makes of creation a movement, a dynamics, easily connected with the flow of intertextuality or the play of *différence* – and it forgets to examine the inscription of himself that the author tries to establish in the midst of the verbal turbulence. Now even if this elaboration of a definite meaning is only a fabric of illusions, it nonetheless has its own laws, the nature of which it may be important to understand. What are these laws? Above all, that writing is enclosure. A desire is in us, as old as earliest infancy, that seeks out in every circumstance what might replace the good which has been missing almost since the beginning; and as it is granted to us, through the ambiguous blessing of words, to keep in mind only a single aspect of things, the author, freer in this than the ordinary man or woman, since he works under the shelter of his white page, is going to select only those aspects which his desire can accept and use, and build with them and only with them the stage where his dream can act itself out. Much will therefore be lost from beings and objects evoked in this manner, and in particular their own inner relationship with themselves, their very act of being, this right they have to be here, in spite of the dreamer and in conflict with his idea of the world, albeit in agreement with the very necessity he denies. Let us call this region beyond our representations

– this ever-censored part-*finitude*, since if we knew how to listen to it, it would assign to us our limits. A world has been destroyed – abolished, Mallarmé would say – the one in which we would be mortal; and, in return, what has taken shape in the poem is a world as well, of course, often a coherent world and, in appearance at least, complete. From this point of view the literary work is a tongue, a sort of personal language, which institutes, which maintains, which professes an autonomous reality felt as substantial, considered as sufficient; and this gravitation which retains this or that thing, this or that value, but shuts out this or that other is an iron law – let there be no doubt about it – under the semblance of a golden age. For one is sometimes led to think, in the face of certain superabundances, that the writer is free to whimsically change his imaginary world, as the scientist might methodically change his hypothesis; but beneath the sea foam which does in fact move about along the shores cut out from this ocean, how still the deep waters lie! There is something immutable about the unconscious; desire only ripens slowly or never at all. Hemmed in by the words he does not understand, by experiences whose very existence he does not suspect, the writer, and this is the element of chance which so distressed Mallarmé, can only repeat in writing that strictly limited particularity which characterises any given existence.

Who was talking then about breaking the mirror? Perhaps one can only set down one's pen, or throw the inkwell at the looking glass. But those who truly desire this are rare, let us say now, because – and here is the second law of literary creation – this world which cuts itself off from the world seems to the person who creates it not only more satisfying than the first but also more real. And for us, as readers, it often seems so as well. Born from the impatience of a youthful mind which was repelled by artificial ways of living, by values which certainly are stifling, writing allows the author to draw out from his memory of beings those features which he thought that society had dismissed. And thus, from these refashioned beings, comes to him the voice – until then never heard by him – of an ardour, a feeling which he can believe is truer; and the earth around these imaginary encounters begins to seem a place for life – where the mountain or the sea multiply those glitterings and those flowers which, in our ordinary world, seem yet devoid of any reason for being. As for finitude, which I said was denied in and by writing, how often it is that one sees, on the contrary, in this glow of words that death is imagined – one might even say loved – as the endpoint of a plenitude! In truth, there is nothing frightening, nothing negative that one does not feel capable of accepting in the magic of the sentence, since everything takes on a new radiance there, even though it be tragic; and especially those experiences of place, of time, of the presence of others which I consider effaced by the act of writing – but which are also missing, it is true, in everyday existence, which is already devastated by so much even more impoverished writing – they seem to gather to a fullness in the sentence, they seem to reveal themselves in their unrecognised value. This impression of a reality at last fully incarnate, which comes to us, paradoxically, through words which have turned away from incarnation, I shall call *image*. Images, world-images – in the sense it seems to me that Baudelaire meant when he wrote, at the most tormented moment of his poetic intuition: 'The cult of images, my great, my unique, my primitive passion.' Images, the radiance which is missing in the grayness of our days, but which is allowed for by language when the unquenchable thirst of dream closes it back upon itself, when it kneads it like a mother's breast.

But what a price for this radiance, and how quickly must the debt be paid! What has been kept in the literary work is what suits desire, it is what leaves it time to drink; it is therefore an infinite, dreamt of within the very limits of things, of situations, or of beings – and it is what will be missing when we wake into real life, which has other laws. Where the writer reigns supreme, he does not live; he therefore cannot reflect upon his true condition; and where, on the other hand, he is obliged to live, he finds himself ill-equipped for this unfamiliar task. How many unhealthy dualisms, between an undervalued 'here' and an 'over there' reputed as richness itself, how many unfeasible gnoses, how many senseless injunctions have been poured out in this way by the melancholy genius of the Image from the very first days of our Western world, which reinvented madness if not love![5] And what an instrument these dreams are for always nihilistic ideologies, for the hunger for power, which will make of them their flags.

---

5   See Rimbaud, 'Délires I – Vierge folle / L'Époux infernal', from *Une Saison en enfer:* 'L'amour est à réinventer, on le sait.'

The Image is certainly a lie, however sincere the maker of the image. Was this the intensity with which I credited the young reader? In any case, it is in the light of this ambiguity that one best understands that it really was time for textual criticism to come along to analyse and even to undermine the ever-truncated perspectives which pile up in the literary use of speech.

Except that there truly is more than the elaboration of these false pretenses in certain writings which I would now like to call to your attention as more specifically *poetic*. And I shall concentrate, in particular, on some seemingly secondary aspects of the fiction in literary works. Every poem, it should first of all be noted, harbours in its depths a story, a fiction, however uncomplicated it might sometimes be: for the personal language which structures its universe can only crystallise in the form of objects or beings which maintain significant relationships with one another and in which is manifest the very law which presided over the act of creation. Now this fiction should, since it is the quintessence of a dream, express the bliss of that dream, and indeed it does so in its sometimes surprising way: for what one might too quickly take for an expression of anguish or a declaration of suffering is often only an exterior, cruelly manipulated by desire, which knows how to use it for its own pleasure – even *Werther* is an Arcadia. But there are other wrenchings in poetic fiction than these superficial misfortunes. It happens that one notices, this time in the very heart of desire, certain hesitations, twinges of remorse – one feels that fear is at work there, that some vertigo is crippling, that an aspiration which aims higher, much higher, than the paltry scene erected is upsetting things; and as a reflection of this uneasiness in the story of which I am speaking, there is therefore some situation, some hidden dimension which cuts back through it and repudiates it.

A great deal of attention has been given recently to the 'mise en abyme' in which, at some focal point of the fiction, the structure of the entire work is reflected. One should also examine the counter-fiction, the *subplot* by means of which, in many cases, the work of abolition proposed by the main action is secretly denounced. What is Hamlet doing up there, stage front, lost in his dreams, lost in the book of himself, if not denying, as Mallarmé says, denying with only a glance, the right of others to exist? – Mallarmé who adds: 'He kills indiscriminately, or at least people die.' People die wherever he passes because he is the dream which only keeps symbolisations and shadows upon its stage. But at the other end of the action, here is Hamlet on the edge of a grave, his project and even his sanity stricken, crying out, with a sorrow whose expression is incoherent, that he loved Ophelia, that he has betrayed her – in a way which remains unclear to him – and that he himself in his consciousness of himself, can now only see a series of endless contradictions. Holes thus appear in the intelligibility which subtends the worlds of speech, blackness in the clear skies of the image, even a complete tearing to shreds, no longer just of the hero in whom the poet is often reflected but of the very stage which had been erected by his language, as in *Phèdre* – while words, sounds, rhythms, all the elements of prosody which one had seen working toward the unity of the poem reveal that they can just as easily attach themselves, in the emergence of forms, to what undermines their equilibrium and create a dissonance where one had believed that one was hearing a harmony.

Now who is expressing himself in this way, who can envisage this failure in the midst of the world dreamt of by the literary work, if not someone who, though moved by this dream, yet refuses to consent to its potential for lying? In writing, which seems totally given over to the joys of its painted rooms, isn't there a captive who is shaking the door? All the more so in that this same author one saw devoting himself, in a first sketch of his book, to the logic of writing is also the person who, one day, has called his book finished, has detached himself from it and criticised it with regard to himself, and begins another where sometimes he attains even greater self-aware-ness. There are not only books, there are literary destinies in which each work marks a stage – which would seem to indicate that there exists an entirely different kind of desire, the desire, let us say, to free oneself from desire, the desire to grow with respect to oneself. And indeed one notices that as the evidence of the autonomy of language increases in our modernity, this maturation of the writer, who calls his writing into question, also becomes more frequent, more vehement – and more listened to as well, more passionately appreciated, as though it were for us, on the threshold of a redoubt-able future, the only act with merit. Think of Baudelaire, who goes from his poems on the Ideal, and on Spleen, to his *Tableaux parisiens*, his eyes as if opened; of Rimbaud who burns up so many stages, though each is fabulous, before disavowing the seer or the angel he had dreamt of being; and think of Yeats, of Artaud, of Jouve, and others of our time whose scruples, whose long silences sometimes are our rallying point, our strength. In the very heart of writing, there is a questioning of writing. In the midst of this absence, something like a voice which persists.

What is the meaning of this persistence? At the very least that poets carry within themselves another idea of what has importance, or of what is, than the idea which emerges today from the investigations of the semiologist. In the very place where for the latter the writer's struggle with words reveals nothing but transitory structurations, shadows where the person speaking has nothing but a shadow to inscribe, there precisely the poets find something very different, since we see that they can sacrifice what they had taken for a more intense form of reality – and this in order to bear witness to an existence beyond, to a being, to a plenitude they don't even know how to name. And one might add to this first paradox that this painful discovery, which cuts into the fabric of sentences, which ravages whole sequences of images – such is the prince of the *Illuminations*, who sets fire to his palace – is not in the least a simple remorsefulness born from the sense of wrongdoing, but a waiting which is feverous, one would say the rising of a yet unknown sort of joy. Poetry is not the account of a world, however magnificent may be the forms which it alone is able to unfold; one would say rather that it knows that these representations of a world are only a veil which hides the true reality. But it is not this remanence of the old ontological ambitions which will render this testimony more acceptable to the new devotees of language. They will simply tell us that so obstinate an assertion is in itself only one more consequence of the suggestion of presence I pointed out a moment ago in what I call the Image. Not the glimpse at last of reality, but further flight into still more delusion.

And yet, my friends, let us imagine that this human community in which we observe today that ontology has been but a dream, the 'main pillar' only a simple congregation of vapours, sometimes even poisonous ones, and the individual nothing but this mask which the Latin people already knew covered only an absence – let us imagine that this community be reduced, through some disaster, to a handful of survivors painfully absorbed at every second by the emergence of dangers. In those moments of deprivation and urgency, the survivors would decide upon a course of action, would assign tasks – but would not the first of these decisions, made without even thinking about it, in the once again uncontested evidence of personal existence, be that *there is being*: these people having no doubt, beneath the collapsing rock, that one's relation to oneself, even if nothing founds it, is origin and suffices to itself? And the horizon around them, though devastated, though unfit for a long while to nurture our dreams, would be, also, would be as one had forgotten a thing could be, from which it follows that in the presence of such things one would therefore be able to recognise that *what is* is what responds to our most basic needs, what lends itself to our project, what allows for exchange, and must first of all have done this to find a place in language: for instance, the main features of a place, the tools of labour, later perhaps the materials of a first moment of rejoicing – one will say then the bread and the wine. Being is the firstborn of emergency. Its ground is the future which calls us to its task, and its substance is the few important categories which we use to formulate this task, that is to say, signifieds which are certainly transitory, but at every moment absolute. Words which name a sacred order, words which welcome us on an earth! Being only exists through our will that there be being; but this will gathers enough reality from outside, even in this winter of ours which will be endless, to build with it this hearth – I no longer say this stage – where those who know they are nothing may come to warm themselves.

And thus it is that we can now better understand the innermost contradiction but also the stubbornness of poetry, which only refuses imaginary worlds because it knows well what our condition is and that our place is this very earth. If being is nothing other than the will that there be being, poetry is nothing itself, in the estrangement of language, but this will understanding its own nature – or at the very least, in dark times, keeping the memory of itself. Let me observe in passing, furthermore, that in so doing it only renews the very act which presided over our beginnings. When words revealed death to men, when conceptual notions put distance between them and things, hollowing out everywhere around them and between them the evidence of their nothingness – which aroused anguish and incited our species to that insane violence which distinguishes it from every other – something in fact like faith was needed for us to carry on with words; and everything indicates that it is also in words themselves – but this time understood as names, cried or called out in the midst of absence – that this faith has sought its way. The most primitive notches are a sign that speaking has always meant asserting oneself – meaning carving itself into meaninglessness; and the gravestone itself, so consubstantial with the aim of speech, is also proof of it, since it preserves a name, since it affirms a presence where one could decide that only nothingness prevailed. Indeed, every monument is the metaphor for this will to be through words and yet against them, to be as a call shouted, answered, and in spite of dream, to be through speech and in spite of the enclosures of our tongues – since the monument is erected in a desert which thus becomes a country, since all art is our way of organising what is close by, since all beauty reflects this light – and as for poetry, it was the very act in which, throughout the ages, these certainties recovered themselves in the midst of their distortions, unity in the heart of multiplicity – at least until the confusions of yesterday, when what today we call the 'text' sprang up from beneath our outworn beliefs, and at the very moment when, from every corner of society, self-confidence was wavering. Let me repeat: the moment when the labour of the signifier was laid bare was not an accident of history. At various great periods of civilisation and of letters, the poets were enough aware of it for criticism to be able to describe it and for anxiety to settle in. But in fact it was then confined to the night of magic rites, it was considered the magician's book which the devil has us sign. The exteriority of words only really appeared, in Dadaism, after the first war which was worldwide; and indeed one could easily believe that in the very ardour which today affirms its irreversible advent, there are a few remnants of hope, and a call for help. You remember: when Paul was going to cross the sea which separated him from Europe, he heard a voice, in the night, which cried out an appeal from the other shore.[6] The gods are dead; very few minds imagine even that the temple for 'the unknown god' is going to receive on its steps, for the second time, some astonishing new gospel – and yet isn't there some chance that the *necessary* idea of being will revive? Is not a boatsman, still soundlessly, approaching our nocturnal shore?

6   See *Acts of the Apostles* 16:9.

★

Ladies and gentlemen, I think that I can return, in any case, to the two questions I asked myself at the outset.

The one regarded the contradiction which we observe today between, on the one hand, the awareness one must have of the illusions of the earlier cogito, and this fact, on the other hand, this fact which is just as obvious – and is a question of such urgency! – that in order to simply desire to survive we continue to need a meaning to give to life. To reflect even a little on this immense challenge of our historic moment, it seemed to me necessary to ask questions of poetry; or rather, having begun in adult life in this way, I was unable to prevent myself from continuing to do so, in spite of the suggestions to the contrary: but now I seem once again to have found confirmed the reason for this confidence which once was instinctive to me. Yes, there is in poets an attitude toward this impasse, an answer to this uneasiness, and it is central in them and it is clear. Whatever may be the driftings of the sign, the obviousness of nothingness, to say 'I' remains for them the best of reality and a precise task, the task of reorienting words, once beyond the confines of dream, on our relationship to others, which is the origin of being. And as for the way in which one might achieve this goal, it is not so unclear, even beneath the level of the greatest contributions of which poetry is capable. For every being dreams his world, let us say at first; every being is imperiled by the words which shut themselves up in him – the writer is not the only one who abolishes, who becomes enchanted by a world-image; he simply runs the greatest risk because of his blank page. Therefore, if he is even slightly aware of his estrangement, and this is within his possibilities, he will feel himself close to others whose situation is the same. In fact, this awareness of enclosure within the sign is the only way which allows one speaking subject to rejoin another and to share – in the void perhaps, but fully and richly – a dimension of existence. It follows that to struggle in our intimate being against the allurements of universal writing, to criticise them, to undo them one by one, to refuse in short to say 'me' at the very moment when the 'I' is asserting itself, is, however negative this might seem, already to go forward toward the common ground. And along this path, which is the path of salvation, poems, the great poems at least, are examples, and more... not the silence characteristic of a 'text', but a voice which spurs us on.

Saying this, I have also begun, it seems to me, to answer my other question, the one I had to raise, this evening, first of all: Can one, when one aspires to poetry, when one strives after it, speak about it authentically? A great many critics of our time would answer no, as I have said, because they identify the poem with the activity of words and not with the search for meaning; but if you have found any merit in my idea of poetry as war against the Image – against the claims of words, against the weight of what is written – you will also have granted me that the poet knows exactly what he is doing, or to put it better, can only be a poet precisely through knowing it. His task, which is to re-establish *openness,* as Rilke would have said, is necessarily a meditation on what encloses his speech. And this project aims, of course, not at words in a manuscript, but at ideas, at experiences in the practice of life, which commits him to a process of becoming that can be, in the case of the greatest poets, a process of spiritual maturation. At the height of its misgivings, poetry is nothing other than an act of knowing.

And in the years to come it could accomplish this act, it seems to me, all the more effectively because for this constant goal it is going to have new means at its disposal. The paradox of the creative act of the future – and this can be its great opportunity – is that the same linguistic and semiological observations that are used today to depreciate the concentration in writing on the writer could – I have already come close to saying this – just as profitably lend themselves, and surely with much greater import, to the opposition that the writer could make, if he is a poet, to the authority of representations, of symbols which contribute to the mirages of writing. How many means have been given to us recently for deconstructing the fiction, for spotting the stereotypes, the *sociolectes,* for following in the web of sentences believed to be uncomplicated the tangle of the figures! And what intuitive shortcuts the new correspondences revealed by the psychoanalyst provide for our investigation of the imaginary! So many keys which were missing in Romanticism, in symbolism, in surrealism, to open by a few more doors the mind's relationship to itself. A lucidity, a short time ago still prohibited, except in moments of extreme tension, could become common currency. After centuries of shame which curbed or distorted desiring imagination, after centuries of ostentation which proclaimed to the four winds the most frivolous eccentricities, we are at last able to recognise the infinitely complex nature of discourse, but also that the self displayed in discourse, while thinking of itself as 'seer or angel',[7] merits – ordinary as it always is – neither Romantic deification nor, if denounced, nostalgia. Never will the 'I' have been better armed for the constant struggle against the intimate, the inexorable vertigo. In my view, poetry and the new criticism are not made to contradict each other for long. They could soon constitute but a single way of living.

And only a word now, to conclude, about the potential that is there. Up until now this evening I have seemed, I suppose, to define poetry, in its relation to the imaginary, as its refusal, its transgression. Without hesitation I defined truthfulness of speech as the war against the Image – the substitution of an image for the world – in favour of presence. But this was only a first approximation, justified I hope by the demonstration I assigned myself, and I would like now to evoke what was behind it in my mind – inasmuch as the few remarks which I have just made go straight toward it. What is this second level of the idea of poetry? Well, it is that to struggle in this way, for a better intu- ition of finitude, against the dosing up of the self, against the denial of the other, can only be to love, since it is presence which opens, unity which already takes hold of consciousness, and thus it means loving as well this first network of naiveties, of illusions in which the will toward presence had become ensnared. At its highest point, of which one can at least have an intimation, poetry must certainly succeed in understanding that these images which, if made absolutes, would have been its lie are nothing more, once one overcomes them, than the forms, the simply natural forms, of desire, desire which is so fundamental, so insatiable that it constitutes in all of us our

---

7   The project undertaken, then deprecated by Rimbaud. See 'Adieu' from *Une Saison en enfer*: 'Moi! moi qui me suis dit mage ou ange, dispensé de toute moral; je suis rendu au sol, avec un devoir à chercher, et la réalité rugueuse à étreindre! Paysan!' ('I! I who called myself seer and angel, exempt from all morality, I am thrown back to the earth, with a duty to find, and rough reality to embrace! Peasant!').

very humanity; and having refused the Image, poetry accepts it in a kind of circle which constitutes its mystery and from which flows, from which rises as if from a depths, its positive quality, its power to speak of everything – in a word, that joy which I said a moment ago poetry could be seen to feel even in its most dreadful hours of anguish. What dream opposes to life, what the analysts of the text study only to dissolve into the indifference of signs, what a more superficial poetry would have torn up with rage, even if perishing with its victim, poetry can refute but listen to, can condemn while absolving it of its fault; it reintegrates it, clarified, into the unity of life. In short, it has denounced the Image, but in order to love, with all its heart, images. Enemy of idolatry, poetry is just as much so of iconoclasm. Now what a resource this could be for responding to the needs of an unhappy society: illusion would reveal its richness, plenitude would be born from deficiency itself! But this dialectic of dream and existence, this third term of compassion, at the highest point of longing passion is, of course, the most difficult. On the level of these exalted representations, of these transfigurations, of these fevers which make up our literatures and which the wisdom of the East would call our delusions, one would need the capacity which the East seems to have – although simply beneath the leafy branches, whereas our place is history – to accept and to refuse at the same time, to make relative what appears absolute, and then to give new dignity, new fullness to this nonbeing. And indeed the Western world, which had a premonition of this deliverance with the *agapè* of the early Christians, then for brief moments in the baroque period and on the peripheries of Romanticism, has, on the whole, made of it the very site of its failure, in unending wars between images. Poetry in Europe seems to have been the impossible: what eludes a man's lifelong search as immediacy does our words. But if it is true, as our time believes, that subjectivity is from now on fracturable, and that poetry and a science of signs may be able to unite in a new relationship between the 'I' which is and the 'me' which dreams, what unexpected richness for hope all at once! At the moment when so much night is gathering, could we be on the verge of the true light?

Translated by John Naughton

Georges Poulet and Poetry[1]

I.

It was not without regrets that I was unable to attend the colloquium in Geneva. For I felt friendship and even affection for Georges Poulet, and I remain much attracted to that fine élan prompting him towards works of literature or rather, perhaps, towards their authors; and I would have liked to hear what the participants, several of whom are my friends, had to say about him.

Moreover, I wished to attend for a more personal reason. Stéphanie Cudré-Mauroux had informed me of Georges Poulet's remark, in a letter to Marcel Raymond, about my writings on poetry – those that he had been able to read at the time. She had perceived this remark as a question that he was implicitly asking me, and she had suggested that I take advantage of the gathering to respond to it. Given the topic of the colloquium, I had already given some thought to the question and was readying myself to deal with it in Geneva, which would have enabled me to take note of my listeners' objections, their comments providing me with food for still more serious reflection.

Deprived of that audience, I am nonetheless going to try to specify my viewpoint on Georges Poulet's comment. And this I will do with an additional regret that you can well imagine: not being able to speak directly to him and encourage him to think about some of the aspects of the problem that he had raised without wholly taking into account the extent of one of its dimensions, to my eyes the most important one.

Had he perhaps brought up this problem, this clearly formulated reservation, long ago in one of our encounters in Zürich or especially in Nice, in that Villa Orangini where he was still living when I held the chair, at the University of Nice for three years (1973–1976),

---

1 First published as '*Georges Poulet parmi nous*', eds. Stéphanie Cudré-Mauroux and Olivier Pot. Geneva and Bern: Slatkine and Archives Suisses, 2004. Collected in *La Communauté des critiques*, Presses Universitaires de Strasbourg, 2010.

that had been his? It is not impossible. Georges enjoyed talking with his friends about critical questions and methods that preoccupied him, but I remember no conversation about this issue, a fact which, however, means nothing, since I have always had a bad memory and have never jotted down anything after such encounters, even important ones. However, I doubt that we would have given much thought to the bewilderment that he had conveyed to Marcel Raymond, even if he had informed me about it. First of all, I am little inclined to those kinds of discussions, which risk taking up too much time during too rare meetings between friends. Given my ways of thinking about poetry, which are little known to many of my interlocutors, I need, once two or more of us seek the truth about it, a whole array of preliminary explanations that burden the spontaneity of such conversations. And I appreciated the fact that Georges Poulet, putting aside his critical and philosophical preoccupations, feared no more than I do 'small talk' of the kind that scandalises minds taking themselves seriously, whereas carefree, bemused chatting sometimes enables one, indirectly but almost as well as many other kinds of dialogue, to attain the essential, which is to make decisions about what is and about what is worthwhile.

On an occasion such as ours, I fear I also need to resort to some preliminaries about my personal ways of thinking, but this can be done more briefly by writing. And first of all, I will return to what induced Stéphanie Cudré-Mauroux to draw my attention to Poulet's remark, which, moreover, she had cited in her contribution to the special issue, of the journal *Oeuvres et critiques*, which was devoted in 2002 to Swiss literary criticism and to the Geneva school.

In that issue, our friend published pages she titled 'Georges Poulet, Critiquer, c'est se souvenir'. I will now summarise what she reports. In a letter written in 1976 to Marcel Raymond and reprinted in the volume of correspondence between the two critics, Georges Poulet, who was preparing the essay about me that would appear a few months later in *L'Arc*, in France, mentions a problem that troubles him. And Stéphanie Cudré-Mauroux, who outlines Poulet's critical methods and principles, and shows his need – by means of a sympathy that had become second nature to him – to become one body, or rather one mind, with what he sensed was the most intimate movement of an oeuvre, underscores the fact that at the time, in the presence of my writings, well, 'the author who is being studied offers,' she says, 'some resistance to this movement of total adherence, which is the genuine motor and *credo* of criticism according to Poulet'. She specifies: 'The symbiotic itinerary that the critic ideally attempts to follow with his subject matter is, in this case, broken off – or rather hindered – by the impression of a contradiction in Bonnefoy's oeuvre. 'I feel […] in an awkward position', explains Poulet, '[the position] where the poet has placed me by making his poetry explicitly depend on a rejection of any kind of conceptual thought, and by himself having fallen into the trap too often, without his being aware of it, of conceptualising when writing poetry.'

Stéphanie Cudré-Mauroux then recalls that Georges Poulet reveals nothing of his reservations in his subsequent essay, as opposed to a Leo Spitzer who, in a similar circumstance, would have taken his footing in such a contradiction and perhaps raised a controversy. Yet it nonetheless remains that, in this case, my remarkable reader both shows and mentions a misgiving that I must take seriously.

I indeed believe it to be an important one, not because it touches upon what I write or who I am, that is, my particularity as a writer, but rather because it clarifies what interests us at present: Poulet's thought and sensibility; and also and especially because it can help us to become aware of the essential nature of poetics, brought to the fore by the difficulty that this reader, who was so subtle and well-informed, and so obstinate in his questioning of others, experiences when recognising what I myself believe is the fundamental nature of the writing of poetry: an ambiguity and a 'double postulation' that both require a break with conceptual discourse and wholly maintain the obligation to use it for at least some of its demands. I believe that this important remark in fact goes well beyond both a critic and he whom he criticises. And I am thus going to try to clarify this remark even more, in order to put forth to Poulet, in a manner as thoughtful and justified as possible, an objection that strikes me as necessary.

II.

Let me therefore come back to Poulet's remark, which expresses his 'discomfort' in the presence of pages that he would have preferred more purely 'poetical', in the sense that he gave to this word, that is, driven, stirred, by intuitions directly born from the relationship between an existence and the world.

First of all, let me say that I well understand the discomfort that he felt when facing a way of being in the world to which he nonetheless had the generosity to pay attention with his habitual capacity for sympathy. Like me, Georges Poulet was not wrong in thinking that theoretical reflection hardly prepares one for the intuition that founds poetry. And he could indeed have been surprised to see me resorting to big, completely abstract categories, beginning with those of 'concept' or 'knowledge through the concept', in pages such as my 'Tombeaux de Ravenne'[2], in which a concern with immediate reality nevertheless appears and in which supposed encounters with it are even recorded.

But doesn't this bewilderment, I wonder in return, betray an at least partly erroneous idea of poetry? I must now attempt to characterise the poetics that the author of *Métamorphoses du cercle* (1961) made his own, consciously or unconsciously, all the while seeking to understand if what he liked in the great works of literature – that they had been freed from what he considered the vulgarity of ordinary existence, thereby attaining what he would have called a 'transparency' – is, or is not, what I myself recognise as the work of poets and their most specific quality.

What did Georges Poulet like in Nerval, in Baudelaire or in the other poets to whom he devoted attentive and often penetrating studies? There is no doubt that the élan bearing him to great minds – his need to identify with them, to discover how they were born to themselves through writing – gave him the opportunity to think about poetry as such, to seek it out in what makes it different: Baudelaire, for example, was not of the same species as Stendhal. And we will not err if we follow Georges Poulet along this path running from an initial affection for a literary work to retracing how it came into being.

---

2   'The Tombs of Ravenna' (1953). Extracts from this important essay are included in Yves Bonnefoy: *Poems*, (Carcanet, 2017), which constitutes the first volume of this *Reader*.

It's clear that what interested Poulet in an author whom he was studying was not what first strikes, and would suffice for, other critics, in other words those aspects of natural or social reality that the work had retained because of the tastes or happenstances of the writer's existence: what one could call the 'world' of the writer, or his particular way of being in the world, and which expresses a subjectivity but not necessarily a spiritual search. Many scholars wish, and know how, to sketch these personal universes to which some writings can be reduced, and they have the right to characterise them as such because the desires that they detect in literary work are not without truth that can be meditated on. But Poulet felt not the slightest propensity for any form of hedonism; as Jean-Claude Mathieu recently recalled, he willingly said that the body is merely a 'stupid ol' saucepan'; and if on certain occasions he noticed and could describe how authors behaved at the sensorial, sensual, and even sexual levels of their existence, this was only because their behaviour revealed, in such cases, the path through which 'thought' or 'experience' – he did not fear this word that our day and age dreads – freed itself from ordinary entrapments.

A writer's thought, wrote George Poulet in *La Conscience critique* in 1971, is 'the act by which the mind, making a pact with the body and those of others, has united with the object to invent itself as the subject' and thereby place itself on the path towards more reality. This 'more' was, to his eyes, of a spiritual nature, the dissipation of matter within a transparency, the sudden expansion of a light. And in the presence of this effort, which is as difficult as it is praiseworthy, the chore that Poulet assigns to the reader and, consequently, to the critic, was, of course, to ponder a way of thinking, but, even more so, to re-experience the thinking by going back up through the superposed strata of representations and images, those fundamental experiences that constitute the germinating cell, towards the liberation, the unchaining, that make up the intention of the creative act.

Re-experienced and understood in that way, the genesis of the literary work is therefore, according to Poulet, what provides this attentive reader with his own spiritual maturation. As he put it in his conclusion to the colloquium on 'The Current Paths of Criticism', in 1966, pages as firmly self-confident as they are modest: the critic, as opposed to great writers, is 'one who is incapable of seeing some things directly. He can see them only indirectly, when they are mediated, […] a blind man to whom eyes are lent, a deaf man who acquires the sense of hearing, a non-poet who receives the gift of poetry'.

Notice this word: 'poetry'. Let us compare it to another of Poulet's statements, this one made in his major letter (1960) to Marcel Raymond, pages to which I will return since he put so much of himself into them: 'The poet is a human being who has the mission, not to make a poem […] but *to be* and to *make* us *be*'. And let's note that with this idea of a literary work and of one's reading of it, Georges Poulet is not far from poetry, in fact, from poetry as it seems natural for me to understand it, since, on the one hand, he wants to free a deep consciousness from the illusions of a simply superficial ego, and because, on the other hand, he senses that the mind is a unity, from which it follows that the highest attainments of the mind, through the work of a few people, can be everyone's common good.

A concern for poetry sufficient enough to make Poulet seem sympathetic to those who are preoccupied by it. And this is how I myself approached him, and in several cases sensed his concern as veridical. But to come back to my initial question: had he in fact understood the poetical act in its most radical aspects? And was he thus able to speak of poets as poets without being somewhat mistaken about their intentions and methods? I think that he was unable to do so. And it is to justify this surprising judgement that I am now going to apply myself.

III.

First of all, I will observe that in his reading of literary works, and of the most diverse kinds of literary works, Georges Poulet regularly came up against a question that he nonetheless refrained from considering in a truly serious way, holding forth on it with remarks more instinctive than thoughtful, and even adopting, in front of friends who would debate with him or had the desire to do so, extreme and occasionally provocative viewpoints. Besides Jean Starobinski, his friends were Jean Rousset and Marcel Raymond; and at least for the latter two men, this question – that of the function of form in the genesis and manifestation of literary works – was as central as it was pondered without intransigence by means of conceptions that partly diverged but that possessed the same sentiment of the importance of this aspect of creative work. Wholly to the contrary, Poulet did not wish to hear about anything, in a literary text or even in the work of an architect or an artist, that was a matter of form. He denied that forms had any reality on the level where, to his eyes, great works are real and even the supreme reality.

He explicitly expressed his thinking about form, his vehement denegation of form, in the letter to which I have already alluded, the 'eight mighty pages' – in fact, some 5000 words – that he sent to Marcel Raymond on December 9, 1960. For some time, the correspondence of the two critics had closed in on topics that had become more and more essential for them, Poulet having read in Raymond's diary passages about his illness and recovery. More specifically broached on in these confident and affectionate letters was the question of transcendence, of the 'bridge' spanned by transcendence, or not, between its locus – its elsewhere – and a human being in his mortal condition; and Raymond, referring to a decisive period of time for him, ten years earlier, had conveyed to his friend, at some point during the autumn, his feeling that transcendence could descend into what is experienced and that a human being could thus commune with a divine presence.

To this, Poulet had expressed, on November 14, his surprise that his friend was not musing about 'rereading Calvin'; then, on December 9, he mustered himself for his 'mighty reply', which, from the onset, returns with emotion to this debate about transcendence, which thus appears to be at the heart of his thinking about life and literary works. As Poulet points out, Raymond wants transcendence – by which he means the being of God in His relationship to oneself – to remain for us mortals an 'essential strangeness' destined to stay 'other', but he cannot keep himself from sensing it as 'nearby', 'accessible', 'incarnated', 'incomprehensibly present'. In this respect, Raymond thus distances himself, as his friend puts it, from the 'religion of the Father', a transcendence closed in on itself, and attaches himself to the 'religion of the Son', which is also a transcendence but one that opens itself up to the strictly human mind.

And facing this kind of immanentism, Poulet vehemently sets out to explain, as he phrases it, 'my religion'. He remains with the Father, a father forever turned away from his sons who have failed, and in his unworthiness Poulet consoles himself, as he puts it, 'by musing that up there, over there, there is *an intact being* whose perfection exempts us from anything and everything except for acknowledging this perfection, distinguishing its lack in us, and accepting the just arrangement by which, ultimately, our death gives back to the daylight that we soil 'all its purity'.

Why did he make such an intensely religious profession of faith to this correspondent with whom the future author of *La Conscience critique* had until then above all shared his interests for literature? Because it is, specifically, of literature that this 'contrast' between two ideas of transcendence will allow him to speak, with the hope that his friend will accept what he considers to be the best approach. Indeed, Marcel Raymond's 'immanentism' enables him to see without difficulty beauty in things as well as in the forms brought forth in literary works; and Poulet asks him – it is the heart of his objection – whether these forms that possess beauty do not exist, in his eyes, 'in themselves', like a 'fetish-God' that one can 'adore only from the outside'; in brief, as a substitute for real experience. By perceiving forms and becoming attached to them, one falls back into ordinary reality where the totality that is the work thus becomes an object: one will only be able to analyse it, describing its 'tricks', while the 'mind' that carried it aloft will withdraw from it. 'Tricks', idolatry – Marcel Raymond does not deserve such harsh words. One admits that it would have been better if Poulet had kept them for a critique of Edgar Allan Poe's imprudent speculations or Paul Valéry's provocative ones.

But this is also because he was burning with the desire to make Marcel Raymond understand the differences between him and other critics, and to set down that he was one, with all his being, with this idea of an un-incarnated transcendence that does not unfold in observable forms in paintings and literary texts. What is present and active in worthy literary works, and the only important element, Poulet declares, is the 'cause', the 'creative idea' that produces the elements and carries them off in a vast unique movement of elevation towards transcendence in its 'up-thereness' or 'over-thereness'; and the various parts of a work are nothing compared to this movement; they vanish into it, annihilate themselves in it, nothing being real on this earth except for this idea that one can call, literally, 'creative'; creative of the 'creator' who will remain the only element that matters in his work, which is ultimately effaced in the process. For example, the 'situations' and 'schemes' of Balzac's novels 'hasten' to point to Balzac 'even as creation, as theologians put it, proclaims the Creator': the forms that can be spotted in *The Human Comedy* not being any more real, Poulet could have added, than the structures and the laws that scientists seek in matter instead of seeing, as the only idea that matters, that all creation 'converges' towards he who creates it.

'And one must draw out, understand, admire this convergence, this resorption – and this at the expense even of all the rest – so exclusively that the whole of the creative work must vanish into the miracle of the final resorption because only the creator is left', concludes Poulet, summing himself up well in this astonishing sentence. This 'understand' that immediately becomes 'to admire' is obviously the critic's task as he understands it; and Poulet specifies, to Raymond, that 'forms are made to be sucked out' like simple grape skins worth no more than the juice that swells them, an ever more luminous entity. 'At best, forms are merely a temporary support, a precarious architecture', he adds, thinking this time of Jean Rousset. And then he passionately evokes how he reads the great literary works. Shakespeare, first of all, 'read many a time', and of whom neither Macbeth, nor Lear, nor Hamlet remains for him; only that vast, inexhaustible Shakespeare who transcends the 'strings' that could convince one to take into account – but those would be false paths – the analysis of each play 'per se'.

And Racine! Whose *Phèdre* has no autonomous beauty, for the silence that follows the death of she who has soiled the light still present in the world is 'a thousand times more important than the play itself': 'silence of Phèdre, silence of Racine, *our* silence'. And Tintoretto! Poulet loves 'with passion' all of Tintoretto's works, taken together, 'and him in them'. At the Scuola di San Rocco, in 'this grand spiritual site' that he visited with Jean Rousset while likely worrying about his travelling companion's viewpoint, 'one runs from painting to painting without any of their forms ever coming to a halt in them, and making you come to a halt'; and one can 'forget' paintings even as one forgets the quartet or the symphony 'in the ineffable presence of Mozart'.

Shakespeare, Racine, Tintoretto, Mozart – let's note that they represent four cultures, four traditions that one might consider to be different ones – but beyond each of them, 'poetry', a word that Georges Poulet now pronounces to make it the signifier of his idea of creative work. I have already recalled his remark whereby the poet's mission is not to 'make a poem', even as one makes 'a pendulum', but rather to 'be', to be what 'makes being'. It is at this point in his long letter that this sentence is found; and what the statement more precisely demands is that the poet, when he ventures beyond the 'mediocrity' – and even, 'I do not hesitate to add', the 'vileness' – of everyday life, agrees to think of himself 'as he appears to himself at the highest, the most profound, the most universal or the most simple level of his mental life'. His work or, rather, his act, is to tear himself from the ignominy of life. 'With all my force', exclaims Georges Poulet, 'I do not let myself speak about incarnated poetry [...]. At the limit of the most marvellous verbal exploits of poetry, there are no more words, there is no more flesh, nothing but a transparency which, carried to its supreme point of diaphaneity, culminates in immateriality, the total invisibility of the poem, even as there is an invisibility of pure crystal'.

This long, vehement declaration blazes on the pages of the 'mighty reply' like a veritable act of faith, which is not surprising since absolute transcendence, designated as such from the onset, has triumphantly run through the discourse. If forms do not matter, this is because transcendence has not consented to our finding beauty in the things of the world; it allows only the élan which, by throwing itself at its feet, frees subjectivity – the only conceivable locus of self-consciousness – from the vulgarities and impurities of existence. 'Thought', at its highest level, is immaterial or almost so, and invisible.

IV.

This letter is a grand reply and a grand idea or, rather, a grand sentiment which themselves transcend, one can say, Marcel Raymond's ways of feeling – more truthful perhaps, but quite prudent – and, furthermore, clearly refuse to let them have the slightest rights over literary works, despite the esteem that Georges Poulet sincerely has for some aspects of his friend's research.

As for myself, I admire this clear-cut position that I hadn't understood, until today, as being so radical. Besides, I find validity in it at the very level where essentials are at stake. In other words, my idea of poetry enables me to find meaning in Poulet's intuition, and even to sympathise with what I will nevertheless have to reject, because I do not consider it to be veridical.

Why this sympathy? Because poetry, as I understand it, is also attached, and I will come back to this point, to a kind of transcendence; yet for me, transcendence – much more so than for Raymond – is also completely made up of immanence and certainly does not consist of anything personalised within a divineness for which I have no use, nothing that needs a theology of a Father or even of a Son. And I love as much as Poulet does, in great poems, their vow to completely consume certain aspects of being-in-the-world, even if my idea of the 'ego', which should be extended into the 'I', does not coincide with his conception of subjectivity, within which he evokes absolutely no fractures, simply degrees of transparency. The impression that he senses at the end of *Phèdre*, or at the highest point of some poems, is merely true: words can sometimes attain a kind of silence and act in such a way that one no longer thinks of how they were present in the text. In brief, I appreciate the fact that Poulet judges the poet on his aptitude to be and not on his skill at doing. This is what makes him a witness of the truth and gives him the right to speak critically.

But when facing this kind of thinking and how it is used in specific essays, I am not without feeling some perplexity and even one serious reservation. My perplexity, which is, in fact, not a reprobation and even a nice surprise, is to see Georges Poulet making such high demands; one would have expected him to be a new Savonarola in the city of writers and painters, calling for more than simply art; and if not a controversialist – he would not stoop so low – at least an impatient reader rejecting much in many works of art or music or literature, of which he wants only the whole that he calls Shakespeare or Mozart, or the silence at the summit of *Phèdre*. Whereas in the practice of his criticism, it is the aforementioned sympathy, and the need to identify with authors that instead predominates, and he even takes great pains to follow them in their detours.

This is probably where Georges Poulet benefits more than suffers from what motivates my reservation, which no less preoccupies me. I must now make it more explicit, for this is the point where two paths, two conceptions of poetry, part. On the one hand, it seems to me – and the genre of affectionate criticism practiced by Poulet only confirms this – that there is a contradiction in the assertion of a transcendence that does not open up to our incarnated condition while, at the same time, works of art or music or literature are recognised as being capable to bear themselves to its threshold, in that silence where one no longer knows if one has heard a quartet, or a symphony, or who, in *Phèdre*, was the daughter of Minos or shy, simple Aricie. To rise like that, didn't Mozart or Racine need something to lean on in this world? Isn't it true that there are vestiges, in a birdcall, a child's laugh, a sob, at the very least, of a mode of being that does not let itself be explained and that solicits the mind in a mysterious way? A transcendence already here, in our midst, a transcendence consubstantial with life? The true witnesses of transcendence according to the Father – to cite the words of the major letter – tolerate not even Mozart or Racine, but this is already because they do not perceive the presence of these vestiges when they listen to our world.

On the other hand, one can refuse, like Georges Poulet, to attach value and even existence to those so-called forms that the experts of the structuralist or textualist years sought to extirpate from the very disorder that they had themselves brought into their analysis of the great works; and, for example, to consider not very truthful how 'Les Chats' was read for a while,[3] that second-rate poem in *Les Fleurs du Mal*. But for all this, one cannot agree that the reader, who has followed Racine all the way to the silence that invades the mind when Phèdre dies, has not been led to this brink by the alexandrine, the form that has been worked on by this great poet in its formal depths, experienced in the way it listens to time, ventured in dramatic situations and then reunified in its absolute potentiality in a way that

---

3   cf 'Les Chats de Charles Baudelaire', by Roman Jakobson and Claude Lévi-Strauss, *L'Homme: Revue française d'anthropologie*, Volume 2, No. 1, 1962, pp. 5–21.

the alexandrine alone could assume and carry so far. Like all those for whom *Phèdre* is Racine's final step beyond the dead-end of classical prosody, Poulet was swept away by the incantatory power – let's risk the word – of verse enabling Minos's dying daughter to give that literally sublime purity and stylistic economy to her last words. Doesn't this imply that there are forms in poems? Not only that great generating form, verse, but other forms in poetry that disseminate their echoes, reflections, and even their silence in the subject matter of the text?

To my mind, there is thus a contradiction in Georges Poulet: a debate that cannot be resolved between his otherworldly, vehement thinking, which was almost tempted by iconoclasm, and his incessant affection and ability to love in this world. It is a rather dangerous contradiction because it keeps him from raising the question of forms, which nonetheless exist, at least some of them, in the very best works of art and literature. Yet I will now say that this contradiction is not a simple error, but rather a repressed lucidity, a halt on the threshold of the dialectic that is the truth of poetry. From which it follows that one can keep this contradiction in mind, and Georges Poulet with it, when we return to another idea of the truth of poetry.

From now on, it is not Georges Poulet who will speak, but rather I who will speak to him, with the wish to interest him in a way of thinking about creativity that will not refuse to find meaning in what he says about Shakespeare or Racine – beyond *Hamlet* and *Phèdre*.

V.

Let me now come back to those texts that Georges Poulet was reading more deeply than many other critics, yet without admitting a need to linger, in his reading, over any point whatsoever: 'running' from one point to the next in the writings of Shakespeare or Balzac as he had done at the Scuola di San Rocco in front of Tintoretto's paintings, when he became intoxicated with forgetting them, every one of them, in the 'ineffableness' of their common presence, the locus, as such, of a great artist concerned with the absolute wrenching himself from himself.

Let me return to those texts, but first in order to consider a vast

group of writings that Georges Poulet would rightfully not have
recognised as poetry because, quite obviously, the perceptions and
the volitions are attached only to things reduced to their materiality, to their being-there-ness as simple objects, such as become trees
when they are cut down in order to be sold in places that are merely
a space, where needs are no longer anything but loveless possession. This is the level of having and not of being, a disorder where
various kinds of predation jostle each other, where reason and the
idea of justice try to gain a foothold, but in vain: the field of negoti-
ation, action, the communication of ideas, but also, it must not be
forgotten, that of reveries, sometimes beautiful and even moving,
which replace predation when it cannot be carried out in its direct
or sublimated forms.

Why should one be interested in this prose of being-in-the-world?
From a literary critic's viewpoint, what does it teach us except that
those who write thus lack, at least in such moments, the quality and
the ambition that typically give substance to poetry? Such prose
shows that texts in which poetry is lacking are totally controlled, on
the other hand, by conceptual schemes: and one well understands
why. No concept can obtain, in discourse about empirical reality,
unless an aspect, a single aspect – as delimited as possible – of the
reality has been retained from among the various aspects that the
slightest things show in an infinite number. And from the mind is
then effaced the experience of this profusion nonetheless inherent in
anything whatsoever, and with it the memory of what, in front of us,
is its origin: the thing or the person as they exist, in their uniqueness,
which we can encounter only in the here and now, in a finitude that
teaches us our own finitude.

If the text and the reading of a text confine themselves to sequences
of concepts, their relationship to what in the world is existence will
thus be threatened. A scientific project will be set up, the concepts
will be made into laws, a noble concern with truth will be drawn
from the profusion of things as they are, and from lives. But what
a risk of existential impoverishment lies beneath this science! We
are invited to think and no longer to see, to analyse and no longer
to love. The imagination – of the kind that dreams of possessing,
not exchanging, thus dedicating itself to appearances that will soon
be phantasms – will prosper, but this type of imagination could be

called 'fancy' in Coleridge's distinction; not the kind of imagination that brings together the paths and the powers of life into a grand, soon unitary, vision that is a poetically liveable world.

Conceptual prose implies obliviousness to, one could even say an ignorance of, that network of infinite, absolute existences; of that background that sometimes, however, makes itself known to us again, like the startling sound of an invisible horn in the depths of the woods.

Yet such prose is omnipresent in society and even prevalent in modern consciousness, because thinking by concepts has little by little taken a lead over all other kinds of approaches to what is. And it can thus be surmised that if writers, artists, and musicians have learned how to attain this intuitive intimacy with life and the things that Poulet loves in their works, it is because they have managed, in one way or another, to extricate themselves from that reductive aim, though without being able to truly undo its grip on numerous aspects of their condition. The apprehension of what is immediate remains an ultimate experience in our modernity, and it is never anything but intermittent. For the study of literary inventiveness, nothing would be more impoverishing than to underestimate the entrapment of one's way of looking by the conceptual project whose initial decision, which is constantly renewed, is to simplify appearance.

Can one content oneself, for example, with imagining that by refining conceptualisation – that is, by increasing the number of application points on the object, by bearing its vocabulary ever further into the folds of sensory appearance or the situations of life – the writer can attain more reality? Such is the aim of some narratives, marked by a supposed realism that is unaware of what matters most: the self's intimacy with finitude. What one must explore if one is to discover how great literature attains, practically speaking, the kind of plenitude that it intimates, is not the concept's ability to differentiate itself ever more, to render more precise and broaden its picture of the world, but rather how it is intricately related to the intuition of presence.

Paying attention to the concept and being concerned with its effects on consciousness while it is at work are what need to be deepened, even and, in fact, especially at the beginning of one's reflections about what we call literature. And this viewpoint will soon reveal that this word, literature, covers truly diverse practices, one of which is so important, so much at a remove from the others, that we must not hesitate to designate it by another name. I am of course thinking of poetry. Some poems show that poetry is an experience whereby what is immediate, that is, finitude, almost lets itself be reached. And what I am now going to attempt to show is that, if this is so, it is not because of an extremely rich sensibility, or a particularly intense need for spiritual elevation, as Georges Poulet contents himself with thinking. Surely much of the quality of poetry depends on the quality of the person devoting him or herself to it, yet it cannot be understood other than as the effect of thinking, specific from the onset, about conceptual alienation.

VI.

Poetry is a thought that bears on the concept. This sentence will perhaps surprise those who know what I have myself never stopped repeating, that poetry, which is the memory of a reality not yet undone by the work of concepts, seeks well beyond what concepts make appear and is even something quite different from thinking. But having said this, can I find meaning by seeing poetry as nothing but a supposedly direct way of looking – freed from all analytical thinking – at a babbling brook or a blooming bush?

The brook, the bush, the earth in its majestic standing-forth, the human being in moments of self-presence – this is what matters to poetry and what readers hope to find in poems, even fleetingly. But the poet would not have progressed very far if his words had not allowed him to understand, early on in his writing, that the apparently most immediate perceptions – this brook, this bush – are also subjected to the constraints of conceptual articulation. In regard to nature or society, we harbour emotions and sentiments that the intellect tolerates, even preserves and cultivates, in order not to suffer too much from its abstraction. And in such cases, the affect seems to arise freely, at the sight of a clump of grass or a child's face, but what the concept thus accepts has, all the same, been detached from what exists around it; the concept has brought out and named –

while simplifying it – the difference; the concept has said what will guarantee its place in a botany manual or in a photography album; and soon the lover of graminae runs the risk of collecting specimens without knowing that grasses wither, or else it will be the novelist who will have only psychology in mind to speak about the child at the very moment when it turns his eyes away from what it is being shown and remains silent for a long while.

And the poet will be the one who notices that the conceptual holds sway, beginning at this level of naming – which is, in short, never Adamic and already shaded by the tree of science – but he will not conclude from this that the use of words is, by this very fact, a closed door. Is this because we have not forgotten that during certain moments of childhood, the age at which the concept is only beginning to establish itself in the youthful mind, sounds disturbed us not because of their signification but, on the contrary, because of their absence of meaning, such as the noise of a boulder rolling down into a ravine, after which there is silence, or the mysteriously repetitive blows of a hammer banging in the distance? In any case, we are still able to perceive in the utterance of a phoneme this same in-itself-ness of the sonorous event that made of those noises from back then an appeal beyond the situations and interests of present existence: in other words, an enigma, but one with an obscure hope in it. And from this aptitude for listening will ensue the possibility of a decision which will be, if we make it, the most important one in our life, as it in fact was for humanity itself, beginning with the very morning after the invention of language.

Indeed, what is perceived 'in itself', for example the surface of a stone block with its cracks that cannot be deciphered, its colours for no apparent reason, or the movement of clouds, or this sound now deeper in us than any thought, is the world as a seemingly intact presence, the world as a wholeness – because with conceptual thought the opposition, which it has invented, between the part and the whole, is effaced. Suddenly one fully receives what was subsiding in the brook or the clump of grass when we were looking at them with, already inside us, the lively sentiment of their presence in our life but also already all the words, all the noises of signification in the words. The sound heard in, say, the word 'arbre' ['tree'] makes us penetrate into the depth of the tree, the true depth, into what is, not matter, but rather being. It is a threshold in its appearance which, by the very path of appearance, opens out onto the invisible, everything, the One, to which we thus return.

And is this sound even, with its circles of sound waves in the invisible, a borderline experience, a wall of what is manifest beyond which we could not go towards anything whatsoever belonging to our existence? No, for a lapse of time sets in, beginning with that very moment, while the strange hope of which I was speaking and which has stayed in our memory, again arises. From one phoneme to another in the succession of words and phrases, the sound is indeed differentiated, without losing its potentiality of epiphany, its capacity to be presently and totally that not-undone wholeness of reality that concepts make us forget. Even as a stone seen as stone unfolds in anfractuosities of various forms, in blue or red veins – which remain below signification even if our eyes follow them into their meanders – sounds in speech, however distinct and distinctive they become to facilitate thinking, remain, beneath thinking, the same intact wholeness that makes only its absence heard. And then another immediacy opens out to the mind.

We can pronounce these sounds, we acknowledge them in their differences on the level of listening where this diversity no longer signifies oppositions of words, of meanings, or of thoughts about the world, but simply the night of the depths of the world, also the night of the living bodies that we are, beneath our gestures, and basically, if I may say so, of our voice, which puts the body into a relationship with language.

And the voice can take charge of the sound, and because the sound can vary in its duration and be able to repeat itself – to lend itself to alliterations, to rhythms, to take on importance in an utterance or to stay merely attenuated, sometimes almost forgotten – what a mental revolution will occur if we know how to remain listening to this passage between the sound and the word, between the breath and the meaning! It's true that the body is already, deeply, made of language, of signification, of discourse. As the body has been human for such a long time and so deeply remodelled by such diverse civilisations, it follows that words, with their thought, have penetrated far into its drives, its needs, and that it is not its mannerisms that are going to slip away from the readings that conceptual networks have made of the body: it can even be said that the mannerisms take advantage of those readings, those networks, for example when there is a question of the senses, the five senses, taking advantage of the objects, the places, and other spadework that language has carried out for them and what they offer.

But the body also possesses, and this time in a way as veridical as it is radical, what enables it to reject the gaze that concepts cast on what is. The body is flesh and blood, that is, consists of time heading to death, consists of finitude, and it knows this, instinctively, whereas conceptual thought has only one abstract idea of this. For the body, finitude is not a mental representation, subject matter for speculation, but rather a direct experience, at once an élan, in its desires, and a limit because of what will come of all its endeavours. And the result of this intuition is that an event takes place, in the body's perception of sound, which is both more original than any activity of language and higher in the mind than any other kind of intellection.

VII.

This event is a relationship with the form which, as is so often the case, will no longer be an entirely mental kind of awareness that can be situated in the field controlled by the eyes and easily separated from the events of life, but rather an implication of finitude. The use of sound made by the voice, that is, by the body, has the chance, because of the body, to be the direct expression of a knowledge that the flesh and the blood have of the finite human being, a more radical knowledge than any other knowledge within speech. The durations and rhythms that are established in sound constitute a time which is that of life in its innermost need, its need most greatly aware of its real condition – that of the immediate 'I', vaster and deeper than the 'ego' produced by conceptual thinking to keep the speaking human being there where such thought seeks to build a world. A time that fully and directly expresses the anxiety and also the hope of the acts of life as they occur, that is, in the random happenstances full of uncertainty within which one must make the decision to choose: and this decision is the absolute of the moment. What is experienced, an open-ended activity whose future is never assured, is thus inscribed in words and, in this way, makes itself heard.

And the consequence of this inscription cannot help but immediately show up at the level of the signification that persists in the
terms thus attained by the path of sounds and penetrated by existential time. The words that remain spoken have known acceptations;
many of them evoke, in natural or social realities, a referent of great
importance for the person who is going to speak in this new way.
But their usage must be transformed. Until now, their relations were
regulated by this conceptual knowledge that does not experience the
innermost depth of finitude. But now these networks of signifieds
are dissolved and only their extra-linguistic referents remain – in the
words – or almost: that is, no longer potential representations, available for expressing, in discourse, something one knows, but rather
presences, genuine presences in the place and the moment of the act
in progress. Let us say that the words cease to exist on the level of
signification and appear on that of meaning, which is what gives to
experienced existence its values and its raison d'être. The words can
no longer be the components of a discourse; instead, their possible
use must be called a song, since what institutes them in this new kind
of existing and keeps them there is the insistent rhythm that holds
the sounds together.

By the force of this sonorous form that has extended into words,
the use of words is thus, literally, transmuted. With words in which
the figure that the concept gives to the world has collapsed, one can
see reality in a different way, extract oneself, for example, from the
category of having – which predominates in the space of the reified
– one can struggle, at the very least, against the need to possess and
thus not be what is born of reification. And countless consequences
result from this inaugural event. It is pertinent to evoke them in
passing. One of them, but I'll have to come back to it, is that what
concepts like to produce to respond to the desires that have made
an alliance with them – a certain beauty – loses its attractiveness at
this precise point. That the image-world of the concept be reorgan-
ised in a dream by desires in a way that satisfies them; that there is
no more discordance in this dream, those remaining shadows that
disturb imagined satisfaction; and that an impression of harmony,
of beauty, is thus extracted from the image itself, in which the ego
will be able to mirror itself, even if this means perishing from it, like

Narcissus: such is the beauty that concepts seek. But such is a beauty of representation, not of presence.

There is much to understand about how the intervention of sound affects words. But it seems more important for my topic today not to forget that the very heart of this transmutation, which has begun, cannot help but be marked by the strong resistance of the revoked thought. This will imply ambiguities in the poetry to come. The knowledge of finitude is established by the path of sounds – through alliteration, for example – but sounds themselves, as we know, can signify conceptually; alliteration evokes things as we know them by ordinary thinking, and this thus partakes of the conceptual, the non-temporal, which slips into the sound per se, with an iambic power, to weigh it down, to pull it down into the depths. The form that was used for poetry is now taken up in the networks of signification, reemployed for this beauty of desire, which is characteristic of the image-world, as I was just saying. No aspect of establishing a poem is unlikely to be seduced by these schemes of ordinary understanding.

Let's thus think of rhyme, so natural to the sonorous usage of words. As the recurrence of a sound at the end of lines of verse, rhyme can reinforce the primacy given to sound by accentuating its hold over speech and thus contribute to pushing away the concept, to opening the path of the knowledge of finitude. But rhyme also implies having recourse to a word, that is, quickly the obligation to come back to a limited number of words, and therein lies the great danger of building up a potential vocabulary that conceptual thought controls well and that it will take advantage of to re-establish its idea of the world, with the complicity of many of those who will make verse – who are therefore rhymesters more than poets. This stratagem is all too obvious in classical literature, especially in the theatre, where analytical psychology also reinforces it. But even in this case, nothing is lost for the thought of finitude. The winning adversary is also he of whom one becomes aware, and great battles have taken place about the use of rhyming, poetry sometimes carrying off surprising victories.

But let's leave this and keep attempting to define the main event. Resistances, assuredly, ambiguities, a sonorous use of words that will perhaps never manage to impose its way of looking at the world in speech, but the primary intuition, which has perceived the not-un-done wholeness in the sound, is not lost, for all that, and right where it is embattled, smothered, and I would say censored, it can start up again and often does. In fact – and it's only now that I can put forward a definition of poetry – it is less the inaugural act of grasping a word by its sound than the recommencement of that act, the obsti-nacy to recover the word in its weaknesses: an activity, as close as possible to words, a working on words which, at the level where the work takes place, so close to the existential need, owes its intensity only to this need for the most immediacy possible, in its fever, and does not thus presuppose the presence in the poet, at least at that moment, of those lofty aspirations that Poulet likes to acknowledge in works of literature. Great poetry is never very far from popular songs, from 'naiveté', as Pushkin puts it.

Obstinacy. A perpetual beginning all over again, in writing, in existence. But be wary now of the viewpoint and the decisions that the critic – who is not an average reader – will have to take. Poetry means getting a hold back on signification by means of sound, by rhythm – by a form. But because this élan of form is so often and so strongly hampered and almost shattered by the resistance of concep-tual thinking, what should matter, for the critic attached to specific works of literature, is less the idea of form in its generality, which calls for a reflection more suitable for the philosopher, than the work which, in the actual writing, produces form, starts the form up again, and will stay visible even in the final draft of the poem. A poem is never anything but work left on hold, with unaccomplished poten-tialities that no longer signify anything, at that point, but the poet's relationship with the self or the influence on him of the thought of his times. The poem, or rather the poet's creative work, carried out as it must be until the last day of his life, is not a unique form exhib-ited in an irresistible and irreversible way. Superposed, yet sometimes remaining in a visible state here or there in the various writings, it is a whole ensemble of forms which, having been produced, were subverted, reemployed by the authority who resists them: but forms that have also been taken back up again, reaccepted, and re-elabo-rated by poetic obstinacy. The work of poetry does not cease, the intuition of its great forming form, having the task of maintaining itself at the level of the self in specific forms, formed forms.

And yet we are interested in these formed forms because poetry is an activity – I'm using this word again – not a victory. Whatever the illusions of many poets, the works of poets are never those full uses of sight – 'sight', not vision – that should be made possible by the memory, maintained by sound, of what is immediate. Poetical works are the quest for this, to be sure, at least when the author's work is not mere rhetorical elaboration, but this quest is barred by obstacles that can be bypassed only by reflections and experiences of a conceptual nature, although still maintained under the sign of poetry, their cause.

Moreover, one must not believe that these dubious battles between two viewpoints, two projects, necessarily result in poems – actual poems – being impoverished by the combat. On the contrary, the two viewpoints, while fighting each other, can lead to a quality and a richness that are as remarkable as they are unexpected. The alienation, of one's way of looking at the world, by means of the concept, and the occultation of what is immediate by means of representation, are not only the poet's fate, but also the condition that characterises any awareness of the world; and one's failure to establish a transparent relationship with what is, is thus what can allow reader and author to be in connivance about what is most essential concerning the experience of living. The poet only brings out what others suffer without their knowing so or, rather, without wanting to recognise it. In his words that take on a written form, he faces up to what many others experience confusedly in situations that have remained unvoiced in their own existence. And if he is lucid and honest, that is, if he doesn't try to cheat, to substitute artifice for poetry, he has understood himself as being one who stands by words as they exist in ordinary daily life; and although he is unable to bring salvation, he will be able to offer an example on which one can assuredly meditate: an example of a quest that is carried out with resolve and under the banner of truth. The truth of poetry is that of being the mirror of the alienation wishing to cease, a mirror that can sometimes not flatter, not hide any illusions, nor remain silent about unrealisable aspirations. A truth that will be all the more gripping for the lazy reader – if he is not 'hypocritical', as Baudelaire put it – in that he will watch it being painfully experienced, accepted with difficulty, by the very person who produced it.

In short, *form*, from its birth in the plenitude of sound, is indeed the path of poetry, the first cause of poems that are born from the hope that form originally is. But the specific *forms* that these poems take on, as the poet gropes from level to level within the intermeshing of sounds and meanings, are loci for a truth that is by no means negligible, that of a poetics re-inscribing itself in life, in society, to reveal to the mind the contradiction – and the dialectics – of its relation to language. As an activity, poetry is dual: a head-on attempt to reach presence, but also an inevitable, incessant, falling back down that illumines the human condition and allows men and women, here and there in the world, to share reflections emanating from their disappointed waiting. A duality, and even a path! One can detect in it what, out of bad experience, lay at the origins of the beautiful falsehood of myths. But one also sees in it a lucidity that remains alive and replaces those dreams, thus potentially providing a foundation and a form to societies beyond the centuries of revelations and dogmas.

VIII.

Now I am in a position to make a remark that this idea of poetry makes me think is not useless: poetry has a liking for this conceptual thinking that it struggles against, that it is born to struggle against.

Poetry is attentive to concepts, as I have just pointed out; it cannot ignore that they interpose themselves between it and the presence of the world but also that they cut out from the world the figures through which this presence manifests itself, from which it follows that one cannot go beyond them without making the very experience itself run dry. But saying this is insufficient. It must be added that poetry, in its attentiveness, is not mere mistrust. As the enemy of the claim of the concept to close itself up into a system, or an image, poetry can experience sympathy for its perhaps involuntary way of helping a person who is thus threatened to regain control of himself as a person in the very world that the concept reifies.

What does poetry understand? That many notions formed by thinking have by no means the single effect of putting reality at a distance: they help us to delimit the figures at the heart of which presence persists, those of the men and women with whom we are involved – memorably, as one says – in common endeavours. In fact, language, from the onset, was not a system of representations freed from time and place, but rather the extension to other human beings – obviously also mortal, threatened, and prey to finitude – of the field of a relationship to the world, a relationship that the subject using language centres on the event that is his life. And he and these other human beings will therefore have lived – either helping or fighting each other – within the same presence to the world where nothing prevailed over their sentiment of finitude. The things to which they clung in order to survive, things in which they participated more than thought about, had not yet lost their thickness of reality. The hunter facing his prey instinctively knew the form and the weight of the branch or the stone that he picked up for his attack. Yet it is in this field of thought that the concept took on form. It was there when the hunter spotted the branch or the stone.

And so we must not decide too quickly about the deeds and misdeeds of concepts: because in these original usages, which have not vanished, many notions are still an open approach to their object: retaining a simple aspect of it, indeed, but without the intention of incorporating the aspect into an organised system of thought. Poetically, what must be fought in concepts is when they build themselves up into systems that prefer themselves, that become their own end. Should such structures establish themselves with a concern about extending themselves, should an image of the world thereby take the place of the world, this is when, and only when, one must deem conceptual thinking dangerous and fight against its threat by using poetic intuition.

What I ask of poetry is thus not antipathy for the concept, but rather compassion, because one must love the courage of this approach to the world which, in order to know and transform it, runs the risk of losing it, with exile for a destination. I would prefer an approach that would be less denial – an instinctive, undifferentiated rejection – than a question asked, for example, of those great simple words of life or nature that seem to hesitate about separating themselves from their origins – tree, bush, source, stones. I would prefer? But it is a fact, and is the most constant work of poets.

One observes those who want to undo themselves from the reified

– that is, from the desire to have and not to be – as they head, amid
concepts, toward those that designate the non-object, what cannot
be possessed: the concept of tree will overtake the concept of wood,
the concept of wood will discover, in its differentiations, those that
designated fallen branches, gathered branches, and then the fire that
brings together the weary people arriving. Poetry re-centres vocabulary more than it judges its ingredients.

And when conceptual thinking intuits what it is losing – the full
realness of finitude that knows itself and assumes itself – and seeks to
recover it and, in order to do so, conceives a stratagem to which poets
succumb, the sympathy of which I am speaking does not cease for
all that. This stratagem is beauty, the 'bad' beauty that I have already
fleetingly evoked, beauty in what I will call the aesthetic accepta-
tion of the word. The conceptual system – this world as an image
– cannot prevent itself from knowing that it is only that, an image
– figures that let the infinity inherent in the slightest real things
flee; and now the conceptual system wants the lines or volumes that
constitute these figures to lend themselves to a harmonisation of
their mutual relations that will suggest that, as far as it is concerned,
it is something intelligible, a unity, a path towards the One intimated
in everything.

Which is not the case. Aesthetic elaboration, however diverted
from vulgar craving, remains a desire to have, nothing else: established in appearances, it neither recognises nor ensures to anything
whatsoever this existence outside of language which would allow the
meeting of the kind of experience that can go, by means of love,
beyond the need to possess. And to be lured by this beauty is to
lose sight of the intuition of poetry, which will rebel, reassert itself,
and this will be the major debate in regard to the genesis of verse.
The aesthetic form encouraged by what is conceptual wants to
take possession of the space of writing, to have its idea of harmony
accepted there, to inscribe its references to sensorial reality there,
while suggesting to the mind that its mirror can be found there…
Combats for and against poetry. But also truces, as when Tancrède
fights Clorinde: knowing the iniquity of his adversary, his nostalgia,
the poet cannot prevent himself from being fond of him. Should he
wish to destroy beauty, feel that his salvation depends on it, he raises
beauty up, speaks to it, follows its gaze towards its illusory horizon.

After all, the beauty that poetry denies also knows finitude because it has been born from its attempt to repress the thought of it.

An affection; and in the poem as well, nothing that is ever pure poetry, nor anything that is ever finished. On the page, the poem is displayed in a version that seems final, yet, in fact, all those uncertain debates remain in suspense in its depths, all those kinds of progress made in a mere moment, all those local forms that increase experience but were also its very life and still signify it. Dangerous is the once-prevalent hypothesis of an 'ego of the work', in the sense that it postulated a global form for the work, deployed under the authority of a person, the author. The poet is not an 'ego' managing a world of which he thereby accepts that he is but a beautiful image. He is an 'I' seeking himself in the future of his writing, never truly finding himself and never attaining a full awareness of himself.

IX.

And the critic? It is desirable that the criticism should understand that poetry is this incessant combat between representation and presence. This struggle is not only that of poets, but also the fate of anyone wishing another human being to be a presence for him, not a thing. The combat thus lies at the foundation of society, whose ups and downs reflect the dramatic events of this very struggle. Working as a critic of poetry thus means having the chance to go to the bottom of all social phenomena. Poems have a capacity to elucidate possessed by no other kind of document, no other archive.

And the same fundamental knowledge of poetics is just as necessary for whoever wishes to engage with specific works and define their differences. If the perception of the poetics of such and such a work is lacking in the analysis, the portrait will be inexact, however richly detailed one finds it to be. This lack of knowledge about an author will also prevent the critic from understanding the true nature of the author's relationship with others.

I have encountered this lack of knowledge in Georges Poulet, in his reflections about Rimbaud. 'Better than any other poet, doesn't Rimbaud make my dream come true', he asks in his major letter to Marcel Raymond, 'that of poetry suddenly surging forth, without antecedents, and entirely new?' This is surely Poulet's dream, and it will guide his reading, but Rimbaud does not fit this dream. What Poulet perceives in Rimbaud as an élan that would have no other cause than the poet himself – the sort of ardent consummation that he also imagines in a Racine, a Mozart – was in reality a series of experiments each based on a hypothesis – involving political ideology in 'The Blacksmith' or 'Paris is Repopulated', metaphysics in the case of 'Sun and Flesh' – which is obviously of a conceptual nature and in which the young poet gets trapped, but for only a short while each time. These dreams produced by thought and hindering poetics are surely not an outpouring. One should rather speak of haste: Rimbaud taking shortcuts because of his irrepressible impatience – a fever.

One would then see that this haste, where poetic ardour is so obvious – and yet where one senses imprudence, that is, anguish – signifies well beyond Rimbaud himself: whence the reception that has been given to his intense, lasting poetry. What causes this poetry to emerge, if it is not the pressure exerted on this young human being's hope by a body whose intuitions and rights are repressed, in the society of his day, at the expense of the universal that he could help make blossom? The reason for Rimbaud's haste, which will end up becoming his undoing, is the multi-secular alienation of a continent 'where insanity roams'. And to read him well is to understand the Western World in its unfortunately distinctive characteristics: its impatience, indeed, its way of waging its wars, its illusions, the very thing that Rimbaud knows how to characterise, just as well, in the lucid first pages of *A Season in Hell*. By reading a poet, one can gain access to the meaning of an entire society.

Let me come back to Georges Poulet. He reads Rimbaud in the same way that he reads Racine or Shakespeare, persuading himself that they are each the flame that at once bears and burns up an oeuvre of which it does not matter to know what fed its furnace, for it seemingly gathers its firewood by chance, being focused on its fire, on its light: the light, for example, that is the silence at the end of *Phèdre*. But reading like this means loving poetry but not understanding it, and I see a problem here that relates to Georges Poulet himself. Why does the author of *Métamorphoses du cercle* initially have the thought, when one speaks to him about forms in a work of art or a piece of writing, to refuse their importance, to wish to prove that poets are innocent? If it is true that there is a blind spot in every critical consciousness, why does it have to be that specific one in him?

The question is worth raising, but the answer is simple. It is, in fact, given by Poulet himself – I have already quoted the passage – in his 'mighty reply' to Marcel Raymond. Why doesn't he want to know anything about the importance of forms in the work of poetry? It is because he adheres to the idea of the 'transcendence of the Father' instead of that of 'the Son'. 'Up there', in a God closed in on Himself, is true reality, being. Here below, where a tepid Marcel Raymond senses that the divine penetrates everything that is, Georges Poulet sees only 'vileness'; and as to the body, which Rimbaud exalts, it is a 'saucepan' of which he hears only the clatter: the mature Mozart probably being not a body but an angel, and unexplainable, which is fine. There is no bridge between the hereness of the world and the secret of God except for the aspiration to attain something more than life that sometimes feels the fallen creature. And nothing in this world that has meaning. At the end of *Phèdre*, silence, yet nothing in the play itself but broken chains, by no means forms that signify.

X.

I must now stop speaking about Georges Poulet, for the lack of time would make me unjust to him, preventing me from seeing everything which, in him, admirably contradicts his principles. To do him justice, one would at least have to begin what I have absolutely not undertaken nor am capable of doing, an examination of the analyses that Poulet, in his many essays, attempted to carry out in regard to specific works of art or literature. And I know that one would find there what I would be constrained to call inconsistencies, and first of all this one, as fundamental as it is fortunate: in his disdain for our earthly condition, Poulet is not worried about having to hold in esteem, to admire, as he does so easily, the writers whom he approaches, although they are many in number; he does not see that by studying their works, which he knows how to love, he gives back to the world a good share of what he claims to condemn in it. Works of art and literature are for him a mirror where what he considers to be nothingness, in their surroundings, finds Being again, and it is perhaps even for the happiness that they give him that he wishes to see in them only this reflecting surface, denying that anything else exists below its light. It is much earlier in his own writings that one must meet up with Poulet, for if every critic has his blind spot, and he like any other, it is at least as true that critics are great only through their contradictions. They are aware of and alarmed by them, they are the cause of additional presence in them, as much for them as for others, from which surge forth intuitions that do much more than compensate for their bizarre denials and their biases.

Yet if one listens too much to Georges Poulet, one will lose sight of what seems essential to me, that is, the place of poetry in the mind. And I cannot help but be preoccupied with what is at stake there, in him as well as in other critics. If he wishes to vouch for the 'transcendence of the Father', he has the right to do so, but one can simply conclude from this position that, instead of studying literature, he should have devoted himself to the study of mystical experience, which seeks to rise above the 'vileness' of ordinary existence and leaves works of art outside its purview, with the exception of a few peaks: for example, as Poulet would say, Mozart's or Beethoven's last years. But poetry is not mysticism, and studies of poetry must not devote their intelligence and sensibility to making us forget the difference.

Poetry is not mysticism. At the moment when the awareness of the fundamental sound lets the world appear as presence in words, the poet is he who does not forget that if there are words, it is for another important reason, which is to establish between a person and another person a relationship which, extended to still other people, establishes a common place of survival, which I call an earth. Perceiving what lies outside of language, sensing this depth of what is immediate, the poet could have chosen this plenitude, rejecting within words what diverted him from it, in short, rejecting speech; but, instead, he chooses to continue to speak, that is, to remain within what – thereafter partaking of the conceptual, of what can be mediated, of representation – nonetheless still partakes of existence, that is, a finitude that it will thus be necessary, if not to recover, at least to designate, to make one desire and comprehend. The poet will establish himself in this relativeness, harbour his own hope, bring the community together in a contradictory lucidity where presence and representation cohabit. This is what I call incarnation, and it strikes me as dangerous to forget the fact. Otherwise, one abandons society to the forces that dismantle it.

All in all, it is this uneasiness, nothing else, that I wished to express in regard to Georges Poulet. But once again, I now must stop speaking about him, for he deserves better than a continuing inquisition, as well founded as it seems to be. Let me finish up my questioning of this critic, of this friend, but not without my coming back to him. It will in fact be to prove him right more or less, with respect to my initial point, his remark made to Raymond, saying that I made him uncomfortable because I at once saw in poetry the rejection of any conceptual thought and yet did not keep myself from 'conceptualising in poetry'.

In conclusion, let me say that his remark strikes me as eminently capable of being pondered, either by me, personally, or from the vantage point of the ideas that I have put forward. In regard to the latter, first and foremost, 'conceptualising in poetry' – why not? I have just stated that intuition must speak with the concept, the mediate with the immediate, and this exchange can be carried out at all levels of poetic preoccupation. I believe that I have shown that it can be found at the very heart of writing, where the 'iambic' form collides with a beauty that is of conceptual birth and that one must recognise and reject as such, in other words, on its own terms. Refusing to think conceptually is what befits the mystic, not the poet. But where Poulet is right is when he says that accepting the fact of the concept contradicts some of my declarations, which would make the access to poetry 'explicitly depend', he specifies, on the total rejection, on the contrary, of the concept. It is true that one must not be so radical, and I thus have to wonder if I have ever said that or even thought so. Did I perhaps do so, out of haste or awkwardness, during that period of time when Poulet could read me? All the same, it does not seem to me, ever since obscure meditations on the 'concept of ivy' and others on the tombs of Ravenna, that I was so uncompromising in my polemical writings from that period.

I leaf through the pages from back then, and from more recent times, and I nevertheless see that on a few occasions I insisted too much on the fault line separating, in one's awareness of the world, conceptual thinking and the intuitive knowledge of finitude. It is as if I did not see, in these declarations, what I hope to have better formulated in these pages today, or as if, rather, for a moment, I no longer wanted to see. I interpret this fact less as an earlier, dated, state of insufficient thinking, than as an ambivalence in regard to the conceptual, a resentment beneath the recognition – in both senses of the term – and even the affection that I felt the need, today, to express. Could it be that there is in me with respect to the concept, and in an obvious fascination, vestiges not of an ancient flame but of an original anger? In other words, should I think that, in my too distracted eyes, it sometimes metaphorises authorities of another kind, still related to it, either because it produced them or that they accepted it? I can believe this, glimpsing that behind conceptual speculation looms the paternal figure's shadow, so diluted, the memory as well of churches, 'malicious plumage'.[4] And these facts that I need to recognise obviously constitute a programme for my work, these forms that I must deconstruct from an ambivalence, from some leftover resentment. A two-faced task. To love those who abide by the truth of the concept. To maintain, however, at a distance the dogmas that the concept favours, with their cartload of non-being. And between these two great postulations, to have much to understand and obviously to attempt to do, which means, all the same, to have to 'conceptualise in poetry' for a long time still.

Translated by John Taylor

4   The reference is to Mallarmé's description of the Godhead, the 'vieux et méchant plumage' pronounced dead and 'brought down', in his letter of 14 May 1867 to Henri Cazalis.

3.
POETS

READINESS, RIPENESS: *HAMLET, LEAR*[1]

Just after he agrees to fight with Laertes – but not without a sense of foreboding that he tries to suppress – Hamlet concludes that 'the readiness is all'. And toward the end of *King Lear*, Edgar, son of the Earl of Gloucester, persisting in his efforts to dissuade his father from suicide, asserts that 'ripeness is all'. And shouldn't we suppose that Shakespeare established consciously the opposition in these two phrases that are so closely related and that come at two moments so dense with meaning – and that they therefore speak of one of the tensions at the very heart of his poetics? I would like to try to understand more clearly the 'readiness' in *Hamlet* and the 'ripeness' in *King Lear*.

But first a preliminary remark which, though it has been made before, seems nevertheless useful to bear in mind when we raise questions about Shakespeare's work. As one studies the history of Western society, one discovers at one moment or another, and on every level of life, especially on the level of self-awareness, a deep fissure whose line marks the point of separation between a previous and now seemingly archaic era and what one might already call the modern world. The time 'before' – that was when a conception of oneness, of unity, experienced as life, as presence, governed every relationship one could have with specific realities. Each of these realities thus found its place in a precisely defined order which in turn made of each a presence, a kind of soul alive to itself and to the world, among the other realities endowed with the same life, and assured to each a meaning of which there could be no doubt. The most important and the most fortunate consequence of this fact of an order and a meaning was that the human person, who knew himself to be an element in this world and who sometimes even thought himself the center of it, also had no occasion to call his own being into doubt or the fact that he stood

1 'Readiness, Ripeness: *Hamlet, Lear*' was first published as a preface to Bonnefoy's French translations of these two plays: *Hamlet, Le Roi Lear*, Collection Folio, Editions Gallimard 1978. Collected in *Théâtre et poésie. Shakespeare et Yeats*. Paris: Mercure de France, 1998; and in *Shakespeare: Théâtre et Poésie*. Paris: Coll. *Tel Essais*, Gallimard, 2014.

for the absolute. Whatever may have been the high and low points of his existence, in which chance often came into play, the human person still could and had to honour his essence, which preserved a divine spark – herein is the whole substance of the teaching of the Christian Middle Ages with its theology of salvation. But a day came when technology and science began to mark out – in what as a result became simply objects – features that could not be integrated into the structures of traditional meaning. The established order fell into fragmentation, the earth of signs and promises became nature once again, and life matter; the relation of the person to himself was all at once an enigma, and destiny a solitude. This is the fracture I was speaking of, the final settlings of which have not yet been determined.

And it should also be noticed that the first truly irrevocable manifestations of this crisis out of which was born the civilisation – if this word still applies – that today we oppose to the rest of the planet, this first manifestation took place, according to the country and according to the social milieu as well, at various moments of the end of the sixteenth and beginning of the seventeenth century, which in England corresponds to the years during which Shakespeare wrote his plays. The fracture line that broke the horizon of atemporality and gave over the history of the world to its ever more uncertain and precipitous development, this fracture line passes through *Hamlet* – this is obviously one of the causes of the play – and I would even say runs right through the heart of the work. Without attempting a detailed analysis, for these few pages would hardly be the place for it, I can at least emphasise, as an example of what I mean, the central importance of the opposition of two beings who clearly represent the succession of the two eras, a contrast which is all the more striking for being established between a father and son who bear the same name. On this scarcely realistic stage, where aspects of the high Middle Ages are boldly combined with others that reflect the life of Shakespeare's own time and even its philosophical avant-garde – the references to Wittenberg, for instance, the stoicism of Horatio – the old Hamlet, the king who furthermore is already dead, although he continues to make himself heard, the old king represents, and this is obvious and even explicitly expressed, the archaic mode of being. Not only does he wear the dress and bear witness to the customs of feudal society, even his need for vengeance signifies his adherence to the dying tradition, since this demand that is so full of the conviction of sacred right, implies, among other things, the certainty that the entire state suffers when legitimacy is violated. And beyond this, his status as battling and triumphant sovereign of being is an excellent metaphor for the domination that the Christian of the era before the new astronomy thought he exercised over a world on the peripheries of which the devil might nonetheless be prowling. And finally, the first Hamlet is a father, without the slightest apprehension, with hope even – which means that he has confidence in established values, in continuity. Claudius, who puts an end to the reign, has no children.

And as for the other Hamlet, as for this son called upon to reestablish the traditional order and thus to assume his royal function, it is easy to see that if he is the hero of Shakespeare's tragedy, it is because the values evoked by the Ghost, which Hamlet tries at once to inscribe in the 'book' of his memory, have now almost no reality in his eyes. His goodwill is nevertheless quite real; he burns with the desire to vindicate his father, and he admires two other sons who do not hesitate to take their place in the society they believe still exists; and if for a moment he thinks of marriage, he who had been filled with disgust for things sexual by his mother's new relationship, in my opinion it is in the hope that the very real love he feels for Ophelia might reconcile him to life as it is, and to the idea of generation, which in turn could help him to vanquish the scepticism that saps his energy and turns him from action. But this desire to do what is right sets off even more strikingly the extent to which his vision of the world, like a paralysing, if not completely destructive fatality, no longer recognises its once perfect organisation – that organisation which is, in fact, already in disarray in the comportment of the 'Danish' court, prey to a symptomatic corruption. One remembers his moving words on the earth, that sterile promontory, on the heavens, that foul and pestilent congregation of vapours. Similarly, if he fails as he does with Ophelia, although there is nothing really wrong with their personal relationship, it is because he has not managed to spare her from that vision that seizes everything and everybody from the outside – as is indicated by his mocking cry, 'words, words, words' – and he therefore can see nothing but opacity and lies in every manner of thinking and speaking, including those of young girls. Even if one feels obligated to try other keys – the oedipal motivations, for instance – for understanding the suspicion with which Hamlet persecutes Ophelia, it remains nonetheless true that this suspicion betrays, in its difference from the simple faith of Hamlet's father, the presence of an alienation, of an isolation, a vertigo which the earlier, more united society could never have imagined and would not have tolerated. And it is, furthermore, in his ambiguous relation to his father, who represents – who is, in fact, the former world – that Hamlet's revulsions most clearly appear. He does not want to doubt that he admires and even loves his father; but when he calls him the 'old mole' or thinks he sees him in his nightgown the second time he appears, or lets himself be carried away by the thought of those sins which keep him in Purgatory – the reference to him as 'gross' and 'full of bread', for instance – aren't these simply more signs of his inability to understand the ways of the world and the beings in it, as the old way of looking at life would have allowed him to?

This inability to recognise his father for what he truly is, although he will affirm his worth at every chance he gets, is doubtless one of the most painful of Hamlet's secrets and one of the unacknowledged elements with which he nourishes what is obviously his sense of remorse, and it explains a number of the most obscure aspects of the play, beginning with the other great obsession that structures it. There are certainly many reasons that explain Hamlet's rages against Gertrude – and once again I am not attempting for the moment anything like a systematic analysis – but it seems obvious to me that if the son accuses his mother so violently of betrayal, it is because he himself has betrayed – although he does not realise it – the very person whom, according to Hamlet, she should have kept without rival in her heart. He always insists that it is the majesty of the old Hamlet, his twofold greatness of man and prince, that has been insulted by the new marriage; he vehemently denounces Claudius's vices, especially as they show him to be unworthy of the role he has usurped; but the whole scene of the 'two pictures', during which Hamlet would prove to Gertrude the grandeur of the one and the ignominy and even the ridiculousness of the other, serves only to show that rhetorical device plays a large role in the emotion he tries to feel. Once again in this play we are at the theatre, and perhaps much more so during these moments of accusation and introspection than when the player recites those rather bombastic, if deeply felt, verses on the death of Queen Hecuba. Hamlet tries to live according to the values which have been handed down to him from the past, but he can only do so on the level of 'words, words, words', the obsession with the emptiness of which one now begins to better understand. He who, in order to wreak his vengeance, in order to restore the threatened order, in short, in order to proclaim meaning, feels it necessary to disguise himself for a brief interval that in fact becomes endless, is merely an actor on this level as well – so that his true double in the play is, alas, neither Laertes, nor Fortinbras, nor even Gertrude, who is only guilty of weakness – and Hamlet knows this, as does his father who reminds him of it with insistence – but rather the character who says one thing and thinks another, and merely pretends to respect and observe values in which he certainly no longer believes: Claudius, the destroyer, the enemy ... This is the true core of *Hamlet*, as well as the necessary consequence of that crisis in society of which the murder of the king is only the symbol. Those who appear now, and who can be seen to exist beyond the boundaries of the broken social order, are more deeply imbued with reality, more fully steeped in the denseness of life than their fellowmen, whose obedience to the categories of former times seems only backward and obtuse. They live in anguish and confusion; their survival reactions are cynical and ignominious – as is certainly the case with that opaque being, Claudius, for such a long time the shadow of his brother. He is an undeniably covetous man, as there have always been covetous men, but he is also one who has consciously transgressed the strictest social codes.

All through *Hamlet* there are a thousand signs of the fascinated interest – sometimes bordering on the equivocal, it seems so affectionate – the nephew has in his uncle. One senses that something attracts him in the very person he thinks he detests, without it being necessary to infer from this strange obsession, at least as its essential reason, some ambiguous extension of the complex algebra of the oedipal relations to be deciphered by the psychoanalyst. I would say that Hamlet less loves, than he simply *understands* Claudius for what he is, and that he understands him more intimately than he can understand others, because it is his contemporary he is encountering, and his only contemporary, in these changing times that have suddenly become a thundering storm, a sinking ship. He feels for this man who is nonetheless his adversary according to the reasoning of days gone by – and certainly his enemy according to values that are eternal – that instinctive solidarity that binds together shipwrecked men.

*

In short, *Hamlet* is clearly, deeply, specifically the problematics of a consciousness awakening to a condition that was undreamt of and unimaginable only the day before: a world without structure, truths which henceforth are only partial, contradictory, in competition with one another – as many signs as one would wish, and quickly far too many, but nothing that will resemble a sacred order or meaning. And it is from this perspective that we have to try to examine the idea of 'readiness', as Hamlet advances it, at a moment, it should be noted, that is late in the play – in the fifth act – when Hamlet has had the chance to measure the extent of a disaster that he experiences at first as an endless tangle of insoluble contradictions. And what about Claudius? Hamlet had been so filled with the desire to kill him, and yet here he is still hesitating to do so, apparently resolute, as resolute as ever, but distracted in every situation by some new consideration – this time, for instance, by his interest in Laertes. And Ophelia? It is certain now that he did love her, the news of her suicide has given him absolute proof of it – he loved her, he says at the time, more than forty thousand brothers, and more in any case than Laertes whose grandiloquence is clearly open to criticism; and yet this strange love, poisoned by suspicion, disguised in insult, has only thrown her into despair and death. It is clear now that he is suffering deeply from an evil the cure for which is beyond him, and that he has lost all hope in his ability to arrest the collapse of meaning. Hamlet is acutely conscious of his own powerlessness as he gives expression to his deepest thoughts on the last day of his life in the presence of Horatio, who always seems to incite him to profound reflection and exigency.

What does Hamlet say to Horatio in this scene – preceded, it should be remembered, by their long meditation in the cemetery beside the skull of Yorick, the king's jester, he who knew better than anyone the falseness of appearances? He says that even the fall of a sparrow is ruled by Providence, that 'if it be now, 'tis not to come; if it be not to come, it will be now', and that if it be not now, let there be no doubt about it, 'yet it will come'. And as we do not know this moment, and never can, the important thing is to be ready ... One might suppose that Hamlet is talking about death here, and in a way that does not seem in contradiction with traditional teaching, since the medieval mind loved to insist that God had the final decision about the fate of man's undertakings. Should we draw the conclusion that Hamlet – who has obviously thought a great deal during his trip to England, and after it as well – is in the process of rediscovering the truth of the ancient precepts and is referring, in any case, to those fundamental structures of being of which they were the expression? But Christianity confided to Providence only the final result of an act and not its preparation which, on the contrary, it asked one to subject to careful consideration and to bring within the bounds of established values. Hamlet, however, is taking advantage of what seems fatalistic in the traditional way of looking at things in order to dispense with the necessity, of examining what he has been compelled to accept in this situation which could be decisive for him – his swordfight with a master duelist – an encounter which could easily be refused, especially as it clearly seems to be part of a trap. Why does he consent to risk his life before having brought to successful conclusion his grand scheme to reestablish justice? Neither the ethics, nor the religion of the Middle Ages would have accepted this way of behaving that seems to suggest that a prince is indifferent to his cause, a son to the wishes of his father.

In spite of how it might seem, therefore, Hamlet has not really taken up for himself an adage which in its true significance – 'Heaven helps those who help themselves' – gave such apt expression, in fact, to the old universe with its contrasting poles of transcendence and chance. If he has recourse to a traditional formula, it is to turn it toward aims of an entirely different nature, and this time authentically, totally, fatalistic. The 'readiness' he proposes is not reliance on the will of God as the guarantor of our efforts, the protector of our meaning, it is rather cessation of what the God of former times expected of us: the fearless and unflagging exercise of our judgment in the world He created, the discrimination between good and evil. In place of the discernment that tries to organise and provide, and does so through awareness of values, he substitutes the welcoming acceptance of things as they come along, however disorderly and contradictory they might be, and the acceptance of chance: from the perspective of this philosophy of pessimism, our acts seem as thoroughly devoid of a reason for being as the necessity that comes into play with them. Our condition is in non-meaning, nothingness, and it is just as well to realise it at moments that seem moments of action, when normally our naiveté is summoned. In a word, a single act still has some logic and is worthy of being carried out: and that is to take great pains to detach oneself from every illusion and to be ready to accept everything – everything, but first of all, and especially, death, the essence of all life – with irony and indifference.

And yet it cannot be denied that the Hamlet who proposes this surrender is, as the whole scene will show, also a man who is now much more alert than at other moments of the play, and much more attentive than he once was to the ways in which others behave, for example, even if his observation leads only to mocking and scorn. He can even be seen to prepare himself for a sport which nothing in his past has allowed us to expect from him, a sport that demands swiftness of eye and quickness of hand – and also the encounter with the other, in that true and not entirely heartless intimacy which can exist in hand-to-hand combat. These characteristics, so unexpected in the one once covered by the inky cloak, act, of course, to pave the way for the denouement of the play which must pass through the battle of two sons who are, as Hamlet himself remarks, the image of one another; and yet, so striking and so present are they, that they must be said to play a role as well in the implicit characterisation of the ethics that is developed, and thus it would be a mistake to think that this *readiness*, which is a form of renunciation, is so in a passive or discouraged way. Doubtless because the conclusion reached by Hamlet has freed him from his earlier self-absorption, from his recriminations and his endless reverie, his new mode of being seems also to take on a body, a capacity for sport, an interest, if perhaps a cruel one, for those things in the world he once had fled. This is now an all-embracing consciousness, an immediacy in the way the world is received that is already response, return: and this 'readiness' is in truth so active, one can feel so intensely the need to bring together everything in the experience of the void, that one is tempted to compare it to other undertakings which, though they too seem pessimistic, are nonetheless of a spiritual nature and another form of the absolute. Is the 'readiness' of Hamlet an Elizabethan equivalent of the Buddhist discipline, of the way in which the samurai, for instance, prepares himself – another swordsman at the end of another Middle Age – to accept the moment of death without a shadow of resistance? A way of recovering positivity and plenitude in the very heart of an empty world?

But with the Oriental – be he warrior or monk – the critique of appearances, of the manifestations of illusion, is also, and even first of all, brought to bear on the self, which has appeared to him, not without good reason, as the supreme form of illusion, whereas Hamlet's lucidity, however radical it may wish to be, is the reaction of a man who has considered himself the depository of the absolute, who hasn't as yet resigned himself to the dislocation of that heritage which remains centered on the self; and I see it therefore as the ultimate response of an unrelenting 'personality', a kind of doleful, yet not entirely hopeless meditation on the meaninglessness he himself has tried to prove. Hamlet's 'readiness' is not the Oriental's effort to go beyond the very idea of meaning to attain to the plenitude of immediacy – the person who recognises that he has no more importance than the fleeting blossoms of the cherry tree; no, it is rather the degree zero of a meaning, an order, still vividly recalled – the fundamental structures of which, though lost, are still considered desirable, and the need for which is still secretly acknowledged by that very complexity of consciousness in which all the language existing only for the purpose of hoping and organising still remains in reserve for the possibility of some future miracle. The new relation to the self of this king without a kingdom is therefore not a peaceful one; it is not the great bright burst of laughter that tears apart ancient woe. What should be seen, on the contrary, is a sharpening of unvanquished suffering, its reduction to a single shrill note – almost inaudible and yet ever present – a form of irony not unlike that of which Kierkegaard will write, in which the moments of spiritedness or laughter are always chilled by nostalgia. Not the liberation, but the celibacy of the soul – taken on as a last sign, a challenge full of desire, offered to the God who has withdrawn from his Word. An appeal, and in this sense a recognition of the existence of others, a sign that he who pretends to prefer solitude is in fact lying to himself – in all of which is prefigured, as the enormous vogue of *Hamlet* throughout the entire nineteenth century bears witness, the dandyism of Delacroix and Baudelaire.

I therefore see the 'readiness' that emerges in *Hamlet* as quite simply a negative strategy for the preservation of the soul, a technique useful at all times when humanity strives to recall what its hopes once were. And I think it necessary, of course, to try to understand whether this state of mind applies only to the prince of Denmark and to a few others like him in Shakespeare's bountiful and polyphonous universe, or whether one should ascribe it, in one way or another, to Shakespeare himself and therefore consider it as one of the possible 'solutions' proposed by the poetry of the Elizabethan era for the great crisis in values it was beginning to analyse. One could easily imagine it as such – *Hamlet* is so obviously a personal play, and one can feel so intensely, in phrase after phrase of his hero, a poet's effort to stand in place of rhetorical conventions. But let us be careful to notice that nothing has really been definitively undertaken, even in the play itself, when Hamlet, at the very last moment, affirms and assumes his new philosophy. That he takes it seriously, that he would like to truly live it, can scarcely be doubted, since it is to Horatio, to whom he never lies, that he confides his deepest thoughts on the matter. But mortally wounded an hour later, it is to Fortinbras that he offers his 'dying voice' – and beyond him to traditional values, or at least to the attitude that wills the preservation of their fiction. One therefore has the right to wonder if 'readiness' isn't for Shakespeare simply one phase of psychological insight and in Hamlet the whimsical stance that masks the even more disastrous reason that has led him to accept Laertes's strange challenge so lightly, and with it the possibility of dying.

★

But let us not forget that it is in *Lear*, not more than five or six years later, that one sees clearly designated that 'ripeness' which Shakespeare seems to have wanted to place against the 'readiness' of the earlier work.

The historical context of *Lear* is not without certain resemblances to the earlier play, since the work is set in an England at least as archaic as the Denmark of Hamlet's father – it is even a pagan world, closely watched over by its gods – and yet here, too, one discovers signs that seem to announce new modes of being. And in *Lear* there also emerges a character one can sense from the outset incapable of recognising that the world is an order, rich in meaning – Edmund, second son of the Earl of Gloucester. A son, then, like the prince of Denmark, and one who has, like Hamlet, reasons for doubt about what will be his heritage. But the resemblance between Edmund and Hamlet stops there, for the painful plight of the son, which Hamlet has lived through with honesty and with the burning desire to do what is right, is now studied in one who is clearly evil, and with conceptual categories that remain essentially medieval. One might, at first sight, consider modern this certainly nonconformist personality who scoffs at astrological explanations, at the superstitions of those who surround him, and even at the values of common morality. But it should be observed that Edmund's speeches are accompanied by none of those indications – such as the actors, Wittenberg, the presence of Horatio – which in Hamlet serve to mark, by outward sign, that one is approaching the modern era. What makes Edmund an outsider, far from being seen as symptomatic of crisis, is rather set very explicitly by Shakespeare in the context of one of the convictions advanced by the medieval understanding of man: if Edmund would usurp his brother's place, if he longs to see his father dead, if he thus shows how far he is from the most universal human feelings, it is because he is a bastard, born out of wedlock, the fruit himself of sin. And it is in complete agreement with traditional Christian teaching that King Lear asks us to understand that this sin, this adultery, is precisely the occasion that evil, ever unvanquished, even if always repelled, has been waiting for – the chance to invade once again the order established by God, which order will nonetheless in the end emerge triumphant once more, thanks to the intervention of a few righteous souls. And this being the case, if Edmund evokes nature as his one guiding principle, as the law to which his services are bound, one should not see in this a reflection of the Renaissance humanist for whom the study of matter is unbiased activity of mind, but rather the revelation of the baseness of a soul, influenced, on the contrary, by black magic – a soul that feels at home nowhere so much as amidst the most frankly animal realities. Edmund's actions do not disclose the ultimate crisis of sacred order but rather its innermost weakness. And one knows from the very outset of the action that he will perish – unmistakably, without a trace of uneasiness or regret, without a future in the new forms of consciousness, as soon as the forces of goodness he has caught offguard have reestablished their power.

Far from signifying, then, that Shakespeare's attention is focused on the problems of modernity as such, as was the case in *Hamlet*, the character of the son in *King Lear* serves rather to reinforce the notion that the old order remains the uncontested frame of reference in the play, the determining factor in the outcome of the drama, the truth that will be reaffirmed after a moment of crisis. And it is clearly for this reason that there emerges in the foreground of the play a figure missing in Hamlet, since neither Laertes nor Fortinbras ever attains truly spiritual stature: the figure of the child – girl or boy, since it is as true of Cordelia, third daughter of Lear, as of Edgar, firstborn son of Gloucester – whose purity and moral determination find the means of thwarting the traitors' schemes. In fact, more even than Cordelia, whose somewhat cool and arid virtuousness keeps at a certain distance from those violent, contradictory words, mingled with both love and hatred, through which the action of the play is developed and resolved, the agent of redemption for the imperiled group is Edgar who, at the very moment when he might have yielded to despair or given in to cynicism – hasn't he been falsely accused, attacked by his own brother, misjudged, without cause, by his father? – gives proof, on the contrary, of those reserves of compassion, of lucidity, of resolute understanding of the darkest depths of the souls of others, that can be found in anyone, even quite early in life and without special preparation. Struck in a completely unforeseeable way by what appears to be the purest form of evil, this still very young man, who only the day before was rich, pampered, assured of a future place among the most powerful of the land, chooses at once to plunge into the very depths of adversity, taking on the semblance of a beggar and the speech of a fool to shatter at the outset the too narrow framework of his own personal drama and to bring his inquiry to bear on all the injustices, all the miseries, all the forms of madness that afflict society. He understands instinctively – and here is clearly a sign that this world is still alive – that he will be able to achieve his salvation only by working for the salvation of others, each man needing as much as another to free himself from his egotism, from his excesses, from his pride so that true exchange might begin once more.

In spite of everything, however, the hero of *King Lear* remains the one for whom the play is named – the old king – since unlike Edmund who has been marked from the outset by the sin involved in his birth, and in contrast to Edgar who emerges into his maturity through the crimes of another, Lear is thrown into his troubles by his own free act, and thus his punishment and his madness, his gradual discovery of those truths and realities he had neglected before, become a succession of events all the more deeply convincing and touching. Lear begins, not with something rotten in the state, as was the case for Hamlet, but rather with a mysterious sickness in the soul, and in this case, with pride. Lear admires himself, prefers himself; he is interested in others only to the extent that they are interested in him, and thus he is blind to their own true being; he therefore does not truly love others, in spite of what he might think: and so the ground is laid for the catastrophic act that will refuse to recognise true value, that will deprive the righteous of their due, and that will spread disorder and sorrow everywhere and give the devil the chance he has been waiting for in the son born of adultery. Lear – even more than Gloucester whose only sins are sins of the flesh – has relived, has reactivated the original sin of men, and thus he represents, more than any other character in the play, our condition in its most radical form, which is imperfection, but also struggle, the will to self-mastery. When, on the basis of those values he has never denied but has understood so poorly and lived so little, he learns to recognise that his kingly self-assurance is pure pretension, his love a mere illusion, and when he learns what true love is, what happiness could be, one feels all the more deeply moved as his initial blindness belongs to all of us, more or less: he speaks to the universal. And yet, even though he occupies the foreground from beginning to end of the play, Lear cannot and must not hold our attention simply because of what he is, or merely on the basis of his own particular individuality, since his spiritual progress comes precisely from having rediscovered the path toward others and from having thereafter forgotten about himself in the fullness of this exchange. It is in the modern era, the era of Hamlet, that the individual – separated from everything and from everybody, incapable of checking his solitude, and trying to remedy what is missing through the proliferation of his desires, his dreams, and his thoughts – will slowly assume that extraordinary prominence, the end point of which is Romanticism. In *King Lear* – as on the gothic fresco which is always more or less the *danse macabre* – no one has greater worth merely because of what sets him apart from others, however singular or extreme this difference might be. The soul, studied from the point of view of its free will, which is the same in every man, is less the object of descriptions that note differences than it is the very stage of the action, and from the outset the only stage: and what appears in the play, what finds expression there, are the great key figures of the society, such as the king and his fool, the powerful lord and the poor man, and those categories of common experience such as Fortune or charity, or the deadly sins that Marlowe, in his *Doctor Faustus*, scarcely ten years earlier, had not been reluctant to keep on stage. In short, behind this character who is remarkable, but whose uncommon sides are above all signs of the extent of the dangers that menace us – and the extent of the resources at our disposition as well – the true object of Shakespeare's attention, the true presence that emerges and runs the risk of being overwhelmed, but triumphs in the end, is that life of the spirit to which Lear, and Edgar as well, and also to a certain extent Gloucester and even Albany all bear witness – what is designated by the word *ripeness*.

Ripeness, maturation, the acceptance of death as in *Hamlet*, but no longer in this case because death would be the sign, par excellence, of the indifference of the world, of the lack of meaning – no, rather because acceptance of death could be the occasion for rising to a truly inner understanding of the real laws governing being, for freeing oneself from illusion, from vain pursuits, for opening oneself to a conception of Presence which, mirrored in our fundamental acts, will guarantee a living place to the individual in the evidence of All. One can only understand *King Lear* if one has learned to place this consideration in the foreground, if one has come to see that this is the thread that binds everything together, not only the young man with the old one whose soul is ravaged but intact, but with them the Fool, for instance, who represents in medieval thought the outermost edge of our uncertain condition; and this consideration must be seen to dominate even in a context in which the forces of night seem so powerful, in which the Christian promise has not as yet resounded – although its structures are already there, since it is Shakespeare who is writing; one can therefore sense in them an indication of change, a reason for hope. *Ripeness* emerges in *Lear* as a potentiality for everyone, as the existential starting point from which the protagonists of this tragedy of false appearances begin to be something more than mere shadows; and from the Fool to Lear, from Edgar to his father, from Cordelia, from Kent, from Gloucester to their sovereign, even from an obscure servant to his lord when the latter has his eyes plucked out, it is what gives the only real substance to human exchange which is otherwise reduced to concerns and desires that are only hypocrisy or illusion. This primacy accorded to the inner life of men, with the inevitable shaking of the foundations that comes with it, is what gives meaning to the most famous scene in *Lear* in which one sees Edgar, disguised as a fool, with the fool who is a fool by profession, and Lear, who is losing his mind, all raving together – or at least so it seems – beneath the stormy skies. Those blasting winds and bursts of lightning, that cracking of the cosmos, might well seem to suggest the collapse of meaning, the true state of a world we once had thought of as our home; but let us not forget that in that hovel, and under the semblance of solitude, misfortune, and weariness, the irrational powers that tend to reestablish truth are working much more freely than ever they could in the castles of only a moment before. It is here that true reflection begins again, here that the idea of justice takes shape once more. This stormy night speaks to us of dawn. The brutality of the gods and of men, the fragility of life, are as nothing against a showing of instinctive solidarity that brings things together and provides comfort. And let us also remember that nothing of this sort appears in *Hamlet*, where, if one excepts Horatio, who in fact withdraws from the action, and Ophelia, who, unable to be what she truly wants to be, becomes mad and kills herself, everything in the relationship between people is cynical, harsh, and joyless: let us not forget, for instance, the way in which Hamlet himself gets rid of Rosencrantz and Guildenstern – 'They are not near my conscience.' It is not the universe of *Lear* – however bloody it might seem – that contains the most darkness. This 'tragedy' – but in an entirely different sense from the Greek understanding of the term – is, in comparison to *Hamlet*, an act of faith. We meet in an arena of error, of crime, of dreadfully unjust death, in which even the very idea of Heaven seems missing; and yet, 'the centre holds', meaning manages to survive and even to take on new depth, assuring values, calling forth sacrifice and devotion, allowing for moral integrity, for dignity, and for a relation to oneself that one might term plenary if not blissful. Here we learn that the structures of meaning are but a bridge of thread thrown over frightful depths; but these threads are made of steel.

Ripeness, readiness ... Consequently, the two irreducible attitudes. One, the quintessence of the world's order, the unity of which one seems to breathe; the other, the reverse side of that order, when one no longer sees anything in the grayness of the passing days but the incomprehensible weave.

And the most important question that one might raise about Shakespeare's entire work, it seems to me, is the significance that this absolutely fundamental opposition he has now formulated took on for the playwright himself, in terms of the practical possibilities for the future of the mind and spirit. In other words, when he writes *King Lear* and speaks of *ripeness*, is it simply a question of trying to restore a past mode of being that our present state dooms to failure, and perhaps even renders unthinkable, at least past a certain point: the only path for people living after the end of sacred tradition being rather the *readiness* conceived of by Hamlet, the Elizabethan intellectual? Or, taking into consideration the emotion and the lucidity that characterise the play – as if its author did in fact know precisely what he was talking about – should we ask ourselves if Shakespeare doesn't, in one way or another, believe that the 'maturation' of Edgar and Lear is still valid even for the present – the order, the system of evidence and value which is the necessary condition for this maturation, having perhaps not so completely or definitively disappeared in his eyes, in spite of the crisis of modern times, as it seems to his most famous but scarcely his most representative character? An essential question, certainly, since it determines the ultimate meaning of the relation of a great poetic work to its historic moment. The answer to which must doubtless be sought in the other plays of Shakespeare, and in particular in those that come at the end, after *Hamlet* and the great tragedies.

One will find there – at least this is my hypothesis – that in spite of the collapse of the 'goodly frame' which the Christian Middle Ages had built with heaven and earth around man created by God, this poet of a harsher time felt that an order still remained in place, in nature and in us – a deep, universal order, the order of life, which, when understood, when recognised in its simple forms, when loved and accepted, can give new meaning through its unity and its sufficiency to our condition of exiles from the world of the Promise – just as grass springs up among the ruins. One will also find here that Shakespeare has understood that, with this recognition, the function of poetry has changed as well: it will no longer be the simple formulation of an already obvious truth, already tested to the depths by others than the poet; rather it will have as task to remember, to hope, to search by itself, to make manifest what is hidden beneath the impoverished forms of everyday thinking, beneath the dissociations and alienations imposed by science and culture – and thus it will be an intervention, the assumption of a neglected responsibility, that 'reinvention' of which Rimbaud in turn will speak. Great thoughts that make for the endless richness of *The Winter's Tale*, that play which is, in fact, solar, and which may be superimposed on *Hamlet* point by point – someday I would like to come back to this idea – like the developed photograph – zones of shadow becoming clear, the bright reality as opposed to its negative. The great vistas, also, joyfully dreamt of in *The Tempest* – luminous double of *King Lear*. And grand opportunities, of course, for a resolute spirit, which explains, retrospectively, what has from the outset constituted the exceptional quality of the poetry of Shakespeare – first in the West to measure the extent of a disaster, and first also, and especially, to seek to remedy it.

Translated by John Naughton

MOZART'S STANDPOINT IN THE WORLD[1]

Ladies and gentlemen, as you know, art has always aroused unease in our Western civilisations. When the human spirit is expected to rise towards a God who is beyond appearances, even if these are a necessary aspect of the world He has created, is it not logical to fear that art depends only on the design of such appearances, in other words, the outer wrapping and not the essential reality, and might thus be complicit in our spiritual laziness? Such suspicion adheres to Plato's idea of poetry, according to which poetry seems to be no more than a fiction seeking to sustain, rather than dissipate, the most sensual reveries; the same suspicion adheres to painting, which decks out these fictions in all the charms of the body and its finery, as well as to sculpture with its easy eroticism, to dance and, of course, to music, sometimes the most spontaneous and feverish expression of desire.

It is hardly surprising, therefore, that such suspicion also touches, even more disturbingly, a form of artistic creation that seems essentially to combine all the other arts, enhancing them with the charm of sumptuous apparel, at the greatest possible remove from life's ordinary needs. In opera, which took from the Renaissance both its body and its soul, poetry, painting and music seem to bring together all the possible marvels of appearance so as to hold us in their design, to the point where you might think it was on the opera stage, competing with temples and churches, that colour, fragrance, and sound – through their correspondences, as Baudelaire put it – began to substitute tangible, immediate reality for the symbolic depths that until then had revealed God in His work. Opera is the richest and most complex locus of illusion; might it not constitute the most dangerous use of signs and symbols? And are not the composers of opera thus the henchmen of the great Tempter who prowls the fringes of society? Do they not, by means of décor and fine music, even help him to penetrate the Church and meddle with its great Mass?

It is certainly true that the baroque and rococo saw a troubling

---

1   'Mozart en son point du monde' was delivered as the keynote address at the conference *Mozart et Europe*, held in Strasbourg in 1991. Collected in *Dessin, couleur et lumière*. Paris: Mercure de France, 1995.

erasure of the line between ritual and theatre; the question of opera's legitimacy, from the standpoint of man's highest duty, namely the quest for God, is therefore entirely serious, and it is easy to imagine Mozart debating the matter, given the spiritual yearning coupled with simple pain and sorrow that one finds in the intimate account – the 'bared heart'[2] – of his chamber music. But the same question can be turned around. Even if you do not see yourself as much of a philosopher, if as a child of some intelligence you had been taken – powdered, pampered, adorned, admired, and as such, a plaything – into the salons of society's great figures, would you not be likely to wonder whether human behaviour in real life is not even more illusory, not to say deceitful, than opera is accused of being: apparently serious motives – the good of society, the aspiration to heaven, the supposed love of the humble, love in its pure form, level with the soul – being only a disguise for altogether different desires and urges, unconscious or unacknowledged?

After all, it is easy to see how at its simple, natural level in the real world, the phenomenon of appetite – such as hunger or sexuality – seeks irrepressibly to be satisfied, and it is easy to conceive of a human being as having a primarily animal life rather than being a soul that a god adjoined to matter. The urges that were innate from his beginning, and have probably persisted, have not shattered language, rich as it is in representations and values that seem to oppose such urges, so that one is led to think that the latter have become integral to a notion of society but without forsaking their aim, merely giving up immediate gratification so as to be better gratified later – symbolically, if there is no other way. The human being is just this dissimulation, albeit original and radical. The self, an acceptance of values, is only the construct of one who accepts having less, or less quickly; on the other hand, as eros becomes eroticism, it is a self that better appreciates, and plumbs more deeply, whatever is left to him: having less but enjoying it more.

Is it true that underneath the declared motive of every human action there is another that we do not wish to recognise? If so, then could one say of opera – and of the arts in general, those illusions

---

2   The reference is to Baudelaire's 'Mon cœur mis à nu'.

that help us gain awareness – as is often said of the theatre, that it is the mirror reflecting the face of society, though only, of course, if society so wishes? This question, clearly more pertinent than those posed by painting or the theatre, has become familiar following the soundings prompted by psychoanalysis, but – and here we come to the crux of our argument – it is a question that was already being sketched in the late eighteenth century, when everything that had so long been repressed by Christian culture surfaced all but irrefutably, and not only in the works of Boucher and Fragonard, or Laclos and de Sade. This period, one of discovery of the self, of exploring its flights of greatness and beauty, of affirming its brightness, was also a time when inner space showed itself to be a labyrinth, whether in Piranesi or in Gothic novels; it was a time when the brightness darkened, as in a Neapolitan *veduta* of Vesuvius spitting fire. And, I would propose, it is not impossible that the double game was best denounced in that very place where the mirror sees, leaning towards it, the coquette powdering herself, the seducer trying out different faces – that is, on the stage and in the music and words of certain operas, at least.

Indeed, we might note that if music, given its cadences, has something that can draw the mind towards the loftiest and purest spiritual goals, it is also the sound charged with turbid harmonies as it rises from the strings of a popular instrument or on the breath of shepherds' flutes; music also listens for the voice in men and women that is linked to language but is nonetheless the expression of the body. It is this art that through deepened harmonies can move towards a supra-sensory unity, supreme proof of the validity of our spiritual ambitions; the art that is thus 'musique savante' or the 'chant raisonnable des anges', as Rimbaud put it after hearing a Bach cantata[3], is also more immediately open than any other to the panting breath of restless or triumphant desire, and this makes it more capable even than poetry, that handmaiden of words, of exposing the fevers it even so disguises, and unveiling the unavowed, which music and poetry alike conceal.

And how much more natural, so to speak, it would be when the

3   Rimbaud, *Une saison en enfer.*

author of this music was as well-placed an observer of society's ways and customs as Mozart – firstly the young Mozart I evoked earlier, watching with the astonishment of his innocent soul those great, richly attired figures who lived through music in their theatrical settings. He was outside it all; the comings and goings, the asides and whispers, partings and regroupings were as incomprehensible to him as the rituals of the seraglio. And yet he was in the midst of it, and in the most intimate way since he had mastered and already enriched that language – the music of balls and theatres. Later, as a musician still fêted on occasion but more often exploited, and distracted from pleasures by the weight of debts and commissions unworthy of his genius, he would benefit, so to speak, from the dialectic between being in society – in high society – and the solitude that sharpens the lucidity of moralists. In a Europe on the brink of a crisis that would engulf pleasure-loving society, Mozart occupied an ideal place, where the illusory and the real met and collided, yielding to one and the same glance. And the fact that he was not a *philosophe*, as many readily were at the time, that he was not a man of thought and speculation – though he must have deliberated before joining the Masonic lodge in his final years – only further indicates, in my view, his powers of analysis and synthesis, for the level on which human reality is engaged is not one of concepts, which always lag behind feelings.

Mozart was, from his standpoint in the world, the mirror in which all society saw itself reflected. That at some stage in his life he actively and consciously played this role, that he thereafter merged reflection and composition, and moreover took his quest and discoveries beyond the question he had originally asked himself, once he recognised the means by which lies, traps, vain imaginings and sudden leaps towards truth could all dissolve in the brightness of a single great light – such are the matters on which I seek here to broaden our understanding. In so doing I shall limit myself to one of the high points in this surge of the human spirit: the four great operas, from 1786 to *The Magic Flute*, composed in the final months of a life that was as stricken as it was immaterial.

II.

Ladies and gentlemen, people are often surprised by one of the most important aspects of *The Marriage of Figaro*. The play by Beaumarchais, on which it is based, was characterised by social criticism, and the portrayal of manners was merely an opportunity for political protest, to the point where the play was banned in Paris for a considerable period: it was staged only thanks to public pressure in those pre-Revolution days. Despite some dozen translations into German, it was still banned in Vienna when Mozart began work on his opera – so that neither Mozart nor Da Ponte could have been unaware of how it was meant to be read. Both of them removed from their opera not only anything that might have given it political relevance but also the more explicitly erotic situations, thereby arguably renouncing the question I put earlier, as to a reflection on human behaviour and its motives.

Did Mozart sacrifice lucidity for the sake of prudence vis-à-vis the imperial censor? Or are we to believe that when he composed *Figaro* he did not hold the critical views I have attributed to him? But we have also seen that the ultimate human motive – as people were beginning to suspect in this era of Enlightenment, which could also be called one of Night, with Darkness suddenly perceived as such – is a primal urge that is alive beyond words and mingles with them only in disguise, so that it can be revealed only as underlying performances in words, not least where the words might have a seditious purpose; music, on the other hand, rises straight from the abyss – something that Beaumarchais sensed in his fashion, since the force of his work lies less in spelling out judgements than in the energy sweeping them on: the swelling of sap that has all the irrationality and immediacy of life itself. In a Mozart opera, it is at this pre-verbal level – but even more spontaneously and immediately – and in the music as music that one has to recognise the attention he gave to these instinctive impulses that can reveal illusion or fallacy in the behaviour and values that society regards as being founded, on the contrary, upon something divine.

We might note, for example, Mozart's request – unusual for its time – that Da Ponte increase the number of duets so that they are dominant in the work. The duets are there not just to mark a unison of feeling, as in the old *opera seria*, or to disperse comically a disruptive quarrel, as in the typical *opera buffa*; no, from the outset they now bring together all the voices in all sorts of situations, and since there runs through the notes an ardour, at once light-hearted and violent, that is irrepressible and unblushing as it issues from somewhere beneath the words, one has to understand this musical intuition as a deeply shared intimacy between these beautiful young characters; like a union that, being already sexual, becomes the essence of certain moments in life, unspoken but lived. And at the very heart of this dance of sorts that directs everything is the primal urge that arises in the young page Cherubino, caught unprepared by the longings of puberty that beset him. *Non so più cosa son, cosa facio,* he exclaims; *or di foco, ora sono di ghiaccio,* he declares, his body buffeted by sudden desires he could not anticipate. The cherub of Baroque churches has again become the *amorino*, or Cupid, of classical painting, and delivers the same message, which is not so much eros as the double meaning of the characters: this gives a troubling ambiguity – which Mozart and his audience could not have missed – to certain scenes in the opera, such as that in which, on Suzanne's wedding day, she and the worthy, reserved Countess together dress up Cherubino as a woman, Suzanne making him kneel before her and turn this way and that until for a moment he loses his head. *Ehi serpentillo!* she cries, Eve once again faced with the Tempter. *Finiam le ragazzate!* – enough of this childishness, concludes the Countess sensibly.

The same eruption of something primal, blind and irrepressible can be heard in the imperious song of the Count as he pursues Suzanne, the object of his desire, as well as in the robust voice of Figaro who is moved by a love that is, in his case, legitimate; this takes to its limit the insight that runs through the work, itself a study of the various guises of eros in human affairs, but also a questioning of society that is as yet only mooted, not resolved. In other words, there is a noted difference between Count Almaviva and his valet, though we do not know what, if anything, it means. One character is lying and the other is not, even though they are driven by the same sexual impulse, which of course suggests that the guises of eros in human conduct and values are to be found solely at the level of aristocrats, whereas those they exclude, not to say oppress – and who, along with their womenfolk, are preparing to demand the right to reorganise human relations – would be capable of restructuring social manners in a way which would show that the primal force is not, in fact, so opposed to the needs of those circles that it has to hide behind their masks in order to have the right to assert itself. Might there be, on the horizon of all the turbulence in store, the openness of a golden age? Should the emphasis not be on putting music's inherent energy at the service of a 'new well-being'? It is a notion that gives Figaro's song *Si vuol ballare* distinctly revolutionary implications, which verge on the alarming, given the sharp instruments of even the lowliest barber.

Thus there is an ambiguousness in this music that allows one to interpret its spontaneity and vehemence in an optimistic light, according to which society could, through political renewal, cease being a simple falsehood. For in his travels and his work, Mozart came to know Europe well, having seen its courts but also noted the energy of the people, its great reserve of strength poised to intervene, one might say, so as to reveal anew the facts of nature and of virtue.

But this ambiguousness disappears from the very first notes of the overture to *Don Giovanni*. There are few admirers of Mozart who have not been tempted to set this work apart from the others and subject it to a more far-reaching philosophical or moral interpretation than is usual – speculating, for example, as did Kierkegaard, that in it, music attains its true essence. For my part, I am also inclined to recognise in the work a major event of the human spirit, taking place specifically in the medium of art. But to pursue this point, it seems to me more accurate to see the work as an extension of *The Marriage of Figaro* as well as already anticipating *Così fan tutte* or *The Magic Flute*. If *Don Giovanni* shows a suddenly deeper insight, a radical experience, this comes from the meaning of the earlier opera, which is in turn illuminated by it. Later work would inevitably be affected.

What is there that is new in *Don Giovanni*? Well, it is the idea, suggested for the first time by and through the music, that *all* social behaviour, not just that of a particular class or group, and *all* actions, even those that seem the most noble and disinterested, are no more than the dissimulation of a very basic impulse, predominantly sexual, that may be so blind and primitive, so radically amoral that it could well, one imagines, put paid to any dream of independent and properly managed thinking. Don Giovanni's voice is perhaps the same as that of Figaro or Count Almaviva, but the way he sees himself is entirely different. From the outset the overture seems driven by a force that is more elemental, more expansive and headlong than the process of thought, a surging, feverish vehemence that is both joy and anguish, and in which it is easy to recognise, as many rightly have done, the spontaneity of eros. But the opera that follows will soon, scene by scene, show itself to be something else besides; and to see in *Don Giovanni* only a passion that is usually concealed through sublimation or displacement, would be to miss the essential element. This is to be found not *under* the language, where the basic animality of human nature is revealed, even at the heart of society, but *through* the usage of words, as if consciousness itself is being put on trial.

What, then, does Don Giovanni represent? Is he simply the personification of sexual desire, pure and simple? In one sense, yes, as we see in the way he approaches Zerlina and tries to ensnare her – a scene mirrored 1,003 times in the catalogue drawn up by Leporello. But Don Giovanni, as evinced in a number of famous arias, wants not only Zerlina's body but also her assent, wants a deep-seated admission that she is in accord with him and with desire, and that there is thus no reality, in the strongest sense of the word, other than the pleasure proposed by this stranger. And if Don Giovanni's demand is not much out of the ordinary in terms of how two people relate to each other – such is the aim of every erotic quest – there is nothing ordinary about the cynical, highly provocative frankness with which this new-style adventurer tries to obtain such an admission, declares it to be fated, and wants to impose on society the evidence that it is.

Let us be in no doubt – and this is the nature of Don Giovanni's godlessness, this is the scandal that suddenly turns this story, which for long had been merely a farce, into tragedy, its music as much as the libretto reverberating throughout – if Don Giovanni were simply a 'Don Juan', the term we still use for someone who enjoys erotic pleasures but is no less eager, for that very reason, to go unnoticed in society, society itself would soon tire of his embarrassing presence and might even want to rid itself of him, but would be grateful for the respect indicated by an offer of marriage and would not doom him to eternal damnation. Mozart's hero, however, wants to denounce the contract that primal sexuality has made with society and with language, and loudly proclaims its secret clauses, without any new form of marriage in prospect, as one might have hoped during those revolutionary years. For this sole but fundamental reason, he is the Enemy in the specifically Satanic sense.

And like Satan he testifies to that which he denounces – for why does this person, who defies society with sexual assault and even murder, do so in such a provocative way that he is first in line to be condemned to death? Don Giovanni seems to need to impress and convince, and surely the need to convince indicates an interest in the other person, betrays regret as to the circumstances of the exchange? Moreover, is there not, in the violence with which he proclaims the duplicity practised by men and women, the exigency of a mind more lucid than cynical, turned against itself? Don Giovanni does not resort to claiming any kind of virtue, since he sees only too well that something within him would block the notion. But he has not forgotten that it is the idea of virtue, of its being possible, that distinguishes humankind from the animal kingdom. And in this respect, too, he resembles the Satan he is about to join in the flames: he is less the denial of the idea of God than a longing which cannot forgive itself its inability to rival Him.

Such discussion is all the more necessary in that it delineates the hero of the tragedy for Mozart, the composer who took the character from a tradition that until then had been much more comic, even farcical, than serious. In the proceedings brought against society, as I have said, by this new Don Giovanni, art is clearly one of the accused, since it is party to the travesties and trickery being played out. As a means of illusion and seduction, it can no longer be only, as one might have hoped, the serenade that seducers use to confuse and fascinate their victim, and catch her in their net; this is the serenade that Mozart places notably at a critical moment in the opera. But is it 'en abyme', as the current term has it, that is, an image set at the heart of the work and reflecting its essence? Should we not rather take it in at a distance, at the heart of this music that throughout exceeds the serenade with an energy all the more mysterious. The fact of its creation, the intensity of the composer's quest that it manifests, runs counter to the destructive, cynical thinking that one attributes to the main protagonist of *Don Giovanni*. It does so through the grandeur and beauty that the latter denies to artistic enterprise. The way in which this is done is all the more striking when one senses that the composer identifies with his character: when the Commander, Don

Giovanni's victim, reappears at the end of the opera, it is in the form of a statue, that is, a work of art, so that the hell into which the libertine tumbles has an affinity, at least by metonymy, with the activity of Mozart. Will the vision of humanity arising from the denunciations of Don Giovanni drag the composer, thus corrupted, into hell? Or will the work that he is producing become a hell for him since in it he has to overcome his own temptations, wrongdoings and cynicism, whereas others seek only to master the easy problems of an art that wears disguises and acts out scenes? If that is the case, Mozart identifies with his character only by turning himself – through this uncertain and perhaps hopeless task – into someone who nonetheless believes in moral values and the possibility of good. And the way he does so is all the more heroic in that he shows he has not forgotten that no one will follow his path. We might note that the last scene of the opera, after the arrival of the Guest of stone and Don Giovanni's final defiance and death, has often been described as surprisingly superficial and facile, and even unnecessary. But if Mozart felt Don Giovanni to be a projection of part of himself, and his death and damnation an image of the suffering that art holds in store for him, the scene again becomes necessary and meaningful, ironically making the point – evinced in the facile comments at *vernissages* and the indifference of audiences leaving after a performance – that the artist is forever alone: virtuous characters like Donna Anna or Ottavio are as alien to his quest as the excesses of Don Giovanni.

This *opera buffa*-turned-tragedy leaves us with one central question. At these boundaries of philosophical disquiet, where society seems to be a mere epiphenomenon, no doubt doomed to extinction, of blind, material forces, is art not simply the mirror that can tell – this being the one and only truth or action it can achieve – that society is illusory and deceitful? Or is not the artist, in this instance, the composer – at the cost of working on himself, perhaps with self-sacrifice – in a position to win, for the benefit of human and humanist interests, the proceedings that his own clear-sightedness brought against society? In this case, Don Giovanni's misfortune lies in the fact that he, author of nothing more than a serenade, cannot be the composer that Mozart succeeded in becoming, at the highest point of the human spirit.

But having said, having *hoped,* all this, how can art, and music in particular, discover and designate within human reality – that vain form of matter – the kind of foundation that might establish social behaviour and values upon more than the darkness of primal urges? The answer to this is not to be found in *Don Giovanni*, where anguish prevails, but I believe it gives significance to the fact that the opera is followed by – in the first place – *Così fan tutte*: for in the final *opera buffa* an insight takes shape, once again in the way that the economy of the libretto – its particular truth, the coherence of its articulation, its ultimate contradictions – is detached, or at least distinct, from the composer's own experience at the time.

III.

It has been said that *Così fan tutte* is a comedy without much logic or depth combined with inspired music, but this misstates the problem, for these two aspects make sense only in their reciprocal rapport, which is much more profound and intimate than it appears. The libretto itself is decidedly not devoid of meaning, nor of philosophical implications, for it continues the novel aspect of *Don Giovanni*, and does so in two equally important respects. Firstly, by denouncing the way in which, in Don Giovanni's forcefully expressed view, values are founded simply on the flesh. It might be noted, in reference to the first work, that this charge did not seek validation through any of the female figures: Donna Anna, Zerlina and even Elvira are primarily victims. As I understand it, this signifies the end of a Christian culture that identifies evil not so much with the flesh as with a way of life, a flawed soul, and traces this flaw back to Eve. If *Don Giovanni* had been a serious work in a more Christian era, a period of counter-reformation, the ultimate fact of human existence would not have been associated with the simple forces of nature; it would have been restored to a universe created by God but corrupted by the sin of Eve, and perhaps the libertine would have had to leave the leading role to a figure of temptation, a new Circe or Armide.

Dorabella and Fiordiligi in *Così fan tutte* are definitely victims too, but they are given sufficient opportunity in the situation set up by their fiancés to show, albeit unawares, that the great suspicion cast by *Don Giovanni* on human motivation is as valid for women as for men.

They too are not what they claim, or even believe themselves, to be. And – *così fan tutte* – this is as true of the more pure and sincere Fiordiligi as it is of the more flighty Dorabella: sometimes the path from the flesh to the soul is simply more strewn with obstacles. Moreover, since the two men are worth no more than the women – being faithful, perhaps, but mostly because enamoured of themselves – the new opera confirms the previous one, all the more convincingly since this time it is without tragedy, if not without drama. The harsh truth is well-nigh confirmed by everyone. It takes the form of an adage.

But – and this is the other way in which *Così fan tutte* is a continuation of *Don Giovanni* – this truth at the level of plot is once again qualified if not disclaimed by what the music suggests, music that, as in the other work, resists any attempt to reduce it to an awareness of a world that nothing can safeguard from scepticism. Each moment, and in particular the finale, brings an eruption of potent, mysterious joy, amounting to an affirmation, it seems, which carries the beginnings of a response to the enigma left by *Don Giovanni.*

What is the nature of this response, and can we, with *Così fan tutte* following upon *Don Giovanni,* begin to perceive the way in which Mozart, late in life, puts an end to the dizziness, doubt and despair he had known? This, even when the intense and startling opening phrases of the work are overshadowed by an anxiety that is all the more surprising since Guglielmo and Ferrando do not yet have the least idea of the sad discoveries they will make at the close of day? One would therefore expect a denouement in which the reconciliations are much less straightforward, and some discordant or bitter-sweet element in the music rather than the note of triumph.

Yes, but Mozart's joy in this final scene does not derive from what is being played out at plot level in the relations between two men and two women, but rather – and this is altogether different – from his reaction to the story's twists of fortune, which he sets forth from an entirely different perspective. And there seems to me to be a supremely realistic hypothesis that takes account of Mozart's thinking and experience in these final years, even though it is based only on this final scene, which is in a way so empty and brings to a close a story of so little weight.

Empty? But here are two men dressed with absurd and arrogant flamboyance, who are as gauche in matters of love as they are overly

artful. And accompanying them, these two young women, primped
and perfumed, swept along by this crazy day full of emotions and
surprises, women at the height of their beauty which they deploy so
ineptly, fleeting as it is. Very fine figures, these four, and yet evanescent. Knots of colourful ribbons with barely a thought or intention
to hold them together: like a summer sky at sunset, when great rosy
clouds rise in tiers upon a bed of foam, like actors on some essential
stage, in a theatre of the absolute, their brilliant presence, however,
already traversed, even undone, at every level by a mysterious drift.
How beautiful and how unreal! And this being so, what an opportunity for whoever observes this sublime precariousness and is open
to such an oxymoron; what an opportunity to experience something
that is likewise essential and no longer difficult to define!

Mere puppets, it has often been said of Guglielmo and Ferrando
and of Dorabella and Fiordiligi, puppets that only serve the ironic
purpose, whether kindly or cruel, of Don Alphonso who pulls the
strings. But faced with these figures so burdened by unreality, is one
not, for that very reason – while forgetting all the foolish upsets,
all the various forms of blindness, all the psychology and sociology
– obliged to see that they are human reality laid bare, at its most
tragically exposed? And since they are no different from ourselves,
should we not feel for each of them a degree of understanding and
solidarity – that is, compassion?

Yet this is to recognise in them the fact and effect of time, where
every human being has his great rendezvous with death; it is to have
experienced them as a presence, briefly shared; it is to see that nothing
in and around us can henceforth be considered as anything other
than the profundity of this moment; and it is thus to find oneself on
the threshold of what the instant reveals, the layering of everything
contained in this moment of the world, it is to see the whole that
envelops us, the unity on which it is founded – and this is what helps
us to feel *real*, belonging to the same reality of this universe which
everywhere exceeds us, to feel real at the very moment when one has
every reason in the world to think one is not. And this – it is time
we said as much – is evidently a cause for joy, the joy at the close of
Così fan tutte, the cause of the 'divine gaiety' that Pierre Jean Jouve
recognised. By detaching the protagonists from everything that binds
them to the outer fabric of society and its values, by seeking them

more deeply than the sorry self that encumbers the Fiordiligis and the Dorabellas as much as their jewels and their bodices, one comes – and here is the source of the airy, second-degree eroticism of *Così fan tutte* – to the very body of Being, as whole and impalpable as the clouds in the sky.

The ending of *Così fan tutte,* like many passages in the course of the opera, shows just such compassion, a transmutation from void into being, a wellspring of joy. And now a new light is thrown on artistic creation. Is it this very practice of illusion that helps to corrupt society, or – since at bottom society only illusion, as Don Giovanni declares – is artistic creation the mirror that shows society its true visage? Yes, it is indeed such a mirror, but one that, as evinced in such moments of compassion, can be turned skyward – to the great sky with its clouds and the lessons that clouds hold – so as to take the light and tilt it towards the men and women of this earth, letting shadows proliferate among them but also bright, iridescent gleams that let us recognise their solid presence, and love them. The biological time of desire is replaced by the spirit's own time. Or perhaps we should say: the spirit appears in the world. And society, overwhelmed and flooded by it, can no longer be considered as merely a disguise for impulses born of matter.

So here it is, Mozart's response to the question of Don Giovanni, a response that in the opera's music is as yet without self-awareness and laden with contradictions; it lets us know that brute eros is not the only way of dealing with people and disciplining language. But the response, we should note, is as yet only partially formulated, for even though there is compassion in *Così fan tutte*, we do not know how such compassion came to take precedence over scepticism and nihilism, nor whether it is simply a feature of Mozart in late life, reaching the threshold of a mystical experience. If so, we would see him on that distant horizon but not have the means of joining him.

But another hypothesis comes to mind: that the compassion which carries the music along and astonishes us with its intensity has, through a kind of circularity, been helped into being by the music itself.

IV.

I noted initially that of all the forms of artistic invention – painting, for example, or architecture or music – only music has *time* as its material, time as marked out on clocks, time in which life grows and diminishes in the body, during which desire reaches for its object while death, revealed through language, looms ever larger on the horizon. Since music takes shape through time, it has a more intimate rapport with human reality than any other form of art, given the presence of a person who speaks, suffers, laughs – sings – alone or with others, in songs or in operatic arias, like that of Papageno at the beginning of *The Magic Flute*, which seems to say *I am* from the depths of the music. The musical form is from the outset a person's presence and is open to all that is most secret in that person, even beyond words. And thus when it is heard from the detached perspective I mentioned earlier, that of compassion, many aspects of life can be understood.

In addition to the music that produces this form, where intimacy lets itself be caught unawares, there is also the ongoing act of composing, the space in which someone who has felt compassion can see who he is and work on himself, so that on other occasions in his oeuvre he will sooner or later experience still more intensely or more deeply these moments of attentiveness and compassion. Throughout Mozart's work there are phrases that owe their mysterious beauty to the fact that they are nothing but themselves, seeming to have no meaning and expressing only their simple musical presence – simply *being*, let us say, but all the more moving for that, since these phrases are metaphors for the naked act of existing, the due and the drama of every individual, acknowledged as such by Mozart, and glorified. An architectural form – a façade like that of the Malatesta Temple, of which Alberti said: *Tutta quella musica* – can similarly indicate presence, and there is a musical aspect in all the arts, poetry in particular, which is itself linked to temporality through the sounds of words, assonances and rhymes. But the fact remains that in the rapport with the world to which language pledges us, it is music, first and foremost, that has *the key to love.*

This is a key that Mozart rediscovered and reflected on. It is easy to make silly comments about *The Magic Flute,* given all the traps laid for us – perhaps intentionally – by a story whose purpose we do not properly know, nor even whether it has any serious intent on the symbolic level where it so clearly declares itself to be. All the same, it contains the idea of a character's development, starting with the first encounter at the level of simple desire, when Tamino sees the young woman's portrait while in our ears we still have the striking, naïvely sensual song of Papageno. And this development is explicitly a matter of music, since in order to forget the birdcatcher's panpipes Tamino is given a flute that is at first purely magic, that is, simple art, the simple expression of desire, simple instrument of eros, and which will later grant him access to inner deliverance.

We shall not attempt to follow the various stages of this deliverance in the opera since time does not permit, but let us note that Mozart wove out of his most sublime music the moment when Tamino keeps silent before the unhappy Pamina: not speaking thus becomes the threshold of perception, of the most profound approach. Let us also point out that it is not in the plot of *The Magic Flute* but in Mozart's life, guided by his music, that the initiation took place, or began: and so it is in the music itself that we should look for his life's vicissitudes and moments of defeat or victory. The evidence is, I believe, solely within the work itself: in the entertainment to be found in many of its aspects. It is a fairy-play for children, this opera, while it does not flinch from coarse jokes, does not hide its stage contraptions and enjoys its special effects: Sarastro in a chariot drawn by six card-board lions is as comical as the Albanians in *Così fan tutte*. And this amusing trumpery is something that Mozart gladly accepts because he knows, and does not mind letting it be seen, that the true locus of reflection is not a philosopher's symbol but whatever is resolved in the profound dialogue between a violin, for example, and a cello; likewise, perhaps especially, in chamber music, in a quartet.

It takes the trials of life itself for deliverance to be more than a dream. And even in life, even in the life of Mozart, one has to resign oneself to thinking that moments of liberation and true joy such as those that conclude *Così fan tutte* are, in a sense, no more than dreams since they arise within an artistic work and will not, even in the most noble existence, endure without being troubled by ineradicable melancholy. – But is it so negligible, a dream of this sort, a dream whose magnificent light is rekindled by Mozart? Is it not enough to safeguard us from solitude and nihilism? A final comment: like an evening sky, I said of the four protagonists at the end of *Così fan tutte*, with great purple clouds that are at once unreal and supremely real. But what could have been more comparable to such a sky – its superb clouds gleaming with the colours of Tiepolo and the occasional flash of lightning, though calm, too, in places – than Europe in 1791, which saw a world coming to an end but still rich in all it possessed? And rather than destroy everything in the abstraction of a neo-classical presentation of reason and virtue, surely history, listening to Mozart, should have staged a sort of grand-scale *Così fan tutte*, in which the dissimulations and the lies inherent in humankind would be understood and forgiven, and thus transcended, for something better than virtue – for love. Alas, for a new *agapè* to replace the original eros, one would first have to finish with the religion of Sin; the difficulty that this would present can be seen in Mozart's final months, with his anguish, his hallucinations, his *Requiem* overshadowed by fear of the person who had commissioned the work. It is as if we in the West were incapable of something that is, nonetheless, our great potential: the conclusion of *Così fan tutte*. It is as though we had always to live through the dizziness of Don Giovanni and must therefore always desire, and at the same time fear, the disastrous arrival of the Guest of stone.

Translated by Jennie Feldman

A Writing Prophet[1]

I.

At long last we have an extensive exhibition in Paris of William Blake's graphic work. This in and of itself is an event of great importance since until now Blake was in fact not especially well known here. His poems are translated, in particular thanks to the work of Pierre Leyris, but who in France reads translations of poets? And before the Louvre's recent acquisition, our museums had nothing that would make it possible even to glimpse the strange and powerful imagination of the illustrator of *Songs of Innocence* or *The Marriage of Heaven and Hell*. Much is now exhibited and all made clear in a single stroke thanks to the great many works brought together in the Petit Palais at the instigation of Michael Phillips and Daniel Marchesseau, and equally to the excellent catalogue. It is now possible to consider what Blake thought or, we should rather say, lived; and conceive, this is my feeling in any case, that his exploration, which might seem from a bygone era and astray from practicable paths, remains in fact very near our needs and in its depth even harbours a proposal that corroborates an intuition of now and here, and makes possible a better understanding of it.

What does this proposal consist in? And must one really think that this stirrer of intuitions, at times hardly expressible, this visionary such as we are no longer familiar with nor wish to be, this fanatic who died singing psalms, can have anything to tell us today? But let's simply have a look at *Songs of Innocence*, that slender booklet – thirty or so lightly coloured plates – he published, if that's the right word, in 1789, at the time of an event that may seem of a completely different scope. And let ourselves become bewildered, should we consider what art and poetry was in the society of that era or even throughout the Occident since the beginnings of the Renais-

1   First published as a catalogue essay for the exhibition 'William Blake, le génie visionnaire du romantisme anglais' held at the Petit Palais in Paris, April 2– June 28, 2009 (Paris, Paris Musées, 2009). Collected in *La beauté dès le premier jour*, Bordeaux: William Blake & Cie, 2010.

sance. It was a synthesis of representation and thought. The artist had something to say but, increasingly attentive with the passage of the centuries, studied no less the appearance of those things around him, even if he knew them hardly concerned with his intentions: in fact thought concealed itself behind the coming into existence of the proximate world, which granted some authority to what is known as material reality, to bodies as they are, as one lives with them and loves to live. Whence an entire art of the fortunate gaze practiced by poets as well as painters, who understood them easily, illustrating Ariosto, Tasso and even Milton, whose evocations of Paradise or descriptions of the Fall gave rise to paintings and engravings bristling with fine earthly mountains and forests, if indeed it wasn't aspects of the English countryside. The divine was incarnated in its horizons, its sublimity made landscape painting legitimate. Only popular imagery could cut these standards short.

Here, in the illuminations of *Songs of Innocence*, the contours of things or beings they evoke no longer condense our desire to delve into the depths of sensorial immediacy. Henceforth a line is diverted from these enticements and so no longer merely expresses the thought it conveys. It clings moreover to outlines of tiny twigs and fresh leaves so as to suggest that they are the irresistible sprouting that, from its tendrils, penetrates – in order to take it apart, to dissipate its illusion – ordinarily experienced reality, that which had held Western painters' attention. And even these tendrils envelop the poems' text, written on these very pages; they slip in among its words so as to forge meaning within them or incite this very refusal, to put it briefly, of matter. These tiny illuminations, then, represent a great rupture, for we must not commit the error of seeing in them a decorative course of action embellishing idyllic scenes. True, these involutions seem facile, as much as might appear free of truth the happy shepherd or the lost child happily found, about whom these seemingly naïve poems speak. But soon enough in Blake's next books he indicates that the line which had pared material observation away becomes more autonomous still. He thereby indulges himself in intuitions that leave the insipidness of the pastoral tradition far behind, unless it should be thought, and this is what I for my part believe, and I will return to this, that they bring its nature to light. In these new books intermingling word and image, the brush stroke continues to gain greater independence and audacity, imposes rhythm and cuts across appearances, and frequently imprints horizontals and verticals expressing nothing but thought: the gaze that had alighted on outer things has yielded to an inner gaze, a net in which strange visions are caught. It is as if, sweeping along the poems' words, the hand tracing the brush stroke, which renders the line omnipresent and dominating, dived far deeper than they ever could, into the unknown depths of psychic life and uncovered an extraordinary *cosa mentale*.

II.

It is tempting at this point to try and understand in its very forms and figures what this could well be, what Blake says, what he believed he had discovered in the midst of his night and was bound to record in his lyric; yet this is not where is found, in my eyes at least, that which makes it important for our time, and I will stick to what I see as intrinsic power, infinite potentiality and meaning almost clearly suggested in the line he revealed to himself. Admittedly, his intuitions about what took place within us from below various censures may be pondered, as they are moreover fundamentally true. We may but subscribe to his conception of Urizen, that massive old man trudging through the fen of matter and who has bent reality to the categories of time and space, introduced measurement, instituted laws, fragmented infinity and deadened freedom of the spirit through dogma. What is denounced, as it ought to be, by this radical vision, expressed in such an uncommonly arresting way, is each and every conformity, each and every ideology. But we would be well advised to understand this message in a way that makes it possible to shake loose its imprudence while at the same time broadening its reach.

We observe, for instance, that the name Urizen, like so many others, including Los, Orc, Tel, Oothoon and Theotormon, such that Blake's mythology expresses them, names found only in connection with him, names that nevertheless mingle in its grand offerings of meaning with others we all know, those such as Nebuchadnezzar, Satan and even Jesus, signify foremost the right the poet grants himself simply to be in the whole of his subjectivity at precisely that moment he plunges his eyes into essential reality.

It matters little to him if these names do not garner the reader's approval. He views his subjectivity as a passageway between spirit and truth, he shows us that the relationship of self to the speaking being is the path; and that for a start says a great deal about the nature as well as the locus of a vast continent within the depths of the psyche which till then had been little delved into only by travellers laden with dogma and troubled by religious prejudice, less as good observers than themselves an object of observation for the thought to come. Enlightenment thought had just then brought this continent to light, in contrast to its aims; it thereby begged to consider and visit it, but without making the means available for descending into the abyss; whence dread, vertigo and fascination, as for instance in Sade, pulling up the very roots of social responsibility and morality. And what did Blake do in these circumstances if not to say forcefully what was needed in order to seize the threshold, to settle and abide there all life long, absorbed in truth. As the abyss on the underside of reason is composed of desire, hunger and aspiration, beings such as they are, stripped down to their finiteness and thereby bounded to their subjectivity, must travel this route in order to understand, he tells us, that there exist in this dimension ways of perceiving, feelings and thinking that one must not only endure in the night-time dream, like a Fuseli, or let seep into works of art left conceived at our rational and diurnal level, but boldly add – indeed, oppose, if necessary – to reason's proposals. Blake opens up a field where Freud, Jung, Kafka and other thinkers of the human night will soon confirm the soundness of his testimony.

And as to the unknown realities which appear beyond this threshold, going to the Night as Blake did – and resolutely, explicitly: 'After Night I do crowd', he writes, 'And with Night will go'[2] – doubtless plays a great role, whatever the truthfulness of the formulations he proposes concerning the economy of the mental world. As extravagant as some of his thoughts are, one can board this ship of warranted folly in order to reach the ports that our new science of the depths attempts to establish on the other shore: it would be to the ship's advantage, in the course of its unstable navigating, if it were

2   From 'Mad Song.'

to take Blake seriously. But let's take a further step in the reflection on the part played by the poet who, turning away from the clear horizons of his early images, plunged into the dark in order to shed light on being in the world.

By observing now that at his thought's most extreme, the point where his visions take shape, what has taken place, in fact, and in a sustained and even explicit way, is an indictment of conceptual thought, that approach to things through their outer dimension which assuredly is exclusively destined to geometric space and clock time, condemning the five senses, and all the others, to the illusions of measurement, binding them to Newton. The conceptual is the guilty party because it retains in its necessarily generalising formu-lations the experience of finiteness which nevertheless each human being must undergo if we should wish to remain attentive to our most veridical needs, those which define his relationships to others and might render them harmonious. We find ourselves faced with this concept just like, in the allegory Plato devised, the prisoners of the famous cavern. Urizen is merely the troublemaker of this shadow world. Call it the power in us which out of this concept – which remains worthwhile, if it can put itself into question – panders to the propensity to turn itself into a system, a closed world, forgotten by the face of the Other who, Blake repeats, is the very face of the true god. Urizen is ideology, with harmful consequences. And the author of the *Book of Urizen* thereby helps us understand that it is at the heart of all speech, indeed in the use of each word, that the concept it conveys may, yielding to gross temptation, blind the gaze that might otherwise have known true hunger, true values, and the genuine circumstances of life. Which would have been poetry itself.

III.

But what development must arise from Blake's becoming aware of the peril that Urizen emblematises? Is it but the enquiry into a thought which could then be made plain or explainable, such as with the psychologists and phenomenologists mentioned above? No, and this is where Blake becomes wholly meaningful; something different takes shape within him other than this kind of reflection, in a manner yet again dangerously conceptual, something that our own era has started to understand, moreover, although it hasn't yet been able to draw sufficient lessons from it nor turn it into a veritable practice. It is what one may call writing.

Writing? The use of words which lets them, surely, recall aspects of the world joined to them by society or the person who speaks but further allows them to become associated with other words in the sentence by often unexpected expressions as they aren't prevented from rising out of the subconscious or unconscious; and thus suggest instruments for thinking, symbols, images and, indeed, scraps of visions, which are no longer the ruler and compass of Newton meditating fancifully in one of Blake's most famous engravings. Writing is that freedom given to words to endlessly cross and re-cross the frontier, if indeed there is one, between their memory of what is, in empirical reality, and the memory they have of what we are, in our night of the interior. A Möbius strip which can be but text, written word, even if there originates in it new life for speech, endlessly in existence because these expressions between words need time to settle into place, to reveal themselves, to make themselves heard, to allow he or she who produces them to triumph over the temptation to make systems out of them anew. Ideology may prosper, in fact, even among symbols; it is sufficient that it fixes them in meanings that can be shared. It follows from this that only writing, by its transgressive vocation, may conserve the surfeit of what is unthought which dissuades from giving itself over to this different kind of delusion. And great is the occasion that presents itself as such. One who writes, fully, proceeds into the night and attains finiteness, we contend with it instead of fearing it. This is where we win our liberty.

And writing does more, for in selecting thereby what is worthwhile and what alienates, in disentangling life and its future from their presumptions and illusions, it opens up a field in which the relationship of I to other is clarified in a discussion whose generalising to society would be truth in the making and thus how the human may decide as its being, for our short time on earth. In restoring words to finiteness stifled in ordinary discourse, writing may be the foundation that neither philosophies nor religions have succeeded in discovering in their ontological hypotheses. But it is also a fact that a great many censures exist in order to occult its idea or impede its course. The poetry which should have practiced it and learned from it, clumsily moreover, during the Surrealist period understands nothing of it today, just as yesterday. And we observe that instead of passing through night in order to transform existence into a new day, many thinkers and writers of that period transformed night into the metaphoric name of a world that language had constructed but which we have abandoned to nonsense, remaining interested in it only as language without words. Writing is an open door, but we aren't even capable of catching a glimpse of it.

This is where I meet up with William Blake. This is where I sense what I was saying was his importance. Blake, it seems to me, recognised the writing which, in its specificity, is the path; he brought it to the fore in his work and even singled it out. That is the message that nearly all his books make clear. What, in fact, is this line which – refusing the task of exploring the sensible aspects of empirical reality, lending itself, on the contrary, with the other hand, to the calls that the unconscious displays, lending itself to intuitions ahead of thought in forms – likewise crosses and re-crosses the frontier between outside and inside, between visible nature and the mental, in his drawing? It is indeed writing, at once experienced and displayed. We even observe in its sometimes massive, weighty figures who metaphorise, in the margin of the outbursts of context, the resistances that in its energy all writing encounters, its 'unbreakable kernels of night.'[3]

Blake singles out writing. He who claimed – was certain – that he was a prophet more than a poet, in any case this he is by the act he foresaw as imagination. He even called it 'Jesus the imagination' because he understood that what's in the human would resurrect among those great powers so forgotten throughout history, modern history in any case, powers one had believed divine. We recognise, from each of William Blake's books to the next, the uninterrupted display of this fundamental act. We rediscover in their bizarre, disconcerting and sometimes even repulsive images the movement of authentic writing: it is by no means a cool marshalling of treasures gradually discovered, but a shaking of the whole of consciousness at work, a directionless spinning of his reading of the signs that encom-

3   An allusion to André Breton, *Point du jour* (1934).

passed him. Clinging to the brush stroke sweeping him along from figure to figure, that unrestrained line, Blake is caught up in a maelstrom whose vortex has these incomplete, successive inventions as its torrent-like edges, which his poetry strains to follow and which we would be mistaken to take for a mythology, a system. It is but resurrection.

IV.

Blake, a prophet of the writing that poetry ought to be. Keeping what is self-evident in mind, we may acknowledge the other fact that his work commands: it conceals, text and image, a further instruction which is also important. One which even more than the first was conscious, deliberate; and which the poet and illustrator clearly wished to make heard throughout a life which was its insistent affirmation up through the dawning of the final day.

This affirmation is the book. Too easily in the history of the West do we have at our disposal the book. We are incapable of acknowledging the drama playing itself out in it either because it is merely the written word or because the written word and image have coexisted under the same title without accepting or even glimpsing the offer which, from one age to another, was made to them by the spirit of the possible, never entirely resigned to abandoning the fight.

This drama has been a fact, however, since the end of Greek and Roman antiquity. Consider the illustrated Bibles of the Middle Ages. On one side, a text that repeated a word become law, firm on dogma and its precepts. On the other, images that achieved just as much through signs and symbols become stereotypes. And in these two kinds of pages nothing, consequently, that made it possible for the first to become more deeply conscious of the second than their shared, fixed assertion; nothing that encouraged the painter to lay down at the feet of the child who the Evangelists evoke the goods of this world of meanings which art controls and about which it presages the contribution to life. And yet it is indeed this that the creator of images must do, no matter what the thought the written word speaks to him about. So that his intervention is in line with what I said about writing, it would have to include this expectation and enable him to delve deeper. This haziness of representations and ideas ceaselessly crossing and re-crossing the omnipresent frontier between inside and outside is in fact what, when the mental depths emerge, requires, in order to dissipate what are often merely fantasies, memories of the natural, earthly place, with its further self-evidence. And this is what the painter might contribute, were his eyes to remain open. The truly living written word is an exchange with painting. If this exchange did not occur and, as in those books that religion prescribed, the Bibles and psalters, or tolerated, the novels, Breton or other, it could only be at the price of what Blake called imagination.

Now this is what happens, in any case all too often, even today. The Renaissance understood the affection between poets and painters. The painters' interest bore on the great poems of the poets; in his art Titian upheld Aristotle's sensual suggestions, afterwards Valentino and then Poussin sought through their meditative canvases the meaning of Erminia among the shepherds, for instance. But the book, at the time moreover lacking colour, was for them a forbidden citadel and so it remained, which may be well explained. For the will of the absolutised concept, which today ravages more levels than ever in its view of life, has taken over that of dogmas; Urizen reigns over us, whence in the illustrated book a great many encounters in name only, simply juxtaposed experimentations in which nothing takes shape out of a shared quest. Yes, we can point to Sonia Delaunay and Cendrars,[4] and all the same in our time here and there, a few exchanges (I can attest to this) which intimate the great scheme, which even venture thereabouts. But their numbers are too few to face the crisis in a world whose horizon has already been scorched on all sides.

And at this very point where we find ourselves it is thus essential to listen to what William Blake tells us, the Blake who has not only contributed to opening up the space of writing to our modernity but who wanted this field of conjoined invention and reflection to take the shape of books in which poet and painter would be either of a piece, as in his case, or live side by side in an intimacy large enough so

---

4   *La prose du Transsibérien et de la petite Jehanne de France* (1913) was an illustrated book by Sonia Delaunay and Blaise Cendrars.

that their experiences would become joined together. Blake's books are, in their fusion of text and image, a lesson that is eminently to be pondered. All the more so that it helps to understand what is sought after in them from the first day to the final one, beneath their exploration of psychic energy and the fate of humanity. To understand what remains one of Blake's great thoughts and, assuredly, his most instinctive.

V.

I have no doubt that I'll hear: is not wanting to marry text and image under the banner of this kind of book, in which so many of Blake's own dreams overburden and obscure veracious intuitions, going too far, in the work of writing, into the dimension where it exists as a work of the mind, the obsessive fears of a personal unconscious more than the practice of the world in its unavoidable everydayness? Is there too much night and not enough day? Not in the least, and I must now suggest what I consider essential as much for writing and poetry in general as for the author of *Songs of Innocence*.

What I believe, or rather what I feel, at the heart of what Blake seems to be – and this time I have in mind the man he was, throughout his life, the poet as well as the thinker, the friend of undarkened mores, of women unbound, of revolutions on their first day – was that he committed himself, shutting his eyes in the thick web of his nocturnal intuitions, uniquely to a reform of self, to exploring his own, still latent freedom, which would enable him, once he'd opened his eyes again, to perceive the world he lived in anew, the world we all live in, that of ordinary reality. Despite his aversion to many painters from the Renaissance on (an aversion moreover less resolute than one readily admits, since he admired Claude Lorrain and had an affection for Constable), Blake was in no case the enemy of things of the proximate world. It is simply that he wasn't keen on seeing them represented as oil painting impelled, that is, with, especially visible, their thickness of matter: for about this matter he also knew that, despite its appearance, it is not a fact of the thing; it exists within us foremost as a way of being and thus as a way of looking at what is, measuring and weighing it instead of making it parcel with one's own life. So much so that the natural, the earthly, might reappear in his eyes, he thought, and in a way that was as glorious as legitimate, as soon as this matter, this weightiness and opacity of the soul, would dissipate in him, letting pass through, by means of external things as well as the poet's desires and attachments, the same unique light which is the sole reality. A whole and full presence, within this light. And the beings – all would be being – so completely free henceforth from the kind of study conceptual thought made of matter, that they would be as the invisible emerging at long last into the transfigured visible.

Blake does not turn aside from natural reality; he merely wishes to reach it where, being life, it exists, namely, in the invisible within him of his relationship of loving being with loved things, the invisible quotient of the acts by which the representations of the intellect dissipate and make themselves presences. And it is not preposterous to say this about the painter of so many complex, inventive and unbridled images; it is simply to return to what his point of departure was but also to the expression of his principal intuition, of his field of inquiry: his illuminations of 1789, those of *Songs of Innocence*. Examine the shepherd on the forest's edge, for instance; or better still, the title page, the young mother showing her children the large book. The title is there, with its two large, clear words. But the branches of the tree of life blend in with the words, which themselves have fresh sprouts, leaves, and all this grows in a dawn light whose tones of blue and pink are also well beyond, in terms of their airiness and purity, what learned painting could manage with colour at all levels of its chiaroscuro. Here we observe the creeping penetration of the evidence, which is a locus, the locus of life, the simple one, through quantified, Newtonian space, the one over which Urizen reigns.

Are these plates of *Songs of Innocence* naïve, works of almost popular imagery? No, they are rather a prompting to intimate its spiritual quality, which is more common than one might believe. Naïve? One might just as well say that they are what in the spirit is most extreme, that which – interiorising the relationship of the shepherd to the slightest branches, twigs and herbs, blended into his environment, taking the slightest nuances of its colour to their source in the light – makes the invisible the respite of the soul, the recovery from death; and the petition to society – primed to slide into the abyss – to pull itself together, to try at least to do so by dedicating itself, as doubtless it must first do, to the battles Blake never ceased waging, and in what writing struggles – his work is truly its testimony, with its terrors, vertigo and unreason – but without for all that losing heart when it affirms itself as poetry. The title page of *Songs of Innocence* embodies what we must learn from William Blake: the sign, all but the promise, issuing from a day still shrouded, of a possible simplicity. It is up to the humanity of today to ascertain if he was correct. Or to decide whether his intuitions were but a dream, Urizen forever reigning wilderness over the world.

Translated by Steven Jaron

The Unique and his Interlocutor[1]

I.

Mallarmé's letters are often of extraordinary interest. Particularly during some of his years in Tournon and Besançon and in terms of his exploration of the confines of mind and matter, he provided information on his conception of poetry and on the poems he then was trying to write (including two of his greatest: *Hérodiade* and *L'Après-midi d'un faune*) that his actual work could neither supplant nor even predict. Not only did he articulate a new and profound thought, he also documented its origins, adventures and anxieties, thus photographing a drama of the intellect. Five or six years later, in all seeming serenity, 'Toast Funèbre' (his sole somewhat explicit poem) could only express this drama's denouement. Yet what violence and boldness at certain moments of this search! Only *Igitur* hints at its intensity and, as such, this narrative is in a way confirmed through the search, and it can be read as what we might otherwise hesitate to recognise in it: the faithful and precise recounting of a lived experience.

Let us readily say that, in the clash of the human condition pushed to its limits, a few pages of Mallarmé's correspondence go as far as those discovered sown into the lining of Pascal's doublet; also as far as the letter, so rich in great new intuitions, that Rimbaud wrote to Paul Demeny around the same time, in fact, as Mallarmé's letters; a time when the history of poetry in the West so abruptly turned to crisis. Hence the need to make such striking testimony completely available, which did indeed occur in past years, but not as effortlessly as it should have. Thanks to the work of Henri Mondor along with the support of Jean-Pierre Richard, and then through the admirable constancy of Lloyd J. Austin's lengthy and conclusive work, as of 1959 all known letters had been published. Yet the result was twelve

---

1 'L'unique et son interlocuteur' was originally the preface to Mallarmé's *Correspondance, Lettres sur la poésie*, ed. Bertrand Marchal. Paris: Gallimard, Coll. Folio Classique, 1995. Collected in *Sous l'horizon du langage*, Paris: Mercure de France, 2002.

large volumes in which, once beyond the poet's younger years, the question of poetry only rarely predominates: thus the need for a selection that at first might have seemed rather difficult.

Luckily, two equally obvious facts offer a simple solution to the problem. On the one hand, even the most cursory consideration of the letters in which Mallarmé presents his thought reveals that it is absolutely inseparable from the rest of what he says, even if concerned with rather small events in his daily existence. There are of course passages devoted solely to poetry and that have their own relief, occasionally their own fulguration. As soon as we try to understand their exact meaning, however, we need to have in mind other passages, in these same letters or in others, since the signifiers surrounding a remark on poetry are not made up solely of a few explicitly elaborated grand concepts. By way of metaphor or metonymy, these signifiers also traverse aspects of daily life that Mallarmé could not forget, alas, and thus endlessly evoked. For instance: Geneviève who had just been born and who would soon push him to reflect on language in a new way, the perpetually hated job, the surroundings – reduced, according to Mallarmé, to the Ardèches-like regions of the world whereas art boasts Parthenons. All of this was matter for and means of reflection. We too must realise this and, in a selection process that would preserve the correspondence devoted to thinking about poetry, none of this can be sacrificed.

As such, the project of selection seems to have been made impossible. Yet, the other obvious fact is that it is only in the letters predating the autumn of 1871 – at which point Mallarmé had arrived in Paris – that he shares among a few friends some of the events of this thought and, immediately thereafter, those of his life. In 1871, his closest friends, Cazalis and Lefébure, disappear from his correspondence: the one had become his neighbour and he had fallen out with the other. As for new interlocutors, at this juncture they are numerous, often intermittent and, for reasons we will need to understand, they only were entitled to reflections related to their own person. Or, when the idea of poetry does come up, they were entitled simply to brief remarks that are suddenly distinct from the rest of the letter and from anything related to Mallarmé's existence. In this new era, he even seemed to insist on speaking of poetry only by refraining from speaking about himself.

Hence the solution to the problem: our interest in Mallarmé's poetics requires a volume containing only those letters written up until this period in 1871, which corresponds to the first volume of the Mondor-Austin edition, augmented with the pages later discovered and published by Lloyd Austin. To these have been added a few letters or fragments of letters in which Mallarmé subsequently focused on the question of poetry in a way that is easy to delineate. For this second part, there was a selection process, but about which there is little to say. Bertrand Marchal carried out his task well.

II.

Some comments now on the actual content of the letters, principally on the fact that there are two time periods, which might reveal far more than simply changes in friendly relationships.

Of course to a certain extent the break between the two periods can be understood by way of two or three other chance reasons. From what we can read between 1866 and 1867, Mallarmé clearly had reached a thought that seemed complete to him, and that any number of indices leads us to believe he kept intact throughout his lifetime. During these few decisive months he 'found' nothingness, then beauty. He also perceived that, when all the representations consciousness forms for itself have collapsed, the word remains; and that once the illusions of knowledge have been erased, this same word fills with a light: that of sensible reality, finally recovered in its original state after having been so often ravished by the mind. And Mallarmé devised the method – to detach oneself from the desire of possession – that would allow him to remain with solely this 'pure notion' at the moment of contact with the aspects that, to 'our joy', abound in nature when we no longer seek, through the act of knowing, to distinguish or to introduce objects therein. As he said back then, Mallarmé thought his thought. We can surmise that he had come into his own, and thus came to an end in his life the period of precipitous, exalted discoveries and, along with it, the need to explain himself to those with whom he was close.

In Paris, Mallarmé was also so quickly held for a master and received so many solicitations, books and invitations that he scarcely had any more free time – constrained by his work, beckoned by his writing – than was needed to write brief letters that his courteousness impelled him to devote to the appreciation of others, always attentive, always serious.[2] Yet these facts do not explain everything. For it was not solely the frequency of his remarks on poetry that had changed, but also the way they were formulated.

In terms of poetry, what do we actually find in the letters from this second period? Certainly a few more important clarifications. When, on January 10 1893, Mallarmé writes to Edmund Gosse that he is making 'Music' and he gives this name 'not to that which can be drawn from the euphonic concatenation of words, this first condition goes without saying; but the beyond, magically produced by certain dispositions of the word, which merely remains at the state of material communication with the reader, like piano keys'; and when he adds: 'Take Music in the Greek sense, basically meaning Idea or rhythm between relationships', he was clearly closest to his thought, even summoning us to it with words that seek to connect with us, though, as Mallarmé was quick to add, what he thus expressed seemed 'very poorly said, while chatting'. The implication being: 'we shall come back to this'.

In other ways, the new letters do throw some light on aspects of Mallarmé's work, projects and dreams that otherwise might have remained at the level of conjecture. In July 1896, he writes to his editor Deman: 'By the end of summer, I shall finish *Hérodiade*, and in the autumn I shall publish the Prelude and the Finale separately in the *Revue Blanche*, both of the same size as that which presently exists.' We thus can glimpse the feverish activity and naïve hopes still hidden – and so late in his career – beneath his few publications. Or consider this passing remark that nevertheless suggests another thought: on February 23 1893, Mallarmé congratulated Hérédia for having 'extricated' the sonnet from the realm of the 'bauble' in order to make of it 'the definitive, full and supreme expression of poetry'

---

2   'I have become little more than the correspondent who replies by rote to books received, and these are accumulating in a most scandalous way. Never a letter. Not that I work or, at the very least, publish. [...] Goodbye, this note is hardly anything, even derisory, when everything should be said. Take from it only our handshake [...]'. Letter to Jules Boissière, July 25 1893. [YB]

thanks to his 'shortcut' that 'binds together, under one glance, the extremely rare magical traits that are merely scattered in the most beautiful poems'. Reading this brings to mind 'the abolished bauble' ('*l'aboli bibelot*') of the second version of Mallarmé's 'Sonnet en yx', which predates the letter by six years. And this bauble – the ptyx on the credenza, where belief fades – might suddenly appear not so much as twelve syllable verse, but as the reflective image of the poem itself: a sonnet that, at its core, circumscribes its own absence. In other words, the 'Sonnet en yx' would also be an historical indicator. It is simultaneously a negative verdict on an entire tradition, beginning with Petrarch, of the fourteen-line sonnet that is so vainly turned toward illusory idealities and the renewal of this same instrument. Let us note that Mallarmé did indeed only publish sonnets, contested word for word against 'sonorous inanity', between *L'Après-midi d'un faune* and *Un coup de dés*, alongside such poems as 'Sainte' or 'Prose pour des Esseintes' that perhaps return to some pre-war pages.

Still in 1893, another useful detail comes from Mallarmé's discussing free verse with Charles Bonnier; or, in 1896, the importance of the 'site' with Charles Morice; or, above all, when he writes to Zola on February 23 1898 – the very same day the author of *J'accuse* is convicted – that he is 'penetrated by the grandeur that erupted through your Act'. We do love to see this Mallarmé who can maintain the connection between poetry and ideas of law and justice. We are equally happy to hear him say, on October 27 1896, to Alfred Jarry about *Ubu roi*: 'with a rare and durable clay between your fingers, you have set a prodigious figure on his feet, together with his troop.' A great deal will have been said after all in these letters that were constrained by overwork and politeness.

Yet how is it possible that Mallarmé, who saw Manet almost every day in 1874, never seems to have written anything to anyone about his reaction to the First Impressionist Exhibition nor about painters to whom he said he was so close, and even to be one of them in his study published in the 1876 *Art Monthly Review*. And there are so many other important if not overwhelming events that took place in his life, but also in his thought and writing, that do not appear in these pages; events that would have been the very subject of his letters from earlier years! Not a single letter reveals what was discovered elsewhere among his papers: his poignant intention to poetically transpose his son's interrupted life. Nor does any letter evoke the bizarre project that Jacques Scherer disclosed under what is actually the erroneous title of *Livre*. And nor does any letter reveal what this 'absolutely new' theatre might really have been, even though at the time it preoccupied Mallarmé so greatly – in his words, he was working on it 'madly' – that, on July 31 1877, he writes to Sarah Helen Whitman (who he barely knew): 'Too ambitious, it is not just touching on a genre, but on all those that in my view include the stage: magical, popular and lyric drama. And it is only when the triple work has been completed that I will present it nearly simultaneously; setting fire, like Nero, to the three corners of Paris…'. Whereas the first *Hérodiade* was so present in the letters, the *Noces d'Hérodiade* appears in none. All of these silences do indeed seem to indicate that after 1871, in terms of poetry Mallarmé no longer felt like talking to anyone about anything close to his heart.

As opposed to his previous expansive writing, I would say that there was something unspoken, even a 'will to not speak', judging by the change in his writing style. In his letter to Edmund Gosse, Mallarmé writes: 'Very poorly said, while chatting'. Not all that poorly said, though, and if it was 'while chatting' or seeming to chat, it is less because the didactic intent had let up for a bit than because another intention had taken its place, and not only on this one occasion. In fact, throughout the new correspondence, the way Mallarmé had expressed himself previously, displaying his thought directly and without ornamentation, yields to writing that is rich in interpolated and suspended clauses, layered suggestions, plays on nuances and reflections: a space of words that are all at once written and no longer the notation of a just thought; a system of facets meant to dazzle rather than to illuminate; and a presence – truly the 'complete Mallarmé', it can only be he – but one that slips away beneath the flutter of the folding fan and, in the end, holds back.

Of course, this is often the case when the letter is meant as a thank you note and where, for the naturally amiable Mallarmé, the point was to not hurt anyone without, however, overly praising them either. Yet this also suggests that, on these often-playful occasions, we ought not get too close to the person who is writing in a manner that is sufficiently concerted and subtle to keep the upper hand.

Unless he was writing to Méry Laurent, to his wife or his daughter, in his letters from after 1871 Mallarmé had become little more than a writer engaged in just another of the forms of his continual writing. This no doubt explains the strange, remorseful obsession with the tended or 'given' hand that runs through these pages that simply serve to keep the door ajar. In closing his letters Mallarmé writes 'Your hand'; 'I clasp your hand'; 'this handclasp that does contain my enthusiasm' – an alexandrine to Pierre Loüys in 1894, which also includes 'I wish it would accompany you in your travels'; and again, 'your hand, always ardently'; 'passionately'; 'a profound handshake, profound, rare, delectable, that I offer you now, I wish that it might contain enchantment'. We could go on forever with these formulas that do seem to offer a declaration of truly real friendship to compensate for a self-abnegation that should thus be viewed as necessary for profound reasons indeed.

III.

Being Mallarmé, these reasons can only be his relation to poetry.

I would now propose that what the Parisian Mallarmé wished to hide from his interlocutors was not an old or renewed thought on poetics – he did express it, even if obscurely, in the writings of *Divagations* – but his persistent hope in the effective implementation and sudden success of this poetics in his work; even if this incessant, feverish work – furnished, from this point forward, with all its advantages – showed him ever more clearly that the 'chalice large and clear' of nature-made-word would remain forever out of the reach of his lips.

Indeed, it certainly was not in the poems between 1880 and 1890 – those of *Triptyque* for instance or, nearly eight years later, 'A la nue accablante tu…' – that we see the ferment of words announced by 'Toast Funèbre', this writing that was to have operated or preserved in each word the dispersal of any notional content and of any knowledge: these insufficiencies and prejudices in perception that force the mind to know itself only abstractly and as chance. Far from opening themselves, through pure notions, to the fleeting yet sensorially infinite aspects of our earthly sojourn, these brief late poems owe their existence only to tangled notions that are certainly multiplied, encumbered with countless ambiguities and pushed to the limit of what we might still call meaning. Yet they are in no way freed from the networks of language nor are they inaccessible to interpretation. Rather, through their provocative evasive force they invite inter-pretation. The intellect is still in control in these poems, which is not surprising since the notion only can be pure – which is to say de-mentalised or de-intellectualised – when the poet is 'perfectly' dead to himself, absolutely freed from all personal desire, this anchor in chance. This was not the case for the aging Mallarmé. The cruel paradox is that an ordinary death, alas, that of his son Anatole, ensured Mallarmé could not even hope 'to die', to become disem-bodied and to forget himself. To do so would have been to betray the child's simple desire to live. One of the necessary conditions for the new writing had gone missing, forever.

Today, we can just as easily inventory the reasons for this Mallarméan impotence and their instances in the writings following 'Toast Funèbre' as we can the signs that, to the very end, betray within Mallarmé the survival of a hope that no evidence to the contrary comes to discourage. When Mallarmé wrote the *Triptyque*, when he was forced to recognise the irrepressible presence of meaning in his verse and even when he tried to resign himself to thinking that this verse needed a linguistic armature since it was a product of language, we can understand that he was still dreaming of something else and of much more, given how rarely he devoted himself to this 'exercise' that, as he explicitly wrote to Verlaine, was only 'meant to keep my hand trained'. And when, in the nearly posthumous *Un coup de dés*, he seems to admit that all writing is thought, all thought a roll of the dice or chance and that, for lack of anything better, there thus 'remains no reason' to exclude from the poet's activity some enactments of the drama of the intellect in its most extreme and absolutely lucid situations, he nonetheless also indicates that he still worships 'ancient verse', even if it only reflects the 'empire of passion and reverie'. In his depiction of the great 'shipwreck', he even allowed there to surface on the horizon a vague glimmer of what can only be seen as persistent hope. 'Nothing will have taken place but the place', writes Mallarmé. We cannot escape chance, the reef or matter. Almost immediately thereafter, however – and please forgive my erasing from his words the spacing, with its effects of distance and sky, that distends them – he writes: 'EXCEPT / at the altitude / PERHAPS / as far as a place fuses with beyond [...] A CONSTELLATION', as though Mallarmé were still indulging in the mirage at the end of the 'Sonnet en yx': the structure of the words that, like Ursa Major, would enumerate – determine in the being of the number – a 'total account in formation' of poetry yet to come. An account – the undeclared beyond of his 'exercises' – to which he was attached at the same time as his return to the unending work of *Hérodiade*: '*Hérodiade* finished, if fate so pleases', as he wrote to his family hours before his death, to which he added, 'And do believe that it would have been very beautiful'.

The hope of writing fully supported by the evidence and of 'appeasing Eden's disquieted marvel' never left Mallarmé. Yet we must also recognise that this hope had become progressively senseless. I now can say that it was this painfully lived contradiction, the aporia of a belief simultaneously dead and alive, that is the cause of the silences and the reserve in his 'second' correspondence; for to write about poetry to someone who might then have replied would have forced Mallarmé to admit this impossible situation, whereas in one's inner self, even if the conclusions are the same and even if one is about to set them down in writing, the moment of resignation can also be put off until tomorrow, after the still dreamt of final attempt. Yes, to admit the existence of chance since it must be so, but in such a fashion that – in such texts as those brief inextricable poems or in *Un coup de dés* – it is as though turned away from one's own being and intimate existence. And in one's secret relationship to oneself, rather devote oneself – to drown the anxiety and to delay dying from it – to this activity, this agitation, but without words, which is surprising coming from a mind like Mallarmé's. Thus, as early as 1873, the project for an International Society of Poets in which the most demanding and most ambitious of them all would have gathered together *rhymesters* from every which where; or the project to set the fire of theatrical representations to the 'three corners' of a city that most certainly would not burn. Rather, yes, to choose these reveries of insomnia and anguish. And, in speaking with someone, turn the conversation away from the greatest hope, with nothing left to offer after the Tuesday evening gatherings – which were also dazzling, but by nature of their variations rather than of the theme – than a smile and his 'hand', which was in fact impatient to return to its writing.

In short, Mallarmé had a secret during the years he reigned over avant-garde poetry, a secret that was none other than his madness. And it was not in order to deceive anyone regarding his alchemist's methods that he remained quiet about poetry in his late correspondence, but to leave himself free to exhaust his resources with an eye toward some gold he no longer really hoped for, but of which he still did dream. 'Every man has a Secret within him, many die without having found it', as he wrote to Théodore Aubanel on July 16 1866, immediately famously adding 'I have died and come back to life', whereby we discover his. Yet this secret was no longer the great resource he had thought he could claim as his own in his late years: an ability to detach himself from the desire of possession, to free himself from the hold of matter. Rather, even if it were impossible, he simply wished for this dissipation of desire so violently that no evidence to the contrary on the part of the world or his intellect was able to dispel the haunting or attenuate the pain of seeing this good slip away.

This was Mallarmé's secret. And, as with anyone who carries an incommunicable and unavowable part within, he was alone even among those he loved. Notwithstanding the evenings at his home – to which everyone hastened, and where he hid behind 'several smoke rings' – let us come to understand this master who inspired reverence, and even more so affection, as someone who 'chatted' only to veil this solitude. And should this solitude come to end, he only could die – to die in the simplest sense – of despair.

Let us now also ask if things were otherwise during the time of his discoveries, when his exaltation was so great that it even seemed to outpace doubt. Perhaps even in a time of triumph, even when Mallarmé was discovering the 'key to the final casket', was this doubt as tormenting as after Anatole's death. And perhaps it already appears, though differently, in his early correspondence. Let us return to those letters to Cazalis and Lefébure.

IV.·

All in all, even at a time when Mallarmé truly seemed to share the movements of his most intimate thoughts with a few friends, was there not already in his seemingly so confident words a reserve, a worry and perhaps also a strategy for concealing this background? With this question in mind, we can begin by recalling that, as complete as his accounts of what he had lived through between 1866 and 1867 might seem, to a certain extent they are in many ways elliptical and thus obscure, which is confirmed by the debate among various critics ever since Mallarmé's first publications. We can reconstruct his search, but we cannot simply take note of it. As I already have emphasised, it is true that everything Mallarmé retains, in the margins of his principal statements, regarding the other aspects of his past existence helps with this reconstruction. He made of this existence the very place of his reflection and one of its means. And, in speaking with Cazalis or Lefébure of the irritating conversations in the house next door or of the birth of Geneviève, he was able to intuitively feel that he was elucidating his thought. Yet, I fear we also must ask whether this information, which does explain him a bit better, might not also serve another purpose: to veil, within the great news that he so feverishly reported 'from the purest glaciers of the aesthetic', a certain quite precise question that remained a cause for worry to its bearer.

What needs to be mentioned at the outset is the extent to which Mallarmé hardly attempted – as 'perfectly dead' as he might have said he was – to disappear from the scene where the absolute nevertheless did seem to him to have triumphed over chance. In fact, he did exactly the opposite. If, in the autumn of 1864, Mallarmé affirmed that he was inventing 'in terror' a 'very new poetics', and if he exposed its principle, which was truly at odds with the beliefs of the time period – as in the famous formula 'Paint, not the thing, but the effect it produces' – almost in the same breath he spoke of his weariness, of his exhaustion, of the *baby* who is about to interrupt him, and of his rather dismal and depressed imaginings. In moving from one letter to another – 'So many torments!' or 'I am suffering greatly' – it is easy to see that he complained in each of them, claiming himself overwhelmed before the ugliness he saw everywhere, before his job as a teacher, which he hated, or beneath the claw of physical ailments, such as insomnia if not 'hysteria'. From these angles Mallarmé is hardly fascinating, and we could almost view him as weak of character, impressionable, cyclothymic. And we are almost tempted to take this diary of his lengthy misery for simply an act – a rather commendable one, actually – of sincerity, made all that much easier by the trust Stéphane had in the sympathy of his dearest friends.

But why is it that writing a letter, even when to these friends, which should have been easy since it offered him the outpouring he needed from within his solitude, was always an arduous and dreaded task for Mallarmé; one that, rather than helping him through the relief it brought, competed with his writing? For example, on March 23 1864 Mallarmé writes to Cazalis: 'I have about twenty letters to write per month, perhaps thirty. I put them off every day. These are wounds that have to be reopened. Besides, a letter makes me hate my quill that I no longer can take up in the following days for my literary compositions'. And again, to François Coppée on December 5 1866 – in the very letter where he notes that 'Chance does not meddle with any verse, that is the great thing': 'During an evening discussing anything whatsoever […] we would say much more about it! Especially as I hate letters, and I pencil them as grimily as possible so that my friends will become disgusted with them.' A letter, a letter to a friend, thus seemed to him a terrible or, at the very least, an arduous task. And if he nevertheless did surrender to this task it was no doubt for a purpose that was much more difficult to carry out than simply the need to share his sorrows with close friends. What then was this purpose? Was it really so that his friends would be 'disgusted' with his letters and with him? By simply inverting this hardly credible suggestion, let us say that, on the contrary, it was to seduce them.

To seduce them! The word might be painful, just as it might be painful to imagine such an apparently banal project on the part of someone who stood so resolutely in the vast night between language and the world. Could we not just as well sense that at a very high level of the mind there are points where the existential and the onto-logical need to interconnect? And, according to this hypothesis, can we refuse to notice aspects of those letters written during a period of intense research – from 1865 to 1869 – where perhaps more intentions are at work than even Mallarmé could have suspected?

For lack of time, I shall focus on only one of these letters, but an important one, written to Henri Cazalis from Besançon, on May 14 1867. These are lengthy pages in which Mallarmé again – the repetition is worth noting – immediately exclaims that the two should speak to one another, and he declares that the as yet blank sheet of paper frightens him, as though to not write verse on it were a sort of 'sacrilege'. Mallarmé nevertheless hastens to present – 'My Thought has thought itself' – an extraordinary discovery: God is dead. At the price of a long struggle on Mallarmé's part, the 'old and malicious plumage' had been chased out of the space where the mind forms its representations. In other words, what is clearly indicated and firmly stated as radical and definitive was the laying bare of the human condition, which is nothing since, as a consequence, there no longer is any transcendence – neither above nor within this condition – that might save it from being anything more than one of the 'vain forms of matter'. And, as other earlier letters show, Mallarmé already had drawn an equally decisive conclusion by noting that in this night of the mind or, rather, beyond it, something like a dawn has survived beyond beauty, even more pure and more luminous – for having been extracted from meaning – than in its manifestations throughout centuries of illusion... Assuredly big news, which is formulated as just so many seamless certainties. Mallarmé implied that he had reached a total mastery of those questions that are nevertheless at the limits of the thinkable. 'My Thought has thought itself, and has reached a pure Conception [...] the most impure region where my Mind can venture is Eternity; my Mind', – note the liberty he takes in appropriating the capitalised letter – 'that recluse accustomed to his own Purity, is no longer obscured even by the reflection of Time'.

Yes, but he nevertheless indicates – this time in the same paragraphs as his formulation of this absolute – both the extent to which he had to suffer to reach this altitude and to which this suffering had broken him. He says the year was 'terrifying', everything his 'being has suffered during this long agony cannot be told'. And if he was 'perfectly dead', from this point of view, on the whole it was for the better, 'luckily'. This reminds us of the layer of pathos, the coloration of truly lived experience that must remain attached to the words 'perfectly' and 'dead'; words he normally only offers to us at a highly abstract level of thought. In his 'terrible struggle' with God, 'luckily' laid low – the second time we hear this word – Mallarmé triumphed only by falling almost infinitely into what was perhaps the same chasm. The 'humiliations' of his 'triumph' were in fact truly profound. From this wider perspective, if we read him as he wished to be read, we cannot help but recall the scarcely heroic laments that he had so often expressed before his friends: his insomnia, exhaustion, strange infirmities – the 'horrible delicateness' to which he felt himself reduced. Would Cazalis pity him more than ever for having let himself be distracted so often and so unjustly by so many ailments born of his vigil in the absolute?

Or would Cazalis perhaps admire Mallarmé all the more as a hero of the mind since this explorer of the confines clearly did not possess the necessary force to assign himself this task, and thus had to struggle against its mortal coil – who knows, perhaps also succeeding in using it for the sake of further lucidity? Did not Cazalis in fact admire him immensely, and through this admiration did he not dispose himself if not to believe Mallarmé entirely then at least to listen to him attentively when he related his discoveries, and to do so without wishing or daring to contradict him, eager rather for him to be right. Mallarmé undoubtedly wanted this attention, this approbation and, at the very least, this reserved attitude. Such was the case when, in 1864, he spoke to this same Cazalis of the 'very new poetics' (that of the 'effect' by way of the senses, all the while evoking his 'sad gray days'): 'I do not know if you guess my meaning, but I hope that you will approve of me when I will have succeeded'. And Cazalis immediately granted Mallarmé his enthusiastic adherence and intellectual trust. In his reply, on May 15 1867, for he had reached for his pen the very day after receiving this profound letter, Cazalis exclaimed: 'My friend, I cried while reading your letter. I cried not because you were dead since your death allowed you to rise in life into the tranquil sky you dreamed of entering, but out of respect and admiration. Stéphane, know that you are the greatest poet of your times. And no matter how high you reach, may this homage console in you, my poor friend whose life has been so painful, so saintly and so sad, what remains of the human.'

Cazalis hastens to add that he and all of their other mutual friends are merely children who 'barely stammer' before Mallarmé, and he concludes by writing: 'Finish your work: I ask this of destiny', which reveals that Mallarmé had obtained what he had asked for: in no way the admiration contained in these sentences – he never worried, then or later, about being the 'greatest' – rather the ability to postpone having to examine with his friend the thought that he had formulated, and that he was undoubtedly already ceaselessly questioning. Yet now he was in solitude, in a place where he could dream as much as meditate, so much so that when need be the most senseless hope could unfold its wings. In 1866 or 1867, such exchanges allowed Mallarmé to speak of his poetic project without encountering anything besides the confidence of others as well as their total refusal to judge him. They allowed him to not make an impression or put on a show, but simply, humbly, to continue to be the dreamer – the 'impenitent dreamer', as he once put it – that he indeed needed to be so as to be able to think, for example, that he was suddenly 'perfectly dead'.

What also emerges from his way of being with his friends, as ambiguous as it was efficient, is that the difference we thought might exist between the two periods of his correspondence disappears. Both were for dreaming. All in all, the second period, the glorious period, simply sought to do so in an even more humble way, by avoiding the situations that might arise from interlocutors who, though respectful, were less intimate and less aware of the poet's private life, and who might ask Mallarmé, to his great alarm (not before them, but before himself), about the ultimate leap between existence and the poetic absolute, between chance and the Book. Whereas the first period of his letters, more confident in its correspondents, still could try to save the dream by sharing it.

V.

The difference disappears. And with it – and this is an essential point – the presence of a real interlocutor also disappears from all of these many pages. For, yes, it is true that in the early years the likes of a Cazalis, a Lefébure, a Mistral and many others are in fact close to Mallarmé, truly loved by him, attentively listened to, joyously received and celebrated when they come to visit him in his exile. But at the innermost level, the only one that matters, the level of poetry, which is to say that of hope and doubt, they are reduced to a simple role in the perhaps increasingly dramatic relation of a monomaniac of the absolute to himself. At every moment in his correspondence Mallarmé is involved in a monologue – 'recluse accustomed to his own Purity'. The recluse, that is, of his own dream of purity; the recluse or, better yet, the unique – a word I of course do not use in its romantic sense. Nourished on the pseudo-truths of a subjectivity diverted from the finite, the romantic poets thought they were well above the vulgar, thinking and speaking in a way all too aware of the divine to communicate with everyday life. For his part, Mallarmé dreamed only of being the same as anybody else; this similarity being, as a matter of fact, the necessary key to his poetics of the Book, this work that 'every one' has attempted. But did this make Mallarmé any less of an exception, has there ever been anyone who wished, as he did, to write the book that would unfurl – 'there at this very point and not any further and not otherwise' than it exists in the silent depths of language – the landscape of perceptible reality, and to dream that he could do so, all the while knowing better than anyone that even beginning was impossible? Who in poetry has desired as he did, really desired, the impossible? In *Une saison en enfer*, Rimbaud has the witness that he has imagined or noticed say of himself: 'No man before him had wished for such a thing.' This testimonial to an excess of hope holds even truer for Mallarmé than for Rimbaud, whose dream was less enduring, just as his solitude, despite all appearances, was less profound.

And overall, what a difficult contradiction this inability to express oneself since so attached to the impossible. What suffering – real suffering, though the only kind that went unspoken – in this man who was so affectionate, so enamored with friendship, so eager to reach out to others, his hand extended but his thought held back by the unavowable!

And this background renders all the more moving a certain letter in which Mallarmé finally says everything! I am not, as one might think, alluding to *Un coup de dés jamais n'abolira le hasard*, though it is in fact a kind of letter that this Vasco of the mind, though unable to go beyond the dream of India, wrote before the shipwreck. Mallarmé had read Alfred de Vigny's 'Bouteille à la mer'. In my opinion he undoubtedly also had read *Les Enfants du capitaine Grant*. He also placed, in turn, a castaway's message in the bottle that was meant for something quite the opposite: its 'foam' was to fill the 'chalice' of the inaugural day of the new poetry: that of 'drowned' sirens and of myths scattered by 'personal song'. Yet, as conscious as he might then have been of the reef, as much as he saw himself as a 'hoary maniac', the master of this shore remains too ambiguous in the delivery of his ultimate thought for us to be able to consider this a true confession of what had taken place in his heart. He affirms the failure and he affirms, as I have mentioned, the constellation of irreducible hope. He does not evoke the debate of the two within a man's everyday life; such as on Tuesdays, rue de Rome, after the visitors have left and insomnia returns.

To go through with this entirely, to admit his madness, we might of course expect that he did need a real presence before him, open to the whole of his problem since aware, more than many others, of the stakes and of the absolute nature of poetic creation. And he found this presence on November 16 1885, when he wrote to Verlaine, who had requested some biographical information for his *Hommes du jour*. Asked to reflect on his work but also on his existence, in a lengthy response that is admirable from start to finish, the poet distinguished from his few published poems his grand project for a text, a book, that would have spoken of its own, with an authorial voice, and thereby would have been the explanation – in other words the unfurling, 'fold by fold' – of the Earth: The project for a book or, failing that, for a 'created fragment', a simple parcel but that would have allowed its 'glorious authenticity to scintillate in one place', for which 'one life would not suffice'. This is really where he revealed the whole of his ambition, pursued 'with an alchemist's patience, ready to sacrifice to it all vanity and all satisfaction', as Mallarmé adds. This time, though, the letter writer no longer resorts, as he had previously with Cazalis, to the power of his ailments or of his weakness so as to convince his seduced correspondent to help him in repressing his doubt. 'Here you see the confession of my vice, laid bare, dear friend, that I have rejected a thousand times, with my spirit bruised or weary, but it possesses me and I may yet succeed.' What did he reveal here? Not simply his failure nor his hope, but the battle between the two, admitted – a 'vice', a possession – at this level of the mind where, for better or for worse, pure intellect no longer holds sway.

Mallarmé confided in Verlaine something he had never told his other interlocutors, at least not in such a thought-out and determined manner, namely that he was only a man like any other since driven by the irrational. And if he spoke in this way to Verlaine it was obviously because among all his contemporaries, of which he knew that 'they do not exist' as he notes in the same letter, Verlaine was the only one who, to his knowledge, was able to offer him the example of sincerity to oneself and of lucid courage. Despite big and small lies, drunken sermons and the daily illusions about the past, 'once upon a time' and tomorrow, Verlaine was the one who, more profoundly, did not discount the precariousness of the mind, the limits of his power and the vanity of metaphysical pride. As Mallarmé recalled at his friend's funeral, Verlaine did not 'hide from fate'. He bravely had the 'terrible honesty' to 'harry its hesitations', all the while affronting, 'full of dread, the status of the singer and the dreamer'. It was not because Verlaine had some 'likeness' to 'human ailments' as well as to ordinary passions that he took on greater worth for Mallarmé, rather it was because of his need for truth in relation to the absolute and for his ability to consent to his condition, whereas Mallarmé refused his.

And how could he not subsequently have listened to Verlaine, how could he not have answered him when he implicitly asked Mallarmé about the meaning of his life since, through his affinity for the extreme as much as through his compassionate clairvoyance, Verlaine could fully understand Mallarmé's confession, whereas others only could see the eccentricities of a great writer: one more signifier, in other words, as unexpected as it might be among all those that makes up a work? Those who 'do not exist' go no further than to think that it is this work that matters rather than the useless hauntings of the Impossible. Thus it was indeed to the author of 'Crimen Amoris', but also of 'Sagesse', that Mallarmé could truly speak. It is because Verlaine existed that Mallarmé did in the end have an interlocutor in his life; to whom, in conclusion, he simply said: 'Goodbye, my dear Verlaine. Your hand.'

Translated by James Petterson

OUR NEED OF RIMBAUD[1]

I.

Ladies and gentlemen, friends, it's with some emotion that at this point in my life, rather late in the day, I return to a consideration of Rimbaud. With some emotion, but also in the hope of a glimmer of truth better understood. I've halted at this great poet many times since the 1950s; I've written a variety of essays about him, and on each occasion learned much from him, about poetry, about society, but also about my own person.[2] Only true poetry talks of its readers, whoever they happen to be, and compels them to take stock of a part, at least, of who they are.

I owe a great deal to Rimbaud; few poets have counted for me in such an essential way – a revelation of what life is, of what it expects of us, of what we what are compelled to make of it. Of course, other poets were crucial for me: Racine, who revealed to me the powers of prosody; Virgil, who enabled me to sense the abysses in the simplest evocation of places and things in nature, followed by Vigny, Shakespeare, Nerval, then Yeats and Leopardi; and I must also mention Mallarmé, despite the reservations I've raised – although not without great affection – about his work. Nevertheless, I'm fully aware that two bodies of work, two ways of thinking, have helped me more fully than the others to live, in other words: to attempt to be. In them I found two friends, if I may use this word. Believe me: it's said without vanity. Two friends: Baudelaire, Rimbaud.

Now that I utter the names Baudelaire and Rimbaud together, I should immediately say that both poets present the same quest and lesson, one that seems to me to engage poetry's essential nature. I see

1   'Notre besoin de Rimbaud' was first delivered as the 2007 Zaharoff Lecture in the Faculty of Medieval and Modern Languages, Oxford University, and again in a revised form at the Théâtre de la Commune, Aubervilliers, under the auspices of the Collège de France. An expanded version is collected in *Notre besoin de Rimbaud*. Paris : Coll. *La Libraire du XXIème siècle*, Editions du Seuil, 2009.
2   Bonnefoy's major essays on Rimbaud, the first dating from 1961, are collected in *Notre besoin de Rimbaud*, cited above.

a kinship, a blood-brotherhood between Baudelaire and Rimbaud, underlying the differences emerging from – and how could it be otherwise? – the infinite plurality of life expressed in language.

II.

And what is this kinship at its deepest level? A sign is that they've both experienced themselves and the world – and the other beings in it, if not immediately – under the yoke, but also the goad of an ambiguity that, without doubt, taxes all poetry. In them, however, it has a scope and a stringency – even a vehemence – that are unusual as can be.

For one thing, they allow themselves to get carried away at times by bursts of hope that exceed any particular cause and can't be substantiated by anything specific. These are thoughts, to be sure, with their own kinds of evidence; but which barely conceal the need for a hope able to prevail against any line of reasoning. And then, later, we see them criticising or even denouncing, if not insulting (and suffering for it), the very thing they had previously borne witness to and desired. Under the force of another need, and one just as irrepressible: that of knowing what's really worthwhile, of having done with the illusory. A need for truth.

Hope, then, but equally lucidity, or a need for lucidity, and between these two impulses a struggle in which hope sometimes yields to excitement, and for good reasons, and sometimes loses heart, other reasons having cropped up. Both aspirations become undertakings, experiments with conflicting aims, and this can happen in what are the most routine matters of daily life, far removed from the concerns we're tempted to ascribe to the poetic project. This is the source of the quite remarkable differences between Baudelaire and Rimbaud, their kinship at such a deep level notwithstanding. At every moment of their life and their work, the one indistinguishable from the other, will be the drift and scatter imposed by the randomness of events: thoughts or opinions formed in extremely different sites and settings, dramas which these two strong-willed men will have to live out in their relationship with others, and not without lasting effects in their appreciation of life or even of the dream that seems reality: one with faith in a beauty of almost divine essence, the other with a vision of a society finally freed of its stifling constraints. But the veritable nature of the world doesn't fade from their view except momentarily, and it's this recurrent lucidity that is their closest bond.

III.

Lucidity is usually the chief quality in Baudelaire, or seems to verge on being uppermost. It's easy to spot almost anywhere in the *Fleurs du mal* criticism of the illusions to which many if not all of the poems seem, even so, to have succumbed. Baudelaire dreams but knows he's dreaming; he even perceives the nature of his dream, which is to think it possible to transmute the situations and forms of ordinary existence by working on the colours, the sounds, the odours flaring in the recesses of sensory perception. Under the purplings of the evening sky, in the thrills of erotic relations, the senses breach mines, orebodies not yet touched by picks and probes: Baudelaire dreams such sensations are able to produce a harmony that might allow life to come to terms with itself. And the beauty for which the artist strives, especially when the artist is a poet: this is nothing other than the supreme good, source of the hope that will sustain and guide the celebrants of its absolute value whenever they feel lost in the chaotic mass of the blind millions. This was an intense hope for Baudelaire: since childhood he'd experienced the body of his mother, and her clothes and perfumes, as a joy and a refuge – with a hint of promise.

Never poor in reality, physical or even carnal – this is beauty as conceived by Baudelaire! A quickening of all the senses, almost never a purely mental representation. It can therefore be a moment truly lived, even if this instant is as rare as the gold in the alchemist's crucible. Nevertheless, just as much as he affirms this essentially aesthetic good, Baudelaire is constantly wondering how to deny its value. This denial is far more than a mere act of the intellect; it too is an immediate experience, and a deeply unsettling one. That's why I see ambiguity in this great oeuvre.

An example of this ambiguity, of this ever vigilant 'double postulation', is the relationship of the author of 'Correspondances' to 'my child, my sister', the woman who captivated his desire. She had to be beautiful, and what is played out with her in their lovers' tangle is obviously an occasion and a place for what the artistic project expects of every sensory (but also sensual and therefore sexual) practice: a devotion to the manifestly beautiful, a deepening of what emerges in gestures, ways of being and doing, even looks and glances, that seem aware of more than mundane reality. The woman with whom beauty's alchemist makes common cause must be his partner in a quest for more than the crass lumpiness of other people's lives: a priestess – with cult and liturgies – rather than the kind of mistress familiar from ordinary life.

But this means that Baudelaire's relationship with her will remain at the level of sensations, and that he will experience and denounce other temptations in life (namely procreation) as a trap. It also means that the woman loved in this way accepts to be nothing more than a kind of perpetually sterile sister for her lover, something that could sunder her from herself, provoke discontent and regret, and surely cause the man who clings to her to become steadily more uneasy, for all his certainties. Baudelaire wanted his girlfriend Jeanne Duval to be a 'dandy' just as he was, or thought he was. But is such a thing possible as the days file past, bringing their own truth; or as they now come pell-mell?

Baudelaire was bothered. He had, as we say, a bad conscience, and he bullied Jeanne to hide the fact that he understood the needs she felt and he denied her. He belittled himself and found ways to suffer in order to show her that he knew he was doing her a great wrong. And this drama, which held him painfully in the common condition he wanted to flee, this was the experience, in his inmost self, of a compassion that had no place or meaning in the aesthetic pursuit other than to spurn the ways opened by that pursuit and name it illusion – to spot and denounce the chimeras within acts hitherto imagined as binding for truth, even as grandly heroic. In short, it was the finitude of every individual life that revealed truth in the very place where pursuit of the infinite – an infinity of the outside – in an artist's practice attempted to conceal it. Jeanne sidestepped any approach that misrepresented her.

Ambiguity, the intimate contradiction in Baudelaire's thinking, in his relationship with poetry – these are some of the most straightforward facts of his life at its most ordinary: moments of the greatest immediacy in his self-awareness. It comes as no surprise to find it in his poems not as a wavering that wants to dedicate itself first to the Ideal, then to compassion, but as a questioning – even as they emerge – of affirmations that at first glance seem perfectly assured and resolute. It's as if Baudelaire is listening in on himself. Listening in on his pain when he dreams of beauty, listening in on the surplus of truth he knows resides in pain. Along with the acute awareness, in the great poems, that abruptly dispels hesitations and doubts. Discovering beneath a first level of hope – for which the absolute was 'yonder' and actuality only something fleeting and intermittent – a second level of hope that will only have this absolute here and now, for the length of a mortal life.

A decisive lucidity that might, finally, be true poetry? Yes, except that it's soon if not forgotten then under attack again. When the aesthetic was denounced, in *Les Fleurs du mal,* this dream flared up again very rapidly. There's no tranquillity of mind in Baudelaire. Perhaps there's never any in this fundamentally dual undertaking we call poetry.

IV.

But I'm not going to dwell on the contradictions of Baudelaire other than to search for a key for a keener understanding of Rimbaud.

There's just as much ambiguity in Rimbaud, the same conflict between a hope ensnared in chimeras and a need for truth so stead-fastly upheld by this being who doesn't know how not to see things as they are. Even so, a great deal pits him against so many aspects of the 'over-artistic' Baudelaire, who is mesmerised by the nature of ideas and feelings. With Rimbaud there's no project for a heightened perception, no dream of a higher or earlier world where beauty might flourish, no nostalgia for a 'yonder' on the Earth itself, where this beauty might already be something of a divisible asset. Everything he desires plays second fiddle to a consideration for the ordinary world, for existence here and now, which he experiences as impoverished and etiolated, and which he proposes to reform and rebuild, besides reinventing the male-female relationship. This will be the source of his dream, or rather his dreams, since he will be tempted to give various forms to this goal of social revolution.

And let's remark first of all that, owing to this concern with the world as it is, and of society and other people, Rimbaud has, if I may put it thus, a head start on Baudelaire. From the very outset he enjoys the kind of relationship with others that the poet of 'Cygne' is able to embrace fully only when the aesthetic aspiration, so deeply rooted in him, has to admit its inadequacy. In this respect Rimbaud's hope, regardless of the mirages that will lead it astray and dishearten it, remains more open, under ordinary circumstances, to the truth and the presence of other beings than Baudelaire. Rimbaud has none of the disdain that this self-styled dandy believed he had for many of the men and women in whose vicinity he was obliged to live. Rimbaud looks more directly than the older poet at those he happens to meet, more intimately at those tied to him by his existence. And to understand him it's necessary to take the full measure of that vocation for meeting others, sharing with them, which stands out in his poems from the very first until the final lines of *Une saison en enfer*.

For instance, the two verses of 'Sensation' – which might seem the still naive daydream of an adolescent in a fever of selfhood – are no blue streak. Although the poem displays the desire for a romantic affair, with all its attendant illusions, it reveals even more clearly and more strikingly the presence of paths, cornfields and grass, the mild breeze bathing the uncovered head of the walker: realities that reveal themselves with such felicity in words only when one is blessed to be on the earth, experiencing how the unity of everything that exists passes – 'infinite love' – through the body and the mind that feel so alive, while desiring every bit as much to share this state of happiness with anybody else alive and present at a similar level of intensity. These rhymes of a 'very young man' – the words of *Déserts de l'amour* – yield up to poetry in the end the nature of this sharing, denounce the solitude of the aesthetic quest. And if 'Soleil et chair' from the same period – all these alexandrines demanding a revolution in an entire way of life, celebrating the sensuality that will awaken the Earth as a lyrical instrument – isn't simply ideology or rhetoric, it's because in their every word these pages already vibrate with the gathering commitment propelling their author towards men and women, all of whom, from the very beginning, will stand as plenitude offered and received, like gods.

Nevertheless, this creative upsurge is driven by thought, and a confidence about how thought can take on the thorniest problems: here is what enables the dream to net in its mesh the sweet intuition of immediacy. The latter isn't going to be less intoxicating, but an insight into how to regain a footing in 'ancient youthfulness' has wedged between the feeling of a unity whose light brings everything together and the poet experiencing it. Now it comes with observations on contemporary society, indignation at its uglinesses and injustices, the urge to banish this vileness whenever and wherever he encounters it. Although it's these analyses and hypotheses that give the conceptual instrument such importance they also increase the risk of the generalising idea, opening the way for an ideology of abusive oversimplifications – nourishment for the chimera.

What a paradox! The dream springs from a thought that aims to be critical, a dialectic of which some of Rimbaud's other early poems are remarkable examples. 'Vénus Anadyomène' or 'Les Assis' denounce, with apparent lucidity, the surrounding moral and physiological misery that come to his attention, only for 'Le Forgeron', seemingly at odds with its sarcastic evocations, to indulge the hope that the proletariat will escape the alienation of modern society. His worker faces up, in a revolutionary manner, to the iniquity of power and draws on the vow of 1789 – which was for justice but also and primarily for a love honoured everywhere, shared everywhere. Thinkers only have to understand and show the road to take, and the lyrical instrument that is the universe will resound again!

Utopia looms over 'Le Forgeron', and it risks becoming trapped in a facile idealism in spite of the would-be realistic observations of 'Les Assis', or of 'À la musique', another of those politically minded poems. But we should note here that these denunciations of a wretched society are proof, through their very violence, of a sharp-sightedness that enables Rimbaud to grasp that the visible aspects of things and persons prevail over any preconceived idea: such particulars as he picks out refer less to his prejudice than to his perception of the raw fact, so obvious as to be beyond analysis. And this is a sign that the hope of Rimbaud, however abstract his daydreaming, remains in contact with reality, remains 'in the world'; and that his forthcoming writings will offer a debate – the utopian impulse having to acknowledge its fantasising, the need to hope thus having to plumb deeper. Which is to say, the need to open oneself more immediately, more straightforwardly, to the intuition of unity, in and of everything, that is its starting point.

V.

In 1870, the very year of the poems of sarcasm and protest, this is what happened too in some of the sonnets Rimbaud wrote when he escaped from his mother's house and followed the Meuse in its course towards Belgium: he thought he was already headed for a glimpse of real life. Hope matured in these poems, and it happened because he made himself more attentive to aspects of existence that are valuable in themselves, the obscurities and standstills of the present moment notwithstanding. The violent contrasts of the initial epoch – the blacksmith's grievance sustained but also disturbed by visions out of Daumier or even Goya – yield to a light that seems to emanate from the inmost being of good and wholesome things: for instance, the tepid ham served to the adolescent at the Cabaret Vert in Malines by a most desirable waitress.

The things and beings encountered by Rimbaud in the few days of his fugue were, in other words, the cause of a rapid maturation. At a higher level they were also the symbols, the crucial issues, in hope's work: its grappling with what resists its dreams but can lend it fresh impetus. Things, in all their depth, which is infinite. But also words, whose potentialities and resonances are just as infinite, things and words communicating with one another and even achieving mutual clarification through exchange. This meant that the need to hope and critical reflection on its implications would soon shift their confrontation zones in Rimbaud's poetry, ushering it into a new future.

And the extraordinary thing is that this very young poet – he was only sixteen – immediately grasped what was at stake in the space between reality and speech: we know this because he mentioned it in a manner as explicit as it was intense barely a few months later, in his letter of 15 May 1871 to Paul Demeny, a young man from Douai met during his two recent wanderings.

What has been called 'the seer letter' is fundamental.[3] Today, we are familiar with the thought which was expressed that day.

---

3 The 'Lettre du Voyant', written when Rimbaud was 17. It contains the famous exhortation, and explanation: 'Je dis qu'il faut être voyant, se faire voyant. Le Poète se fait voyant par un long, immense et raisonné dérèglement de tous les sens.'

We acknowledge that poetry in its use of words transgresses what conceptualised statements make of them: they are familiar only with aspects of human or natural realities, not the unity of their being, nor how they are written into the lived time of our existence. We know that, at the heart of its writing, poetry therefore has access to our real needs, which are to accept our finitude, to recognise the infinity packed like a seed within it, to open ourselves in recognition of this fact to relationships of greater immediacy with one another in a society that could, as a consequence, be transfigured. And we no longer forget that it's just as important to close our ears to concepts that pretend to be ends in themselves, in other words we turn away from ideological messages or stifling prejudices, those stereotypes straight out of everyday life.

We've understood all that, and also the fundamental role played by sound, underneath words, and prosody and its rhythms, in this questioning of speech's routines. But look at Baudelaire. He attempted more intensely and concretely than any other poet to transgress the ordinary conceptual world, and yet he wouldn't have been able to decipher these designs and these laws of poetic invention – he wouldn't even have dreamed of doing so. Rimbaud's letter to Paul Demeny is therefore a giant step forwards that expresses the essential aspects of what we were not yet able to say. A step that Rimbaud was fully conscious of having taken; whence the passion and fever of his argument. When his need for hope ran smack into his lucid gaze it turned his thinking and his perceptions upside down; his pen leapt from one startling fact to the next.

VI.

I will focus just on what the letter says about the effect of words on self-consciousness. It's the best way to dwell on this double need for hope and truth which was, for Rimbaud, site and cause of his fundamental discoveries. The 'seer' demands that the poem abstain from phrases that lose the spoor of the immediate in the labyrinths of discourse. He indicates that the spirit level of these phrasings is the 'self', simple building brick of these meanings that are always partial and fatally reductive. And what he knows too, and states with considerable emphasis, is that underlying the self is an 'I' which, well in advance of the need for words, keeps the talking subject in contact with ways of being in the world that are lost to ordinary thought. It's at this level, the immediate level, at which the One becomes perceptible out of which we have to make our happiness. 'I is another', writes Rimbaud, underlining the pronoun to indicate that this level of consciousness transcends the forms and figures imposed upon it by the self. It's in the depths of this 'I' – covered up again but not stifled – that the poet will dwell because that is where his matter is to be found.

And he is able to do so, by a 'disordering' of how the self has construed reality. The negative is put to work in order to reinvigorate the existent by means of the 'torture' it's prepared to inflict: an uprooting, in the mind but firstly in language, of the core aspects, imposing as they may be, of this world of the self. It is, after all, one of mere representation. This torture will make the new poetry as hard-going as it is disconcerting for those who are not poets. 'The thing is to make the soul into a monster', announces Rimbaud. The pains of a true birth, a beauty that cannot be perceived by the shy gaze of the self.

He writes too: 'The poet makes himself a visionary by a long, immense and reasoned disordering of all the senses'. I'll halt for a moment at this phrase which engages as closely as possible with Rimbaud's double objective, in its good and bad effects. 'The senses' are the ways in which the body relates itself to empirical reality at its most immediate, the underside of the mere aspects retained by conceptual understanding. And since these ways are nonetheless partly in thrall to the conceptual world that is our place of exile, they're precisely what must be – to use Rimbaud's verb – disordered, upended, so that those first raw impressions can be rediscovered at a deeper level. But these three words, 'all the senses', may also refer to the meanings – multiple too – which enter and overlap in speech, texts and poems. Hence, in the sonnet 'Voyelles' that Rimbaud will soon write, and whose meaning, he is reported to have said, was to be taken 'literally and in every sense'.

Now, because of our analytical habits – and out of fear of this advanced position of the mind that Rimbaud in his letter called 'the unknown' – readers of poems, especially critics, are rarely tempted, on their side, to disrupt or disorganise meanings. On the contrary: they like to collect perceived meanings in order to adduce a coherent train of thought that is supposedly the main thrust of his texts – and this is where the pursuit of profundity is denied for the sake of surface events, the 'I' throttled , once again, by the self. How many attempts to 'explain' the verses of 'Voyelles', for example, shift with a blithe confidence from the level of open reception to that of reflection or even self-satisfied erudition, the exegetes failing to hear how the abrupt, violent movements of the poetry burst open the net they throw over it!

'The senses': these words designate both the body in contact with the world and the many meanings that shackle its speaking – now the two sites of the disorder advocated by Rimbaud come together in the same thought. To disorganise sight, hearing, touch. But also to discredit in the written text what, for instance, is fabricated there by those rhetorical devices from the literary past: they care nothing for renewal. Why the need to hoop together these two attacks on the ordinary approach to the existent? And why is this need so great for Rimbaud? Mindful of the deep-rooted ambiguity of this poet's being in the world, I believe it's because this loss of reference points, all at the same time, enables the impulse to dream and the engagement with hard facts to struggle with each other more directly: the resultant shocks will be the occasion for yet more and keener perceptions, either in thought or in existence: an opportunity for 'real life', as Rimbaud will put it.

Let's observe what takes place in a mind torn between a dream – a dream beholden to its hope – and the lucidity that refuses this chimera, although it too risks getting trapped in dubious proofs. Underlying the visions and opportunities for daydreaming there are words, but words don't reveal themselves one by one, they're already joined to other, alien words in the language, and by degrees to all other words, owing to habits of thought that are all the more influential because imperceptible. The kind of moral judgements, for instance, that seem self-evident. And more intimately still, the convictions we have about sensory perception which are however only idiomatic habits approved by usage – for example, the way the world is parcelled up by colours, and the impact this way of seeing has on values and even morals. What prejudices, what fears or joys, ride with the words 'red' or 'black' in their scrutiny of things! Language denatures empirical reality as much as it reveals it, and it's precisely for this reason that the disordering of perception can, retroactively, affect the use of words and challenge their traditional contributions to self-awareness.

So, disorder in the chains, at the very least. A little freedom of movement for the prisoner's limbs. And hence a nagging doubt about what conceptualising breaks up and hinders: namely, whether an experience of unity can develop in the poet's relationship with real things. Such an experience makes a poet far more confident in the intuitions of his body, this half-share of the mind, and freer in his life. It's a big chaos of words and signifiers, but suddenly their referents are in reach. The perceptual disorder has created disorder in the language, but opens it up to hitherto unknown channels. And to observe this fact is to grasp that the same revolution can be started at either end. To wreak havoc firstly in the use of the most common words, to disorganise the cultural tradition's master narratives with an arbitrary element that ambushes how stereotypes are taught, and very soon sight, hearing and even touch, and smell too, become confused: the disruption of direct perception might already be under way, but this makes it easier. Whoever questions the order of words criticises the order of things. It's one and the same task for the poet with the opportunity to prepare a great oeuvre.

That is the disordering, the *solve* that hopes to give its true sense to the *coagula* in the alchemical formula: and allows us to use the word 'alchemy' as Rimbaud will use it – its meaning now has nothing fantastical about it and is even entitled to be called a new rationale. Rimbaud's disordering isn't the daydream of an occultist faithful to the notions of the Middle Ages or the Renaissance, nor is it the unconsidered and irresponsible manifesto of an avant-gardiste in thrall to mere literary effects. It's a realistic, materialistic way of thinking, in which something inmost in poetry reveals itself, whatever the limitations and errors that we'll have to note in this particular undertaking.

VII.

And disorder isn't a simple idea either for Rimbaud on this May day, but a true project, experienced in full: even its implementation has been thought through. We can verify this by an example from these same months that also enables us to get a better purchase on the dialectic.

In his famous sonnet Rimbaud seems to know that what he calls 'vowels' – whether they happen to be letters of the alphabet or phonemes, it really matters very little – have colour as much as sound, and that the *a* is black, the *e* white, the *i* red. And this apparent conviction has triggered, as I said earlier, a torrent of texts. Critic after critic, too many to mention, have wanted to understand why a poet might think in this way. Should one refer to the theory of correspondences and dig among the symbols? Should one, on the other hand, proceed by metonymy and associate a poet's declarations with the circumstances of his life, for example an alphabet-book of the bright colours he might have loved as a child?

But how is it possible not to see that even if a particular reason, conscious or not, had played a role in Rimbaud's interest in the colour of vowels or the association of one of these vowels with black, green or red, what is significant – poetically significant – in these verses operates at a completely different level? It's not so much the respective merits of each case that determine the pairing: the poet wanted, from the very outset, to make his proposals arbitrarily, randomly. Rimbaud is after disruption. Is there a better way to scramble the relationship between words and things than to associate some physical quality of words with some apparent quality in things, and to do it in a manner so poor in perceptible or imaginable reason that simply talking about it will disorder reality and allow it to course back retroactively among words, changing how they relate to each other and thereby decomposing the image of the world?

To associate *a* and black arbitrarily is to embed in the word where the sound *a* is heard – or letter *a* noticed – memories of things that have black in them, a jumble of things, and in its train all the unforeseen circumstances this chaos is likely to create in what we expect from and value about the world. Flies and stinks emerge from words with *a* – 'amour', for instance, or 'âme' – to make the poet say what he wouldn't have wanted to say. The 'buzzing', the very disturbing hum of the 'hundred dirty flies', instead of the music once heard in cosmic spaces where thought once delighted itself. The black *a* is at once the ruin of a being in the world, an experience that can be very difficult to live out, part of the 'torture' that the seer wants to inflict upon himself. It's in the prism of such decompositions however that more light is going to appear.

More light because, owing to these paired disorganisations of perception and elocution, 'Voyelles' marks with each succeeding strophe a growing surplus of immediate reality – non-fragmented, unified and therefore luminous – in words which now almost entirely lack any meaning that could fit in a concept. In his letter, Rimbaud called this surplus 'the unknown', but it's more precisely an epiphany of what is intact, of what is not undone, of everything all together and fully present. In these verses it seems to occur all the more convincingly since everything here is flies, stench, spat blood, 'cattle-studded pastures', faces, 'studious foreheads': in short, the bold perception and reception of the hugger-mugger of what ordinarily goes unremarked and unnoticed.

The One emerges from all things, and from everything in all the things, which become 'stridors', dissonances that conquer the weak music – especially mental – of the poetry of the past. To such an extent that in the last lines the epiphany even takes on the voice and shape of the 'trumpet': the ever so brassy trumpet being in music the instrument that has stayed closest to the raw fact of the world, to its abyssal noise that stands out over any harmony. Had the sensory plenitude banned from the West reappeared in 'Voyelles'? And perhaps absorbed in it, that other abyss, those human eyes opened wider by the disordering, allowing a ray of light to issue which Rimbaud, in the poem's last line, observes is 'violet'?

This is what 'Voyelles' announces: increasing disorder in the use of colours is going to ruin all the ways of being in the former world and with them crush the hopes Rimbaud had nurtured until then, in the spaciousness of old-time thinking. There's nothing left of the communist ideas of 'Forgeron', nothing left even of the visions of 'Soleil et chair', for all their cosmic aspirations. But this sonnet has destroyed nothing at all. On the contrary, it has upped the ante by offering him already a glimpse of his grand objective, one Rimbaud had never known how to express but which – as he realised – was alive within him: the hope that the fund of unity and immediacy dormant in things, gestures and existences would swell up in his body and mind just as an immense wave takes the swimmer in its flow, and makes his life at least for a moment 'true life'. Disordering has dislocated the forms of his native experience, which were concepts and therefore impoverished reveries, but it seems to have confirmed an immense underlying intuition. It's as if the lucidity that had conquered these chimeras, in becoming more radical, did not so much dissipate them as in fact discover within them an underlying truth that legitimated the élan which, one after another, they had allowed to go to ground.

Rimbaud, in the spring and summer of 1871, emerges from the debate between his illusory desires and his critical exigency with this impression of victory: the indication that what speaks in him has the power to gain access, through a disordering of his old language, to his centre of gravity and his *raison d'être*. That he thinks in this way is surely a topic of meditation for people who have just discovered poetry, hopeful but disconcerted by the forms it has taken (wherever such forms are still to be found), in ossified words that know nothing of hope and express it only from the outside, through lures. They instinctively understand the fundamental value in them and through them, of a force that calls and lifts them up, but all they can do is confess the illusions, not to say lies, that emerge in what they say. It's this old lyricism that Rimbaud in these months allows himself to breach, and this fact already produces poetry. After 1871, it will no longer be possible to talk about colours and flowers as before.

VIII.

But for all that can we still hold fast to this promise? Should we not consider the categories of thought or our ways of relating to the world, and to life, which are at stake in the disordering advocated by Rimbaud – but which it has misunderstood, and dangerously so?

Should we not, in other words, ask ourselves questions about 'rock, coal and iron', since the seer tells us that such 'taste' as he has is for little more than them, or for earth and stones? Shouldn't we recall that rock and iron exist as such only for physicists, natural scientists and engineers, and in their own idiolect, which is distinct from that of ordinary existence? It's true that artists and musicians view the emergence of raw matter from that perspective as a source of colour or sound. But they have no *telos* other than to repatriate in their lives these glimpses of what lies beyond the human scene: if they nevertheless wanted to hold fast to these glimpses, in this beyond, it would be the start of a mystical experience that would quickly turn away from the dealings between persons that nourish life itself and even, it might be imagined, 'true life.' Nothing in language expresses the beyond as such: everything in it is conditioned and even constituted, structured by the human need for a scene we can adopt as the world. And if our words sometimes seem to designate the purely sensorial, names like 'black' and 'violet', these signified colours are still abstractions, aspects of things cut loose from their intrinsic endlessness for the sake of a human project where the first impression is a paradoxical one: that they're about to plump for impoverished desires and superficial reveries. Are these apparent epiphanies dwindling into fantasies, as is perhaps already happening in 'Voyelles' with those 'dazzling flies' hovering over 'gulfs of darkness'?

It is incumbent upon us, from the viewpoint of poetry and its true needs and ways, to reflect upon the worth of the 'long, immense and reasoned disordering' that Rimbaud proposes at a decisive moment in his quest for himself. And it bears upon us all the more so since Rimbaud was the first to ask the question, hardly two months after his letter to Paul Demeny, in other words at the exact moment he was exploring the virtual aspects of colours.

In saying that, I'm thinking of the dramatic reversal which takes place in 'Le Bateau ivre', those strophes initially so vehement and packed with images, so vivid in their colours and so strongly smelling of effluvia brought up from the seabed or from marshes full of things rotting and fermenting. 'Le Bateau ivre' reads as if we had embarked aboard 'Voyelles' to be brought before the 'Trumpet' of the second tercet, become 'low sun, flecked with mystic horrors', with all around it, on flanking waters, 'congealments' of the same 'violet' of the eyes mentioned in the final verse. Besides, the will to turn everything upside down is clearly stated. 'The crews and cargo meant nothing to me,' writes the 'I' of the poem, a metaphor for its author, an 'I' in which 'the other' regains the confidence repressed by the former self.

The brutality of the assault he launches against the former constraints is forcefully substantiated: the 'haulers' of the stolen boat, these masters of ancient thought, he has 'nailed them to painted poles' in the same way in which 'Voyelles' had nailed to black, green or red the representations, ideas and values of the traditional way of saying things. Whence it follows that the hoped-for unknown appeared to offer thousands of liberating visions, 'amazing Floridas', beauty of a new kind in which the immoderate, the hideous, the tempestuous are all currents swirling in a sudden apparent unity, poetry's sky 'fissured by lightning'.

'Le Bateau ivre' knows how to say these things, and as it were from the inside – the discoveries and joyful moments of a soul become a kind of proud monster. In its first part it's a genuine illustration of the poetics for which the May letter had been the project. Rimbaud has set his bow moving, as he said in the letter, and the symphony had made 'its stirring in the depths.' But why, right at the start, is this evocation of the great future which is all set to open in the ruins of the former time written in the past and not the present tense – the absolute, new present of the 'true life'? What a paradox, that an experience of immediacy, meant to dispel the very notion of time, should be depicted as a mere moment of existence!

And why, among these images that jostle to account for the superabundance of the unknown, are there traces of the previous existence? – those 'trembling shutters' which recall the rooms of the family house where, as the child looked on, rays of sunlight cut through the slats in the blinds, too often closed. These 'congealments' closest to the 'low sun' can then be described as 'figures in an antique drama': they seem to recall scenes from the first few years of life, with clashing protagonists who would be a cause for alarm were they not to leave lasting marks on a small witness's future. Drowned men pass on two occasions close to the boat, 'backwards' in relation to him although momentarily entangled in his 'frayed ropes', what's left of the mooring. And one of these drowned men is 'pensive', sealed on a thought quite opaque to us, which suggests that he is less a dead man than a consciousness unable, in the unleashing of visions and ecstasies, to join in getting drunk.

And what is more, abruptly interrupting the paean to the 'power of futurity' – and its 'million golden birds', what an extraordinary

vision! – Rimbaud exclaims: 'But it's true, I've cried too much!' A
wholly different kind of thinking emerges from beneath the exaltation of these last months.

IX.

'I've cried too much'? Let's first take the measure of the chasm which
opens in this exclamation and goes on to widen in the ensuing
strophes. Let's note that it's no longer a matter of 'unmoored peninsulas', of a limitless horizon, of storms overlaying the infinity of the
sky with the infinity of the sea, but the evocation of a very narrow,
very exposed place, and of a child's growing awareness of what a
place is – in its intrinsic being – as place. Even where the grown-up
Rimbaud seemed to have broken with any localisation of his experiences, the very world and its stars not being big enough to take
them in, now 'European' waters shimmer before him, the 'puddle'
on which an unhappy child plays at launching his toy boat. A place,
yes, and even a poor place, since in this village dusk there's nothing
to catch the gaze but a few houses and their overhanging trees. Were
there to be a boat, 'on this lugubrious eye of water', it would in any
case be motionless. What other bank would it make for? The only
boat which counts here is this simulacrum, 'frail as a butterfly in
May', a simple fold of paper perhaps, and short-lived. There's no
more striking manner of contrasting two kinds of dreams. One kind
which straddles the limitless, this other kind that cannot gainsay –
they are too close for that – such palpable constraints.

Now – and at one stroke it overturns all the thoughts of the 'Bateau
ivre' – this next-to-nothing is vehemently proclaimed the object of
desire, and even of true desire. 'I yearn for Europe and its ancient
parapets': that is what he has just written, this poet who nonetheless
had revolted, refusing any historicity and culture; and Rimbaud adds:
'If I long for European waters, it's for a pond'. He knows, however,
that this water is 'black and cold', especially since in this same land of
misty evenings he'd learned the nature of his mother, primary cause
of his childhood distresses and his later adolescent rebellion.

What is there to understand, other than at the very moment when
the great disorder ran riot, he couldn't forget that he wasn't going

to succeed in prevailing over the evil for which he once seemed the remedy; and was perhaps even going to stumble down roads that in the end might prove fatal? Let's read now the account that Rimbaud left of the few months of 'Voyelles' and 'Bateau ivre', the chapter 'Delirium II, Alchemy of the Word' in *Une saison en enfer*. 'My turn now', he starts. 'The story of one of my insanities.' And he's clearly talking about his project of May 1871, since he states: 'I invented colours for the vowels!' and: 'I imagined that I would invent a poetic language that would one day be accessible to all the senses'. He adds that in the way he looked at things he'd become used to 'basic hallucination', and knew the relationship that it bore to 'word hallucination'. Word for word, the programme of the letter to Paul Demeny.

But what holds him back now are the negative aspects of the undertaking. 'I became a bitter person', he writes. He observes that he'd succumbed to a 'leaden fever', been in an idleness that made him envy 'the happiness of the creatures'. And it's true that he'd known joys, even ecstasies; he'd felt like 'a golden spark of *natural* light'; but this happiness was a worm that was racking him, a 'leavetaking of the world'; he regrets it all, and besides, from beneath, 'terror was closing in'. Rimbaud concludes: 'I was dead to the world for several days, and when I woke my dreams continued to be as sombre as could be. I was ready to die; my weakness led me along dangerous roads to the ends of the earth, to the land of Cimmeria, home of shadows and whirlwinds'. The 'drunken' boat was being dragged into the maelstrom of the abyss.

'I had been damned by the rainbow', continues Rimbaud, recapitulating in this striking image everything that transpired in 'Voyelles', from the infra-black to the ultra-violet. Above the 'drifting peninsulas' the colour spectrum failed to produce the sign he was hoping for, the rainbow of a new alliance. And in a poem which he reproduces in this same 'Alchimie du Verbe' he makes it clear as well: 'Through my tears, I saw gold – and couldn't drink.' Had he been during these months 'the sickest of the sick, the great criminal, the great accursed one' that he pledged to be in his letter to Paul Demeny? At any event, today he would no longer add: 'and the Supreme Knower'.

X.

And for us, it's easy to understand what the 'seer' was lacking in order to find himself living the true life. When a child cries, sobs his heart out, it's always because he believes more or less directly, more or less genuinely, that he's no longer loved, that he's been abandoned by his nearest and dearest; and because he senses too that this lack of affection will make it difficult or even impossible to love himself in turn. He is or thinks himself to be an orphan; he suspects that he will also be a 'crippled heart'. That is the twin cause of his despondency. The origin of his deepest despair.

I ought to say now that in the disorder of the senses as experienced by Rimbaud in these months no situation, either explicitly or merely hinted at, revealed him to be involved in an affectionate or amorous relationship. In this supposed intensification and upheaval of everything that is human, in this invention of a language which ought to be 'language [...] of the soul for the soul, telling the whole story, perfumes, sounds, colours, thoughts hooked on to thoughts and pulling', one of the most vital ways in which a person can participate in life has not been taken, indeed would hardly seem to have been noticed other than with impatience and disdain. If Rimbaud feels hunger, at this moment of his poetry, it's only for 'earth and stones' – we know the lines. He loves 'vacant plots, burned-out orchards, sun-bleached shops, tepid drinks', all places or circumstances in which he is alone with himself. 'Eyes closed', he offers himself up 'to the sun, the god of fire': it still means being alone. And to live as 'a golden spark of *natural* light' is to be separated from any kind of presence, from beings even more than things. Beings – in this 'study', in this 'madness'? Yes, the wolf which howls from the cover of the leaves, the hedge-spider, and once, very far away, carpenters under the Hesperidean sun, but nobody in the foreground, not even the spoor of a serving girl from a green inn.

Is it true, what I've just said? Had Rimbaud really turned his back in these months on any kind of affection, any urge to share things? I believe so. It's true that he sent Paul Demeny a poem titled 'Mes petites amoureuses', but these forty-eight lines – very weak lines for once, being racked by so much anger and sarcasm – signify only that he imagined, on that particular day, that this solitude was something desired, not suffered. Concerning this solitude, and precisely from this perspective, he'd also asked the question in his great letter in a manner that wants to be taken for an *a priori* decision, the outcome of a considered thought. As long as 'the infinite servitude' of women has not been broken, he wrote, and as long as they remain alienated in what enchains them but also denatures them, depriving them of their own words, they cannot be admitted into the work of poetry. As he puts it in another poem of that period, 'Les sœurs de charité', woman is 'unconscious and blind' in spite of her 'immense pupils'. Aspects of that thought might be defendable, but it sounds as if it failed to alert Rimbaud to a personal problem.

Yes, but 'Mes petites amoureuses' exclaims 'How I hate you!', where he contrives to see these 'dogs' only in terms of their physical ugli-nesses and physiological miseries, mocking the objects of his desire with an extreme bitterness, insulting them: evidently 'the woman, transfigured a moment, the frightener' reopens a wound he has suffered and would like to be able to forget, and in his 'disordering' he intends to be alone. Which is hardly contradicted by 'Ce qu'on dit au poète à propos de fleurs', other lines from the 'Bateau ivre' period, since the flowers he speaks of there aren't worth 'a seabird's crap', being no more than 'enemas of ecstasy' to be hunted from poetry in order to be turned into gums, sugars, even 'chairs': these are, whether the author understands it or not, metaphors for young girls.

Rimbaud was alone during all these months which nonetheless held out so much hope for the powers of poetry. In this great agita-tion of words – and things – he will fail to encounter a living soul. And that is something we're obliged to register, but it's also some-thing he understood himself, and regretted. What does 'I cried too much' mean if not that he ended up seeing that the sad and forsaken child on the edge of the puddle was his own personal reality, his 'real truth', not the 'million golden birds'; and that if he wanted to restore sense and value to his existence he had to ground himself in how he related to others, those on account of whom he wept: only there could he act in a way that will be decisive – and hence poetry. The disordering had only applied to words and things misappropri-ated from this true field of experience. It had helped him to believe that the real was in raw things and not in human situations; in coal and iron and not in the despondency of a child or the neurosis of a mother or the alienations of a society. But its effect was to leave him more exposed than he was before, being himself only an aspect of the distress that had to be overcome.

XI.

That is in any case what the events of the following months clearly seem to confirm.

In the autumn of 1871 Rimbaud went to Paris, and in spite of the conclusion of 'Bateau ivre', it was still with great hopes, since he was confident about the welcome he would receive from the poets, principally this man Verlaine who had encouraged him to quit Charleville for good. And I think his life would have taken a quite different course, in these months and perhaps for years after, if he'd found some support, some serious colluders in the Paris milieu. On the contrary, what he experienced was both a surprise and a disappointment. Face to face, for starters, with the person who had been his main reason for believing there would be a poetry after Baudelaire.

Rimbaud called Verlaine in his May letter 'a true poet', successor of the author of the *Fleurs du mal* who was himself, the 'first seer', 'a true God'. And it was common knowledge that he, Verlaine, held his young correspondent 'equipped for war': words which made of poetry a combat, a revolution, exactly what he hoped and prayed for.

But one decisive evening he saw with his own eyes the man behind the poems, after which it took him very little time indeed to grasp that his new friend was weak and foolish, that his way of dealing with things was all too often ineffectual and that he was in an evasive if not downright deceitful relationship with his timid young wife and her bourgeois family. Pitiful! And then he'd had to follow Verlaine among puerile pen-pushers indulging in smugly irresponsible games: this was really what he most detested even as he allowed himself to be caught up in their laughing and drinking.

And all this scandalised Rimbaud, struck at the very quick of his idea of poetry. He'd been 'certified poet', ready to go in search of the 'unknown' through the most 'enormous' sufferings. Whatever his own contradictions and concerns, and in spite of his liking for provocation (reverse side of the shyness born of an excessively demanding nature), he was a person of severity, rigour and revolt: and now he discovered Verlaine was also addicted to every kind of appetite and egoism, this man whom he once called 'a swine'! Was this the Paris of which he'd celebrated 'the huge stirring of strength' and shouted about its 'supreme poetry'? And since he himself didn't break immediately with these obvious fakes of poetic ambition, wasn't he bound to conclude that his nature too was a papery one, if somewhat on edge? That, beneath the illusions which had strained his first poems, there was yet another, and the worst one of all: imagining that he was truly a poet?

In any case, there is no doubt in my mind that it was these observations and especially this worry about himself, this great alarm, that account for the strange behaviour which marked Rimbaud in the following months. Temper tantrums, made up of bitter parodies and aggressive sarcasms, of slurs against one or other of these disastrous young people whose company he was keeping, as well as self-directed anger, took on clearly punitive forms. He evokes what can only be this moment in his life, writing 'I lay lengthwise in the mud' at the beginning of *Une saison en enfer*. 'I summoned executioners so that I could gnaw on the butts of their rifles as I lay dying.' And again: 'Spring has brought me the hideous laugh of the idiot'. All his actions at that time show Rimbaud to be racked by an enormous anger at everything, and in a miserable situation that rapidly destroyed the hopes that had brought him to Paris. 'I succeeded in purging all hope from my mind', he observes, on the same page. Which might suggest that hope wasn't the constant thought for Rimbaud that I said it was; and that at least at certain times his lucidity didn't allow him to fortify it by helping him work out its nature.

But that isn't how I interpret the months before the departure of Rimbaud and Verlaine for Brussels and London.

In point of fact, there was too much violence, in the way he lived then, for another interpretation not to interpose itself. 'I pounced with the stealth of a wild beast in order to wring the neck of every happiness. [...] Despair has been my god. I lay lengthwise in the mud. I dried out in the stench of the crime': these are words that speak of something more than a great, all-encompassing disappointment. And further on in the *Saison*, in 'Delirium I' where Rimbaud is clearly the

'Infernal bridegroom' of the 'foolish Virgin', he adds: 'I shall cut gashes all over my body [...]: you'll see, I'll run through the streets shouting my head off. I want to go raving mad'. Is that the voice of unhappiness, despair? By all means. But it's also a desire, obscure perhaps but active, impelling, a desire to take the feeling imposed by this sad state of affairs to its utter limits. A desire, fascinated, to reach rock bottom – still in life but now made unlivable – where the dissociation of all representations, judgements, everything that gives meaning and coherence to a worldly existence could be experienced in the moment they fall apart: at the point, then, where he has to look at everything from underneath. Underneath words even, underneath the illusion of words. Has hope gone? Yes, but one essential thing should be pointed out: it's because Rimbaud has 'succeeded' – it's his word – in purging it. He sought the abyss as much as he was led into it.

Why? Because beyond his terrible setback he has sensed instinctively that the decomposition that can be accelerated in how a person relates to himself, the annihilation that clings to ideas, affections, lived emotions – all of this harbours possibility, and it isn't straightforward renunciation, death, the 'last *squawk*' as he says, portraying himself in that expression as a dying animal. For this night which now inhabits every part of the mind, this death not of the body but of ordinary consciousness, this could be the first phase of a dialectic through which, with the defeated self expunged, an absolutely new consciousness, a new reason might be able to take shape. Once again, we have the *solve et coagula* of the alchemic intuitions, the idea of a transmutation of leaden life into gold: except that, this time, what would enable this gold to come up from the depths would no longer be the simple disordering of words under the effect of disordered sensory perceptions, as in the 'Voyelles' period, but the 'strangling' of every form of discourse, no exception made, in use until then. The void thus created in the self would now open perhaps on another level of human possibility. When everything is dislocated – ambitions, judgements, values – on the scene of the self, isn't there in fact still a residue, a sort of ultimate evidence, a consciousness of self, naked now, nothing but a feeble sound in the encompassing silence? And isn't this the point of no further reduction too, and a new beginning? In this degree zero of life a second degree for the mind, a future inaccessible by any other means?

Yes, it's possible to see things this way. We can even consider that decomposition of the self is the sacrificial act which the poet, as the great 'worker' he still wants to be, is duty-bound to accomplish. And it's precisely this intuition which seems obvious to me in the cries – the howlings, the intended self-mutilations – of the Rimbaud of this season. So I conclude that, in spite of all his turmoil, what he experienced in such actions was still hope. That what he 'succeeded', as he says, in destroying, were solely those forms he recognised as being illusory. That this Rimbaud enraged at everything and himself, this Rimbaud, throwing himself if not under horses' hooves then beneath the catcalls of the assembled company at some banquet of the Vilains Bonshommes, is a Rimbaud who hopes, still hopes. I believe, in short, that once again it was lucidity, simply and finally brought to a pitch, which preserved in him his innate, and reckless, commitment to hope. Which enabled hope, in extenuation, to accede to the most essential aspects of what it is, as potential.

XII.

Let's return to the first page, already cited, of *Une saison en enfer*. The page which depicts the decomposition of the self that I've just spoken of. Rimbaud confirms my hypothesis there since he indicates that, in his flight, it's to 'hate' and to 'misery' that he has entrusted his 'treasure'.

His treasure? Nothing other – in fact nothing more – than his capacity for hope, which he now knows is his asset. This capacity isn't dead, it's simply in the hands of 'sorcerers': those claws tearing it out of him, cruelly but exactly as they must, the utterly chimerical substance of the ancient spirit, the substance of that beauty 'happy and radiant' as people used to say. And it appears too that this hope is placed – as was the case at the time of 'Soleil et chair' – in relations with other people. It's a 'banquet' for which Rimbaud is seeking the 'key', and he says of this banquet – life at the moment of its origin – that there 'all hearts opened' at the same time as 'every wine flowed'. 'Once', he states. Once and not yesterday? Yes, since in the months when all the senses were disordered, months of solitude, his heart, as we have seen, was closed to other hearts. This 'once' shows that, now, he understands more clearly what the essence of hope is. It isn't a matter of 'every wine', as he wanted to believe at the time of 'Soleil et chair', or of 'Voyelles', or of the first stanzas of 'Bateau ivre'; it fastens to 'hearts', that is to feelings and affections, even the most humble and naïve. The intuition of 'I've wept too much' of his great poem finds itself here confirmed.

These first lines of *Season* do more however than just discover what hope is at its deepest, they also say how Rimbaud sought to restore it in his life. 'Just lately,' he writes, 'finding myself on the point of croaking my last *squawk*, I thought of searching for the key to that ancient banquet.' And he adds, quite specifically: 'That key is charity.'

Charity? The word is certainly a difficult one. But it shouldn't astonish us, since what else can the 'I' do which frees itself from the self in a world emptied of all its bearings? It can only turn towards the sole reality that subsists there: other human beings seen as if back-lit by the obscure rising sun. And isn't it the most natural act then to ask these others for a 'helping hand' so as to be able to get up and stand on new ground – a reason for existing as much for them as for oneself? Charity, at this moment in Rimbaud's work, is the offer made to others to participate in the sacrificial act of renouncement that enabled the 'I' to free itself from the self: for them it means a task to be pursued or which they might begin to understand, where they can dare what previously they hadn't known how to dare, or wanted to. Charity? The proposal is made to undertake a quest, but he brings to it this gift of encouraging people to pursue the task with stringency, rigour, even severity. Here again, in fact, 'the suffering is enormous', as a corollary of the existence that takes on form again – not without a number of poorly closed wounds, anxieties and hesitations, and with constant occasions for relapse.

And could it be this kind of charity which Rimbaud is talking about in this prologue to his big book of considerations and new projects? Yes, to judge by the events which happened at the end of these few months of indignation and shame; the departure from Paris, Verlaine uprooted from his miserable existence, and then the way in which Rimbaud behaved in London with the man he calls in 'Vagabonds' – one of the two accounts that he left of their shared life – his 'pitiful brother', his 'poor brother'.

He had despised Verlaine, but no more than he had despised himself. He had loved him, equally, because, as 'sickly' as he was, his heart opened in the presence of victims, and he would have been able to work out quickly that Verlaine was one too. He shared pleasures with him which he'd thought futile, indeed humiliating, which meant considerable distress. And there had been moments too to learn what miseries, even physical, can weigh down the exuberances of the body or the emotions of love; so distant then, at least in appearance, from the intensity of the true life that poetry deemed possible. What could be less surprising that, henceforth, raising his eyes from his own dereliction, he called on Verlaine to join him in his 'venture' – this will be his word in 'Vagabonds' – to rediscover together the 'original state of a child of the sun'? To turn charity into a key, this for Rimbaud meant to reclaim, at its origin, his relationship with this poet who had so disappointed him on his first day in Paris, the city that had to be abandoned now they were making a clean slate of it. This was an attempt to transmute his anger, to upend the 'badness' that had accumulated in him since as far back as his childhood. And this was the watershed moment in his life.

A remark, here, seems essential to me. This passage to the limit, at least ventured, this effort to restructure self-consciousness into fractured ways of understanding or even to live framed in our very being by the prejudices of conceptual thinking – this is evidently poetry itself. Beyond the insufficient operations mounted by the glorification of sensory perception in 'Soleil et chair' or the disordering of the same in 'Voyelles', poetry attempts to be a direct experience of unity – of its presence at the heart of all the acts of existence and in all the ways words are used – in this single true infinity of everyday reality. And in the spring of 1871, Rimbaud got rid of every happiness and every value, but also and perhaps above all of Beauty, now experienced as 'bitter' – it's simply an attempt whenever confronted with situations in life to take as his starting premise a steep and dangerous route (but also the only direct one) in this quest for the poetic absolute. After which, dedicating himself to charity, he simply found himself at poetry's second moment. Once the One is recollected, recognised in all that is, the meaning of this second moment is to perceive it too in those close to him, and attempt to give it features through them. Through this double experience of 'the hideous laugh of an idiot' – a laugh which was headed straight for death, a poor man's ecstasy – and the offer to others of unity as a goal, Rimbaud was brought to the centre of poetic intuition, which is fundamentally ambiguous or, better said, *dual*: the affirmation of the One but also that of others. Redressing himself after his errancies, the young man who in his letter of 15 May proclaimed himself 'officially poet' had plainly become one.

But we know too that 'becoming' a poet doesn't necessarily mean being able to remain one. That it's only in fleetingly brief moments, or as simple scrapings of verbal gold, that poetic inspiration yields itself. Making use of words which are necessarily conceptualised, absorbed in the endless flow of representation, the poet can very well imagine presence in what exists. Nevertheless he cannot remain long under this sign; and even Verlaine plus Rimbaud didn't add up to a tertium quid. After their departure as a couple, what happened? With his lucidity now fully developed Rimbaud reports the event, in *Une saison en enfer*, and it's only to register another 'delirium': through Verlaine's voice, which Rimbaud chose to do the talking, we learn that his violence against him, which he hoped would completely purge him, hasn't freed him from his old self-hatred, a pain which he tried to assuage by turning it into a glory. Nevertheless, disappointed to betray in this manner the friend he wanted to help, and punishing himself in front of him for this shortcoming, he frightened him, made him suffer, and finally enslaved his opposite number instead of setting him free, reinforcing his childish dependency. He sorely loved to infantilise him, the child unable to resolve the thorny problems of his own life.

'Perhaps he knows secrets for *transforming life*? No, I told myself, he's simply trying to find them. His charity is witchcraft', concludes the partner that Rimbaud has taken on: he doesn't save him, but he lends him, for a moment, his extreme lucidity. Overcoming the old Adam is decidedly no easy task. Wounds sustained, it may be thought, in his earliest years – think of the 'I've cried too much' – and not closing as straightforwardly as some idea of hope might dream, rapidly become naïve again. Especially since it's no longer possible for Rimbaud to imagine that his 'crippled heart' will be restored by a 'divine master'. The 'charity' which he is talking about isn't Christian: it depends only on him. Instead, he will soon find that Christ, the 'thief of energies', is responsible for his unhappiness, having delegated his message to persons less generous than himself.

Why, indeed, does Rimbaud struggle so much to go where he wants to go? Because when he was a child or even a young adolescent, he was a person who still trusted, needed loving, who wanted to believe and share. He'd yet to discover other people's lies, their double-dealing: his mother beholden to the local tittle-tattle and preferring her pauper's morality to her own son, a priest preaching love but not believing in it, both of them therefore perverting the signs that ought to have served this poet as meeting place and occasion. There he is, bewildered and unhappy in his seven years, forced into a distrust now every bit as complete as his trust had been, and what a disaster that was in the years to come! And distrust of course gave birth to anger at those other liars and his own too credulous self. And then came pride, which combats self-loathing by a feeling for personal and innate talents, those same talents to which people in the past wanted, and still today want, to bring offerings. Can one acquit oneself of such a burden, despite the evidence, and call of the poetic vocation? 'Once a hyena, always a hyena', cries Rimbaud, on the same essential first page. He adds: 'Go to your death with all your appetites, and your selfishness and every deadly sin.' Did he want to make a key of charity? He then concludes, or thinks he should conclude: 'This inspiration proves that I've been dreaming.' 'Charity', the movement by which, even poetry, the 'I' meets up with the other – without complaint, without reproach – in the fugitive absolute of finitude is certainly the supreme, or rather the only reality. But to think that one can gain access to this reality, and get a foothold on it, is still just a dream.

The fact remains: poetry doesn't need to perfect itself in a life in order to express itself through a body of work. What already counts, in the writings of some poets, is the dissatisfaction manifestly at work, the lucidity when they find their dreams being drilled into routine, the sincerity of their judgements when they succeed in avoiding the pitfalls of the writing life. And how razor-sharp these gestures of impatience, these illuminating contradictions were in Rimbaud's work! I'll give you only one example. At the same time as 'Mes petites amoureuses', the failings of which I've already mentioned, he writes 'Les Premières Communions', this time a great poem, which shows how aware he is of the alienation suffered by the feminine condition, crushed by the mendaciousness of words, and his sympathy for it. Women are something fearful for him, and in these months he even insults them. But the victim moves his heart and he straightaway befriends her; he discovers in the scared, disturbed child taking her first communion and condemned to misery a humanity that transcends the sexes, this poor reading of existence. The 'rotten soul' and the 'saddened soul' meet each other.

And beyond *Une saison en enfer*, where these aporias of his condition are analysed and understood, it might seem that some of the *Illuminations* no longer reflect, explicitly, this concern – a concern I would term specifically poetic – and so much so that they might legitimately be abandoned to simple lovers of literary qualities. I've no doubt everything would be lost if we didn't glimpse in their depths the glow of that great non-resigned hope: this faint light of the smithy in the forest, to quote Marceline Desbordes-Valmore, always so close to Rimbaud, who, as it happens, admired her poems. Hope may end up by losing itself in his work even as his energy – most certainly 'stolen', as he once said – runs out. What remains of this faith in poetry, which was extraordinary, when the person who had written 'Le Bateau ivre' flees Europe, 'where madness prowls', on various merchant ships? Until his last writings however – I'm thinking of 'Vagabonds', 'Ouvriers', 'Génie' – this hope, this faith will have been the gold in Rimbaud's voice, the ray that casts its light. Which is what makes this oeuvre even in its failure, if that's the word, exemplary. And makes of this example a way.

XIII.

A Baudelairean way, this, which turns away from the metaphysical dream in favour of existence as most physically present in the vagaries of a life; which shifts from the lures of language to the tasks of the word. A way which passes through anger, fecklessness, confusion, but which keeps on trying, in its meanderings, to move towards what 'Matin', at the end of *Une saison en enfer*, calls 'the new work', 'the new wisdom': 'Christmas' finally on earth. A way which has to be taken otherwise 'the Kings of life, the three wise men, the heart, the soul, the mind' will no longer lay their presents before this child, this merely human child, who, still denied his great possibility, keeps asking to be reborn.

And a way which, today, is obstructed. I'm not thinking of those among us who deal with the strictly textual or historical aspects of the poetic work, and sometimes imagine that poetry is simply one kind of literary activity. That they think in this way is clearly to misjudge Rimbaud's nature although such approaches can also help to read him, and don't misrepresent his deep meaning. Those who love his voice can still readily hear it; they aren't disturbed by this form of listening although they expect much more of it.

But there is now another way of considering the poetry, and this approach presents a danger: Rimbaud provides me with an occasion to take its measure. I'm referring here to the impact produced by the changes that have taken place since the mid-nineteenth century in the consciousness of world and existence, in its relationship with language. Since then, scientific and industrial revolutions have multiplied the contributions made by conceptual thinking, diversified its levels of communication, and thus added enormously to the networks of thoughts and even perceptions that constitute a distinctive self – the distinctiveness that enabled Rimbaud to recognise an 'I' fully aware of the assets of a finite existence. This is an entirely new situation, and not without major advantages. Beneath this wide-open gaze, myths and beliefs dwindle away, the divine withdraws from empirical reality, God dies or survives only as the unknowable, which is good.

One consequence of this kind of thinking, which has fortunately managed to become secular, has however been bad. If concepts fragment objects and displace the inner infinity of the individual existence with abstract schemes, however complex they may be, we're going to start believing that there's nothing anymore in the world (or indeed ourselves) than things, than the thing itself: in other words matter, a void vibrating and sounding just as the immense cosmic lyre did in 'Soleil et chair'. It's true that it's hardly possible any longer, among so many objects – manufactured, consumed, discarded, repackaged, purchased, sold – to feel oneself participating in the great unity that used to caress in its flow and ebb the finite life of beings, imparting presence to them and their immediate surroundings, giving meaning to their life. And it's tempting to see only enigma and silence in this fragmentedness, in the disorder 'out there' – to decide that it's a vast, unbreathing, starless night; pure absence and nothingness. Which obliges us to seek cover under the canopy of language. Is there nothing else, then, than these words and this syntax through which we act and imagine? To know this and live with this knowledge – isn't that the ultimate experience?

It's a paradox: a human being thinks himself unreal within the very heart of his own spoken words. Then he attempts – this is where danger lurks – to make words accountable only because they are fictions, perceived and valued as such, to render them a substitute for life or a source of pleasure by running the gamut of vocabulary or syntax, in considering them in their own terms, in making abstract art out of them, without knowing or wanting to know anymore that they are made for a quite different task, namely to grasp the reality beyond language – finitude – so that we can enter our existence in it by devoting ourselves to the places we inhabit: these places may be laden with a meaning that the simple concept is unable to utter. The 'I', which knows in Rimbaud that it has to be 'in the world', loses itself again in the daydreams of the self, sustained for the sole non-utilitarian reason of writing. And in so doing magnifies literature – the right word this time – but only by radically misunderstanding poetry, the essential transitivity of which is perceived to be an illusion. Such a thought, and its fundamentally aesthetic creations, claiming no less than the right to call itself a 'poetics', simply because of the etymology of this word – and yet it turns out to be the old dressing down of poems in rhetorical terms.

So be it! But we, readers of Rimbaud, can we accept to think in this way, abandoning the idea of poetry, allowing its name to mean something else, renouncing the intuitions and hopes that were Dante, Shakespeare and Baudelaire? And were so fiercely and so tragically and obstinately the quest of the author of *Une saison en enfer*, the last words of which still speak of a reality 'to embrace'?

I prefer to point out that beneath the level of the intellect that puts a simple image of the world into conceptual patterns and gets trapped in their non-being, there are situations in which we're still governed by the needs arising from the brevity of mortal life, the aspirations that turn these needs around and to good account, the fundamental desire to encounter others in the few days accorded us – and we don't want to encounter them recomposed by systems of representation or terrorised by the kind of reasoning that proves that they don't actually exist: we desire to love, in a word. And then I see that these needs and desires, and the acts that cut through the so often frozen waters of utility to give them body and even happiness – all this offers a ground beneath our feet, a ground that continues to exist with its own light emerging from it for all the surrounding darkness. It's true: we moderns, stragglers on earthly footpaths, are riven by two forms of knowledge: under the umbrella of conceptual knowledge we still have a propensity for dialogue that establishes another, more essential kind of speech. In space, as science understands it, we're no more than shadows. But at the forefront of this space we can establish the locus where our body is reconstituted, through dialogue: opening the debate between us will be our being. And this fact confirms poetry's intuition; it explains its hope and its obstinacy in hoping.

My feeling, my claim? We shouldn't allow ourselves to be intimidated by this thought of the night, which can be so aggressive, in proportion to the fear it engenders. I've nothing against conceding to it so many lyric flights that were mere dreams, sometimes poor disguises for lies. But we should defend against the night the memory of the 'I' beneath the Self, the task of 'reinventing' it. We should know – let's decide – that being exists; let's hope – we should prepare – for its advent. What must be understood, above and before all else, is that even if hope is often, or always, an illusion, its essential nature is not illusory.

And let us remember Rimbaud, since Rimbaud is one of those who, as things continuously fall apart, attempted with the greatest courage their permanent redress: he expects an awakening on our part when he says in 'Adieu', at the end of *Une saison en enfer*, that he has 'his feet back on the earth', but that it is necessary 'to hold the hard-won ground.' Let's remember Rimbaud; we need him in order to be true to ourselves. We need, if I may say so, our need of Rimbaud.

Translated by Iain Bamforth

Yeats's Poetics[1]

Poised on the threshold of this book of translations of Yeats, I feel the need to express first and foremost the admiration and then the affection which carried me toward this body of work that I would like to bring alive in our language, in French. Indeed, I'd like to note that my focus here is on not only a set of texts, of course, but also on a person, since Yeats is so present in each of his poems, in so intense and as one might say so transparent a way that one can't really read them without giving oneself over to his personal drama, none of which contradicts serious research concerning his poetry: rather, such concern may organise it. Yeats never shied away from writing, its marvels, its pitfalls; but he was also someone who, at critical moments, detached himself from it, because he never forgot that the meaning, the value of lived experience is more important for the soul than the uncountable labyrinths that open up among words.

Moreover, I'm not eager to add to the work I've already carried out, a commentary that one often thinks translation requires, since those texts – necessarily elliptical – seem to require more words to illuminate (perhaps at little extra cost) their apparent obscurity. I am not certain, after all, that this clarification after the fact leads much further than the first breakthrough, if it is really a breakthrough. Translation is already not much more than explication, though it is all the same an explication made with images and symbols, and intervenes just at the point where the rhythms of our language and the burning materiality of its words keep these symbols alive, active, capable of an intuition that cannot be expressed in prose. The sequence of critical notions, which tries to lay out the literal sense of a thought and is thus necessarily piecemeal, is inherently ill-adapted to capturing poetic truth, which seeks a kind of unity. The sole point that perhaps needs to be made, when the translator has completed for example 'Among School Children' or some other poem with

---

1 'La poétique de Yeats' originally appeared as the preface to W.B. Yeats, *Quarante-cinq poèmes suivi de la Resurrection* tr. Yves Bonnefoy, Paris : Editions Hermann, 1989. Collected in *Théâtre et poésie. Shakespeare et Yeats*. Paris: Mercure de France, 1998. This translation was first published by *The Hudson Review*, Autumn 2016.

similarly extraordinary meaning, is that he was keenly aware of his own audacity in wishing to bring to life such an enormous network of thought and sentiment. And he must acknowledge that he has not forgotten that such audacity is a risk, and that he must accept the possibility of being judged harshly in proportion to the outlandishness of the task, which cannot be cautiously avoided or justified in advance by describing all the decisions he had to make for each line and indeed often for certain words.

All the same, it does make sense, on the occasion of the translation of a particular work, to make some general remarks, since if the latter are true they may prove useful for future translations, and it's only by examining particular texts in detail, as evidence, that we can show such general claims to hold. And yet, more important than all those considerations, we must also extract certain traits of Yeats's character, because of an ambiguity in his poetry which may surprise the reader and lead him astray just at the moment when he might have encountered in Yeats's verse one of the most essential laws of poetic creation in its relation to life. The ambiguity I'm pointing toward is certainly not one of those which open up a single text and insist that we rest within it, among those effects of the senses that don't properly belong to writing. Rather, it is inherent in existence, at least Western and modern existence, and it is only worth calling up, apropos Yeats, because it is the poetic dimension of life, which is so misunderstood, neglected and rebuked in our society.

I'll attempt to define two terms, two kinds of ambiguity which we can find in Yeats, but emphasising from the very beginning that though they may sometimes be violently opposed, indeed almost ready to destroy each other and to discourage his spirit so greatly that he almost wishes for death, nonetheless the tension between them most of the time has a largely positive and creative effect. That tension allowed his sensibility, at first too captivated by the mirages of Symbolism and later by the traditions of Ireland, finally to disengage itself, to become true. The first term is a passionate protest against the material world, against life as we must live it. Yeats never ceases to accuse birth of making promises without following through, and of suggesting a plenitude which then quickly dissolves in the disappointments of fate. One example of his thought, amidst many others, is this sentence from his journal, in 1909: life, he says, 'is a perpetual preparation for something that never happens' – an idea which appears seventeen years later in the draft of a great poem: 'no possible life can fulfill our dreams'. Human beings dream, and Yeats himself dreamed as much and more than anyone, so much so that at certain moments he seems to resemble someone like Auguste Villiers de l'Isle-Adam, who came to think that the imaginary is the only reality. 'The Circus Animals' Desertion' confirms the point again, during the last months of his life: for a long time, after 1910 and always after that, he was also among those (a much rarer breed) for whom lucidity overrides illusion, even while illusion stubbornly persists.

But we should note that Yeats reproaches life only with respect to situations where it seems, in his words, 'to prepare', to support or develop its own specific aspects; in fact, the wildest reveries that spring from his imagination are only a kind of mist that envelopes (as in the case of a faery) a body that rests strictly in this world. In sum, what Yeats wishes for when the universe as we have it disappoints us, is not something superior, some sort of transcendence that will allow us to pass upward to another plane; it is only ordinary reality writ in just those characters that others would condemn as expressing precisely the imperfection of the earth, since in his eyes those characters express its sufficiency and its glory: that is, supposing that they might be accessible here where they reveal themselves, which alas – and here is Yeats's problem – isn't possible and will never be possible. When a moment of happiness allows him to pluck the fruit which he sees shining on an earthly tree, Yeats thinks right away that he is in Paradise: he can't imagine anything better. And this capacity to feel himself in support of the world, he feels above all else for whatever concerns eros, which he recognised since his childhood when he had 'the long summer day to spend' in the quiet countryside as that which extends to everything that shines under the great sky, in the light which is divine. Yes, I want to assert this with particular emphasis, it's here that we find what is most intimate and most constant in Yeats. If we follow the author of 'Sailing to Byzantium', a poem which calls on us to flee life to some alternative opposed to it, what do we find right away: the things of this world, each badly disguised as an Ideal, poorly repressed, never forgotten. There is for example plenty of mythology in Yeats, as there is in the writings of many of his contemporaries, who see there an opportunity for the most facile kind of sublimation.

But it isn't those figures elaborated in Greek art that Yeats uses in his fables, those forms on a Grecian urn that drove Keats to desire only pure Beauty; rather it is the aggressive, sweating bodies of Celtic heroes, or the young Faeries who seem only to dream of seducing youths. And if he thinks of Helen, as so many other poets have, it's in terms of her physical and indeed sexual beauty, that beauty that drove Paris mad and so ruined Troy without leaving the combatants any reason to complain, since, as Yeats said, truth is just that very beauty.

And when he seems at some, rather rare, moments to let himself recall certain aspects of Christian culture, we should still keep in mind that the Byzantine ascetic he admires is in his mind God's athlete, a substantial figure, an energy that uses the body all the more in transcending it; and that Hagia Sophia is not only a place harbouring those mosaics where the Eternal weighs upon us, but first and foremost the dovecote of souls, which he imagines as a flock of doves in flight, with heated blood, cooing, desiring. The bird that Yeats evokes in his reflection on Byzantium ('Sailing to Byzantium') may be a work of art studded with gems and set upon a golden bough, yet this bird-Idea speaks nonetheless to the Lords and Ladies of the court about what has been born and will die, and even as well what will be born: 'what is past, or passing, or to come'. And in the other poem 'Byzantium', the strange bird that is half-metal, half-living, cries out its wrath against the inconstant moon and the ordinary birds, as if it had never managed to overcome in itself a longing for that sensual music made by the latter up in the trees. The true object of Yeats's poetry is the being of flesh and blood, those 'birds in the trees'.

But it is nonetheless true – and this is precisely what frustrates him, and to use his own word, enrages him – that these birds in the trees are 'dying generations', death infuses birth, and as soon as the object of desire spreads the peacock-feathers of its glory, old age is there, 'decrepit age':

> that has been tied to me
as to a dog's tail,[2]

and even when youth and force are there to back up desire, that which one wishes for may be refused, more often than not, and

2   See Yeats's poem 'The Tower'.

makes of this world (which is the only one) a field of bitter disillusionments. To signify the absolute, Yeats inevitably turns to the figure of a woman, whose attractiveness easily combines the terrestrial and the spiritual; and we know what poetic worth he recognised in Maud Gonne, the beautiful and fierce militant, committed to Ireland's independence, who was from the time they were both in their early twenties his dearest, but distant, friend: he didn't hesitate, in 'The Rose of the World', to set Maud next to God before the world had even been created, like the archetype of the true good. But Maud Gonne never wished to be more than a friend, and the fact that this was so and remained so all his life: here was the clear and indelible sign of the insufficiency of this world.

Let no one object that Maud Gonne obviously was not simply a natural being who would have chosen someone who celebrated the most instinctual ardour; that point is granted. The refusal of life was just as strong in her as love for the people of Ireland, from which stemmed that quality of impatience, of a drawn bow, that Yeats recognised in one of his great poems. Maud Gonne was animated by the desire to reform, by violence, a world she judged to be disappointing. Kin to Helen of Troy, to whose fatal beauty Yeats compares her, she wanted to push forward the contradictions of her era rather than to spark a man's desire. In 'A Bronze Head', the very last poem Yeats dedicated to his friend, towards the end of both their lives, he cites the idea of destruction as her essence, although – as 'Among School Children' suggests – that violence bore above all upon the heart and the body she so heedlessly inhabited. Maud Gonne was certainly not mere humble, carnal life; and one can't help but suppose that Yeats himself sought in her that shadow of the Absolute for which he never admitted his desire. But to pursue that thought is to misunderstand the immediate sensual attractiveness that he said emanated from her, as he evoked her with those infinite words that name simple things. Is she one of God's familiars, a new Beatrice? Yet God 'made the world to be a grassy road / before her wandering feet', where her life would be at one with the intoxicating unfolding, under the ceaseless sky, of the mountains of Ireland, at the end of which – a long journey for two – 'The Rose of the World' was written. And the poet recognised in his friend, and indeed emphasised with deep and deeply moved attention – which we find for example in 'Before the World Was Made' which takes up the idea that beauty precedes the world – the coquetry, pride and narcissistic fervour that characterised the young woman. In fact, if something in Maud Gonne aroused a desire in him for more than the world, it wasn't so much an epiphany of the Absolute, but rather the fact that the young woman wanted it just as much as he did and was just as unhappy at having been denied it – from which arose a complicity between them, a solidarity in the heart of their mutual exile, which must have made the distance between them all the more difficult for him. Both of them suffered in the same way from the contradiction that imposes its stamp on life. It was this shared experience, which began at the end of childhood, to which Yeats refers metaphorically in 'Among School Children', the story still overwhelmed by the pain that Maud Gonne visited upon him – at the beginning of their friendship, 'bent / above a sinking fire' – in a troubled childhood memory: after which, he writes, they experienced themselves for a moment, or perhaps all the rest of their lives, as 'the yolk and white of the one shell'.

In sum, both of them (he directly, she by the detour of her passion for politics) thought that in life there is a knot we can't untie, binding plenitude and night, glorious immediacy and death. Yet constrained as he was between two opposed thoughts, bound to love the world he detested, Yeats was certainly not (despite the waverings of some of his first poems) one of those who in his era believed that they could call themselves 'Symbolists', because they plucked from the world they did not love a few scraps of sensation capable of aesthetic purification, in order artificially to reconstruct a reality supposedly superior to our own. Yeats was never able to speak of that imaginary life, despite his metaphysics and bizarre mythology, and even despite his occasional experiments as an amateur magus. And he moreover never indulged in the dream of some kind of wisdom that would bruise the body to pleasure soul: instead, he mocked its pretensions and called the Paradise of the ascetic Plotinus a copulation in sea foam, in sunlight, on the shores of Greece. He notes, fearfully, that weakening of the intellect often accompanies physical decay; he thinks that the sole lucidity that comes with age is to be able to assert what was illusory in those dreams of the past, which left him all alone at the heart of his own oeuvre; and he expects, from the company of that woman who has also aged, even though in the old days she was his inspiration, only some conversation under the lamp whose light they have veiled, apropos an art and beauty which remained enigmatic. This world has no other end or upshot, because it is in itself the meaningfulness that, he suggests, one has opposed to it. And the only conceivable truth is thus to affirm the world in spite of everything, as the old bard does in 'The poet, Owen Hanrahan'. He too might have allowed himself to complain, Yeats tells us, were he not old, already a bit removed from the world:

> But he calls down a blessing on the blossom of the May
> Because it comes in beauty and in beauty dies away.[3]

While beauty might well be the sign of what we are missing, it lies nonetheless at the heart of life, and the only poetic task, the only future for the dream, is to reaffirm that fact, here, now, among us – and the meaningfulness, however enigmatic it remains.

Two remarks might be added here, apropos the two great concerns which traversed both Yeats's work and his life and might seem to contradict my philosophically pessimistic conclusion. The first was the country and countryside of Ireland, which was for him early on the key or code around which many of his most cherished perceptions were organised. In his youth, Yeats heard the old farm women or tramps on the great roads singing the ancient songs of the folk – some of them already half-lost – which gave him the impression of a mysterious intensity or transparency of life at the time of Celtic culture, a life which had passed away. He also discerned in certain of his contemporaries, like John Synge or his friend Lady Gregory, who collected the old texts, eminently poetic powers, in those places of great natural beauty like Coole Park, where they all gathered in the summer, so he could not help but dream that if they could only save their country, countering the alienation from its own culture brought about by history, by foreign domination, they might create a new, privileged space where the world and the absolute might find common cause. Perhaps the contradiction from which our life suffers, put another way, was simply the effect of a misinterpretation of one's relation to self and world, an error which a certain wisdom (not the wisdom of experience or philosophical wisdom, but of youth and of origins) might one day banish with the aid of some great myths? But it's significant that in the

3 From 'Red Hanrahan's Curse' in Stories of Red Hanrahan (1905).

song of ancient Ireland that Yeats loved the most, and which he turned into one of his first poems, 'Down by the Salley Gardens', there is not only a young man who is a dreamer – recalling the illusion that attends poetry – but also a young woman animated by a kind of common sense permeated by melancholy, as if already in this originary world they already recognised that life is a furtive plenitude, which we have to take as it comes in the very moment!

> She bid me take love easy, as the leaves grow on the tree;
> But I, being young and foolish, with her would not agree.[4]

When Yeats heard a fragment of this song which a peasant woman of Sligo had preserved and often, he said, sang it as she went about her chores, he was carried away and never paused until he had reconstituted the old air. Why? Because these words spoke marvellously to his nostalgia, and to his growing lucidity, and suddenly came to his aid. Ireland didn't have to be an idealisation that might quickly turn into a sophistical invention without substance, as the Middle Ages decked in Pre-Raphaelite imagery; rather, the task, however difficult it might be, was to discover Ireland in the features of the young woman who knew instinctively what existence is. And, in fact, Yeats's patriotism wasn't fundamentally different from his poetic lucidity. Conscious of Ireland's beauty, of the quality of its culture, though always ready to denounce its weaknesses – see 'Nineteen Hundred and Nineteen', among other poems – he only asked of his unhappy country that it be a consciousness just as alert – and just as lacerated as he was himself, and in that existential relation, compassion was married to unreasonable demand.

And the second remark brings in Christianity, which was also for him a call which might disrupt existence preyed upon by finitude but which Yeats early on dismissed from thought because that God, who had all the means and love, didn't expect enough from the earth. There is an astonishment that we find in this thinker who was after all accustomed to religion – his forebears included Anglican pastors, as he recalls in 'Under Ben Bulben', the last of his great poems – an astonishment at the figure of Christ whose project he did not under-

---

4   'Down by the Salley Gardens', first published in *The Wanderings of Oisin and Other Poems* (1889).

stand very well, above all that it was a divine project. Though Yeats knew that it was compassion – a number of his poems attest to this – and could thus understand the sacrifice of God, he nonetheless had too instinctive a sense of the plenitude of the flesh. He so wanted a deepening of the relation between being and nature that he couldn't understand why Jesus only taught a kind of suffering charity, for which what can be shared is only what can be separated from the body, whereas it was precisely the body which seemed to Yeats to be the true locus of life, from which stemmed an entirely different ethic, one of eros as much as *agapè*. The Saviour according to Yeats is not the god who died on the cross – the Three Kings in one of his poems are astonished by the 'agitation on Calvary' – but rather the one who is born on the 'bestial floor' among the animals of the stable, rich in mystery that remains beyond understanding. In fact, if it is a matter of self-sacrifice, one ought to carry it out in art: because the artist is the one who renounces the small amount of terrestrial satisfaction that remains accessible to us, in order to realise a work in which intensity itself is produced, perhaps opening a pathway.

II.

In sum, the locus, the place, is poetry, as much for recovery as for the assessment of the contradictions from which we suffer. And it follows that such creation according to Yeats was certainly not that which Mallarmé – whom Yeats in his youth wanted to meet when he visited Paris, and whose *Hérodiade* he loved in English translation – wished for himself, in his own critique of the world's illusions: that is to say, a text, taken as an end in itself. Since Yeats had no objection to what takes place in existence when it attains the intensity of which it is capable, why would he have been tempted to devote himself to relations that could only be established among words? It wasn't because he didn't attach the highest importance to the quality of language, to verse which rises to the limits of the aural possibilities of language: the proof of that is the way he reads his poems in a firm, highly accented manner, in the recordings of him that we have. But this verbal beauty was for him, after his earliest period, only the flash in which spirit escapes – for an instant, nothing more, and simply by means of a reflection – our ordinary inability to live in the absolute. And such beauty is accompanied by what for a 'Mallarméan' poet would be terrible negligence, like the meaningless repetition of words, by means of which one returns to the ordinary condition of life. Illuminating, transforming, beauty in Yeats's work organises itself around an image, an abrupt and fleeting flash of light – 'the dolphin-torn, the gong-tormented sea' – because it is the unity that suddenly flowers and the surprise that responds to it – an instant of passionate attachment – before nostalgia repossesses it. And it thus expresses only its own precariousness, always with something very rapid as well as marvellously luminous. 'They came like swallows, and like swallows went…'. There Yeats was speaking about certain poets, in 'Coole Park, 1929'. But more deeply, in this line that sweeps by like an arrow, he was saying that poets only allow us to hear brief cries, unlocatable in the light, like those of the swallows in the summer sky.

This radiance itself has moreover a history in his poetic work, which reveals that it was a discovery for him, before attaining its highest expression, so that its recurrence (easier at some moments and more painful at others) had something of existence in it, not just art. In Yeats's earliest works, *The Rose* (1893) and *The Wind Among the Reeds* (1899), the imagination still lingers in places where one supposes faeries might appear, fragile figures which require for their survival quite a few aesthetic precautions, as in the tapestries of William Morris where interlaced foliage surrounds the hieratic deeds of heroes. It is a matter of planting the invisible in the visible; a lovely haze of supple rhythms is just as useful for that as mythological references and precious vocabulary, and the lightning that one senses lurking within is deferred for a while. But Yeats soon ascertains that all that 'famous harmony of leaves', all that strenuous weaving of a thousand flowers, reinscribed by the Victorians,

Had blotted out man's image and his cry

and in the famous poem, 'The Sorrow of Love', there is one line,

A girl arose that had red mournful lips,

a new kind of line, where the too-artistic writing starts to undo itself: these words are moreover an evocation of Maud Gonne, which clearly shows the contradictory, paradoxical nature of Yeats's experience of beauty, at once plenitude and death. In fact, it was his fascination with a creature who herself broke with conventional and artificial idealisation; it was Maud Gonne who bestowed on his poetry its first moments of illumination – it was she who was the 'burning cloud' that drove away the lovely mists. In 'No Second Troy' (1912), there is a bolt of lightning of just this kind:

Was there another Troy for her to burn?

This line acknowledges and performs the very fact that it expresses; it reveals that Symbolist poetry, with its parapets of archaic words and its machicolation of symbols, is precisely the new Troy that this new Helen, endowed like the ancient one with a terrible beauty, is going to put to the flames and destroy. And it is also Maud Gonne who permits Yeats in consequence to deepen the intuition of finitude that lies at the heart of these radiant visions: simply put, by aging. And though formerly he, like Rossetti and so many others, loved the Italian painters who lived before Raphael for their quality of joyful sprightliness and sought in their bright, intense colours traces of a Golden Age, in any case he afterwards paid more attention to what, in the work of the later painters Mantegna and Botticelli at the end of the latter's life, is tragic sentiment, an apprehension of death. And so he could write of his friend, apropos her 'present image',

Did Quattrocento finger fashion it,
Hollow of cheek as though it drank the wind,[5]

which finally reveals how one arrives at poetic joy via the nothingness at the heart of life. After the First World War, Yeats wove between moments of deliverance articulated in admirable grand lines, and ordinary stanzas, which don't oppose themselves to reality as it is and make their revelations by evoking the most familiar words and places and lived events – friends like Augusta Gregory, for example, her house at Coole Park and his own at Thoor Ballylee, and the political situation, veering towards tragedy with the Irish revolution. Ireland itself might be the 'burning cloud', whose fire carves out a fault line between the absolute and speech just before poetry reunites them in the great arc of a lightning strike.

5 'Among School Children', first published in *The Tower* (1928).

A bolt of lightning that moreover cuts across many symbols, in these poems: which leads one to think that their author accepted all the same a good portion of fin-de-siècle speculation about the invisible world and its reflections in our own. It's true that great traditional symbols lie at the heart of Yeats's poetry, and he himself often adhered to interpretations of them which suggest, in covert but insistent terms, occult societies. But even in his occult researches, we see him quickly turning away from anything that only builds castles in air, ideals without substance; rather he always tries to relocate these symbols in his most immediate, everyday existence, at the risk of sometimes getting himself involved in acts that today would not be considered credible. It was not in order to arrive at some Mallarméan 'book' that he proposed at a meeting of the Hermetic Society to collect the affirmations of poets 'in their most beautiful moments', but rather a sort of liturgy, with some passing fancies of white magic. And we see him consciously invoking the moon, and noting his visions of centaurs and naked women appearing at night upon pedestals, then asking his hermeticist and cabalistic friends what they mean. But even there his lucidity intervenes, in the form of a return to ordinary reality in the midst of the space of speculation. Is he really talking about communicating with the dead, in 'All Souls' Night'? No, Yeats rather brings back to mind what constituted the true being of certain beloved people (not perhaps without some agitation); he lingers upon what once mobilised them, with pathos, against the thought of nothingness; and it is in sum compassion without hope that dominates that admirable poem, along with the slightly crazy humour which is the modesty of courage. Symbols, indeed, but they return us to the ground of life lived, not to dream-worlds substituted for it. The setting sun and the clouds, but only because they recall heroic destinies, grandeurs that foundered between foolishness and malevolence. And then the swans, traditional signs of the poetic state, but they appear because Yeats so often encountered the real swans at Coole Park, who testified in all the brilliance of their yearly return through twenty years or so of his visits there that the visitor had grown old. Yeats's swan was moreover not so much immaculate whiteness as wild sexuality, blind and cruel impulse. It stands only for the instinct that leads up to the wish for truth, the desire for wisdom, which means that it can also become over the years the epiphany of non-meaning, still discerned amid the ruins of those dreams of transcendence with which it had been associated. This is just what those sublime lines that open the third part of 'Nineteen Hundred and Nineteen' reveal:

> Some moralist or mythological poet
> Compares the solitary soul to a swan;
> I am satisfied with that,
> Satisfied if a troubled mirror show it,
> Before that bright gleam of its life be gone,
> An image of its state;
> The wings half spread for flight,
> The breast thrust out in pride
> Whether to play, or to ride
> Those winds that clamour of approaching night.

And as to the deficiency of the symbolic, or the intensity of Yeats's opposition to it in the end, one should read, to be convinced, 'The Circus Animals' Desertion', where, not long before his death, the poet who had once celebrated the supernatural heroes of Ireland, and nourished so many of his works with these dreams, compares them to old empty bottles, broken boxes that the wind sweeps randomly along the streets, cast-off clothing sold at bazaars. If there is any symbolism here, it's only to indicate that any symbol is a lie, if it doesn't take into account our finitude, and even our non-meaning, our irrationality. 'Fifteen apparitions have I seen,' Yeats also wrote in 'The Apparitions', from his final years, 'The worst' (that is, the only real one), 'a coat upon a coathanger', the absence beneath the fine clothing.

Yet the poetry of Yeats is not just what the fear of death traps inside the network of the internal relations of these texts, supposed to be the only beauty; his poetry is too crisscrossed by bedazzlements that come from the outside, from beyond, which is to say the finitude where the frustrations, the unhappiness and the only joys that matter exist together. It's a dream, that begins again every time we catch the shadow and not the quarry, but it's also the courage that makes us throw ourselves into nothingness, because it's there we encounter the true light. And the extraordinary thing, Yeats's great accomplishment, is that in this tension between two forms of consciousness, his poetry, that use of words that are so tempted to detach themselves from the finite, to fall back into mere writing, not only avoids the temptation but also remains song, an instinctive song, produced by the whole body, as the rhythms show. What is the music of words, in the work of Yeats? Often, doubtless, in his early writings, it is an incantation without an object outside of itself, in the imaginary world. It is tempting to offer as an example 'The Lake Isle of Innisfree' (1890), where he claims to hear the waves of a small forgotten lake beat suddenly, in the secret recesses of his heart. And yet already in this poem, written in London, in other words far from the places of his childhood, in the wake of a quite Proustian experience, a typically Yeatsian movement occurs, which both pulls away from the present circumstances and also clings to a reality which is nothing other than the fact of his own presence as a thing in nature. Of course, Yeats also reveals that he is still fascinated by the echo of the otherworldly on the island in the middle of the lake, surrounded by legends. But he is also moved by the idea of 'nine bean-rows' which he might plant next to his cabin, a new Thoreau, as if ahead of time he were already inebriated by the humming of the bees! 'I will arise and go now, and go to Innisfree'.

Born in ambiguity – which is seductive and explains the enduring popularity of the verse – Yeats's music ceases early on to be some kind of greenhouse that protects the frail seedlings of myth from their own haze. It is troubled: it often hesitates but then starts up again and recovers its unity, that is, its rhythm, at a deeper level, in which a force appears which is, in the spirit and even in the body, something more than ordinary desire:

> An aged man is but a paltry thing,
> A tattered coat upon a stick, unless
> Soul clap its hands and sing, and louder sing
> For every tatter in its mortal dress.

So Yeats invokes it in 'Sailing to Byzantium', and if he thinks in that moment of reflection that he only wishes for the Platonic elevation which tends to break up desire, the words that he uses reveal, upright and dancing as they are, that this ambition may prevail in someone without memory losing sight of his place on earth.

Precisely because Yeats only describes sensory reality in terms of his own fascination with it, his poetry despairs in vain, it departs all the more quickly for the Isle of Innisfree, the deep rhythm of the universe; and since it is an ongoing song arising in situations of deprivation usually dominated by the vocabulary and habits of prose, his poetry acquires an unusual degree of freedom, despite Yeats's adherence to prosodic conventions which moreover in the English language were always more supple than they are in French. I could give numerous examples from these poems, to evoke that 'final joy', that joy beyond everything, which Yeats claimed to have heard in the speeches of Hamlet – perhaps when he offers his 'dying voice' – or in the farewells of Cleopatra, or in Lear's outbursts beneath the thunderstorm? And because of this freedom and this joy, Yeats's greatest moments attain a precisely Shakespearean quality, since in Shakespeare's lines the pentameter so clearly pervades and commands the full variety of the human condition. Impetuous, limping bravely forward because it must, Yeats's twentieth-century poetics recaptures a familiarity with the One, which the still medieval cosmology and anthropology of the Elizabethan era made easier for Shakespeare to attain, and it also reveals what allowed that continuation into an era where perhaps the world was falling apart, as before anyone else Yeats declares in 'The Second Coming' or 'The Gyres'. This reasoning, this loyalty to the blossoming of May, to clarity, to the earth: it is there because Yeats's poetics is not reasoned or reasonable or corrupted by some Ideal, but rather violent and instinctive.

All the same, it was just that joy that Rimbaud, who was only eleven years older than Yeats, also sought, wishing to reanimate it through a forceful stroke of the spirit, but doomed to remain in the shadows, though his verse shines a bit in 'Ma Bohème' and a few other early works. And it was also what Mallarmé specifically judges and refuses, when he opposed embodied life to an elaborated system of pure notions that artistic sensibility, detached from the sensual, sets aside from lived reality. Thus neither Rimbaud nor Mallarmé, for different reasons, were capable of the true happiness that resonates in the strongest of Yeats's poems. Nor do we find it in the writings of T. S. Eliot, the younger poet who was close to Yeats: just a few years before the Irish poet attained his zenith, with 'Sailing to Byzantium', 'Two Songs for a Play', 'Among School Children', Eliot published 'The Waste Land', in which the epoch recognised itself. In the English poetry of the era, this work is matched only by the poems of Yeats and originates in the same locus of the spirit, which is the perception of the contradictions of existence and the loneliness of human beings, so that consciousness is out of joint and things once full of meaning are now devoid of sense. But 'The Waste Land' doesn't know how to resist the disorder that it exhibits; the signs and symbols are opaque and as if dead, and the text is a poem only in virtue of a certain nostalgia for unity, which animates it but in a lacerating way that never arrives at redemption. Why do we find this inability, among so many testimonials to a new moment in history, to achieve the redemption that we find in Yeats? But what is really at stake is the capacity to love, which is always much more difficult – being in a way too simple – in eras of crisis. 'But I do love thee,' cries the Elizabethan Othello, 'and when I love thee not, / Chaos is come again.' And even before, he exclaims, with the kind of anguish also found in *Une saison en enfer*, 'Perdition catch my soul'. Everything is in play, it's true, as if it will always be so in this fundamental alternative; and being doesn't exist and poetry doesn't have a place, apart from this act of faith which triumphs in the midst of the self-mirrorings that we call language.

III.

And it is clearly this élan, this burning desire of the spirit to rebuild what spirit itself breaks, to speak in spite of words, which anyone who translates Yeats must re-create or at least try to revive, which is a problem if he takes his task seriously. The courage, the freedom won back by Yeats in his lofty struggle must vibrate, at however low a level, in the translation; but then for that very reason doesn't the translator have the right to decide that he isn't going to trouble himself with concerns that might be legitimate from the point of view of philological exactness, but which might elicit in him for that very reason too much devotion to language? The poem was a miracle of resolved contradictions, a mastery suddenly lived as natural. Does one not have the right to sacrifice word for word accuracy in order to preserve better that authority which is the poem's meaning and reason for existence?

But first a remark about the structure of a poem by Yeats. There is a kind of transport, as I've emphasised, an irrational élan, like our most instinctive actions; but one finds there no less a well-managed thought, a series of articulated and precise ideas, which might seem surprising. How many writers in the last century aimed to dissociate the poem from any intention to speak and turned away from any such attempt unless its import was fractured and hidden. Mallarmé, for example, viewed discourse as an object to deny or refuse, at least theoretically. His 'Sonnet in *yx*' wishes only to evoke appearances, become once again irrelevant to our human aims, where consequently the conceptual relations disappear. And so these fourteen lines have lent themselves to a wide variety of interpretations, many more than is usually the case: but it seems impossible to me that a writer who creates a text can prevent his mind from formulating meanings or his unconscious from calling up fantasies. Some thought is always active – I mean seeking to articulate itself – throughout a poem, even if poetry itself is an act that transcends thought, since it is a witness to unity and a search for presence. The function of this thought is precisely to articulate the experience of what lies beyond language in a memory, in consciousness, in a life that remains always singular.

Now this kind of meditation which is thus the characteristic activity of any author, whether he knows it or not, whether he wishes it or not, leaves its mark on Yeats in a way that, especially in his case, can only be complex, since it touches upon the very essence of his relation to himself, where speculation and disillusionment loom so large. What is present in these pages, first of all, is the kind of thought that might be called *a priori*: metaphysical or cosmological – or magical – which fed his dreams. An example would be his theory of 'gyres', set forth in *A Vision* and cited also in his poems, after 1918. But still more important, since it is now a matter of the very invention of texts, is the highly self-conscious reflection which is born in the very first words or even a bit before them, following upon an emotion felt by Yeats, which led him to certain judgments which he would right away set down. In 'Mad as the Mist and Snow', for example, he knows that outside the mist and the snow are turning about in the night wind, but he himself is in a cosy house, next to a burning fire; and there we might think that he is concerned only with physical impressions and half-memories: only with another 'Sonnet in *yx*', in fact, much less rigorously reduced to the being-there of objects and with only sketchy and floating thoughts, like a bit of light snow, momentary in the penumbra of the heavy lamp and the peat fire. And yet an act of reasoning is no less active in the poem's furtive images; indeed it frames the whole. For the closed house with its warmth and its books, is the safety and comfort which the poet and the man or woman with whom he speaks have managed to attain, thanks to experience, culture – and the reasoning which led them there. They are no longer the ones who could call themselves mad as the mist and the snow. Nonetheless, the poet suggests, they were so once, but they are no longer, and so they have ceased to be young, and what value has their wisdom amounted to since then? Such wisdom comprehends, with a shiver of fear, what Cicero and Homer knew: nothing is worth more than simple youth, however foolhardy it was.

The poem is thus only apparently disconnected: and even if it invites interpretations different from mine, and above all sets us before a presence, with its flakes of snow in the night, with a silent world where all thought is reabsorbed, it nonetheless imposes a light of sense, a summation, which we cannot neglect without deeply impoverishing our reading of it. Moreover, Yeats himself formally attested the fact of this thought, which arises in the first lines and is developed in all three stanzas, without for all that losing touch with what makes the poem specifically poetic. That was also the case in 'The Lake Isle of Innisfree', for in a letter he wrote that the poem arose from his perception of the sound of drops of water falling and his longing to leave the city called up by the sound of the droplets. So too apparently the line of thought developed in 'Among School Children' was conceived in advance of the poem, since Yeats wrote three months earlier, in a notebook, 'Topic for poem – School children and the thought that life will waste them, perhaps no life can fulfill their own dreams, or even their teacher's hope. Bring in the old thought that life prepares for what never happens.' In his new role of Senator of the Free State of Ireland, Yeats visited a Montessori school. And one can hardly doubt that he thought of Maud Gonne there, noticing a small schoolgirl, as the poem suggests: confronted by the child, the painful memory of an ancient emotion naturally surfaces, from which right away the thought proceeds, not without recognising deviations and diffractions which unconscious associations provoke in a work of literature. In 'Among School Children', perhaps more than in any other poem of Yeats, the suite of ideas gives the impression of comings and goings, of wandering, to the edges of the contradictory, as Cleanth Brooks showed so well in his celebrated study. But this wandering doesn't indicate a lack of rigour in the leading idea, but rather the implication of a whole existence within it, from which it follows that what might have been only a theme – and versified philosophy – moves ahead of the mystery and in the last line names it. Thought, in Yeats's work, and this is what makes him a great poet, is the collaboration of the conscious and the unconscious, the fruitful mastery of their fusion, which our era seems so seldom capable of achieving.

And so the translator must capture the thought, the reasoning, as well as capture the emotional intensity from which one sees them arise, and that might seem to add to the difficulty of the task. But Yeats's reflection always has something of the universal, so independent of this or that language, like the books near the fire in the house beneath the snow showers, that it is almost possible fully to recapture them in words other than those of English. And rather than being an additional obstacle, it is thus the key to the temple where an epiphany may have taken place or a ritual may be celebrated. In order to conform to what it says, one can also take some steps to approach the temple, in French. But it is still necessary to follow certain principles.

The first principle is that the translator must be absolutely faithful to the pathway of meaning in all its rigour, which is to say, not so much by attending to ordinary meanings, those which the dictionary offers, but rather by staying close to the debate that words carry out in the text with the facts of life or the marks of thought or dream. And I must admit my irritation with many translations that match up the words of a text with words from their own language without retracing the pathway of the conflict between the conscious and the unconscious – and sometimes the peace which follows – as if the translators thought that the poets weren't saying anything and were only concerned with mixing up the words. Nothing is worse than those phrases that starve sympathy; an interpretation with errors is preferable to that glue of vagueness where no living form emerges, and where the primary requirement is rendered superficial and banal. It isn't right to translate a work if you are only going to put something into circulation that doesn't recognise that the life of poetry lies in the tension between meaning and words, between things that are signified as well as signifiers. The multiplication of translations available now, the majority of which don't take into account the importance of rhythms, of the brisk rhythm of phrases – of the 'state of singing', as Valéry would say – has accustomed readers to texts in which we no longer hear a vibration in their depths like the strings of a musical instrument. It's as if the libretto had been substituted for the opera without anyone mentioning the fact or even being aware of it.

And the second principle is that while it is important to be faithful to the meaning which carries the text toward the unsayable, one should never hesitate to follow the thought of the poet where it goes forward in words, but sometimes hides itself by obscurity or ellipse under the entanglement of sideways meanings, even though one senses that the poet has never lost his or her ultimate aim. And that effort, which in a reader is called understanding, in a translator is explication, which one must never fail to do, even if it means running into certain dangers. From the moment when one has carried out the analysis just to the point at which the primary intuition, the meditation, has been covered over by the ebb and flow of writing that is in part unconscious, the translation should be clearer and more coherent than the work itself: which is of course a distortion. But is it preferable that the translation break with the original – leaving the non-Anglophone reader without recourse – while the reader of the original poem always has the linguistic means to follow or to knit the meanings back together: which is to say the threads of reflection that Yeats has finally brought to fruition? What good would it do, if instead of preserving that ardent continuity of 'reasoning', we let ourselves believe in a Yeats who was simply a juggler of ideas, employing 'themes' which he forgot to pursue whenever they constrained him? In truth, that would be an insult, to him and to what we call the text, leading readers to believe that his own words are just as disjointed as they are in such superficial translations. It would be better to resign oneself to the necessary violence of explication, at certain points, and then ask oneself if that violence can't be repaired in some other fashion.

Happily, this is the case, because to interpret a poem, where it is really necessary, to go beyond thought where it is expressed as no more than an enigma, is to involve yourself personally, because of

the choices that you must make, and so to take on the obligation to
know yourself better, that is, to change, to become. From this stems
an abundance of problems, which will interfere with those inherent
to the work, and charge with the pressure of lived experience, the
unconscious, the imaginary – in this case one's own – the translation
that the search for meaning threatened to make too conceptual. To
give just one example of what can arise under these circumstances,
I return again to 'Among School Children', this time to its decisive
moment, the beginning of the last stanza.

> Labour is blossoming or dancing where
> The body is not bruised to pleasure soul,
> Nor beauty born out of its own despair,
> Nor blear-eyed wisdom out of midnight oil.

Thus wrote Yeats, and therein lies, I think, one of those points where
a thought – since evidently there is one – moves by ellipse and ambiguity without for all that being chased away in favour of the crowd
of signifiers that encompasses and assails it; thus the translator must
intervene, for if not he will undermine the equilibrium of the text.
What is the issue here? It is the ambiguity of the word 'labour', which
is entirely necessary to the meaning of the poem, while at the same
time obscuring it. And it is also the obligation that results for the
translator, because in French the ambiguity can't be expressed in
the same way, to reverse the hierarchy of the two meanings that are
united in the original text, and to say more, spelling out the ambiguity, than Yeats apparently does.

The word 'labour' means work, which is what interpreters and
translators usually understand by the word in this passage. So 'work'
blossoms, 'work' dances in the situations indicated in the lines that
follow, and which are the search for beauty that should never be
born out of its own despair, as Yeats explains, nor the search for
wisdom from the aridity of abstract speculation – without taking
into account the harmony and plenitude of the body. But why does
Yeats here restrict himself to the evocation of what is only an effort of
consciousness, especially since from the very beginning of the poem
– and in accord with his earlier notes – he seems preoccupied with
existence in a rather biological sense, with promises that life seemed
to have made but never kept, and even with the alarm that mothers

feel? So must we not understand, just after the stanzas that describe their alarm, the word 'labour' in its other, less frequently used sense, which is the labour of giving birth: those pangs that can only be suffered in vain if every existence is the shipwreck of a dream, but, who knows, may recover their meaning thanks to a different way of living? It is life itself and not just the labour, it is being born into a life capable of re-flowering and becoming a dance, if beauty, wisdom, and the body are given over to the joy inherent in them, if we put our powers (we really have some) and our values in harmonious order, in the unison that the chestnut tree exhibits – which is only a confident immediacy – instead of tearing ourselves apart in quest of the Ideal. In sum, Yeats may well have offered, in order to conclude his reflection on Maud Gonne, now become old, thin and tragic, the idea of a divine birth of which humanity is capable, even if he never recognised it – as his poem on the Magi shows – in the sufferings of Christ.

Thus I translated 'labour' as '*enfanter*', 'to give birth', in order to retain the thought that to me seemed the most important – and which also seemed to me the main thrust of the poem, in spite of all the embellishments one can find in the richness of the text. But arriving at this decision made me feel duty bound to go back over my thoughts and my unarticulated intuitions here and there, to reflect on poetry, to retune my own strings. That's to say that my experiences, memories, nostalgia, and a few more things, went into my reading of the other poet. And so my translation is also marked by my blindness, impatience, and ignorance, which is regrettable but tends to reestablish in the words the kind of continuity and density, which characterises poems that really matter. An advantage, in the midst of undeniable dangers. The more a translation interprets, which it must do if it seeks to clarify, the more it is also a reflection of the one who undertook it, with all those differences. But to be faithful one must also be free, and could one arrive at that liberty unless one had lived through those occasions where it is legitimate to go forward, while reading, toward one's own self? To translate is not merely to repeat, it is first of all to let oneself be convinced. And one is never truly convinced unless one has been able to verify, along the way, one's own thought.

Translated by Emily Grosholz

The Other Language in my Head[1]

I.

I never cease to be amazed that when people write about translation – and there are very many different opinions upon the subject – the problem of translating poetry is not addressed as it should be. By this I mean we need to recognise from the outset that the language of poetry is radically different from all other language and therefore can only be translated by following laws that are properly suited to it. I am equally surprised to see that it is possible to critically examine the translation of certain poems, as Antoine Berman has done, and very astutely, but without, apparently, being aware that we first have to consider the very nature of poetry, if we are to appreciate the worth of any version into another language.

I personally am convinced that there is something very specific about poetry's aim in its relationship to words and to the text which emerges from these aims; and so it must also be when it comes to translating poems.

All this, however, requires me to explain what I mean by poetry, because without doing so I won't be understood, all the more so since many don't share my point of view. But these preliminary thoughts don't influence only my reflections about poetry, for truly poetic intuition underpins many other endeavours and behaviours of artistic activity and even other areas of social life. I have said and explained this often enough not to wish to repeat myself again here. The reader can find quite a few examples, for instance, at the beginning of 'La traduction de la poésie' or throughout 'Langue, verbe, parlar cantando'.[2] I will limit myself to one or two clarifications, more especially that necessitated by my different usage of one particular difficult word.

This is the word 'utterance'. At the conference 'The community of

---

1   'L'autre langue à portée de voix'. This is the introductory essay for *L'autre langue à portée de voix*, Paris: Coll. *La Libraire du XXIème siècle*, Editions du Seuil, 2013.
2   Both these essays are collected in *L'autre langue à portée de voix* (see above).

translators', which happened some time ago now, in Arles in 1996, I used the term the 'utterance' of the poem to denote the kind of knowledge poetry gives to the relationship the speaking subject ought to have with him or herself. This cuts across conceptual discourse, which seeks to encapsulate knowledge at the risk of failing to understand what it is to be finite. Some poems at least exhort us to consider changing our life; they increase our capacity to perceive what is, what matters; if this happens, the poem will indeed have spoken to us. This notion of the utterance of the poet is in fact an ancient idea with a long and venerable pedigree. The poem makes us think, as if it was thought trying to utter itself.

But this poetic utterance cannot be summed up in a simple formula. The proof of this is that it has been expanded from many different quarters down the centuries, even to the point of self-contradiction. One of the prime examples is the German word 'Dichtung', which contains these contradictions better than any word in the Romance languages. To speak, yes, but also to imagine, venturing into myth, taking delight in fairy stories, exploring very personal desires which may lead as easily down the byways of error as towards the paths of truth. In what poem has the speech of poetry truly found its expression, the words which would really bring it to life in language? If truth be told, the act which would genuinely allow poetry to come to fruition is impossible or at least impossible to achieve. This fact only serves to make all utterances in a poem, even the idea of poetry as utterance, suspicious, even though we do think we find it in this or that particular poem.

Yes, poetry reveals a certain kind of truth; and so, if poetry were truly to be realised, it would be a manifestation of that truth, it would utter it. But one individual poem? This is only ever a gathering of diverse harmonies in which the ray of poetry is often barely perceptible. Yes, the poem speaks, but in a thousand ways, involuntary as well as intentional, sometimes impoverished, sometimes full of simple everyday truths. In order to hear what poetry is saying to us, we must beware of favouring the speech of any one particular poem amongst the thousands that exist. We will not find an authentic formulation of poetry's essence, even in the apparently gnomic utterances of Hölderlin or Rainer Maria Rilke, no, not even a metaphorical one. Even in these poets, who nevertheless hoped to reveal this essence, we find nothing but a purely personal idea, the fusion of genuine intuition and the preoccupations of an 18th or 20th century mind.

II.

So it is perhaps better not to talk too much about the utterance of poetry; this is all the more true since there is another kind of speech, which I will call 'prose' for simplicity, that is manifestly part of what utterance is. In vain have our ordinary words, the ones we use to think or act, but also to dream, been invaded by unconscious and uncontrolled elements; they are structured by notions, ideas, figures which are conceptually defined so as to allow them to grasp and control the objects of these words. Now, these words are the result of collective decisions; they can only be used if we continually make adjustments on this level; they are immediately caught up in the process of exchange, of communication. Everything that comes into being in this 'prose' world rests on formulations in which conceptual thought plays a necessary part. This is a fundamental fact that retains all this intellectual work of elaborated and communicated meaning within the language. Prose is constituted of meaning – in definitions, descriptions, information given, questions asked, reveries; we can only conceive of it in these terms, it speaks, it is made for speech. This is very evident in the discourse of science but just as much, despite appearances, in the language of desire. For desire only becomes aware of itself and takes shape in response to the real or imagined echoes which come back to it from another person; and it will only withdraw if it comes to understand that it has fixed itself upon an object which will remain for ever beyond its reach.

In the word as prose we do indeed sometimes sense that the very meaning which constitutes it may not always be adequate to seize certain actual or supposed realities or ways of being. In saying this, I am not forgetting that certain types of discourse which identify themselves passionately with meaning and speech only do so by recognising that what they are discussing continually eludes them. This is the experience of theologians when they try to talk about God; they have called this inability to speak about him his ineffability. Prose knows when to acknowledge its limits: this is as clear in the case of the believer who sinks into silent prayer as it is for the demonstrator in the street shouting an indignation which goes beyond words.

This inability to grasp the object of one's discourse has been perceived by contemporary critics and philosophers as they themselves approach the borderline between prose and another sort of speech. But they have not been able to meet or understand this other way of using language that I mentioned at the beginning of this essay and which I call poetry. What are these thinkers going to do with what some of them call literature? – I think of Maurice Blanchot here, for example. They remember events where the vast network of meaning that makes up their awareness of the world and of existence, this network of prose they speak, has been suddenly, from one minute to the next, reduced to nothing, emptied of itself. It has been crushed by the overwhelming evidence of something beyond all this, a beyond which cannot be known, a night infinitely surpassing our day, the destruction of the illusions which shored up our naïve existence until this moment. It is an experience of an absolute beyond that is impossible not to recognise without being frivolous. After Mallarmé or Georges Bataille we cannot lay claim to truth without living that truth or, at least, without acknowledging and bearing witness to it. One would otherwise be quite rightly accused of lying, to oneself and to others.

Blanchot has realised this. But, having recognised this fact which seems set to destroy everything that man can or hopes to achieve in the universe, beginning with language, he comes back to language with the thought that we can – we should – continue to speak. This time, however, it is to try and utter an event which has transcended utterance. This is because he cannot imagine that using language could have any aim other than to produce meanings to be communicated and understood. He envisages a paradoxical, impossible act, the act of saying the unsayable; and he gives the name of literature to this attempt, which he sees as our only opportunity to attain both to truth and to nobility. A literature which gives new life to the age-old questions raised by theologians, although emptied now of faith.

III.

It is important to stress that this project, which harks back to Mallarmé, but also to Lautréamont, even Sade, is in practice a negative one that defines itself solely by the deconstruction of the illusions with which we bolster our existence. An obvious correlative to this effort to say the unsayable, arising from our perception of the nothingness of everything, is that we must detach ourselves from the joys, the sorrows, the hopes, the mistakes, which make up the commons of everyday life, since we can no longer find any meaning in them. But then with them also disappear the colours, the scents, and the sounds that belong to the sphere of the human; the warm evening sun sinks from the balconies. This literature that touches truth, it is also that matter which pierces the surface of things; the violence betrayed in our actions; the scepticism that mocks what we nevertheless want to do at those times in life we have difficulty in believing are in vain, and the responses they elicit. Nothing remains, in this negative obsession, of what could give meaning to beauty; nothing remains either of the terrors and fears that bound us but also pushed us on, because they were accompanied by hope. Nothing remains of that way of life before the collapse; nothing remains of the agonies and ecstasies that moved Keats, Leopardi, Baudelaire. This writing that empties itself of everything that seems vain also sweeps away on its flood all that life loved to hold precious in this world. It is not surprising, therefore, to see that it has no idea about poetry.

I have noticed this (it is what has prompted me to write this essay) and I have concluded that, while assuredly we should not overlook the evidence of this terrifying beyond, the realisation of the illusory nature of our world, what the writers and philosophers I mentioned have made of it inclines me to think they have drawn the wrong conclusions.

Let us look for a minute at the moment when the beyond opens up, rises up, when night arrives from every direction, when we awake from the sleep of the just to see everything that we thought had truth or meaning rolling over the edge into the abyss. Is it true that the only practical alternative is either to go back to sleep or to let out that scream that destroys hope? Let us not forget this scream has no future in words. Mystics may well, and with good reason, try to interiorise it, to transmute it into something at the very edge of consciousness, to substitute, for the evidence of no meaning at all, the experience of nothingness. But to do this they will have to detach themselves from words, one by one, by emptying them, not only of their physical but also their emotional content, in short, by ceasing to speak: metaphysical fear inhabits silence. But how do we say the unsayable, how do we convey what is beyond words while yet remaining within them, while continuing to be mindful of the diversity of languages? Any text that thinks it can do this will only be cut down to size by its readers, who bring to it all their anxieties, hopes; they will use the text, they will subvert it, and the unstoppable force of this appropriation means that the original sense of horror will be lost... Surely it is obvious that we open the door to a different kind of distraction for the mind when we claim to bear witness to the 'dark side'[3] of our being in the world? And this distraction is analogous in its aim and its methods to the discourse of religion, which is not so much a testimony to transcendence as a collection of beliefs, myths and fictions that imagine they can show us its ineffability.

IV.

And yet, on the very edge of the abyss, something else may occur. The scream of metaphysical horror may be succeeded by a kind of recovery that manages to come unscathed out of the collapse of everything. This is because we have not denied the evidence or failed to recognise it, even though we set ourselves completely against this collapse. This decision rises up out of the very depths of our awareness of self which, let us not forget, has remained alert and intact even in the very moment of total collapse.

In another essay on poetry I have already discussed a famous passage in Gerard de Nerval's *Aurélia*.[4] There can be no doubt that the poet who cries out elsewhere in the book 'The universe is sunk in night' had a profound experience of this. And the dismembering

3   In English in the original.
4   See 'La poétique de Nerval' in Yves Bonnefoy: *La Vérité de parole*, Paris: Mercure de France (1988), p.63.

of all meaning which results from this understanding of nothingness explains his mental state extremely well, at least on those days when the dreams that ran alongside his everyday life prevented him from shaking off the weight of this 'sunk in night'. So what does Nerval say in the 'Mémorables' just before the end of *Aurélia*? He evokes the Himalayas, an obvious metaphor for the chaos that ensues when thought is stripped of meaning. Yet on a slope he spots a tuft of forget-me nots, as solitary as the broom blossom in Leopardi. And he writes, 'On the mountains of the Himalayas a tiny/little flower is born – Do not forget me! – The glimmer of a star fell for a moment upon it, and a sweet, strange language whispered back 'Forget me not!'.

What do this flower, this star, this 'sweet language' mean? I think they signify, unconsciously perhaps and yet clearly, the decision I have just mentioned or at least what leads up to it. Because the myosotis is called 'forget me not' in English; it is the little flower that demands to be noticed, whose entreaty is embedded in the language we use to talk about it. Its ' forget me not' is like the task of the poet, which is to recall the true reality of beings and things, so often veiled by their schematic representation in words normally used to convey conceptual understanding. At the moment when the world built by conceptual understanding collapses, to notice this little flower surrounded by non-being, to see in it, not the abstract entity of the dictionaries, but *this* particular flower, in *this* place, in *this* admittedly illusory but sentient existence that believes it is real, well, that is something which is not illusory, but new, radically new. It is the birth of a new – or perhaps we should say, a primordial – reality.

There can be no doubt that we are made of nothing, nature shifts our bodies as water does the shoreline sands, but we do exist at the instant and in the place when we become conscious of each other. And is it not a reality to decide that this other being, however much a creature of nothingness, is nevertheless an absolute who can become our companion as we turn, not this time towards that terrifying beyond, but towards the interior we uncover when we choose the things around us, giving them names, places, a help for our survival? Is this not the sole conceivable reality, is it not being itself? Being which exists because we have said no to the nothingness we might otherwise see in everything and everywhere. And if it is true that this being is only there because we have decided it is, and not because its existence is shored up by some divine prop, some support from the world of meta-sense, well, isn't that enough: an absolute made from the absolute reality of another being in our time and space? Being human is not a mere material fact, any more than is the communal effort of the shipwrecked in their boat. No, it has being. Matter can undo us as much as it likes, but consciousness and its decisions will forever fundamentally escape this process. The fact of being human depends on nothing but itself.

What I am describing here, clearly, is what happened when language began, the founding act whereby a sign was plucked from the flux of being to be shared, in the endless storm, with shadowy presences who gradually became human, formed a world. The word was from the beginning a communion, it was born as communion. It renews the pact each time one person turns to another, choosing to see that person as he or she is, and not as the reports we hear from the world of concepts. This transport is what we call love, and it transforms the abstract noun into a proper name, the word into an appeal. These are the commitments one human makes to another in the supreme moments of their lives, acts which may often seem tiny, which pass unnoticed. And yet each time they happen, they remake our being. They are the way we have being.

V.

In other words, they should be taken seriously, because they give force to all the words that they renew. The danger in this enterprise is analytic thought's constant turning in on itself, onto a schematic world which has forgotten it is rooted in matter and so discourages the need to love. This world needs to remember, even be taught, that the task of words is not only to establish laws or analyse essences. These are vases that can overflow with sense while yet not becoming human, confusions where at any moment that dark beyond can catch fire like flames in kindling.

The task is clearly difficult. Every day so many events show that, even when humans dream of new skies or a new earth, what inevitably follows is massacres, tongues and eyes cut out, deliberate famines, endless wars. These are so many fractures, chasms in language, everywhere it is the carnivore blindly leaping on his prey, no, worse, because we take a hideous pleasure in it that animals do not. It is as if language, which allows us to foresee the future and thereby reveals the inevitability of death to us, an inevitability that purely conceptual thought cannot penetrate, has become a gaping hole, driving the being who utters it mad, so that he adds the violence of nature to the perversity of his own spirit and its swirl of nightmarish dreams. In such conditions, how can we not acknowledge that hope's message is constantly traduced and betrayed?

We must recognise this, there is no doubt; even if I wanted to forget it, it's not just the evils of society that would remind me, but also the cracked soil of an increasingly dry planet, the extinction of species and of innumerable languages. But how I can tell all this to a child who is about to go to sleep and who wants the help of songs, of fairy stories to carry him across night's threshold? Wouldn't I be right to give him a story with a happy ending and say, 'No, don't be afraid, you can feel safe'. Isn't this just as true as the lucidity that has given up hope? It is certain that mankind will never sufficiently open up the clearing he inhabits in the 'dark wood' of the universe. It is certain that the 'leopard'[5] Dante met in his first canto will always bar the way the spirit wants to go, which no star illumines. But is this the right question to ask? Does the fact we can gain no external certainty in this dead wood mean that there is no point in bringing light to it?

No, because it is precisely and solely our need to imbue the actions and events of our ordinary existence with meaning, a need born of hope, that keeps these events from sinking completely, immediately, definitively and for ever, into something worse than animals merely devouring each other. Worse, since we would have language to turn a simple assuaging of hunger into enjoyment, the horrible pleasures at the end of time. We should not conclude, just because we have no future in time and space, maybe not even in the short-term, that there is no value in living in the present moment: we can exchange a glance or that handshake that Paul Celan, justified in despairing if anyone was, called a poem. Are we

---

5   YB uses the Italian terms *selva oscura* and *lonza* in the original.

just shipwrecked passengers in a boat? Let's behave as if we knew a shore will soon appear before us.

This kind of faith without belief or illusions is, let us admit it now, what we call poetry; its aim and task is to prise words sufficiently successfully from the grip of conceptual language so that men and women are able to use them to show affection or love at crucial times in their lives in a manner which I adjudge spontaneous. In the language of ideas poetry is born from our recollection of being mortal, something of which the language of ideas has no notion. Poetry frees words from the burden of having to signify so that the mind can see the forget-me-not on the edge of the abyss; poetry helps us to think of place, of the being that exists through place, which I have tried to define.

This is a very different thing from what Maurice Blanchot concluded from his experience of the abyss: this 'saying the unsayable' that got no further than mere signification. Poetry is the complete opposite of this idea of a linguistic oxymoron, and so it restores to the reader everything that this kind of writing had taken away. You'd have to really despise existence in the here and now, and think affection naïve, so to place nothingness at the centre of words. No, on the contrary, poetry recognises in the affections what is at the origin of being and what creates place. Poetry sees the world as the affections see it, through their eyes, with all its colours, noises, lights that can turn to storm shadow, nights that are never the black ink of nothingness but often the soft summer dusk where John Keats listened to the nightingale's song.

VI.

Poetry enters words because of the need to be, of the desire to be. And, as Keats shows us in his great poem, this doesn't mean the poet does not experience acute doubt about what he is doing or his ability to keep faith with his vision. In fact, he is assailed at every moment by the arguments of the 'dark side'; he is on the point of giving up on his essential intuition and turns to very mundane dreams to drown out or at least mask the incessant voice of his disquiet.

But this argument of the spirit with language and its apparently insoluble contradictions doesn't only happen in poetry. The body too, which desires, loves, wants to create, has its own truth, a truth that is more basic and even more sure. Writing poetry, with its myriad ways in sound and rhythm of confounding explicit meaning, is also the means by which the body can make itself heard in the word, offering to the poet, however frightening it seems, the chance to connect to that real mortality in him that he was in danger of forgetting. The body in verse re-centres and even broadens the spirit. Rhythms arise from it to support our flagging will with their awareness of the immediate and of unity. Images appear in the words that commingle the invigorating evidence from our senses with the vagueness of our thoughts. Poetry takes on new life but also reveals what its place is in the poem.

This place is definitely partly in the words, for they represent the dialogue between despair and hope, an exchange that is always troubled because words inherently conceptualise, and syntax maybe even more so. But it is also the expression of the body, the rhythms that lift up words and feed them from wellsprings they are not even aware of, although this process sometimes fails when language gets in the way of these primordial needs and desires. Rhythm is often iambic, rich in hope-giving energy, but it can also be broken or collapse before starting up again. Rhythm can be a harmonious, serene movement, when what is profound in life conforms to the wishes that we beings have; but it also often, in the greatest poems, resembles a racing pulse, like a fever.

This, then, is poetry, a concern for words, an attentiveness to rhythm. It is not, I must insist, what one might call an utterance where the poet's struggle with himself dominates, on every level, the convictions he thought he had acquired, including his key intuitions. But neither is it a text, mere verbal material abandoned by a poet frustrated in his intentions, that the reader has the right to decon-struct for his own ends. For the argument with which it is freighted continues, it bears up the piece of writing that is forming even as it lets itself go, it never ceases to drive these restless currents. The printed poem is an accidental interruption of the work of poetry, the poet's concession to artistic beauty, a beauty that flatters the dream.

So does poetry represent a horizon beyond a text perceived as inferior? That horizon, those few great presences which the poet is trying to see and love and persist in showing, in witnessing to, when he remains faithful, despite many false trails, to the tuft of forget-me-nots, the flowering broom plant, the nightingale's song, the sunset hour on the balcony? If the poem were only trees, rivers, hills, fields and sky gathered up by men and women as they travel, it would become indistinguishable from the evidence of a place, from the life given that place by memory; it would be like a landscape with figures, a painting by Poussin. That is, of course, some of the truth of poetry, the sort of beauty one glimpses in the far distance of a poem: those misty, blue, remembered hills.

But time is also an actor in every piece of writing, the time of the lived life, the time of the irreparable, the irredeemable, of tenacious hope, of life's unremitting busy-ness that stops the picture taking form and sticking in the mind of the reader. Changes in the poet's life make this particular bit of land that the poet loved fade from him; this house, this scrub, these oaks start to take second place in his writing when other aspects of the world make claims on his affection. The idea of place remains but the place we would wish to serve as a cipher for a presence in the world is just a sketch we constantly rework; and it is the human hand that draws the figure in the foreground.

So what is poetry? This time I'm not talking about the essence of poetry, but the way in which its work is present or not, perceptible or not, in a finished poem. Well, I *think* I would say that the poetry of a poem reaches the reader in the same way that a voice does.

A voice, with its tremors, its exaltations, its calm or its fevers. The work of poetry is in its words; it needs them to combat the conceptual world but it also feeds on impressions that cannot be put into words, often visual memories, secret emotions or indelible hurts. Writing cannot contain these in words alone; it is flooded by a tide that wells up from below, a tide that is full of truth and borne along by the rhythm that mind and body have decided upon together. This overflow is what I call voice, whose tremor expresses the inexpressible without any mediator. Voice is what the unsayable adds to the sayable. It is the sound of words caught up in what goes beyond words. It is the space where poetry can keep alive its ambition to capture in words the infinite inherent in everything that exists. Voice is the prow of the word, its vanguard, the most active part of poetic invention. It is also the unifying principle in the poet, where the temptations, the errors, the delusions of his daily life are fused in the fire of his deepest desires.

And it is to this voice of the poets that those who are in greatest need of poetry listen. The critics read Baudelaire and analyse his texts in their different ways: here he is in fragments on their table. But the friends of poetry hear the voice of 'The Swan' or 'The Balcony'. Not his fleshly voice, that mortal vestment which he has put off. But the poetic voice which flowed in his ordinary voice as blood flows in our body. 'The Traveller', recorded by Guillaume Apollinaire, is an example of this voice within a voice, a flame despite the cinders. Who could claim that the great poems of Keats, Leopardi, Vigny, Nerval, Yeats are not this prow opening up the deep of words? What witness to poetry would not want to make Shakespeare's voice relive in his translation?

VII.

Did I say translation? Maybe we should think a bit more and harder about what voice in poetry is but for now we need to return to the problem of translating poems, because thinking about voice casts this problem in a new light, I feel.

If by translating poetry we are referring to what poetry in a text is, rather than that part of translation which is concerned with its manifold meanings, can we imagine that it is even possible, when other kinds of writing already present so many difficulties? For example, how can we move from one language to another, from one network of ideas to another, without substituting the direct thought of one writer with another which, necessarily distanced from the original by virtue of its own ideation system, can only be an imitation, a commentary? This causes us to lose that connection with the immediate that most writers have, even in prose.

Nevertheless, this kind of shackled translation can give us a hint of what poetry is. It helps us to understand, word by word, the disparate nature of the ideas that attach themselves to apparently similar or analogous problems in different languages. Thus we can identify an 'inadequatio rei et intellectu'[6] which has led some translators to deduce that there is a reality beyond our understanding of conceptual representations, the reality of the living being, the possibility of presence.

What is more, poems cannot be reduced to the language of mere meaning; I have just said they are a voice. Because of this, their translation may in fact be much more directly and intimately possible than works of prose. That is of course assuming that we rethink what we mean by translation, and to look for it elsewhere than in the common solutions of line by line or *testo a fronte,* facing page.

Let us not forget that for a work of literature to present itself as a voice, rhythm is essential. Now, this succession of long and short sounds, of alliterations and assonances on which voice is based, is audible all over the world independently of the sense of the words that carry it, as is the music of instruments, which partakes of the same nature: the flute or the oboe receives the voice of Mozart or Mahler just as words receive and animate the meditative rhythms of, say, 'L'Invitation au voyage'. The word of the poem is music, its *parlar* is *cantando,* its voice is a singing voice. Even if the text is in Italian or German or some other Western language, we can hear it in France.

And the rhythms in this text in another language may be a key to the investigation of the self that happens in poetry. What we can hear casts light on this movement. If we listen carefully to the hesitations and the tremblings in Hamlet's voice, we will get straight away to the central experience in Shakespeare's tragedy, the one Hamlet recalls in a famous scene: that he saw the lights of the starry sky put out, and heard discord in the heavenly spheres. This is the presentiment of non-being, the meeting with the great beyond to which Blanchot and others refer! With Ophelia, Hamlet tries to give some basis to being as Nerval had done, by recognising one of the lives in his intimate world, – the young girl in fact does actually say 'Forget me not' – but doubt paralyses him, he cannot get up the resolve needed, soon Ophelia will scatter the flowers that could have been symbols

6 In Latin in the original. YB is mischievously altering (and misspelling) Aquinas's famous formulation *adequatio rei et intellectus,* the adequation of the object and the mind.

in a world full of meaning. The iambic pentameter is an extraordinary instrument for conjuring up existential angst, for glimpsing the possibility of receiving the experience of presence even in the situations of a life wrecked by futile endeavour. It is the same verse form, or almost, that Yeats uses, a poet torn between the lure of all sorts of attractions and a passionate need for incarnation.

Why is it that the rhythmic play of verse, the secret of its prosody, allows a poet in another language to reach the poet who wrote the original? It's simple. When writing has turned into voice, it is because the world is no longer perceived as a mere jumble of things but as a collection of presences. These presences are the essential realities that correspond to the fundamental necessities of life and that consequently inhabit a territory beyond specific idiom which is common to all peoples: a territory where no-one is on foreign ground. Rivers, trees, shores, mountains, houses scattered under heaven, Nérine on her balcony singing softly at nightfall: all these are archetypes of being in the world, admittedly always checked and everywhere in chains, but real and springing to life the minute that we desire being. This is our common treasure property, what used once to be called the sacred.

It follows from this that these points of reference in our world –which have been replaced in prose by simple montages of signs, each different according to country and never entirely translatable – re-appear in verse, in the voice it bears, as something universal, something that we can immediately share. This explains why we are able to follow Leopardi's gaze when he sees the broom flower or to listen to the invisible nightingale with Keats. Thanks to these shared referents, we can understand the thoughts of these poets, relive the way in which they created a place for life out of what they saw occurring in nature around them. And each of these ways is a sign of that desire for being which is the essence of poetry.

The best poetry cares nothing for the barriers separating languages at the basic level of words. The ground of resurrection is present in every one of us, even though it may seem like a mountain peak endlessly receding from us as we approach it. Since we can understand or, rather, hear these poets in another language, is it not possible to imagine being able to translate them? The only thing is, this translation would have to have the same care for the sound of words and the same experience of rhythm as in the poets being translated. This might produce some disconcerting results for those readers who are used to ordinary translations, that is, ones that offer no more than a mere transposition of meaning.

The first movement of this new mode of translation would no longer be an act of the intellect, that is, choosing a word by thinking about the meaning of another word. The translator of poetry is a witness to the work that he loves; he will want to try and convey its meaning through the struggle between his experience of non-being, of nothingness and his desire to create a place to share. He will have to put his whole existence into this quest, which is addressed to everyone and to himself as well. What will count will be less his ability to retrace the steps of his interlocutor, the original poet, than how much he is able to accept or reject another way of constructing the world. This translator poet is going to react, become aware of himself by listening to the other, abandon or reaffirm aspects of his own thought; in short, write in the true sense of the word, which is to use everything in individual words to renew voice. So there are no strictures here about sticking close to the text, as is expected in ordinary translation. There is a lot, however, to encourage him to keep faith with his own text, where his relationship to himself is played out, where he thinks, where that transgression called poetry may illuminate him.

Does this mean translation won't work because the translator has to remain true to himself, while nevertheless under the influence of a work that has called out to him, perhaps even shattered him? Surely he's going to continue to think about it even though it's in his own words now; he will draw on his own work, the life of his own preoc-cupations and ideas, that may reflect or copy or undo, but surely meditate upon, the poetry and the poetics of the other author. He loves the latter too much to traduce his efforts. It may be that the fictions that come most naturally to him will allow him to present, to imagine, through figures, images and symbols, what he cannot fully understand in the other writer. I am thinking of Baudelaire or Mallarmé writing 'The Double Room' or 'Sonnet in –yx', each of which in its way is a meditation on the poem 'The Raven' by Edgar Allan Poe, their master in poetry, though they don't in fact follow him to his logical conclusion. Are these reflexions, these mirrors –

and there are others I could mention – a betrayal of 'The Raven'? I don't believe so, because they help to show Poe's thought beneath the new things they add, beneath their critiques; they manage to keep the poetry alive for once, because the voice lets the poetry be heard. This way of listening to poetry by interweaving different works is what I call translation in its broadest sense. I think it has a right to exist next to more literal translations.

Translated by Hilary Davies

4.
MEMOIRS

LETTER TO SHAKESPEARE[1]

Supposing I wrote to you, Shakespeare – but why? If they should bring you my letter – whether on the stage where you speak to your actors, or on the construction site of your theatre, or at the tavern where you trenchantly discuss the events in your society that worry you, as I well know – you would stick it in your pocket, you would forget it. And besides, why should I ask you questions, or make remarks that do not interest you? It isn't that you don't care about what gives us pause when we read you ourselves. Still, your way of thinking about it doesn't lie on the plane of self-aware thought, but in your highly disorganised work on your plays, in those hours when subconscious intuitions or the demands of the unconscious are no longer repressed – at any rate not as severely – by the words and convictions of the intellect.

I see you: you're standing in a corner of the theatre. It's cold, and a wind seems to be blowing. You're talking to several men, young and old. One of them will be Hamlet; another, Ophelia. Do you have an idea to explain to them? No. *Hamlet* is being written here, at this very moment, in the sentences that come to you, that take you by surprise. It's virtually an improvisation, over several days divided between your table – I don't know where – and the stage. A text, certainly, but one you cross out off-the-cuff, as when you understand – for example, at this very instant – that your future Hamlet doesn't grasp all that well what you're trying to tell him. You cross things out, since you hardly know better than he does what the prince wants – this sketch of a character whose ready responses are still so evasive. What appears of him in your words comes from underneath what you have imagined or projected. And of course, that is because great thought is what I like to call 'figural' – made of symbols that catch us unawares, of impressions that inflame our entire body. If you had prepared *Hamlet*, had meditated on the meaning you would give to its characters and their relationships, we would no longer read you today: you would have produced nothing but a Ben Jonson play. Ah,

1 'Lettre à Shakespeare' was collected in *L'Hésitation d'Hamlet et la décision de Shakespeare*, Paris: Coll. *La Libraire du XXIème siècle*, Editions du Seuil, 2015.

I see you so well, intuitive as you are, and luckily! You rush through the text as you will later rush through the city, looking for money or adventures. You dash off (as Ben Jonson might say) responses, fears, appeals, soliloquies, because you feel – obscurely, but this is your genius – that you must do things quickly to keep from bogging down in ready-made ideas. I think you wrote *Hamlet* in just a few days. You won't refute me.

Did you ever ponder something consciously? Yes, you did, but it was only at the time when you stepped back from your work on the stage – and because certain people fairly near to you, at the University, at the Court, looked down on you. They called themselves poets, and sometimes they were. This happened, I can even make note of it, only a few years before the *Hamlet* of today, which according to me is the consequence of your thoughts. Your meditation continued for quite a while, and allowed you to understand that you had been right to place your trust in hasty writing, already so easy to discern in your dramas inspired by the history of England.

This reflection came to you before your new period – the reason we still love you so much today – the phase that begins with *Julius Caesar*. What was it, then? To start with, you cast a sceptical, ironic eye on the sonnets being written everywhere in those same years, among the lettered and the learned. As you perused Spenser, as you read even the poignant and noble Sidney, and as you skimmed the bloodless pages of their brazen imitators with such impatience and contempt, you became aware of this: that what springs from a poem governed by predetermined forms, closed on themselves, can only be a simplification of feelings and beings – a focus for stereotypes that above all seem laughable, but in fact are dangerous, destructive.

Assuredly, in these fourteen idealising, exclamatory verses, the grand encounters that you had created – in *Richard II*, for example, or in *Henry V* – are quite impossible. In fact they occur often in your history plays: men and women overflowing with desires, passions – unpredictable in that – but allowing us to perceive similar ways of being in ourselves, that this time harbour within them the full and brutal authenticity of life, often unpleasant. Those sonnets are a renunciation of truth. And writing them is easy: you can show that you know how to turn them out as easily and even better than anyone else – better, because you can make harmonics (which only you understand) vibrate in the sound, the beautiful sound of words. You can write them – harmonious, eloquent, mellifluous, and easy to recall. But this was your spontaneous reflection: that you could verify for yourself, in your momentary adhesion to a fixed form, the illusion that it substitutes word by word for the presence of beings; the temptation that it instils to observe man through the prism of dream, woman through that of prejudice, and society through that of a more or less cynical consent to its injustices.

Better to flee this supposed poetry, which is only useless literature... And with a renewed confidence in its powers, and thus with a greater ambition – and even, you have come to sense, with a higher one – better to recover on the stage that open, shifting form which the emotions lift but do not break, in constant dialogue with life's unknowns. This is the vivid, febrile language you had learned to love and practice, fired by the political or martial action of your chronicles. Iambic pentameter, that breath of being in the world, deserves something more than the beauties of simple appearance as chiseled by the versifiers: it is and has to be our key to the essential finitude of life, that relation with ourselves which means true joys, true sufferings – true love. And then the work becomes not merely the mirror of society as it is but of life as it ought to be, a lesson of existence.

Supposing I wrote to you, William Shakespeare – no, you wouldn't read me. You have too much on your hands with this language of truth that has already arisen within you, so to speak, two or three years before the *Hamlet* of today. Tomorrow and the day after tomorrow, it will become Lear's harrowing cries, Macbeth's shouts of horror – and also Cleopatra's sublime declarations, Perdita's exquisite words. You wouldn't understand me, and that is certainly a shame; I would have so many questions to ask you. But what I can do, all the same, is to dream that I slip you a note. Yes, take this sheet, folded four ways, asking you a favour: admission to the theatre, one of the evenings when your play will be performed. Admission through some hidden door, if there is one, since we of another time – at any rate your best readers of late, writers, critics, often women – don't like to mix much with those strapping rowdies, loud-mouthed and easy with their swords, who jostle on the threshold of the Globe. Those fellows don't make way gladly for people who're different from them. Unlike you, who have read Montaigne, Ariosto, Machiavelli. Who have even read

Goethe or Baudelaire, and taken a look at Freud – though his mode of thought seemed a bit simple to you, if I understand you rightly.

But there's the rub: the reason I'm asking you to help me get in this evening is so I can sit near that young man I recognise, Lord Chandos.[2] He comes from another era, and is accompanied by two other gentlemen who also interest me. One of them doesn't seem to be from London or from your century, any more than I am. His features are marked by the furrows of an unquiet subjectivity. In your time it didn't surface so clearly on people's faces – didn't flare up the same way. At any rate, the portraits we have of you don't show a trace of it. But the other man is obviously one of your contemporaries, perhaps even one of your friends. Above his small beard, his beaming eyes shift with the mischief of a free and beautiful philosophy. It so happens that the first of the two men holds a letter, another one, which he is trying to slip into Chandos's hand – without much success, since the young man visibly has his mind on something else. Take it, he whispers to him; give it to Francis Bacon in a little while: this is the right moment, because we are about to hear a work by Shakespeare. But will Bacon be able to decipher Hofmannsthal's text? It's not likely, since these two or three are only – like all of us, this evening at least – shadows among shadows.

I turn my eyes to the stage, still empty. Empty? I will even say vacant, offered unreservedly to all the winds of the mind – because there are hardly any objects on these boards. A dodgy chair, that might serve as a throne if need be; a piece of artillery that later you'll have to keep from noticing too much, since it's here for another play tomorrow. No stage set, no demands made on facets of the visible world to support the lines of the actors; but on the other hand, this trapdoor in the floor to communicate with the invisible world – in other words, the unconscious.

This stage with nothing but itself – this metaphysical place, in short – mirrors the dimensions of the hope we peg to language. It offers itself unreservedly to what is sought by poets, always much

---

2   A reference to Hugo von Hofmannstahl's *Chandos Letter*, published in 1902. This missive from the fictional character Lord Philip Chandos to Francis Bacon, dated August 1603, laments the author's mounting inability to express himself in words, though he had once been a fluent speaker and writer.

more than the letter of their work. It permits us to glimpse what is unsayable in their perception of the world, or hidden in their relation to themselves: two things that are inexpressible. Their conjunction, their mutual consumption, is the event of poetry: as sometimes in your theatre, for example in the radiant light of certain moments in *The Winter's Tale*. – Shakespeare, you are at the Globe before this bare stage. You even have the lucky find of the proscenium, which allows Hamlet to move forward into himself, meeting his great questions. Shakespeare, you are alone, deep inside yourself with those questions, those anxieties. Nobody is here to place a small Victorian table next to Hamlet, as if his grand speech needed somewhere to set the skull of 'poor Yorick'.

And I think of that extraordinary invention, staging: when did it come about, and where? This addition of content, schematic from the outset – that profile of a tree on the garden side, that little table on the courtyard side – in this place and at this moment when the actors' voices are overcome by content, from the depths of a text which is life in the making: those presentiments, those terrors, those vows that no reading of the work could ever wholly identify, ever completely grasp. All the same, the director has an obligation to understand; to pass through meaning before (from time to time) arriving at presence. And when he is great, which may occur, he will know instinctively that for poetry this detour is a peril, one he owes it to himself to face with a good deal of ardent exigency towards his own unconscious. In fact, as I am aware, it's only natural that staging should have made its appearance at the end of the Enlightenment, when the audience was banned from seats or small armchairs on the boards, but also when a number of prejudices were unseated from their positions of command over thought. When subjectivity could thus begin to become aware of itself in the Gothic novel and the poetry of those young people we have called the Romantics.

And how many problems arise from this time forward that didn't exist on your stage in the era of Elizabeth or James! You see, today this late afternoon is autumnal, or so it seems to me; in any case the light outside is already foggy under the lowering sky, and what's left of it inside the theatre is quite feeble. A torch brought on stage, or the brief flame of a musket, will stand out against this background with all the intensity found in red – all its tragedy, all its appeal to the thought of the tragic. This was perfect for performing *Julius Caesar*, in which a torch appears at the most decisive moment, when Brutus finally accepts that he must confront his unconscious, must raise the trapdoor. And it works well for performing *Hamlet* right now, as the watchmen move on the ramparts at night, casting glimmers on the faces of those who arrive. Or when a king who has blackness in his heart calls for torches, still more torches – *lights, lights, lights* – after which his fascinated witness cries (and this must be marked by a lighting effect again), *'Tis now the very witching time of night...*

Night, deepest night, with all its meaning, can be signified on your stage, Shakespeare. And by the same token it can denote its contrast as well – through the rebounding of the mind, through hope free at last to express itself. Yes, it also implies the purest day, the light of moments of reunion, of hardships ended, of truth recaptured – of Perdita no longer lost. Your highly intimate experience of light, my friend, the secret vow of your theatre and its denouement – which we possess as a legacy from you – everything that takes place in words is preserved on these boards. They do not substitute any particular content for the universal roots of your English language, as it comes into its own. A privilege, we should note, that painters did not enjoy even in your era. No doubt they had an inkling, in their gaze and in their hearts, of those epiphanies of a truer light in the midst of the everyday. But it was expected of them that for lack of words, they should explain the situations they evoked by means of things – and regrettably, these ran the risk of absorbing our attention.

All the same, they expressed their intuition of the possibilities of life, or at least the greatest of them did. Among your contemporaries, Caravaggio already succeeded – almost as much as the extraordinary Goya, your kindred spirit – in representing night, utter night, and hope in the thick of night. Fittingly, he did so with torches, and faces that suddenly loom in their glow. As to Veronese, or Titian already in his *Bacchanal of the Andrians*, they almost attained in their own right that irrefutable and irresistible light of fusion, of happiness, of peacefulness that all of us dream about in the heart of night. And to that end they did not take the tragic course of the chiaroscuro painters, which Goya as well still follows at times, in his deaf-man's house; instead they chose the path – obviously so difficult, so daring – of trust.

These are your contemporaries, Shakespeare: Caravaggio, Veronese. Caravaggio is painting at this very moment, in Rome. He has placed his confidence in religion: in his *Vocation of Saint Matthew* the light comes from without, from the upper right side. But other works will follow, tremendous zigzags; and perhaps in desperation, he will die on that savage coast in the very days when you are writing *The Winter's Tale*, your vision of true resurrection, your victory. And I perceive that you have essential links with him, but even more so with one of his disciples, Adam Elsheimer – who also died in 1610, strangely enough. In my view, Elsheimer pondered the night of being more deeply than Caravaggio. And this is because he had in mind the buried light that you, ultimately, will know how to deliver from the quicksand of language. I look at his *Judith*, which he will paint next year, or two years from now. She's your Lucretia! With the same idea of murder but – no matter how scorned she may be today, or tomorrow – the same faith in life. Shakespeare, this painter is similar to you, the dramatist: you foresee that your moment in history, when Galileo returns the sky to us, might open on this intuition, on poetry itself. With that conviction unknown to your conscious thought, but exigent and bold, in a while you will descend from the high ramparts of Elsinor into utter blackness – where you will found the world anew.

I look at this stage where members of the audience are taking their seats, but which is empty, metaphysically – as empty as the blank page where the human voice risks itself in poetry, though so full of disquiet, so deeply wounded, so ridden with doubts. A last pale ray of this sun from who knows where, in the city where my dream still lingers... But there's already enough penumbra to allow someone hard to discern – in the presence of someone else who is just as hard to read – to cry out *Who's there?* After which the action will begin: the dead king will appear with his ambiguous claim, the archaic element of the world will reaffirm itself for a moment, only to go swiftly out of joint when shadows emerge on the boards of the theatre within the theatre – shadows within shadows. They as well will sink so fully into the commonplaces of language – a last glance at the sonnet, no? – that they cannot help this time but beg from us the question of words within words... And those torches then, do they really come forward? No, because Hamlet sees the clouds drifting by in the sky, taking whatever shapes – a weasel, a whale – that words may want. *The very witching time of night?* The abyss, are we meant to understand, that is the core of language? I say to myself that your bare stage was your good fortune, Shakespeare, preserving for you – who was worthy of that gift – the great, the only true possibility of words. Were you an eclectic spirit, passing from comedies to tragedy, from Venus to Lady Macbeth, from contented bodies to the worst sufferings anyone could evoke? No, you thrust your hands into language, stirring up felicities and afflictions, surprises and certainties, good and evil, senselessness and the hopes that persevere.

And how did those hands go about moving this mud, these colours, this coldness, these mysterious beginnings of warmth – I'd very much like to ask you this. That was the reason for my letter. Or no, instead I'd like to tell you what I think, to explain to you what you did; after all, I have my idea about the matter, and perhaps you would acquiesce… But this isn't the moment, as I can readily see. Other members of the audience have already sat down next to us on the stage, and I look at Chandos – it's you he's watching, in fact. Distractedly, he sticks the letter into his pocket: the letter that someone from another era, like me, caused him to write. The shadow spreads over my page as well, in my words. And someone – is it you? – has called out *Who's there?* The performance has just begun.

Translated by Hoyt Rogers

A Dream in Mantua[1]

In the early summer of 1961, Jackson and Marthiel Mathews arrived in Paris. They were on their way to Egypt, then Greece, and Sylvia Beach had decided to make the journey with them. One evening, Jackson said to me: 'Couldn't we meet in Athens?' I discovered I was free to leave, and looked forward to joining them.

Sylvia was tireless in Greece, but there were times when we thought she wasn't so much below as beyond – henceforth – the threshold of fatigue. She would walk on ahead, in silence, perch on stones, gaze round, climb higher, in the sun, dressed in black, with unblinking attention. Early to bed in the evening, and away so early in the morning! On one occasion, in Nafplio, I was watching the waking harbour from my window. Before long, among the still-silent fishermen in the pools of still-blue shadow, stepping briskly over coils of rope, Sylvia appeared in a hat, her slender silhouette and quick small feet all dauntless, unweighing grace.

I also recall a large, dark room, in a restaurant at Delphi, again at a very early hour. No Nescafé even. Little help to be expected from a handful of waiters in the distance, hard to make out, soon nowhere to be seen. 'No matter', says Sylvia. On a shelf she has spotted – God knows when! – a tin that does indeed contain ground coffee and she adds a bit of the powder to the lukewarm tea water, stirs it and drinks. 'It's not so bad', she concludes, under no illusions but with that steely resolve which is the most self-effacing aspect of humour.

Never, in fact, have I seen a traveller so unselfregarding and so joyously stoical, and I genuinely admired – wondering at times from what deep need she drew her strength – this frail-bodied trust in the world. What did Sylvia hope to find in Greece, which came so late in her life? I remember that in Mycenae she wanted to go down into the great well, the bottom of which is reached along an endless flight of winding stairs, with only a slender flame to guide you. The

1 'Un rêve fait à Mantoue' was originally published in the *Mercure de France* of August–September, 1961, as part of a memorial issue for Sylvia Beach. Collected in *L'Improbable*, rev. and enlarged edition, Paris: Mercure de France, 1992 and also in Paris: Gallimard, Collection Folio/Essais, 1992.

steps are slippery, the walls close, the water when it appears will have only the narrowest and most silent of shores, but Sylvia, who had gone on ahead of me, was courageous, I felt, a little awe-struck but very much alert, and I could recognise in her, the colours faded but the spirit intact, sister to that water which leaks away, the timeless young woman with something English about her, who, released for a moment, goes off with a backpack, sleeps in a tent, takes notes in museums (she no longer did this, however, though she would sometimes jot a word down on an old envelope) and strolls through the small village streets in the early hours of the morning. Sylvia Beach was the very figure of ingenuousness, which is the intelligence of the free. She went from childhood to working life and old age paying no heed to the gloomy side of things. Like the Korés she so admired, who look everything squarely in the face, without prudishness but intact, like the robust but melancholy art depicting the decisive battle, on the pediment at Olympia, she wanted to submit the steeps and rubble, the dreary undergrowth of life, to her unbending ideals.

And perhaps our driver had understood that Sylvia was of the non-magical race which turns its back on the labyrinth and ascends into the light, since each morning he would bring her a bundle of heavy September jasmine, bright with dew. For my part, I couldn't help thinking, in much the same way, that she really had little in common, in her moral choices at least, with the Joyce whose memory she sought out everywhere in the land of Ulysses. One morning – Sylvia clearly belonged to the rising sun – I was strolling around the National Museum and saw her coming towards me in the distance. I had a camera. 'Yves', she said, 'look, it's the spitting image of Joyce. Could you take a photograph?' Preserved in the funerary stele that she pointed out to me was the likeness of a sixth-century warrior, helmeted, naked, steely, muscular, and yet – how the devil, and drawing on what fund of mythological awareness, had Sylvia seen this? – it's true that Joyce was there, there was even the brow weighed down with myopia.

Sylvia, of course, nurtured the idea of going to Ithaca, and it came as a great disappointment to her when she realised, in the last week, that even today the island is difficult of access, and that she had missed the boat which would have taken her there. That final visit had to be postponed for another year. Sylvia was most put out by this mishap. She brought forward her return to France. Suddenly, she didn't have time, she would never have time now, Sylvia Beach.

★

A few days later, I too left Greece, on the boat to Venice. I had decided to stop over in Mantua, to visit the Mantegna exhibition, and in no time at all was there, travelling overnight on an *accelerato*. I wanted to stay near the railway station, but there were no rooms free in the neighbouring hotels. I entrusted myself to a taxi, only to discover that all the other hotels were full as well, even the *pensioni*. I was surprised by this, as it was October. 'Why are there so many travellers in Mantua?', I asked the cab-driver. – 'For the big Mostra, of course', he said. His answer gave me an extraordinary feeling of well-being. As I had come to see Mantegna, it was as though it was I myself, multiplied a million times over, living in the rooms of the town. Meanwhile, we wended our way down, step by step, still to no avail. All that was left in Mantua was a small *locanda* that my guide was loath to recommend.

As it turned out, there was a huge room for me at the Locanda al Giardino, reached in the dark along some stone steps under the trees. Gleaming in a dim light were large pieces of dark, nineteenth-century furniture beneath colour prints of scenes from Verdi's *Otello*. I rushed off to see the two Alberti churches. Then I fell asleep and had one of those beautiful dreams which, from time to time, stand out with the clarity of a poem from the blind scrawlings of the unconscious.

Here is the end of that dream. It was spring or early summer, I entered a rather squat white house at the end of a garden, and from there made my way down a wide spiral staircase, but without losing any of the radiance of the late morning, where the green leaves were dappled with flecks of ripe orange fruit. In the room in which I suddenly found myself the light was scarcely less intense. French windows gave onto what appeared to be the deepest foundations of the same garden, while the room itself, which was rather narrow, turned out to be an old-fashioned kitchen fitted with polished wood and copper. Little girls were milling about, laughing, in front of gigantic ovens, and a delicious odour of fresh oil wafted from the black frying-pans where eggs were gently cooking. I watched these tiny suns crackling in the odours and shadows. And I saw that, from time to time, one of the young girls would scoop one up and toss it into one of the tubs on the floor, where many more were lying about, vegetating or about to go out. I was taken aback by the bizarreness of it all. 'What else can we do?', I was told. 'We are fairies, we don't have needs. We cook for pleasure. This is the house of immortality.' Whereupon more laughter, and the full, mutable faces of childhood that is drawing to a close.

After this, I was in a busy thoroughfare, or a lane rather, the walls of which were hollowed out with shops fronted by grey stone arcades. Outside one of the shops, surrounded by passers-by, was Sylvia Beach. She was holding a book or a journal. People were explaining that she had suffered from an ungrateful publisher. She looked pale, infinitely old, endangered. So I told her she had to leave this place and come with me. I even took her by the hand and led her away along the winding, slowly descending street to the young girls' abode. Yes, I knew that she had only to enter the house and her life would be saved. But it was also obvious to me, and more urgently with each minute that passed, that we had to hurry. A mysterious new reality – daylight, finitude, awakening – was seeping into the trees from all sides, obliterating them, together with the street and this whole place of hope. We ran on, the door stood before us, and I struggled with all my soul to ensure those presences remained, for a minute at least, in the burgeoning whiteness; then just as everything was about to be swallowed up, the stone threshold was there beneath our feet. Did I manage to smuggle Sylvia Beach into the house of immortality? On waking up *al giardino* on a sunny morning, in a thicket of birdsong, I was almost willing to believe it.

★

But then one year later, on a morning of cold mist and rain, I was making my way down the steps of the Columbarium at Père-Lachaise, with Sylvia's friends, to a derelict garden. The whole of reality that day was black and white, with glints of yellow perhaps, of the kind seen on old photographs. And at that moment someone who had known James Joyce well during his Paris years said to me with a start, pointing out suddenly a gaunt, stooped old man with a high brow, his eyes partially concealed by thick narrow lenses of a kind I would have thought were not made any more; a man who was standing apart from our group, and as it were colourlessly between us and the trees: 'Look! It's extraordinary. You would swear it was him.' And indeed, though I wasn't thinking about him, I recognised him at once.

It wasn't James Joyce. But to have caught a glimpse of him in this man walking away seemed to me rich with meaning. It meant, of course, that some of us at least continued to be haunted by his memory at this sad time. But in a more profound sense, and more than anything, it meant that it was easy that morning to cross over into the fluid world of dream, to disregard the hidden anchor that keeps our world at harbour and to believe in one's heart of hearts – a guilty thought, it's true – that there is no reason to shield the narrow realm of lived experience from the symbols that rain down on it from elsewhere. When you lead a loved-one away into the void, especially one who like Sylvia Beach has been so present in your life, and so natural a focus for the truest labours of an era, you can almost believe that reality is just a dream. Was it not the illusory essence of our existence that my Italian dream had sought to signify in the fading away, at the end, of all appearances? A phrase that ebbs and flows, with its shifting erasures and unreal horizons, a mist like today, and nothing but the beating of a small Delphic bell. And the true world beyond in that inaccessible awakening which my own awakening in Mantua, in its concern for poetry, could never do more than imitate.

I also thought of some photographs I had taken of Sylvia Beach – at Delphi, at Mycenae, in Arcadia – and understood more clearly now why they would become, like all photographs from another age, a silent epiphany, eroding the objects that make up their horizon, or simply their backdrop perhaps. In the faith that gathers it into unity, our humanity, our ancient will to selfhood, can only experience fullness of Being *from within*. Seen through the eyes of another, in the incessant past, how motionless, and how mysterious, a gesture soon becomes: she walks towards the camera like a daemon of the twilight hour. Yes, what hollows out great conceptual pathways between things – our keen interest in their appearances – is also what makes them so unusual in our eyes, because of that other hollow, that other subsidence, this time at the very centre of our being: the emptiness of our name. I take a photograph, I immortalise a moment of Sylvia Beach, and the trees change, as though by following a procession in summer, and looking high up all of a sudden, I was seeing them anew, in and through the uncertain movement, like that of a small boat pitched about by a noiseless swell, of this smiling and slightly weather-beaten black statue which we carry away under the branches.

Translated by Mark Hutchinson

THREE RECOLLECTIONS OF BORGES[1]

I.

In my memory, I turn the pages of one of my keepsake books. It holds some images of a man whose life hinged on a suffering, old and profound, which his quiet reserve never allowed him to mention. That was my impression of him, right from the start.

Three recollections, beginning with our first encounter: in Cambridge, Massachusetts, in 1967. Borges was slated to give the Charles Eliot Norton Lectures at Harvard that winter. I admired him, convinced I'd like the man I guessed he must be. Jorge Guillén was living in Cambridge, too, and I saw him often - either alone, or for lunch with Paul de Man. When I spoke to him of Borges, Jorge said: 'He's here already, settling in. Write him, and ask if you could meet.'

I wrote him; but ten days went by, and still no reply. At last, Guillén reported to me with a laugh: 'Guess what? I called on Borges yesterday, and Elsa took me aside. "Do you know this woman?" she asked, in a low voice. She had your letter in her hand. Borges had said your first name out loud, so she decided to keep him from seeing you.'

My first name? It's pronounced like the English name, 'Eve' – a temptress who fouled up everything on earth, reputedly. That Borges should have a wife was a novelty: it was rumored his mother had forced her on him, when she'd grown too old to travel with him herself. True or false, Elsa only shared his existence for very few years. It would be hard to imagine two beings more dissimilar; and the author's old friends, several of whom resided in Cambridge, felt unhappy and disconcerted about her role.

'You're mistaken,' Guillén informed her. 'He's not a woman; and he happens to be a friend of mine. He's no threat to you. So please let Borges answer him.'

---

1 'Trois souvenirs de Borges' was published in *Dans un débris de miroir*, Paris: Editions Galilée, 2006.

One evening, Borges phoned me; he agreed to come to dinner at our house on Francis Avenue. For that stay, which lasted about a year, my wife and I had rented a small frame house; it adjoined a larger one, raised by four or five steps, that surveyed the street between two wooden columns. We'd fallen in love with the creaking floors, and the windowpanes flush against the trees. This modest place exemplified a way of being in the world - which is why those who leave New England feel such a homesickness, ever after. We laid fires in the chimney: now it was spring, with leafy branches on every side; and now it was autumn. Then all those leaves turned red and gold before they fell, in such profusion they crackled softly under our feet. And soon enough, there was snow; it had snowed the day 'the Borgeses' came to dinner.

Even though I'd never met him before, he conversed with me openly right away – he always placed that trust in those who sought him out, I gathered. He'd just returned from Concord, he explained. He'd been eager to visit Hawthorne's house, since he revered him enormously. Out of devotion to this great writer, he'd knelt on the doorstep, despite the bitter cold and heavy snow. Perhaps he'd done so in part because of the life Hawthorne had led there, in a community imbued by faith – though a faith Borges himself certainly didn't profess. Then he asked me: 'Have you ever read "Wakefield"?'

Since I hadn't read 'Wakefield', Borges summarised the tale for me in French. A man tells his wife he's going out of town for a day or two. He takes leave of her with a 'sourire idiot' – a 'stupid smile'. But a few streets away, he stops. Why travel any further? he shrugs. He takes a room in a nearby hotel, planning to go back home the next day.

But the next morning, Wakefield thinks: why should I go home right now? And so he postpones his return for days, months, years. All this time, he remains very near his house – just a stone's throw away, so to speak. Vaguely disguised, he often strolls in front of it. Now and then, from a distance, he catches sight of his wife on the street; he can see she's growing old, Borges noted. Still, it's not that Wakefield's up to anything unusual; for twenty years, he doesn't see a soul, and doesn't have a clue.

Then one day, he's walking down the street again. It's raining, and a gust of wind happens to push him against his door. Why not step inside? he says to himself. He rings the bell, goes in, and takes up his former life, with the same 'stupid smile' as when he left, many years before.

The story made its mark, especially since Borges was visibly moved as he recounted it. The winter, already severe, found us sheltered by a house from Hawthorne's time, as well. Our guest's companion was kneeling on the hearth before the fire, with a wine-stopper stuck to the end of a poker; she wanted to prove you could make mascara by charring cork. I think one thing that drew Borges so strongly to the United States was the houses of that country. They'd offered an austere comfort to Hawthorne, so he could ponder God, society, and his own existence. This may be why Borges thought of 'Wakefield' that evening, on his return from Concord. But what of the 'sourire idiot'? He'd repeated the words, with an emphatic flourish. The adjective sounded oddly harsh, in a narrative that seemed so nuanced. I wondered what English term this accomplished reader had translated there, since he knew his French so well.

The next day I read 'Wakefield', and I've reread it again today. In Hawthorne, too, Wakefield's smile is the touchstone of the tale. At one point, he depicts it through the eyes of the character's wife - who believes she's a widow - as she recalls her husband's sudden, unexpected departure. To grasp that strange smile, she even tries to impose it on his death-locked features, his rigid face. But the word used by Hawthorne isn't at all the English twin of the French modifier, 'idiot'; in fact, he speaks of a '*crafty* smile'.

'Crafty' is a rich and beautiful adjective. As opposed to the French 'idiot', it conveys the idea of a certain intelligence, a cleverness, the lucid mastery of techniques that are often quite precise; but over the centuries, irresistibly and irreversibly, the term has acquired a pejorative stamp. Even so, the related substantive, 'craft', has largely escaped that connotation. It's as if we sensed, instinctively, that in the mastery of a practice, we might attain our freedom: that through a potential evil, we might achieve a genuine good. To sum up, 'crafty' reflects the evil-obsessed Christianity brought over on the *Mayflower*, freighted with archaic fears; whereas 'craft' preserves the even-keeled know-how of specific trades - often handicrafts - that lie at the heart of society.

So I inferred that when Borges said 'idiot' in French, he must have had 'crafty' in mind. 'Stupid' is a word that comments, rather than condemns: the unguarded translator had wanted to excuse Wakefield - as though he felt compassion for him, along with fascination.

I couldn't help recalling that the Norton Lectures Borges was about to deliver at Harvard – that Mecca of sophistication – bore the title: *This Craft of Verse*. I found the title provocative, since it seemed to defy a whole tradition of thought: that poetry could be the occasion, or the cause, of a spiritual experience. Instead, it implied the poem was just a product, a montage of figures - a verbal object we could entrust to rhetoric, however bogus its devices.

The lectures duly took place, and the first one, at least, convened the leading minds of the entire East Coast - from as far away as New York, and beyond. The notoriety of Borges was then at its height, after several years of unaccountable delay. But it rested on an image of the author as highly subtle, even convoluted, and many of the listeners were taken aback by his talk. Is my remembrance of it just a dream? No doubt I'm about to distort his lecture, even betray it; people will complain that I'm mistaken. Still, I can't erase the impression made on me by his first remarks. Borges spoke without notes, since he couldn't use them. In fact, he didn't go on for long: from time to time, he picked up a large watch from the table, holding it close to his eyes. Once again, he expressed himself with what appeared - to me, anyway - like a simplicity meant to provoke. 'The Chinese have observed there are only a thousand words,' he said. 'After that, there's not much to add. Maybe just this: that there are ten metaphors.'

Then he counted off the ten metaphors. For example, time is a flowing river, or battle is an inferno. 'Oh, maybe there's another metaphor worth our while,' he threw in at the end. 'An American poet, E. E. Cummings, has dared to write: "The face of God is shining like a spoon."' But on further reflection, he concluded: 'No, that one shouldn't be admitted to the list.'

I may have oversimplified, in turn; but at any rate, some of his listeners were more than a little nonplused, when the lecture came to a halt. I met up with Borges afterwards in the hallway. 'What do you make of Mallarmé, then?' I asked him. 'Oh, Mallarmé - he's too complicated.' 'Then how about Baudelaire?' 'Baudelaire? He's too arrogant,' he replied, in all earnestness.

They belong to that handful of poets we've acknowledged in

France as the source of our modernity: we often contemplate their thoughts on poetry, and its role in our awareness of the self. But Borges liked to claim their work wasn't the best of French verse; he preferred Verlaine, or even Paul-Jean Toulet, for whom he felt a special fondness. This rebuff of his - which he extended to many attitudes and values he conceived of as French - was easily understandable. Poetry owes a debt to what's truly important: compassion, and the humility that it instills. Those who want to raise poetry to some loftier plane of the mind are arrogant: they refuse to accept the narrow limits of the human condition. Their excesses make poetry fall prey to evil, which may win out because of their meddling. They'd be better off just being stupid, like Wakefield; then we could more readily show them the indulgence each of us deserves, on the vain stage of this world.

I believe that kind of criticism is well-founded; indeed, it's what appealed to me in Borges. In my view, it underpins the grandeur of a writer who's often been taxed as incapable of love. On the contrary, he was ravaged by the pain and mortality of those around him, appalled that by merely being ourselves, we might inflict an irreparable hurt on our fellowmen. He said as much, plainly and boldly, in 'The Garden of Forking Paths'. Compassion - and the sense of helplessness it entails - surely underlies the suffering I invoked from the outset as fundamental to Borges. This stance has every right to pass judgment, even – or above all – in literature.

But obviously, such strictures don't apply to either Mallarmé or Baudelaire; they weren't complicated or arrogant, and Borges knew this as well as anyone. His rejection of them that evening, as so often, didn't take aim at those great poets at all, but rather at the great man he was himself: he feared complication, and refused arrogance. He considered writing a person's walling in of the self – or in other words, the murder of everyone else - and all the more so, the more important the writer. Through Mallarmé and Baudelaire, he worried about his own dilemma; and since they clearly rose above such a grave indictment, he could feel reassured about himself.

II.

A second recollection, from several years later: 1974. The nadir of Watergate; the interminable dusk of the War in Vietnam. A mood of insecurity haunted New York, and after dark the streets lay deserted. That night, on my return from New Haven, my nerves would seem slightly rattled, even while waiting for a taxi at Grand Central. All the same, many young people, though no longer the 'flower children' of some time back, still dreamed of renovating society through a moral experiment. Reacting to Puritanism and its obsession with evil, they wanted to believe that evil doesn't exist.

I'd boarded my train to New Haven in the early afternoon; and soon I reached the edge of the campus, with a friend who'd picked me up at the station. At five o'clock, I was supposed to give a talk at Yale on something – I no longer remember what. As we were walking past the churches, we ran into a group of three or four people, Borges among them. He'd also come to the university to speak, later on that evening. But it wouldn't be a lecture, he told me, just a round-table with an audience of students, there to ask him questions. 'By the way,' he went on, 'since you're free at that hour, why don't you join our discussion, too?' I accepted the invitation, and each of us continued on his way. We knew we'd see each other again later on at the Faculty Club: he'd be dining there before the roundtable, and I'd be eating the meal that followed my talk – a repast we could cut short, if need be.

The two tables were side by side, and before long we heard a faint hubbub: stirs and rustlings that reached us from the street. After a while, we went outside. As in a dream, we were engulfed by an unaccustomed crowd; it ballooned larger and larger, the more we neared our destination. Borges was traveling with a secretary who carried his briefcase, and they were separated in the crush. We also lost sight of the elderly writer, and fretted over his whereabouts for several minutes. But in the end, we all converged in front of the hall where the roundtable would take place.

We were then advised that the 'full occupancy' rule forbade us to hold it there: the public was already too numerous for a hall that could only accommodate two or three hundred, at most. In the midst of this confusion, we couldn't expect people to forgo their right to attend; we had to head for a bigger venue, located in due course. But the throng kept growing steadily – somewhat out of curiosity, by now, since the event appeared to be exceptional. At the second hall, we were shunted away with the same announcement: insufficient capacity, no entry allowed. The whole tide had to swerve, and flow back again.

What next? There certainly was an amphitheatre vast enough for our purpose, but would they unlock it for us? We stood around waiting for the people in charge, in the courtyard behind the building; by now night had fallen, and it was cold. Hearing the uproar on every side, I said to Borges: 'It looks like you're inciting the second American Revolution.'

Borges was not a revolutionary. He turned his beautiful face to me, on which a gleam of astonishment never ceased to roam. 'Do you know what I'm thinking of, right now?' he asked me. 'I'm in Geneva, at Bourg-du-Four.'

Bourg-du-Four, the central square of old Geneva, is the quintessential setting where orderly lives coincide, at intervals, during a day which repeats the one before. It's not a place that could spark revolutionary urges in a teenage Argentine, working toward his high-school diploma in the prosperous city of Calvin. Even so, several years later I read a story by Borges called 'The Other', which portrays him back in Cambridge again: there, on a bench beside the river, he comes across the young man he'd once been himself, long ago. He learns from the student – in fact, he remembers – that he's started writing a series of 'Red Hymns', because he wants to sing 'the brotherhood of all mankind'. I suspect that on that evening in 1974, too, Borges was thinking about this facet of his life. In the nearby street, he could hear the rising wind of a hope; but today it was he himself, strangely, who'd inspired it. And he wondered, all over again, what we're to make of the beliefs we cherish at age twenty. Are they merely figments of the eternal illusion? Aren't they, revealed for a moment, the only experience that gives meaning to our life?

A few minutes later, we sat down at the table: the hall was truly immense, and immensely packed with overexcited young people. The moderator introduced the participants by name, and each of us received a goodwill ovation. But this was nothing compared to the cries of joy that greeted Borges, who politely agreed to answer questions, if submitted to him on slips of paper. And so it went: questions and answers swung back and forth; all evening, the auditorium seethed like an ocean-swell in a rocky cove. But the moment arrived when Borges had to say he'd reply to a final question, and the last scribbled note was handed up to the front.

Was it that badly scrawled, or was the author's vision really reduced to almost nil? As I'd seen him do in Cambridge, Borges held the strip of paper right against his eyes; he deciphered a single word, followed by a question mark. He pronounced it out loud, with the trailing tone that precedes a response.

'Love? Yes…' he said, gearing up to go on. But the hall preferred to take this yes in its strongest sense – as an affirmation of absolute trust. The crowd jumped up as one, to hurrah Borges with a wild acclaim that never seemed to end. It was still resounding, late into the night, when I set out for New York, gripped by its anxiety. Friedlander claims that in the history of art, we kill our father only to find our grandfather again, who moves us to deep emotion. Never had his rule of thumb been proven so well: Borges emerged from Nixon like Phoenix from his ashes.

(That evening at Yale was very different from the tumult over Borges at the Collège de France, seven years later. There again, the crowd had expanded bit by bit, until at last people were climbing into Auditorium 8 by breaking the windows. But this time, the curiosity far outstripped the fervour, and I even whiffed some hostility in the disparate, unknowing multitude. In any case, that's how I interpreted a question shouted from the back of the hall: 'Monsieur Borges, since you're blind, what do you think of the cinema?')

III.

A third recollection: our last meeting, at the cantonal hospital in Geneva. Borges, who'd elected to round out his life near the Bourg-du-Four, was treated there for several weeks.

Shortly before his death, I visited him with Jean Starobinski. In the small room, we were seated on either side of his bed. Though weakened, Borges was as gracious and benevolent as ever. I can't recall why or how, but I brought up the subject of Virgil, who'd always signified so much to him.

'Virgil?' said Borges. 'Yes, but don't forget Verlaine!' And he spoke about Verlaine, once more in this life; after that, we passed on to something else, and finally took our leave. Borges propped himself up on his elbow. 'Don't forget Verlaine,' he told me. Then, as we were walking through the door, he raised his voice: 'Virgil *and* Verlaine.' By emphasising the 'and', he'd pointed to an equivalence; but above all, he aimed to stress a complementarity, crucial to our meditation of poetry.

When we were already in the hallway, a few steps down from the room, Borges repeated in an even louder voice: 'Virgil *and* Verlaine.' These words - a message with so much meaning, so briefly expressed – were the last I heard him say.

Translated by Hoyt Rogers

Acknowledgements

Grateful acknowledgement is made to the Estate of Yves Bonnefoy and to the publishers and copyright-holders listed below; for fuller publishing details please refer to the title-footnote at the head of each essay.

© Mercure de France/Editions Gallimard for 'Byzance'; 'L'humour, les ombres portées'; 'Terre seconde'; 'L'Acte et le lieu de la poésie'; 'Shakespeare et le poète français'; 'Transposer ou traduire *Hamlet*'; 'La Poésie française et le principe d'identité'; 'La Présence et l'image'; '*Hamlet, le Roi Lear*'; 'L'unique et son interlocuteur'; 'Un rêve fait à Mantoue'

© Mercure de France for 'Henri Cartier-Bresson et Giacometti'; 'Mozart en son point du monde'; 'La poétique de Yeats'

© Editions du Seuil for 'Notre besoin de Rimbaud'; 'L'autre langue à portée de voix'; 'Lettre à Shakespeare'

© Editions Galilée for 'La stratégie de l'énigme'; 'Poésie et photographie'; 'Trois souvenirs de Borges'

© Editions Flammarion for 'Le Baldaquin du Bernin'

© Editions William Blake & Cie for 'Art'; 'Un prophète de l'écriture'

© Presses Universitaires de Strasbourg for 'Georges Poulet et la poésie'

Grateful Acknowledgement is also made to the Publishers that hold the foreign rights and first issued some of these essays in English Translation:

The University of Chicago Press for 'Byzantium'; 'Humour and Cast Shadows' in *The Lure and the Truth of Painting*, ed. Richard Stamelman © 1995 by The University of Chicago; 'The Act and the Place of Poetry'; 'Shakespeare and the French Poet'; 'French Poetry and the Principle of Identity'; 'Image and Presence'; 'Readiness, Ripeness : *Hamlet, Lear*' in *The Act and the Place of Poetry*, ed. John Naughton © 1989 by the University of Chicago; 'Transpose or Translate' in *Shakespeare and the French Poet*, ed. John Naughton © 2004 by the University of Chicago

© Seagull Books for 'The Horizon of the Early Baroque'; 'The Shepherds of Arcadia'; 'Poetry and Photography'

© Yale University Press for 'Three Recollections of Jorge Luis Borges' in the translation by Hoyt Rogers

The publisher and editors are grateful for the translation grant bestowed by the Institut français du Royaume-Uni as part of the Burgess Programme.